The Makings of Indonesian Islam

PRINCETON STUDIES IN MUSLIM POLITICS
Dale F. Eickelman and Augustus Richard Norton, editors
A list of titles in this series can be found at the back of the book.

The Makings of Indonesian Islam

ORIENTALISM AND THE NARRATION OF A SUFI PAST

Michael Laffan

PRINCETON UNIVERSITY PRESS

PRINCETON AND OXFORD

Copyright © 2011 by Princeton University Press

Published by Princeton University Press, 41 William Street, Princeton,
New Jersey 08540
In the United Kingdom: Princeton University Press, 6 Oxford Street, Woodstock,
Oxfordshire OX20 1TW

press.princeton.edu

Jacket art: "Hadji Baok," as drawn by Muhammad Yasin of Lombok, ca. 1900. LOr. 18097s1.
Reproduced by permission from Leiden University Library.

Library of Congress Cataloging-in-Publication Data
Laffan, Michael Francis, 1969–
    The makings of Indonesian Islam : orientalism and the narration of a Sufi past / Michael Laffan.
        p. cm. — (Princeton studies in Muslim politics)
    Includes index.
    ISBN 978-0-691-14530-3 (cloth : alk. paper)   1. Sufism—Indonesia—History.
2. Islam—Indonesia—History.   I. Title.
    BP188.8.I5L34 2011
    297.409598—dc22   2010053108

British Library Cataloging-in-Publication Data is available

This book has been composed in Adobe Carlson Pro

Printed on acid-free paper ∞

Printed in the United States of America

10 9 8 7 6 5 4 3 2 1

For Mum and Dad

Contents

Illustrations

Preface

Clifford Geertz and Christiaan Snouck Hurgronje

It was with genuine sadness that Indonesianists and Indonesians alike reflected on the passing of the anthropologist and humanist Clifford Geertz in late October of 2006. Even though he had long since moved beyond Java and Bali and embraced far broader horizons, there was a sense among Indonesianists that, whether we agreed with his ideas or not, he was one of us. Certainly he had given the field a lot to think about. In such contributions as his *Agricultural Involution* of 1963, *Islam Observed* of 1968, and *Negara* of 1980, which all built on the reputation formed by his highly influential *Religion of Java* of 1960, his ideas were unfailingly stimulating.

In life and in death, though, his legacy has often been contrasted with that of another scholar whose contributions I will argue have been crucial to the ways in which Indonesia continues to be seen. One major Indonesian magazine even named them as two of but eight foreigners in a list of one hundred people to be adjudged "Indonesian figures of the twentieth century." This second (or rather, first) figure is Christiaan Snouck Hurgronje (1857–1936); Dutch Orientalist, outward Muslim, colonizer. And while Geertz was warmly embraced by his Indonesian biographers in the edition in question, Munawar Khalil declared the Dutchman to have been "the muskrat who slipped among the Muslim community to steal the 'secrets' of the people's resistance towards the colonial government."[1]

While this book is neither a critique of Geertz nor a defense of Snouck, the Dutchman's key contributions to the making of Indonesian studies will be addressed as it explores its major theme, namely: What are the supposed ingredients of Indonesian Islam? And who can we say has made it? As I shall argue, the process, or rather processes, that laid the foundations for a consensus on these questions have been driven by the long-standing engagement of Southeast Asian Muslims with coreligionists at home and abroad, both prior to and under the Dutch colonialism that made them Indonesians. And far beyond a mere fact of background hegemony, the direct engagement of Orientalist advisors like Snouck, acting on behalf of the colonial state and, ostensibly, for the benefit of Muslims, is a major strand complicating that story.

Sufism and the Modern

With the benefit of hindsight one can easily say that Geertz's amused scepticism about the long-term vitality of the process of Islamization, expressed in his *Islam Observed*, may now be seen to have been misplaced. But we might also challenge his characterization of the history of Indonesian Islam as having been "until recently, remarkably malleable, tentative, syncretistic, and, most significantly of all, multivoiced."[2] If, for Geertz, it was the multivocal nature of Indonesian Islam that was most significant, looking back some four decades later, one might argue that it was his conditional "until recently" that was actually his most relevant observation on the subject. Geertz was arguably reading his fields in light of the modernist scholarship and explications given by informants who were apparently detractors of many of the local practices he documented. As we shall see, such informants and their Western spokesmen had entwined histories.

In a recent critique of the field of colonial studies, Frederick Cooper has questioned the usefulness of the holy trinity of "identity," "globalization," and "modernity," arguing for greater specificity in academic discourse and for studies that read colonialism less as a story set against the backdrop of rising modernity than as encounters in which concepts like "nation," "the modern," and "religion" are given meaning.[3] This book is intended in part to rise to this challenge. Whereas I have previously aimed to demonstrate the Islamic contribution to the creation of Indonesia, I want to turn now to examine how Islam was interpreted and fashioned by the region's diverse actors; Dutch Christians included. Central to my inquiry will be disputes about the place of *tariqa* praxis— the rituals of mystical reflection organized under the guidance of a preceptor known as a *shaykh*—which represents but one aspect of Sufism as a field of Islamic knowledge. On the way a much larger and often political story has to be told that implicitly questions the current notion that Sufism is the form of Islam most amenable to Western contact. That said, I am not offering a narrative about how Sufism and anti-Sufism played out in the twentieth century as a whole, nor yet how Islam and politics intersect in Indonesia today. Rather, this will remain a colonial story, though one that will seem at times not so different from the one being played out for very high stakes today.

Narrative Outline

To say that someone or something has "the makings" of something else already implies an ongoing process of formation, and I would argue that Indonesian Islam remains just such a national project that is constantly redefined by its citizen adherents. At a more obvious level, however, the title of this book indicates that there were multiple processes at work on the way to the declaration of independence of August 17, 1945, of which the reformist and colonial projects were perhaps the most explicitly stated. But while the colonial looms large in this book, I felt it important not to commence by privileging the Western experience. Hence the first three chapters (Part One) describe major trends in the formation of Southeast Asian Islamic discourse, beginning with the first steps toward the Islamization of the region in the 1200s, and continuing into the 1880s, when the Dutch would make more explicit *de jure* interventions in Muslim Law. This background is necessary to throw elements of the later colonial story into proper relief.

Chapter 1 documents what we know of the process of Islamization across the archipelago and argues that our present knowledge is informed in large part by our acceptance of the retrospective framings and validations of seventeenth-century Sufi teachings that emphasized a mystical connection between the Prophet and a learned elite patronized by regal authorities. Chapter 2 considers how, in the eighteenth century, more formalized structures of learning were established in the archipelago as Southeast Asian scholars began to participate increasingly in Middle Eastern networks. I will argue that there was now an even more explicit regal attempt to move the Islamizing public away from the attractions of speculative Sufism and towards a stronger commitment to Islamic law (and thus governance). Chapter 3 then considers the rise, largely in the nineteenth century, of a new form of populist authority that expanded the scope of Islamic activity beyond the reach of ever more marginalized courts. In particular it examines the practical import of the use that some of the mystical fraternities with newer Meccan connections were making of the lithographic press.

The second quarter of the book, by contrast, deals with the parallel longue durée of Dutch (and, to some extent, English) experience with Islam in Southeast Asia, placing equal stress on the interactions in the Indies and the way in which these interactions were viewed in the metropole. Chapter 4 focuses on the very hazy notions of Islam that were formed in the course of the first voyages of the 1590s, emphasizing the place of Protestantism in the evolving understanding of Islam and its problematic relationship with the East India Companies. With the decline of the trading empires at the end of the eighteenth century, chapter 5 considers changes wrought in the nineteenth under the impact of new cultures of science and new concepts of empire fostered by the governments of The Hague and Batavia. These intellectual developments resulted in a more active attempt by the Westerners to measure and understand how Islam was organized in the archipelago and to educate their officials in Islamic Law in preparation for their deployment in the field. Chapter 6 is then at pains to show that a parallel framing of the Indies as a missionary field was crucial in informing, and sometimes challenging these colonial enterprises.

Having accounted for the two major strands of Indonesian history—the Islamic and the Colonial—the book turns in its the third, pivotal quarter to consider the implications of the entwining of indigenous and Dutch scholarship on the question of religion. Here our focus is on Snouck Hurgronje and his network of allies and informants, and we will examine their activities in detail and over a rather brief period of years, for we are now indeed in the realm of years, rather than decades or centuries. Chapter 7 commences with Snouck Hurgronje's interventions in the field in Holland, his criticisms of the juridical and missiological attacks on the orthopraxy of Islam in the Indies, and his alliance with those whom he deemed to have a more scholarly interpretation of Islam, and whose views he therefore promoted as beneficial to public well-being within a still Netherlandic Indies. In particular the chapter will consider the distaste of Snouck and his allies for the varieties of populist mysticism that rival, and rather less juridically concerned, Muslim teachers could turn to their own purposes. Chapter 8 explores these relationships in greater depth, following Snouck as he arrives in Batavia in 1889 and conducts fieldwork in Java and Aceh, examining his place in both Dutch and indigenous society. Whereas he was seen by his superiors as an informant on Muslims, the Muslims themselves could see him as a mediator and authority for their interests. Chapter 9 then lays out the position of those who were not so enamored, and who opposed Snouck's authority, seeing his "ethical" policies (as they were known) for the modernization of the Muslim Indies as a part of a longer-term project of Christianization.

The final quarter of the book considers relationships between Dutch scholars and Muslim reformers in the first half of the twentieth century and their apparent consensus that a new Islam was coming into being in the Indies, and that this new form would supplant the region's assumedly ancient tradition of "Indic" mysticism. Chapter 10 continues where chapter 3 left off, tracing the ongoing debates about Sufism in relation to changing notions of orthodoxy. Chapter 11 will consider how, meanwhile, Snouck's successors, trained in the history of Islam through the use of manuscripts he had collected, favored a particular strand of Muslim activism in what people were now increasingly calling "Indonesia." It will also examine how that support was problematic for the colonial authorities even as they relied upon the relationships formed between advisors and local religious leaders to keep a lid on potentially explosive situations. Chapter 12 will then show how, with the rise of a national movement couched by some of the actors in terms of Islam, the advisors and their reformist fellow-travelers would be blamed and marginalized by a reactionary colonial state, just in time for the Japanese occupation.

Acknowledgments

The seeds of this project were sown during a three-year fellowship in Leiden and have finally germinated not so far from Nassau Street, Princeton. Some of the ideas, since altered or elaborated, have come out in various venues over the past seven years, notably at seminars held at Oxford and Bogor in 2005, UCLA in 2006, Tokyo and Kyoto in 2007, and Amsterdam in 2008. The project as a whole nonetheless remained obscured from view, including my own view, for some time. I am grateful to many for their support, questions and encouragement. I first wish to thank the former director of the International Institute of Asian Studies, Wim Stokhof, and his vibrant staff for an excellent start. In particular I acknowledge my colleagues in the "Islam in Indonesia" project, which the Institute facilitated with funding from the Royal Netherlands Academy of Social Sciences (KNAW): Nico Kaptein, Kees van Dijk, Martin van Bruinessen, Moch. Nur Ichwan, and Noorhaidi Hasan. Similarly helpful were Jan Just Witkam, Hans van de Velde, and Arnoud Vrolijk at the library of Leiden University, and my many good colleagues at the Royal Netherlands Institute of Southeast Asian and Caribbean Studies (KITLV)—Henk Schulte Nordholt, Willem van der Molen, Tom van den Berge, Rini Hogewoning, Jaap Anten, Lam Ngo, Liesbeth Ouwehand, Peter Boomgard and David Henley— under whose auspices the final pieces of the book fell into place in 2009. Holland was also a warmer and sunnier place thanks to the fellowship of Rosemary Robson in Leiden, Jaap Plugge and Karla van Boon in Westzaan, and Luitgard Mols and Harold Abu Biff in The Hague. Princeton, too, has been a rich field, and I am indebted to my present and former colleagues, especially James McDougall, Helen Tilley, Michael Gordin, Angela Creager, Sheldon Garon, Michael Cook, John Haldon, Bhavani Raman, and Yaacob Dweck (yes, Yaacob, I named you). I am furthermore indebted to the University Committee on Research for generously funding the extended field trips that helped bring this book to completion, and to good friends at the Asia Research Institute in Singapore, then under the eternally generous Tony Reid. My appreciation also goes to Michael Feener, Bill Roff, Duncan McCargo, Merle Ricklefs, Annabel Gallop of the British Library, Aunal Abied Syah in Cairo, Henri Chambert-Loir in Jakarta, and Bob Elson and Deb Brown in Brisbane. Final thanks go to Barbara Andaya for some key interventions, Tsering Wangyal Shawa for drawing the maps, the Leiden University Library and the KITLV for permission to reproduce images from their collections, and, most especially, to Judy, Faridah, and Daniel for their long-standing patience with me and with New Jersey.

List of Abbreviations and Archival Referents

AA	*Ambtelijke adviezen van C. Snouck Hurgronje 1889–1936*, E. Gobée and C. Adriaanse, eds., 3 vols. (The Hague: Nijhoff, 1957–65)
Ar.	Arabic
Archief	*Archief voor de geschiedenis der oude Hollandsche zending*, J. A. Grothe, ed., 6 vols. (Utrecht: Van Bentum, 1884–91)
b.	*Ibn*, or *Bin*; i.e. the Arabic designation "son of"
BB	Binnenlandsch Bestuur, Netherlands Indies Civil Service
BKI	*Bijdragen tot de Taal-, Land- en Volkenkunde*
CSI	Centraal Sarekat Islam, the coordinating body of the Sarekat Islam
Du.	Dutch
EI²	*Encyclopaedia of Islam*, Second Edition. P. Bearman et al., eds., 12 vols. (Leiden: Brill, 1954–2005)
EI³	*Encyclopaedia of Islam Three*. Gudrun Krämer et al., eds., (Leiden: Brill, 2007–)
f	Dutch gilder
GAL	Carl Brockelmann, *Geschichte der arabischen Litteratur*, Jan Just Witkam, introduction and ed., 2 vols. 3 supp. (Leiden: Brill, 1996)
GG	Gouveneur Generaal van Nederlandsch Indië, the Governor General of the Netherlands Indies
Hazeu*	Collectie Hazeu, KITLV, H 1083
IG	*Indisch Gids*
IJMES	*International Journal of Middle East Studies*
ILS	*Islamic Law and Society*
IOL	India Office Library, the British Library
IOR	India Office Records, the British Library
IPO	Overzicht van de Inlandsche- en Maleisch- Chinese Pers
Jalal al-Din*	*Maleisch leesboek voor eerstbeginnenden en meergevorderden; Vijfde stukje; Bevattende een verhaal van den aanvang der Padri-onlusten op Sumatra, door Sjech Djilâl-Eddin*, J. J. de Hollander, ed., (Leiden: Brill, 1857)
Jav.	Javanese
JESHO	*Journal of the Economic and Social History of the Orient*

*Please note that *Hazeu, Jalal al-Din, Kern*, and *Pijper* are set in caps throughout to differentiate the source from the person

JIB	Jong Islamieten Bond
JMBRAS	*Journal of the Malaysian Branch of the Royal Asiatic Society*
JRAS	*Journal of the Royal Asiatic Society*
JSEAS	*Journal of Southeast Asian Studies*
Kern*	Collectie Kern, KITLV, H 797
KIAZ/KIZ	Kantoor voor Inlandsch en Arabisch Zaken/Kantoor voor Inlandsch Zaken; Office for Native and Arab Affairs, later the Office for Native Affairs
KITLV	Koninklijk Instituut voor Taal-, Land- en Volkenkunde; Royal Netherlands Institute of Southeast Asian and Caribbean Studies, Leiden
LOr.	Leiden University Library, ms. Or.
LUB	Leiden University Library
Mal.	Malay
MCP	Malay Concordance Project, Australian National University, http://mcp.anu.edu.au/
MinBuZa	Nationaal Archief, Den Haag, Ministerie van Buitenlandse Zaken: A-dossiers, 1815–1940, nummer toegang 2.05.03
MR	Nationaaal Archief, Den Haag, Ministerie van Koloniën: Mailrapporten 1869–1900, nummer toegang 2.10.02
MNZG	*Mededeelingen van wege het Nederlandsche Zendelinggenootschap*
NBG	Nederlandsch Bijbel Genootschap; Dutch Bible Society
NU	Nahdlatul Ulama
NZV	Nederlandsche Zendings Vereeniging; Dutch Mission Organization
ONOI	F. Valentyn, *Oud en Nieuw Oost-Indiën, vervattende een naauwkeurige en uitvoerige verhandeling van Nederlants Mogentheyd in die Gewesten, enz. met meer dan 1050 prentverbeeldingen verrykt . . . en met . . . kaarten opgeheldert,* 5 vols. (Dordrecht [etc.]: Van Braam, 1724–26)
ONZ	*Orgaan der Nederlandsche Zendingsvereeniging*
Pijper*	Collectie Pijper, notes, LOr. 26.337
Plakaatboek	J. A. van der Chijs, *Nederlandsch-Indisch plakaatboek, 1602–1811,* 16 vols. (Batavia and The Hague, Landsdrukkerij and Nijhoff)
PNRI	Perpustakaan Nasional Republik Indonesia, The Indonesian National Library
PS	Correspondence between G. F. Pijper and C. Snouck Hurgronje, in Collectie Pijper, LOr. 26.335
PUL	Princeton University Library
Q	Qur'an

RIMA	*Review of Indonesian and Malaysian Affairs*
SB	*Amicissime: Brieven van Christiaan Snouck Hurgronje aan Herman Bavinck, 1878–1921,* J. de Bruijn, ed., (Amsterdam: Historisch Documentatiecentrum voor het Nederlands Protestantisme, 1992)
SI	Sarekat Islam, The Islamic Union
TBG	*Tijdschrift voor Indische Taal-, Land- en Volkenkunde*
TKNM	Tentara Kanjeng Nabi Muhammad, The Army of the Lord Prophet Muhammad
TNI	*Tijdschrift voor Neêrlands Indië*
Vb	Nationaal Archief, Den Haag, Ministerie van Koloniën: Openbaar Verbaal, 1901–1952, nummer toegang 2.10.36.04
VBG	*Verhandelingen van het Bataviaasch Genootschap van Kunsten en Wetenschappen*
VG	*Verspreide geschriften van C. Snouck Hurgronje,* A. J. Wensinck, ed., 6 vols (Leiden: Brill, 1923–27)
VK	*Orientalism and Islam: The letters of C. Snouck Hurgronje to Th. Nöldeke from the Tübingen University Library,* S. van Koningsveld. ed., (Leiden: Faculteit der Godgeleerdheid, 1985)

A NOTE ON ORTHOGRAPHY, NAMES, AND ITALICIZATION

In writing a book that deals with sources in numerous languages and spelling traditions I have had to make some decisions in the interest of readability. I realize that in many instances I have done violence to modern Indonesian conventions that are derived from their Dutch predecessors, and most especially by adding the Arabic letter *'ayn* here and there where Indonesian resorts to glottal stops, silence, or the occasional k. I have also inserted the odd "of" or made use of Arabic adjectival designations to aid readers unfamiliar with Indonesian geography. Hence someone generally known today as Abdussamad Palembang will be referred to as 'Abd al-Samad of Palembang, or 'Abd al-Samad al-Falimbani (as he is represented in Arabic texts).

In many instances I did so in order to reconnect Indonesia to its Islamicate past that was communicated through the Arabized *jawi* script. By the same token, however, Arabic terms have been stripped of various macrons and subscript dots that are only of interest to specialists. Hence names—whether Arabic or Indonesian—have been rendered in this same system, though I have naturally not applied it when citing or translating original passages in roman script. Of course this compromise, especially considering the preponderance of Dutch sources employed, still leaves quite a few names and terms that are opaque to the Anglophone reader. Few will recognize *sjech* as *shaykh* at first sight, though hopefully the flow of the discussion will ease such transitions. Also, in the hope of easing the jarring caused by many foreign terms, italics will usually be employed in the first instance rather than throughout, and in the hope that I managed to include all the usual suspects in the glossary.

PART ONE

INSPIRATION, REMEMORATION, REFORM

ONE

Remembering Islamization, 1300–1750

To the Mountain of Fire

Seen from above, the great archipelagic world of Indonesia, the scene of much of what follows in this book, drifts eastward from the Bay of Bengal into the Pacific Ocean. The Malay Peninsula, too, has long been an integral part of this world. Its ports, and those of the mainland from the Gulf of Thailand to southern China, were tightly linked to states located on the major isles of Sumatra, Borneo, Sulawesi, and the Moluccas farther to the east. South of these islands, and sharing in that same nexus of trade, lie Java and such eastern islands as Bali, Lombok, and Sumbawa.

From the opening of the Common Era, the rulers of the western half of this world shared an Indianized court culture and profited from the presence of foreign traders. This is because Southeast Asia lies at the intersection of two trading zones of significant antiquity. The first encompassed the Indian Ocean while the other skirted the South China Sea; indeed our knowledge of some of the earliest Southeast Asian kingdoms comes from Chinese records that note the arrival of emissaries with seemingly Muslim names. From the other direction we have Arabic accounts of sailing routes from the Persian Gulf to the ports of Southern China that had the Malacca Strait as their fulcrum. There captains would await the change of monsoonal winds to carry them either onward with their journeys or back home, while the intra-archipelagic trade injected costly spices, gums, rare plumage, and aromatics into holds already brimming with fabrics, ceramics, and glassware.[1]

Though there are suggestions of early Muslim sojourners in the region, Islam was a late arrival as a religion of state. For much of the second half of the first millennium, the ports along the Malacca Strait seem to have paid tribute to the paramount estuarine polity of Srivijaya (or those states which claimed its inheritance). Based around the harbors of East Sumatra, Srivijaya's rulers supported Mahayana Buddhism, making pious bequests as far afield as the monastery of Nalanda in Bihar, India, and sending missions to China by way of Guangzhou and, later, Quanzhou, the great southern port established under the Tang Dynasty (618–907). On the other hand, Arab accounts, which refer to Quanzhou as the ultimate destination of Zaytun, appear only vaguely aware of Srivijaya at best, and merely mention a great "Maharaja" who claimed the islands of a domain that they called "Zabaj." Its capital was distinguished by a cosmopolitan harbor and an ever-simmering "mountain of fire" nearby.[2]

More mysterious still are the identities of Southeast Asia's first established

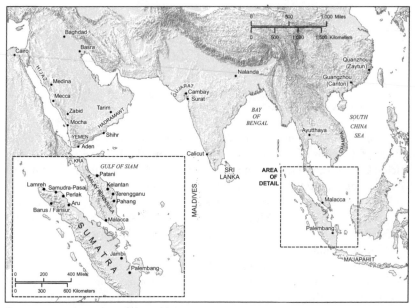

Figure 1. Southeast Asia's Malay Hubs, ca. 1200–1600.

Muslim residents. In part this is a result of the successive rememorations of Islamization that seldom tally with the physical traces left in the soil. Marco Polo referred in his account of Sumatra (around 1292) to a new Muslim community founded by "Moorish" traders at Perlak, and one of the first dated Muslim tombstones (which gives the Gregorian equivalent of 1297) names "Malik al-Salih" as having been the contemporary ruler at the nearby port of Samudra-Pasai, but some see evidence of even earlier communities further west at Lamreh, where badly eroded grave markers suggest a connection both with Southern India and Southern China.[3]

While we know little of the mechanisms underlying their deposition, whether they were middlemen acting for the China trade or perhaps even the Chola kings of Southern India, by the early thirteenth century, the spice traders of Aden, in Yemen, had at last become aware of Muslims inhabiting a place they now called "Jawa."[4] It also seems that, by the fourteenth century, the rulers of Samudra-Pasai were either competing or colluding with those of Bengal for the right to have their names invoked in Friday prayers in Calicut, where Jawis (as the peoples of Southeast Asia were known to Arabic speakers) often met Indian, Persian and Arab coreligionists.[5] Hints of a Muslim Jawa appear in the writings of an Aden-born mystic, ʿAbdallah b. Asʿad al-Yafiʿi (1298–1367), who devoted much of his life to recording the miracles of ʿAbd al-Qadir al-Jilani (1077–1166), the Baghdadi saint adopted as their axial master by many mystical fraternities. Known as *tariqa*s, by al-Yafi'i's day these fraternities had evolved into groupings under the leadership of specially initiated teachers, or *shaykh*s, who claim successive positions in an unbroken lineage or "pedigree" (*silsila*) of teachers that extends back to the Prophet. Whatever their particular line of spiritual descent, whether of the Qadiriyya, which is traced back through 'Abd al-Qadir al-Jilani, or the Naqshbandiyya of Baha' al-Din Naqshband (1318–89), the tariqas provide instruction in the techniques of being mindful of God—whether through silent contemplation, spectacular dances, or self-mortifications—that are commonly termed "remembrance" (*dhikr*). Perhaps one of the most famous forms of dhikr is the "Dabus" ritual favored by the Rifa'iyya order, which takes its name from the Iraqi Ahmad al-Rifa'i (d.1182), in which devotees seemingly pierce their breasts with awls without injury. By contrast other tariqas, such as branches of the Naqshbandiyya, are known for their silent contemplation. Regardless of the specific mode of dhikr, it is held that such activities, when led by a knowledgeable master, can generate ecstatic visions and moments of "revelation" in which the veils of mystery separating the believer from God are swept aside.

Writing in the fourteenth century, al-Yafi'i recalled that as a youth in Aden he had known a man who was especially adroit at such mystical communications. He had even inducted him into the Qadiriyya fraternity. This man was called Mas'ud al-Jawi; that is, Mas'ud the Jawi.[6] We would seem to have proof here of A. H. Johns' famous theory of a link between trade and the spread of Islam to the archipelago at the hands of the tariqa shaykhs. But while al-Yafi'i's works continue to play a role in the spread of the stories of 'Abd al-Qadir al-Jilani in Southeast Asia, any local memory of this process, if it was occurring in Sumatra in the same way as it was occurring in Aden, is lacking. Instead we often have regal accounts of how the light of prophecy was drawn to the region. In several cases, an ancestral ruler is said to have met the Prophet in a dream, to have had his somnolent conversion recognized by a Meccan emissary, or else to have been visited by a foreign teacher able to heal a specific illness. Perhaps the most famous example is found in the *Hikayat Raja Pasai* (The Romance of the Kings of Pasai), in which King Merah Silu (who would become the Malik al-Salih commemorated by the headstone of 1297), dreamt that the Prophet had spat in his mouth, thus enabling him to recite the Qur'an upon waking, much as the Persian-speaking 'Abd al-Qadir had been rendered an eloquent speaker of Arabic in al-Yafi'i's *Khulasat al-mafakhir* (Summary of Prideworthy Acts).[7]

Merah Silu is further said to have received a shaykh from Mecca to validate his conversion, a story that might at first seem to point to some form of tariqa connection. However the emphasis on Meccan validation more likely reflects regal concerns with genealogies of power and a long-running fascination for that city as the eternal abode of the family of the Prophet. Perhaps the most famous of the many Malay royal lineages, Malacca's *Sulalat al-salatin* (Pedigrees of the Sultans), incorporated sections of the *Hikayat Raja Pasai* and preempted the line of Muhammad by asserting that the dynastic founder had the blood of Alexander the Great.[8]

Regardless of how it was achieved or subsequently justified, Islamization brought the power of international connections that linked the Indian Ocean and China Sea ever more closely together. Even though the rulers of Malacca claimed descent from Alexander and Pasai, they nonetheless considered themselves Ming vassals right up to their conquest by the Portuguese in 1511. To be sure, there is much that remains mysterious about Malacca. Whereas the Tangiers-born Ibn Battuta (1304–77) claimed, around 1345, that the ruler of Samudra-Pasai was committed to the Shafi'i juridical method (a school of interpretation of Islamic Law attributed to Muhammad b. Idris al-Shafi'i [767–820]), the later navigator Sulayman al-Mahri (fl. 1500s) doubted whether the people of Malacca were Muslim at all. He would have had some reason for his doubts. Even though the famous code *Undang-undang Melaka* (The Laws of Malacca) ranked "the laws of God" as more lofty than local custom, they often favored the latter.[9]

The *Sulalat al-salatin* for its part has little to say about either juridical particularism or the texts in use at the sultanate. It only refers to the sending of questions to Pasai concerning the eternity of God's reward or punishment, as well as a specific request for the explication of a text brought to Malacca by one "Mawlana Abu Bakar." The question would seem to relate to ongoing arguments concerning the views of the Andalusian mystic Ibn al-'Arabi (1165–1240), who had claimed that while Hell was eternal, there would be an end to the suffering of those languishing there, for God's mercy transcends his anger. Meanwhile the text brought by Mawlana Abu Bakr, which he is said to have personally taught Sultan Mansur Shah (r. 1456–77), seems to have been called *al-Durr al-manzum* (The Strung Pearls), a title that the scholar G.W.J. Drewes (1899–1993) attributed to Abu Hamid Muhammad al-Ghazali (1058–1111).[10]

Then again, there is no one text or agreement. Another version of the *Sulalat al-salatin* published by the famous Singaporean printer, Munshi Abdullah ('Abdallah b. 'Abd al-Qadir, 1796–1854), declares the *Durr al-manzum* to have been by "Mawlana Abu Ishaq" from "above the winds" and lays out its contents as a treatise on the Essence (*dhat*) of God and his Attributes (*sifat*), to which a further section on his Actions (*af'al*) had been added. It has been proposed that this is suggestive of a work of mysticism, though it sounds more like a primer on dogma (on which mystical works certainly depended).[11] Whatever the secrets of the *Durr al-manzum* were, it is clear that Malacca, joined by the northern peninsular ports of Pahang and Patani, played a role in the conversion of the Moluccan islands and that the process was linked to the ongoing extraction of spices for the global market.

Figure 2. *Sharh umm al-barahin*, ms ca. nineteenth century. Author's collection.

FROM CHINA TO JAVA?

The kings of the Moluccas were not only in touch with Malay Muslims in the fifteenth century. Trade with China remained the key to ongoing success in Southeast Asia, just as much as conversion to this latest of world religions. Hence Muslim Chinese and Javanese were also on the scene, sailing out from newly converted ports like Tuban and Gresik, which had found their way onto Arab sailing itineraries. The emergence of Patani as a Muslim polity also owed a great deal to Sino-Javanese contacts. This is recalled in the name of its harbor, also known as Gresik. Similarly the German naturalist Rumphius (1627–1702; see ch. 4) would later comment that the Javanese in Ambon were known as "Tubans."[12]

Ports like Gresik and Tuban had emerged on Java's north coast under strong-men now remembered as *walis*, from the Arabic word implying both saintly proximity to God and the worldly exercise of power. Certainly no discussion of the history of Islam in Indonesia can be complete without mention of the ca-nonical "Nine Saints" (Wali Sanga) to whom the Islamization of Java is as-cribed. They include Malik Ibrahim and the "Lords" (*sunan*) Bonang, Ampel, Drajat, and Kalijaga. The first of these men, also known as Mawlana Maghribi, is remembered today as an Arab who arrived around 1404 from Champa in modern-day Vietnam and who died in Gresik in 1419. Few of the others were Arabs, however. Perhaps the most famous is Mawlana Maghribi's Javanese adept, Sunan Kalijaga, who has been seen as the archetypal avatar of an Indo-nesian Muslim, being "malleable, tentative, syncretistic, and, most significantly of all, multivoiced," in contradistinction to the land after which his master took his name, which Geertz characterized by "saint worship and moral severity, magical power and aggressive piety."[13]

Often cited as examples of Indonesian malleability, some of the Nine Saints are alleged to have created artistic forms to explain Islam in the local idiom. Sunan Kalijaga is said to have invented the shadow-puppet theatre (*wayang*); Sunan Drajat is credited with composing a melody for the traditional percus-sion orchestra (*gamelan*), and it is claimed that Sunan Bonang invented the poetic instructional form known as *suluk*, a term that comes from the Arabic word meaning one's "wayfaring" in quest of divine knowledge.[14] In addition, however, there are Javanese narratives about Mawlana Maghribi and his peers that suggest they relied upon the same trade links with China that would en-rich Patani, where Mawlana Maghribi is also claimed as a founder saint. An account from Cirebon, on the borders of West Java, even credits the Ming ad-miral Zheng He (1371–1433) with seeding the island with communities of Muslims belonging to the Hanafi school of legal interpretation.[15]

On the other hand more recent Arabian genealogies, such as that composed by ʿAbd al-Rahman al-Mashhur of Tarim (1834–1902), claim that the Nine Saints were all descendants of the Prophet (Ar. *sayyid*s). More specifically al-Mashhur's genealogy asserts that they were, rather like the genealogist himself, of the family of a man called ʿAlawi, whose grandfather had migrated to Hadramawt in 951.[16] Still, the Chinese have not been written out of Indone-sian history, as may be seen in the story of Sunan Gunung Jati, a Malay born in Pasai as Nur Allah, who traveled to Mecca after the Portuguese conquered his hometown in 1521. According to Indonesian legends he returned to the archi-pelago and married the younger sister of Sultan Trenggana of Demak around 1523, moved to Banten around 1527, and finally settled in Cirebon. There he married a local Chinese whose heritage is strikingly referenced by the cloud pattern on the doors of her tomb and the particular style of batik fabric for which the town is famous.[17]

The eagerness of various latecomers to appropriate the saintly histories of Java reminds us that the founders had great political importance, regardless of whether they came to the archipelago as Arab adventurers or as handlers of Chinese business. Regardless of their origins, each saint now has a mortuary complex, often the source of their present-day renown. For example the hilltop of Giri, behind Gresik on Java's east coast, was once the site of the gleaming sepulchre of Sunan Giri, whose clan produced leaders known to the Dutch as the "popes" of Java.[18] Such tombs remain pilgrimage sites and are visited by believers seeking a share in God's blessing, or else active mediation by the saint on their behalf.[19]

In both the reputed genealogies of the Nine Saints that are found in pamphlets handed out to pilgrims and the scholarly works on Indonesia's Islamic heritage, most writers are quite convinced of the saints' contribution to the making of Java. That inheritance, as we shall see, has been revived in part by virtue of the interventions of Dutch scholars, whose research led them to manuscripts that found their way into European collections. It is from these texts that at we gain some insight into the teachings of the saints as they were understood within the first two centuries of their advent. Despite the common attribution of cultural flexibility to the Nine Saints, it appears that their concern was often to sternly inculcate behavioral norms in societies where by no means everybody was Muslim. A Portuguese apothecary, Tomé Pires, noted in the early sixteenth century, for example, that the coasts of Java may have been Muslim, but the interior population was not.[20]

One representative of such coastal Islam was Seh Bari, who left his students a series of teachings framed as the "fundaments of traveling on the mystical path." Judging from this work, the Islam being promoted was most definitely not a syncretic teaching that would have accommodated local practices. Rather Seh Bari advanced propositions for an elite community that sought knowledge of (1) the nature of God based on Qur'anic interpretation; (2) whether God was distinct from creation; and (3) how the believer might come to know of his transcendence. In exploring such questions Seh Bari referred above all to al-Ghazali, whom he invoked against the esoteric theology of Ibn al-'Arabi, especially against "the unity of being" (*wahdat al-wujud*), the notion developed by Ibn al-'Arabi's followers who took his teaching to entail that God and creation were in fact identical.[21]

Similarly, another early teacher, Seh Ibrahim, urged his pupils to remain at a distance from earthly temptations, and to take inspiration from Khidr, a prophet-like figure mentioned obliquely in the Qur'an (18:65–82) and many Alexander romances. Questions have been raised about the dating of Seh Ibrahim's text, but his views may perhaps be taken as representative of attitudes during the formative period of Islamization on Java. The works of al-Ghazali and al-Yafi'i are cited against instances of extreme heterodoxy, and transgression of the Shari'a. This is made plain in an appended text that describes a meeting of eight saints who were each to provide an explanation of his understanding of gnosis. When one of their number, known as Siti Jenar, dared to proclaim, "I am Allah. Who else could I be?" he was censured for revealing Ibn al-'Arabi's doctrine to the public.[22]

Siti Jenar would not be quiet, however, and was executed. Similar fates are said to have befallen other imprudent teachers. While these stories are far from verifiable, they are often taken as catalysts for discussions of the meeting of Javanese (and, by default, Indonesian) and Arab mysticism. In European scholarship parallels have even been drawn with the execution of the famous Mansur al-Hallaj of Baghdad (858–922). Curiously, similar comparisons with the story of al-Hallaj are ready to hand in today's Indonesia, but it is worth noting that they postdate the publication of Western works on the subject. It is also worth pointing out that even if Siti Jenar and al-Hallaj shared the same fate for the same crime, there need be no link to the lineage of any particular tariqa, or at least not to one with deep roots in society beyond the courtly elite.[23]

From Hamza al-Fansuri to an Ottoman Moment

Whereas we have some limited sense of the teachings of the Nine Saints on Java, there is little comparable material for the peininsular port of Malacca. We have only tangential references to the philosophy of Ibn al-'Arabi concerning God's mercy or seemingly under-emphasized juridical elements in the *Sulalat al-salatin*. Malacca's capture by the Portuguese in 1511 ended any pretensions it may have had to being a center for Islamic knowledge, and created instead an opportunity for other entrepôts to channel passing Sino-Muslim trade. The rulers of what would become the Sultanate of Aceh were among such beneficiaries who set about enlarging their territory at the expense of Pasai, the port that had once supplied Malacca's scholars and perhaps even its narrative of conversion.[24]

Like Malacca and Pasai, non-Muslim Majapahit was soon in turmoil. After an abortive Javanese siege of Portuguese Malacca, the kingdom was overthrown by a force from Demak in 1527, to be reconstituted in time as Muslim Mataram. This state would reach its apogee the next century under Sultan Agung (r. 1613–46); though he would commence his reign by subduing the north coast and cap his victories with the sack of Surabaya in 1625. His court would then sponsor works that M. C. Ricklefs argues represent evidence of an emergent (rather than incipient) "mystic synthesis," fusing non-Javanese Islam with a domestic form that seems to have developed after the Nine Saints had done their work.[25]

The lords of Java's north coast had also had an impact elsewhere in the archipelago, where trading centers were drawing more and more Islamic territories ever closer together, including such ports as Gowa (Makassar), the first of the principalities of Sulawesi to be Islamized (in the early seventeenth century). With the encouragement of the lords of Giri, Gowa became an active Islamizer both of its neighbours and of the more distant isles of Banda, Lombok and Sumbawa. Some argue that, by the late sixteenth century, Sulawesi's rulers had begun to construct their authority on the Sufi model of "the perfect man" (al-insan al-kamil) while looking to Mataram and Aceh for practical models.[26] Certainly there is evidence of Sufi ideas permeating local traditions in the archipelago, given the evident popularity of Khidr, notions of the perfect man, not to mention the possibility of becoming truly aware of God by passing through the "five grades of being" formulated by ʿAbd al-Karim al-Jili (1365–1428). It seems that such ideas were made known to many Indonesian societies through the works of a certain Malay from North Sumatra, Hamza al-Fansuri by name. Much like the Nine Saints, he is credited with the invention of an artistic form, in his case the Malay poetic syair (from the Arabic word shiʿr). Hamza's peregrinations took him far away from his home. A recently interpreted funerary inscription even suggests that he ended his days in Mecca in 1527.[27] This new dating has radically altered our understanding of the history of Malay literature and Sufism, as Hamza al-Fansuri has usually been placed at the court of Aceh under Iskandar Muda (1607–36). Whatever the truth of the matter, the preponderance of the literature shows that al-Fansuri's poetry was suffused by Sufi images resonant with the maritime world of the Malays. In one case God is presented as an all-encompassing ocean to be traversed by the ship of the Shariʿa en route to the islands of paradise. Another explanation likens the relationship between God and humanity to that of waves and sea, waves being of the sea, but not the sea itself.[28]

Based on the extant manuscripts and references to al-Fansuri's anthologies, it is clear that he attained widespread popularity. It is further tempting to place the future Javanese saint Nur Allah in his Meccan entourage, before his venture to Java and ultimate interment as Sunan Gunung Jati, for it appears that al-Fansuri's own tomb may once have been a site visited by other Southeast Asians, who referred to him as "the master in Mecca," and who may well have been numerous enough there to simply inscribe his headstone with the relatively precise attribution "Fansuri" rather than the more general "Jawi." In any case, his headstone declared him to be a "master," "ascetic," "the mine of reality," and the "Marabout shaykh," all titles appropriate to a master of tariqa Sufism.[29] Al-Fansuri himself alludes in his poems to joining the tariqa of ʿAbd al-Qadir al-Jilani in Ayutthaya, Siam.[30]

Unfortunately, and like the earlier Masʿud al-Jawi of Aden, there is no proof that al-Fansuri ever inducted anyone else. Still, some of the foreign visitors drawn to Aceh's increasingly prosperous shores over the course of the sixteenth century may well have maintained affiliations with particular tariqas, and the example of al-Fansuri could have made it *possible* for them to think of a Jawi being so affiliated. One potential pointer to a general knowledge of tariqa spreading after the passing of Hamza is the apparent adoption of the Arabic word *murid* (Sufi initiate or disciple) for "student." Whereas it is found but once in Hamza's poems (and in a different sense), it appears in the modern sense in three Malay romances of the mid-sixteenth century. These are the *Hikayat Amir Hamzah* (The Romance of Amir Hamzah), the *Hikayat Inderaputra* (The Romance of Inderaputra), and the *Hikayat Iskandar Zulkarnain* (The Romance of Alexander the Two-Horned), though all are in fact translations, which leads us to wonder about antecedents and influence.[31]

In any case, 1527, the year in which Hamza apparently died in Mecca and the Muslim forces of Demak overran the Javanese interior, should be seen as a crucial one for Islam in Southeast Asia. Despite taking Malacca, the Portuguese failed to supplant their Old World rivals and they failed to undo the work of the Muslims who had preceded them in the Moluccas. By the 1570s, the Iberian position would be decidedly weak. There have been suggestions that this was the result of Ottoman policy put in place once an anti-Portuguese faction had gained influence in an effort to firm up relations with a number of disgruntled sovereigns in the Indian Ocean. Much as the Rasulids of Yemen had previously been important suppliers of patronage across the seas, Ottoman aid was certainly attractive to Muslim rulers or pretenders in the networked sultanates of Gujerat, Bengal, and the Maldives, as well as in the autonomous Muslim communities active under non-Muslim rulers like the Zamorin of Calicut. For their part, the increasingly confident rulers of Aceh had even sent ambassadors to Sulayman the Magnificent (r. 1522–66) seeking Ottoman cannon to use in more determined actions against Portugese Malacca and for their own regional ambitions in general. That said, and despite repeated promises, actual Ottoman intervention was limited. Whereas numerous Turkic mercenaries and their allies from Abyssinia, Egypt, and Gujarat were indeed to be found engaged in combat from the Batak highlands of Sumatra to the Moluccan isle of Ternate—where Sultan Bab Allah (r. 1570–84) even succeeded in expelling the Iberians in 1575—the famous "Ottoman" cannon of Aceh were actually cast by Turkic rulers in Gujarat. It also appears that Acehnese pledges of allegiance to the Ottoman sultan were probably concocted by an ambitious spice procurer, who gave but little hint of the doctrinal debates being played out at a court that would become the venue for some very famous arguments indeed.[32]

ACEH, BANTEN, AND MATARAM IN THE SEVENTEENTH CENTURY

And so, among the throngs some spoke to others saying, "How splendid is the assembly of our All-Exalted Ruler. Many of the lands below the winds and those above the winds have we seen, yet of all the palaces of great kings, none can compare with the assembly of our Excellent Ruler. Verily, the state of Aceh Dar al-Salam is the forecourt of Mecca![33]

Seventeenth-century Aceh is often seen as the template for Indonesian Islam, especially during the long sultanate of the bellicose Iskandar Muda, a near contemporary of Java's Sultan Agung. Modern historiography has sometimes presented Aceh as a center of power and learning to be equated with the Ottoman Empire.[34] There is some truth to this. Acehnese sovereigns like ʿAli Mughayat Shah (r.c. 1514–28) may have already started commissioning replacement headstones for the old tombs of the kings of Pasai in an effort to claim continuity with the regional cradle of Islamization. Whereas such early rulers were most likely conscious of their parvenu status, a century later they had become confident of their place in the (Muslim) World. Iskandar II (r. 1636–1641), whose port was sending spices to the Mediterranean in Gujarati ships, would even lead visits to the graves of the "ancestors" at Pasai in the late 1630s.[35]

Such rulers also dispensed their largesse among the Islamic scholars, known as ʿulamaʾ (some of whom claimed links with the older port), who would travel on the same vessels. It is fairly certain that among them was Shams al-Din al-Sumatra'i (a.k.a. Shams al-Din of Pasai, d. 1630), who might be identified with a ranking "archbishop" seen at the court of Aceh by John Davis (c. 1550–1605) in 1599, and perhaps with the same Arabic-speaking "chiefe bishope of the realme" met by James Lancaster (d. 1618) in 1602. Either way, the Arabic-literate Shams al-Din presided over a period of intensifying Jawi contacts with the western end of an increasingly Muslim Indian Ocean. He was instrumental in directing a doctrinal shift from al-Jili's five grades of knowledge towards the ascendant notion of seven grades. This had been advanced in 1590 by the Gujarati Muhammad b. Fadl Allah al-Burhanpuri (d. 1620) in his epistle al-Tuhfa al-mursala ila ruh al-nabi (The Gift Addressed to the Spirit of the Prophet).[36]

In this schema, recognition of God ranges from the possible to the impossible. At the innermost core is God's impenetrable and unknowable being, which is enclosed by six subsequent emanations culminating in the final world of "the perfect man." Scholars often divided these seven stages between the inner three concerned with God's immutable "eternal essences" (aʿyan thabita) and the surrounding four "external essences" (aʿyan kharija) that could be perceived in some way. Perceptible or not, this was a theology not intended for the masses. Only accomplished scholars like Shams al-Din were able to debate its merits with peers across the Indian Ocean or yet explain it in detail to their royal patrons, who may well have wanted to know more of the methods of such Sufis as al-Burhanpuri, known as a master of the Shattariyya tariqa.[37]

Orders like the Shattariyya and Naqshbandiyya were active in India, Arabia, and Yemen, but there is, once again, little surviving evidence of a specific tariqa connection among Jawi scholars and their patrons prior to the seventeenth century. While Shams al-Din is reputed to have inducted Iskandar Muda into

the fraternity of the Naqshbandiyya, there is no verifiable mention of the latter's having made a pledge to a Naqshbandi shaykh. Nor is there any surviving
pedigree predating the nineteenth century that connects him to that, or indeed
any other, tariqa subsequently active in the Malay world.[38]

Even so, one need not necessarily have been a member of a Sufi order to
have been an exponent of mystical theology, which Shams al-Din propagated
until his death in 1630. He was then succeeded by a local scholar of apparently
extreme inclinations called Kamal al-Din, whose tenure was threatened with
the arrival of a scholar from Gujarat in May of 1637. This was Nur al-Din al-
Raniri (d. 1658), a member of the substantial and important Hadrami community of Surat, whose family already had connections with the Malay world.
An uncle had taught elementary subjects at Aceh under ʿAlaʾ al-Din Perak (r.
1577–85), and there are suggestions that he was already known to the Pahang-
born Iskandar II, who had recently succeeded Iskandar Muda.[39]

It appears that al-Raniri was especially disquieted by Kamal al-Din having
advanced the notion (perhaps even in public) that much as God was "our soul
and being," humans were "his soul and being." Although there is no evidence
of this phrasing in previous Malay or Arabic sources presently known, al-
Raniri linked the enunciation to the writings of al-Fansuri and Shams al-Din.
This is all the more surprising given that al-Raniri had previously praised
Shams al-Din, who is also known to have urged that mystical works should be
kept out of reach of the unlettered. In any event it was guilt by association.
After a series of debates before Iskandar II, an apparently unrepentant Kamal
al-Din was executed, while the books of his Jawi predecessors (which might
have contained the phrase) were consigned to the pyre.[40]

Al-Raniri would henceforth rule on practically all questions of religion and
state under the sultan. With the latter's death in 1641, the accession of his
widow Safiyyat al-Din (r. 1641–75) caused him no particular qualms. In fact
he was likely gratified when she began her reign by honoring the established
trading commitments with Gujarat to the momentary consternation of the
Dutch. It was instead a renewal of the debate over theology that justified al-
Raniri's expulsion two years later with the return, in August 1643, of a student
of Kamal al-Din. This man was an ethnic Minangkabau from West Sumatra
called Sayf al-Rijal (d. 1653), said to have studied in Gujarat himself. While
this may well be the case, a recently identified document indicates that he also
styled himself Sayf al-Din al-Azhari, implying that he had had some experience at Cairo's premier teaching mosque, al-Azhar.[41]

Founded by the Fatimids in the tenth century, al-Azhar became famous as a
major center of Sunni juridical authority after their unseating by the Ayyubids
in 1171. It was subsequently patronized by the Mamluk rulers of Cairo (1250–
1517), who supported the holy places of Arabia until their displacement and
incorporation by the Ottomans. As the ultimate destination of the Indian
Ocean spice trade, Cairo was well known to Southeast Asia's traders. Sumatra's

early sultans seem to have emulated Ayyubid regal names, and the Acehnese welcomed Egyptian scholars in the sixteenth century. Aceh's *Bustan al-salatin* (The Garden of Sultans) reports that the court had hosted a certain Muhammad al-Azhari in the 1570s, followed in the 1580s by an authority on the *a'yan thabita* who was implied to be the kinsman of the famous Egyptian jurist and Meccan resident, Ibn Hajar al-Haytami (1504–67).[42]

The identification of Sayf al-Din as Sayf al-Rijal is supported by the fact that al-Raniri later recalled how his enemy had declared that his approach was "that of all the saints of Mecca and Medina."[43] There is as yet no evidence of any Meccan and Medinese saints ever having publically proclaimed that the doctrine of the unity of being entailed interchangeable souls and beings. Rather, the statement appears to be a uniquely Acehnese contribution to Islamic philosophy, and one doomed to an oblivion almost as complete and that of its originator once the tide of more orthodox tariqa learning washed over Aceh's shores. Perhaps the next attempt to suppress its enunciation after al-Raniri came in a short treatise written by Cairo's Muhammad al-Manufi (d. 1663), who was asked (probably in the wake of al-Raniri's expulsion) whether the partisans of Kamal al-Din were true "men of realization" (*muhaqqiqun*). In his reply, al-Manufi used the utterances of Imam Nawawi (d. 1277–78) and Ibn Hajar al-Haytami to suggest that there were many "ignorant pseudo-Sufis" who busied themselves with the works of Ibn al-'Arabi at the expense of the formal sciences of Shari'a *and* tariqa alike, ignoring the law and even frolicking with the opposite sex. Still, once he turned to consider the explicit claim that "God is our soul and being," he remarked that the lack was less in Ibn al-'Arabi's books than in the deluded antinomians themselves.[44]

The remainder of al-Manufi's treatise recapitulated debates over the meanings of Divine Unity and God's perceptible attributes, critiques of pseudo-Christian misinterpretation of scripture, and condemnations of the gatherings in which mystics claimed to experience the wonders of revelation and visions of heavenly gardens. As we shall see in this book, the sorts of concerns raised by al-Manufi will arise again and again. And again and again the defense will be made in terms of local Islam being the true *Meccan* form, even if the locus of juridical authority will so often be vested in Egypt or Egyptian scholarship, where the tariqas had become a crucial part of the social fabric under Ottoman rule. Be that as it may, the later Acehnese scribe who made an interlinear translation of al-Manufi's tract had his own ideas regarding such gatherings and made sure to expand the Malay gloss on al-Manufi's mention of "Ibn 'Arabi and Ibn Farid and their followers," to append, "as well as all the *ulama muhaqqiqin* of Aceh Dar al-Salam, such as Shaykh Hamza Fansuri, Shaykh Shams al-Din Sumatra'i, Shaykh Kamal al-Din Ashi, and Shaykh Sayf al-Din Azhari, may God Almighty's grace be upon them all!"[45]

Setting aside the apparent line of scholars (which reflects a post factum desire to claim all four men as exponents of *Acehnese* Islam), the repeated reference here to the (plural) *muhaqqiqin* is important. Essentially an individual *muhaqqiq* is one who, following Ibn al-ʿArabi, is engaged in seeking the ultimate "reality" (*haqq*) of God. Certainly the term and its verbal form *tahqiq* abound in tracts concerned with Sufism in the Jawi world and with the Arabian Sufi masters the writers came to admire, but we should perhaps look to Egypt in the early seventeenth century to understand its genesis and importance, much as the Acehnese arguing about Kamal al-Din did. This is because debates about *tahqiq* and its application had recently become of interest there in a more technical sense as "verification" of the intent of scripture. It has been suggested that this stemmed from a twofold influx of scholars into the Arab East. On the one hand there were the Azeri and Kurdish masters of "the books of the Persians," fleeing the expansion of the Shiʿi Safavid state; and on the other, there were scholars who came from the Arab West, popularizing works of earlier logicians, such as the Moroccan Muhammad b. Yusuf al-Sanusi (d. 1495).[46] In some respects it is strangely fitting that a Javanese transcribing al-Sanusi's gloss of his own primer, the *Umm al-barahin* (The Mother of Signs), slipped momentarily when describing the author as the "the glory of the sainted *muhaqqiqin*" (see fig. 2, line 9). Still, not all the ʿulamaʾ of the Arab East were favorable to the new *muhaqqiqin* and their heirs. The Acehnese copyist of al-Manufi's *fatwa* regarded the views of the Cairene *mufti* as opposed to his own, and called on God's protection "from the evil of the ones who reject the sayings of all the ʿulamaʾ *muhaqqiqin*."[47]

Certainly we should be cautious in stating here that the arguments between al-Raniri and Kamal al-Din represented a showdown between an irenic and mystical Malayo-Indonesian Islam and a scripturalist Indo-Arab intolerance. Arguments for and against the *muhaqqiqin* would rage in all parts of the Muslim world. Even if al-Raniri's tenure was controversial, it resulted in the writing of works of Islamic jurisprudence (*fiqh*) that remained in the Malay canon well after his expulsion. It is also clear that later writers appreciated al-Raniri's insistence on the proper use of attested Muslim traditions and his rejection of Malay romances like the *Hikayat Seri Rama* (The Romance of Seri Rama) and *Hikayat Inderaputra* (The Romance of Inderaputra).[48]

Perhaps the root of the problem lay in the apparent willingness of aspirant *muhaqqiqin* to wed their teachings to just such writings. Seen from today's perspective, there was much to reject in many of the romances personalizing the names of famous battles of early Islam, or having heroines rather than heroes. Still, al-Raniri had little interest in pursuing the question of female agency given his collaboration with the independent Queen Safiyyat al-Din, who was described by a later visitor, Mansur b. Yusuf al-Misri, as "a gracious and perfect Muslim woman." Female rule evidently caused no problems for this Egyptian, whose stories reached Yemen by ca. 1662. In fact Mansur b. Yusuf had been impressed by the commitment of the Jawi peoples to Islam, declaring that those of Banten and Java "looked to Islam" under kings who were "just and aware."[49]

Certainly they had been looking ever westward. The *Sajarah Banten* (The Chronicle of Banten) recounts how one sovereign, ʿAbd al-Qadir (r. 1626–51), had sent a mission to Mecca in the 1630s. This has often been explained as an effort to obtain the title of Sultan from the Sharif of Mecca, but this reading privileges the politics of titulature above the stated aim of the mission, which was to gain an understanding of key doctrinal works. After stopping at the Maldives, the Coromandel Coast, Surat, and Mocha, the emissaries traveled to Jeddah for an audience with Sharif Zayd (r. 1631–66), who was asked to explain the contents of three tracts.[50] These have been identified as a text on Sufi eschatology, one of al-Fansuri's anthologies, and perhaps even a repost by al-Raniri. Indeed recent scholarship raises the possibility that the dispute between Kamal al-Din and al-Raniri may well have been stirred up by the passing of the Bantenese mission or perhaps its return from Mecca. Whatever the case, the *Sajarah Banten* indicates that the issues being debated in Aceh were almost immediately of concern in West Java. Certainly the Bantenese remained in communication with al-Raniri once he was back in Gujarat. Although the mission was to have proceeded to Constantinople, with the death of their leader, the party took their leave of Sharif Zayd, who gifted them with a stone with the Prophet's footprint, a piece of the covering of the Kaʿba, and a banner said to have belonged to the prophet Abraham. To their regret he was unable to spare a scholar to accompany them, nor was the Shaykh "Ibnu ʿAlam" (perhaps Muhammad ʿAli b. ʿAlan, d. 1647) prepared to leave the Holy City.[51] Gratified nonetheless, the Bantenese returned to a rapturous welcome in 1638. The *Sajarah Banten* even implies that the Sharif had given the Bantenese the right to distribute titles to the lords of Mataram and Makassar. These rulers preferred, however, to send their own delegations to Mecca, which seems to have been the order of the day in the seventeenth century. The Meccans for their part were well aware of the potential largesse on offer, for they dispatched a delegation of their own to Aceh's Queen Zakiyyat al-Din (r. 1678–88) in 1683.[52]

It has often been said that factional politics would ultimately see letters sent to Mecca resulting in a fatwa urging the deposition of the last Acehnese queen, Kamalat al-Din (r. 1688–99), in favor of her husband, Sayyid Hashim Jamal al-Layl. While there is no evidence of any such fatwa, the ascendancy of a Hadrami dynasty has played its part in completing the vision of Aceh as the most Islamic of Islamic states in early modern Indonesia.[53] Some scholars also point to the proselytising role of the ʿAlawiyya, a tariqa from Hadramawt that traces its pedigree back to Muhammad b. ʿAli (d. 1255). The ʿAlawiyya has even been referred to as an "expanded family tariqa," which is no doubt appropriate, at least to some degree. We should keep in mind that the bonds of family often linked people like al-Raniri to the Hijaz, Gujarat, the Maldives, and Aceh. This is certainly a theme to return to, especially in relation to the widespread popularity of the numerous prayers focusing on the person of ʿAbd al-Qadir al-Jilani as a descendant of the Prophet.[54]

That said, the oft-touted diffusion of ʿAlawi grace overstates the role of the men of Hadramawt in Southeast Asian history before the eighteenth century, and we should look to Egypt and Mecca, too. Moreover the driving force for ongoing Islamization should not be seen solely in terms of the presence, or absence, of foreign visitors like the Hadramis. Not to be neglected is the role of Jawi scholars themselves in venturing to the holy lands and either returning to, or writing for, their homelands. It is arguably these figures who should be seen as key to the final transmission and elaboration of the ascendant "Meccan" complex of Islamic institutions under Ottoman rule, institutions that included tariqa practice. Perhaps the most influential scholar in the history of Islam in Southeast Asia has been ʿAbd al-Raʾuf al-Sinkili (1615–93). He was born not far from Pasai, and from his own brief notes we know that this "Jawi" left Aceh (and al-Raniri) in 1642, embarking on an overseas venture that would last some nineteen years.[55]

After moving from teacher to teacher between the Gulf, Yemen, Mecca, and India, it was in Medina that al-Sinkili found his masters, Ahmad al-Qushashi (1583–1661) and Ibrahim al-Kurani (d. 1690), who both had extensive links to Egypt. The first, born in Medina, had had a series of mystical experiences in Yemen, where his father had taken him in 1602. He later returned to Medina and established himself as a teacher of the Shattariyya order after the death of his key Sufi preceptor (and father-in-law) Ahmad al-Shinnawi (d. 1619), who was linked to many Egyptian scholars. Ibrahim al-Kurani was born in Kurdistan and joined al-Qushashi after numerous travels in the Arab East. In 1650 he traveled to Cairo and linked himself to a number of Egyptian scholars. He then returned to Medina in 1651 and became al-Qushashi's deputy for the Shattariyya, though he is today better known in Arab biographical dictionaries as a Naqshbandi. Whereas ʿAbd al-Raʾuf claimed to have affiliated himself to several tariqas, it was the teachings of the Shattariyya that he would take to Aceh and pass on to his disciples like ʿAbd al-Muhyi of Pamijahan (1640?–1715), who established himself at the West Javanese town of Karangnunggal sometime after 1661.

Al-Kurani was also responsible for a tract, the *Ithaf al-dhaki* (The Gifting of the Clever), which he addressed to those Jawis whose enthusiasm for al-Burhanpuri's *Tuhfa* had never abated. Mustafa b. Fath Allah al-Hamawi (d. 1712), who met al-Kurani in 1675, claimed that the questions of several Jawis concerning the interpretation of the *Tuhfa* in their "religious schools" led Kurani to write his text.[56] It seems, however, likely that we can identify a more specific theological issue behind such requests, for al-Kurani also produced a shorter epistle about the reported views of "some of the people of Jawa" who averred, "by virtue of learning and piety" that "God Almighty is our self and being and we are his self and being." These had been the very words of Kamal al-Din; indeed it seems from the context of the reported question, addressed now to "the ʿulamaʾ of verification," that Kamal al-Din's theology was being reframed in terms of a general debate between "some of the people of Jawa" and "some of the [foreign] 'ulama' [now] heading there."[57]

Al-Kurani was more generous in his responses than al-Manufi had been. He argued that the Jawi in question had not deserved death, but that both he and his attacker had misinterpreted the esoteric meaning of the words of Ibn al-'Arabi relayed by al-Burhanpuri. In the *Shath al-wali* (The Utterance of the Saint), al-Kurani further proposed that only an individual possessed of a weak faith would come to such a view, and then only if he applied an overly rationalist reading of the Qur'an. The ultimate aim of the mystic was a "return" to the divine Creator, while recognizing that one's being was still a part of creation, and hence inescapably separate.[58]

Al-Sinkili's own contributions on matters mystical seem to have begun when Safiyyat al-Din asked him to write his *Mir'at al-tullab* (Mirror of the Seekers). That al-Sinkili in this work sought a middle path between local ecstatic antinomians and the Shari'a-centrists heading (back) to Southeast Asia is shown by the fact that he paraphrased the poetry of Hamza al-Fansuri without citing his name. By the same token, and like al-Raniri, he was no opponent of al-Burhanpuri's seven grades. Rather he argued in his *Daqa'iq al-huruf* (The Details of the Letters) against confusing the inner, eternal essences with the external, perceptible ones, for that would equate creation with God.[59] Certainly his Bantenese emissary 'Abd al-Muhyi was a teacher of the *Tuhfa*, as was another deputy, Shaykh Burhan al-Din (1646–1704), who is now remembered as the Islamizer of the Minangkabau (regardless of the existence of many older Muslim graves) and founder of a school at Ulakan. Perhaps most famously al-Sinkili is known for his translation and exegesis of the Qur'an, the *Tarjuman al-mustafid* (The Beneficial Translation), the first fully fledged Malay exegesis based on the treatment of "the two Jalals" of Egypt; Jalal al-Din al-Mahalli (1389–1459) and his student Jalal al-Din al-Suyuti (1445–1505).[60]

Quite unlike the situation in the sixteenth century then, when it seems that there was simply an eagerness for the knowledge of "Sufism" that foreign guests could impart and a willingness to philosophize about the eternal essences, seventeenth-century Aceh would become a center of scholarly industry and a regally sponsored clearing house for tariqa learning in the Shattari tradition. But it was not the only polity to produce a scholar of international calibre, witness Yusuf al-Maqassari (a.k.a. Shaykh Yusuf Taj al-Khalwati, 1627–99). Born in the newly Islamized Kingdom of Gowa, on Sulawesi, Yusuf left for Arabia in September of 1644, stopping off at Banten, where he befriended the crown prince, and then Aceh, where he may have rued the absence of al-Raniri.[61] Like al-Sinkili, al-Maqassari spent years in the teaching circles of the Middle East. He linked himself to the Naqshbandi fraternity and transcribed a work of Mawlana Jami (d. 1492) under the guidance of al-Kurani. Ultimately, however, he determined that the Khalwatiyya was the order for him, and was inducted at Damascus by Ayyub al-Khalwati (1586–1661).[62]

On his return to the archipelago in the late 1660s, al-Maqassari, better known today as Shaykh Yusuf, was welcomed in Banten, where his old friend had since taken the throne as Ageng Tirtayasa (r. 1651–83). He married into the royal family and corresponded with the elite of his birthplace. It was this perhaps that made Banten an obvious place of refuge for many Makassarese after a combined Dutch and Bugis alliance sacked Gowa in 1669. Shaykh Yusuf is perhaps best known to Indonesians today for having led the resistance against the Dutch in Banten after the Dutch East India Company intervened in 1683. After the capture and exiling of Ageng, Shaykh Yusuf took over the command for some weeks from Karangnunggal. After his capture in December of 1683, he too went into exile, to Ceylon. He continued to write for his home community from that island until 1693, when he was sent further west to the Cape of Good Hope, where he died in 1699.

Throughout this time he remained a conduit for tariqa authority to the region, and became, ultimately, a pattern for retrospective emulation in the specific locales where he had been active. The *Sajarah Banten* and its Malay variant, the *Hikayat Hasan al-Din* (The Romance of Hasan al-Din), seem to retrofit Shaykh Yusuf's Khalwati connections with notable *muhaqqiqin* onto Sunan Gunung Jati at the opening of the sixteenth century. It even trumps them in certain respects by making their particular saint a sayyid, who regularly communicated with his ancestor the Prophet, not to mention with various famous Sufis who were not necessarily alive at the same time or in Mecca during his alleged Hajj. These included Mawlana Jami, as well as the Cairene jurist Zakariyya' al-Ansari (1420–1520) and his pupil 'Abd al-Wahhab al-Sha'rani (1493–1565).[63]

The works of the last two scholars would arguably become of greater influence in the eighteenth and nineteenth centuries than in their own lifetimes (see below). In any event, a more reliable royal account from Gowa, written some time before 1729, chronicles the arrival from Banten in 1678 of Shaykh Yusuf's principal vicegerent, 'Abd al-Basir (a.k.a. Tuang Rappang, d. 1723), who was followed by members of his retinue from Cirebon in 1684.[64] There is clear evidence of Khalwati activity in Sulawesi by 1688, when a French priest, Nicholas Gervaise (c.1662–1729), published an account of Makassar, largely based on his interviews with two princes whom he tutored in Paris. In his account Gervaise described how local religious leaders, known as *Agguys*, presided over well-maintained stone mosques. These were equipped, what is more, with a staff of celibate mendicants called *Santaris* tasked with serving the mosque.[65] In order, Gervaise noted:

> that they be the less expos'd to the danger of becoming unfaithful to their Vocation, and to their Vow of Chastity, they Live Night and Day in little Cells, separated one from the other, and which are all built in the Mosque: There they receive every Morning the Alms of the Faithful, upon which they are to enjoy nothing in Propriety; and when they want any thing

necessary for the Support of Life, they think it an Honour to go and Beg from door to door. Their Number is more or less, according to the bigness of the Mosque; they wear neither Locks nor Beards; a plain Bonnet of white Linnen covers their Heads, and the Garment of the same clour, with which they are cloath'd, reaches no farther than their Knees. If they are forc'd to go abroad upon any urgent Affair, they beg leave of the Grand *Agguy*, and then they put on what cloathes they think convenient; nor are they distinguish'd from Seculars, but only that their Heads are shaved, carry a white Turbant, and wear neither Scimitar nor Cris by their Sides.[66]

This is perhaps the first clear Western reference to tariqa devotees in the archipelago, and one replete with echoes of Cairo, especially in its terminology as communicated by two young members of the learned elite. The word *Agguy*, for example, is very close to the Cairene variant of *Hajji* (*Haggi*), the title by which many Southeast Asian teachers would be known, while Friday services are referred to in Gervaise's text as *Guman*, perhaps from the Egyptian pronunciation of "Friday" (*al-gumʿa*).[67] Still, this should not be taken too far as it does not necessarily bespeak anything beyond the presence of a scholar of Egyptian origin or Jawis having been trained by Egyptians. In fact Gervaise was at pains to point out that the devout Makassarese aimed to emulate one form of Islam alone, and it was not that of Cairo:

And now it is not to be imagin'd, with what exactness the *Macasarians* acquit themselves of the Duties enjoyn'd by their new Religion: They would not miss of the meanest Holydays which it prescribes, without signalizing their Devotion, every one in particular, by some Good Work or other, of Supererogation; the neglect of a Bow, or any slight Washing, is look'd upon them as a considerable Crime. Some of them out of meer Sentiment of Repentence, abstain'd all their Lives from drinking Palm-Wine, tho' it be not forbidden by the Law: And some there are, that will rather dye for Thirst, than Drink so much as a Glass of Water, from Sunrising to Sun-setting, during the whole time of their Lent. More than this, they are far more devout than all other *Mahometans*; because they observe an infinite number of Ceremonies that are not in use among the *Turks*, nor among the *Indian Mahometans*; because they believe them to be practis'd at *Mecca*, which they look upon as the Center of their Religion, and the Pattern which they ought to follow.[68]

The *Santari*s were not the only members of the *Agguy* elite described by Gervaise. There were also the junior members of the clerisy, known as *Labe*, and the all-important *Toüan*s, a.k.a. "Tuans"; whose very authority rested on that same "Meccan" Pattern:

The third Order is that of the *Toüan*, which cannot be conferr'd in any other place than at *Meca*, and that by the Grand *Mufti* himself. Whence it comes to pass, that there are very few *Toüans* in *Macasar*; because that every body will not give themselves the trouble of going far to be Ordain'd, nor engage themselves in so great an Expence. This Order, which they receive from the Grand *Mufti*, renders them all equal, as to the Dignity of the Character; but the inequality of the Jurisdiction, makes a great difference between them. They who serve the biggest Mosques, have more Credit and Authority than the others; and he who has the Honour to be near the King, is the highest of all, as it were the Patriarch and Primate of the Kingdom; nor does he acknowledge any one above him, but the Grand *Mufti* of *Mecca*. They may all Marry, and if their Wives happen to dye, they are permitted to take another. But they forbid Polygamy, under very severe Penalties, which they cannot escape, if they are convicted of it. As they are beloved and respected by all the People, who load them with Presents every day; and as there is not a Wedding, nor a Feast, to which they are not first all invited, and honourably admitted, the Life which they lead seems very commodious and easie.[69]

More crucially, we begin to see evidence that the cult maintained by the *Ag-guys* took on distinctly regal, and localized, tones. In 1701 the Gowan annals report that the kings began to visit the grave of Dato-ri-Bandung, said to have been one of the first preachers of Islam to the Makassarese in the 1570s. Soon, however, they began to favor that of Shaykh Yusuf after his body was repatriated from the Cape in 1705, perhaps in response to urging by his son, who had returned in June 1702.[70] Certainly his son was welcome at court, and future royal genealogies of Makassar would incorporate the lineage of Shaykh Yusuf with the same alacrity as the Bantenese showed in making Sunan Gunung Jati into a Khalwati and a descendant of the Prophet. His mortal return even seems to have occluded the roles played by earlier *Agguys* and such sojourners as an Arab shaykh, ʿUmar Ba Mahsun (1634–93), who had also arrived in 1684 (some weeks after Shaykh Yusuf's followers), and subsequently served as a prominent *Tuan*.[71]

CHAOS AT KARTASURA

Azyumardi Azra argues that Shaykh Yusuf consistently emphasized the need for a balance between the requirements of Shariʿa and Sufism in his teachings, but that, unlike al-Qushashi, he held that the novice had to be utterly loyal to his shaykh. Such loyalty must have played on Dutch minds when they sent him across the Indian Ocean, or as they watched over coronations where regents initiated princes such as Mallawang Gawe (d. 1742) within the walls of the Dutch fort in a manner reminiscent of a Sufi pledge.[72] It was to prove an issue too when, over the course of the next few decades, their formal allies in Mataram seemed to come under the influence of other Sufi masters.

By the beginning of the eighteenth century, the Dutch had eaten away the domains of Mataram in exchange for promises of military assistance against the rebellious north coast provinces. In the process they gained the right to collect taxes on behalf of the descendants of Sultan Agung. Still, the Javanese chronicles betray but little concern with the Dutch, who were, it seems, poorly apprised of what was going on at court in respect of Islam. Much of what follows appears to have entered little into Dutch calculations, and has only been made known to us through the work of Ricklefs on Javanese accounts and from tangential observations made by the Dutch.

According to these sources, in 1731 a teacher was tried under Pakubuwana II (r. 1726–49) for revealing mystical truths to the uninitiated. This was Hajji Ahmad Mutamakin of the village of Cabolek, near Semarang, who claimed to have been instructed in the Naqshbandi techniques by a Shaykh "Zayn al-Yamani," perhaps the son of a teacher to both al-Sinkili and al-Maqassari. Certainly his foreign pedigree was regarded with suspicion. In the *Serat Cabolek* (The Book of Cabolek), Ketib Anom of Kudus mocks Mutamakin for his Arabian credentials and preference for foreign books. As far as Ketib Anom was concerned, true knowledge of Sufism was already to be found in kawi texts like the *Ramayana*. It would seem then that there is some evidence of a conflict between synthetic local understandings of Sufism and the Sufism being imported from Arabia in both Arabic *and* Malay, the other scholarly language of ʿAbd al-Raʾuf, Shaykh Yusuf, and ʿAbd al-Muhyi.[73]

Hajji Mutamakin apparently escaped ultimate sanction, and a follower of Ketib Anom, Pangeran Urawan, showed the bemused yokel how true Sufism was to be found in the Indo-Javanese works. Yet Urawan may himself have had links to the same current of Arabo-Malay influence. The son of a royal exile sent to Batavia in 1721, Urawan was at the center of a clique forming around Pakubuwana II around 1729 that seems to have been especially active from 1731 to 1738, at which time, and at the insistence of the Dutch, he was exiled to Ceylon, an action that occasioned considerable disquiet in pious circles. Urawan had, however, hardly acted alone. His allies included the future chief minister, Natakusuma, and two other men from Batavia. One was a teacher called Kyai Mataram, who had arrived in 1735. The other was an Arab called Sayyid ʿAlwi, who had come in 1737.[74]

What teachings this clique supported are at present less than clear, though it seems that they were opposed by a faction backed by Pakubuwana II's grandmother, who sponsored the rewriting of several texts held, since the time of Sultan Agung, to possess a magical power that united the Javanese and Muslim worlds. Among these was a reworking of the Qurʾanic tale of Joseph; the *Kitab Usulbiyya* (The Book of Usulbiyya?), which was heavily influenced by the *Isra' wa-miʿraj* (The Night Journey and Ascension) of Muhammad (see below); and an Alexander romance translated from a Malay model brought from Champa.[75]

Beyond importing a more pronounced opposition to the Dutch, there are suggestions that at least one member of the young faction was affiliated in some way with the Qadiriyya order.[76] Even though there are Qadiri links in the story, a case can be made that they are affiliated with the Shattariyya brought to Java by ʿAbd al-Muhyi. The outward-looking proclivities of Natakusuma and Sayyid ʿAlwi arguably became clearer once the so-called China War commenced in October 1740. Natakusumaʾs faction commissioned the writing down of a series of Shattari pedigrees following an early Javanese victory over the Dutch garrison of Kartasura. These pedigrees were also accompanied by a wayward interpretation of the *Fath al-rahman*, first written by the warrior-Sufi of Damascus, Wali Raslan, and redacted by al-Ansari. There must have been some global resonance here, as al-Ansari, the famous Shafiʿi Qadi of Egypt under Qaʾit Bey (r. 1468–95), was already imagined to be a fellow in Mecca of Sunan Gunung Jati.[77]

Despite such compositions and prayers, however, ultimate victory did not ensue for the Javanese. With the loss of the court to Madurese forces, Pakubuwana II returned to the Dutch fold and, after wanderings into the wilderness near Ponorogo, even handed over his erstwhile mentors to exile. In so doing he turned his back on the competing pietisms of his late grandmother and his Batavian allies alike. The stage was now set for other voices to challenge the legitimacy of the Dutch in Java.

Conclusion

We have seen that numerous difficulties beset any attempt at plotting a straightforward history of the conversion and Islamization of Indonesiaʾs many diverse peoples up to the middle of the eighteenth century. What does emerge is a sense that certain key courts took on the mantle of defenders of Islam (regardless of their actions against Muslims of neighbouring polities) and regularly sought validation from beyond their shores, most preferably from the person of the Prophetʾs lineal descendants in Mecca and the scholars associated with them. As a part of the mix, the latest form of high orthodoxy as embodied by Sufi praxis would appear to have been embraced as well. Far from being a mechanism of conversion, however, Sufism was formally restricted to the regal elite, while adherence to the Shariʿa was commended to their subjects. Moreover, as the singular case of Kamal al-Din makes clear, we begin to perceive the intense gravitational pull of Cairo in our story; which is only natural when one considers that Egypt supported the holy places under its Mamluk and Ottoman rulers. By the eighteenth century it even appears that the works of several Egyptian scholars, some of whom had a dim view of the Medinese tradition and its advocates, would begin to find a fixed place in the curricula of Jawi scholars throughout the region, and especially where sultans still reigned, if in name only.

CHAPTER TWO

Embracing a New Curriculum, 1750–1800

LEAVING THE COURTS

Compared to Aceh, Banten, and Mataram, we know little of the argumentation in the other, often warring, Muslim states of the eastern half of the archipelago, though it seems to have followed the lead of Sumatra. Makassarese legends claim, for example, that it was an Acehnese queen's use of diplomacy that convinced their king to embrace the Islam of Mecca. While spurious, such tales nonetheless echo the trajectory of Muslim knowledge as it spread throughout the region.[1] Certainly they give us little information about the means of conversion, barring surviving hints that iconography and oral performance may have had a part to play. Just before describing the spiky and putrid-smelling fruit we know as the durian, Mansur al-Misri, the Egyptian who had called at the court of Queen Safiyyat al-Din, wrote of how he had once been asked by some Dutchmen at Batavia to don the dress of a local religious scholar (which he noted was not the costume of the Egyptian or Ottoman ʿulamaʾ) and to pose for local artisans whose normal trade it was to depict their "messenger/prophets" (*anbiyaʾihim*) carrying the Qurʾan under their arms. Perhaps their more usual subjects were saints like Sunan Kalijaga, for at least one early nineteenth-century Javanese source appears to indicate that the line between the saints and prophets was often blurred.[2]

A much later echo of such a depiction would seem to be found in a sketch sent to the Dutch Orientalist Snouck Hurgronje by Muhammad Yasin of Kelayu on the island of Lombok. It shows a bearded figure of somewhat Arab appearance, bearing a spear in his right hand and carrying a bag of scriptures under his arm.[3] He resembles Sufi dervishes, who could still be photographed in the Middle East in the nineteenth century; though a figure of this kind is also emblematic of the traditional north-coast saint depicted as a holy messenger, lawgiver, and warrior. In any event, we will need to ask yet again what other texts such missionaries might have carried with them, and where (and indeed when) tariqa Sufism had a place in their missions. Whereas the influential scholar A. H. Johns once saw the profession of Islam as "practically synonymous" with membership in a tariqa in Southeast Asia, he later moderated his views. Even if the teachings attributed to Malik Ibrahim and Seh Bari are suffused with mystical speculation, they make no allusion to tariqa practice, leading us to wonder just what texts other than the Qurʾan may have been under the arms of the saintly messengers who preceded ʿAbd al-Raʾuf and Shaykh Yusuf.[4]

Sites of Learning

Sufism as embodied in tariqa practice is not the only form of Islamicate learning that is often asserted as having been a part of the first offerings of the
saints. They were also allegedly responsible for the founding of religious
schools, known individually as *pesantren* (lit. "the place of the *santri* [religious
students]") so often linked to figures like Mawlana Maghribi, though we have
no corraborative accounts of religious education being delivered by such institutions in the early centuries of Islam's spread, nor in fact anywhere beyond the
verandas of the mosques sanctioned by a given court. Despite the observations
of travelers like Jacob van Neck (1564–1638), who saw a school run by the
state preacher of Ternate in 1599 (and whose illustrator showed the ruler proceeding to its mosque with prayer beads in his hand, see fig. 5), and John Davis,
who noted the existence of "many schooles" (and the use of prayer beads) in
Aceh in the same year, there is little surviving evidence that such sites were
anything like the large residential complexes of today.[5]

At first sight Gervaise's second-hand account of Makassar in the 1680s
would seem to provide evidence of a relationship between rulers, teachers, and
tariqa mystics. But then again he was told that the *Santari*s were adult ascetics,
rather than the young students of elementary primers who are more normally
known as *santri* in Indonesia today. For their part the youthful members of the
community took their lessons in huts in the company of the *Agguy*s for two
hours a day in between learning more practical trades. Unfortunately we do not
have similar descriptions for Java. To the contrary, Ricklefs has argued that
there is no evidence of any pesantren on that island prior to 1718, when Dutch
East India Company reports mention the Surabayan enemies of Kartasura establishing a "training school." Even then he is suspicious, as he is of claims that
Pakubuwana II later established the great pesantren of Tegalsari, near Ponorogo, in quest of renewed spiritual power after his defeat in 1740.[6]

A lack of evidence for royal sanction need not invalidate claims that independent Islamic schools existed in the eighteenth century or earlier, but such
sanction must have been crucial to maintaining the structures required by the
partisans of Shaykh Yusuf or ʿAbd al-Ra'uf if they were engaged in the sorts of
practices that we have seen on Sulawesi. Indeed royal recognition in Southeast
Asia was in general highly desirable as it would usually release a teacher and
his retainers from all demands for taxes or corvée labor. By the mid-nineteenth
century there were numerous stories of Javanese rulers, such as Pakubuwana II
and Mangkubumi (1749–92), following ancient precedent and making particular villages associated with religious teaching or sacred graves *perdikan*, or
"free" of all tax and labor obligations. In this respect it also seems that Shattari
teachings had by now become accepted by more and more members of Java's
courts and the particular perdikans they supported.[7]

To be sure, not all perdikans were connected to the Shattariyya order at first, if indeed ever. The charter of Tegalsari only had Pakubuwana II urging the founders to read religious texts, without any mention of what they were, nor yet of any particular tariqa. Still, by 1789 there is evidence of a regally backed Shattari orientation, with the mention of Pakubuwana IV of Surakarta (r. 1788–1820) as having come under the influence of a faction whose praxis deviated from the now hegemonic learning of "Karang." Even if it is unclear what learning this rival clique represented—whether it was domestic "deviation" or perhaps even the challenge of the new "Meccan" learning of the Sammaniyya order (see below)—the reference to "Karang" is in all likelihood to the network linked to ʿAbd al-Muhyi, whose grave, grotto, (and school) were to be found in the region of Karangnunggal, Banten.[8]

Perhaps the most interesting suggestions regarding the emergence of Shattari-oriented perdikans relates, once again, to the issue of nomenclature. Even in the late nineteenth century the sort of Islamic school the Shattaris supported was seldom known as a pesantren, but rather as a *pondok*, a word assumed to derive from the Arabic word for a place of lodging (*funduq*, itself a borrowing from Greek). Just as Venetians and Portuguese were lodged in the *funduq*s of Cairo in the sixteenth century, so too were Acehnese emissaries, leading one to wonder if the Ottoman-style mercantile "lodge" had found its way into Southeast Asia, where it was transformed, by virtue of its inhabitants, into a nucleus for the inculcation of Muslim learning. Once again, however, there is little evidence for specifically religious institutions on this model prior to the eighteenth century. Instead one finds brief references to verbs based on the pondok being a general "shelter" in seventeenth century Malay chronicles from Borneo, which add weight to the suggestion that the independent boarding school is indeed a recent innovation.[9]

Sammani Reformism in Palembang, Banjarmasin, and Banten

One source that projects the pesantren back in time is the nineteenth century *Serat Centhini* (The Book of Centhini), in which a hermit explains that he had studied at Karang under ʿAbd al-Qadir al-Jilani. Leaving aside the legendary nature of most such claims, scholars have shown that this particular account, with its mention of various Islamic texts, remains of value when read in conjunction with the reports of L.W.C. van den Berg (1845–1927), compiled after a tour of Java in 1885. Both sources make it clear that the scholarly diet of Javanese Muslims was becoming ever more stable and bound to standards set in Mecca and perhaps at Cairo's al-Azhar mosque, led between 1794 and 1812 by ʿAbdallah al-Sharqawi.[10]

Though there are hints of a Southeast Asian presence in Cairo during the later life of al-Sharqawi, his popularity may well reflect his earlier years in

Mecca, or his regular visits there. It was probably in Mecca that al-Sharqawi inducted two Jawis into the Sammani brotherhood, founded by the Medinese Muhammad Samman (1717–76), who had cultivated tariqa links with Cairo in 1760. One of these Jawi initiates was the ecstatic Muhammad Nafis al-Banjari (fl. 1770s–1820s), the other was the more sober (and prolific) Da'ud al-Fatani (d. ca. 1845).[11] As we shall see below, both men had predecessors who should be seen as the instigators of a shift toward Egyptian scholarship at the (public) expense of the more speculative Medinese *muhaqqiqin*. Perhaps the most famous of these forebears were ʿAbd al-Samad al-Falimbani (1719–89) and Muhammad Arshad al-Banjari (d.1812?). Both had sat with Shaykh Samman himself in Medina and both should be seen as having played a crucial role in pointing Malay courts towards the writings of al-Ghazali and his Egyptian interpreters.

ʿAbd al-Samad and Arshad were themselves building on trends being set in the archipelago. ʿAbd al-Samad's hometown of Palembang was emerging as a center for scholarship in the eighteenth century, eclipsing Aceh and perhaps complementing Patani to the North.[12] No longer the vassal of Mataram, by the 1750s Palembang outshone its old rival Jambi and soon would be competing with Banten for control over the lucrative pepper-producing areas of Lampung. Whereas Java became ever more fractured and ever more firmly in the grip of the Dutch East India Company after the China War, Palembang's Sultan Mahmud Badr al-Din (r. 1724–57) appears to have embraced both Chinese miners of tin and Dutch traders alike, joking on one occasion that he would "fire pepper and tin at the Company," which would bombard him in turn "with good Spanish rials."[13] The long peace enjoyed by Palembang under Mahmud and his successors also seems to have attracted numerous Arab visitors and allowed some members of the court to become preoccupied with policing antinomian mysticism. The crown prince who would later reign as Sultan Ahmad Taj al-Din (r. 1757–74) before stepping down to act as Susuhunan (1774–76), sponsored a translation of Wali Raslan's *Fath al-rahman* which offered a far more accurate expression of the latest form of orthodoxy encountered in Mecca or Cairo than the variants composed at Kartasura in the 1740s.[14]

G.W.J. Drewes first drew sustained attention to this issue when he demonstrated the contributions of two Palembang scholars, Shihab al-Din b. ʿAbdallah Ahmad and Kemas Fakhr al-Din, who were active in the 1750s and 1770s respectively. They were also anticipated by an Acehnese active in Mecca, Muhammad Zayn al-Ashi, who should be seen as a Sufi working to restrict the teachings of the Wujudiyya to the elect; though he criticized both the sorts of attacks made by al-Raniri and the claims of his own countrymen to understand the writings of al-Qushashi, al-Kurani, or even al-Sinkili after a mere two or three years' study. While he advised his fellow Jawis against reading the works of al-Fansuri, Shams al-Din, and Sayf al-Rijal, he did so only because he felt they were not competent to comprehend them. Back in Sumatra, Shihab al-Din argued against a "Malay" tendency to follow incompetent teachers and place themselves above the Shariʿa. He similarly urged that (assumedly Shattari) books about the seven grades be removed from the reach of unqualified people, much as Kemas Fakhr al-Din paraphrased the *Fath al-rahman* in the 1770s, making essentially the same call, and perhaps under the personal influence of one of the many Arabs drawn to the Sultanate.[15]

Much has been made of the rise of the Arab community of Palembang. It is claimed, for example, that ʿAbd al-Samad was the grandson of a Yemen-born mufti of Kedah. Born in Palembang around 1719, his early periods of study and teaching were spent in Zabid, where he formed connections with such scholars as the Indian polymath, Murtada al-Zabidi (1732–90), who went to Cairo in 1766. Such encounters would seem to have drawn al-Falimbani on to Egypt as well—together with three famous colleagues: Muhammad Arshad al-Banjari, ʿAbd al-Wahhab al-Bugisi, and ʿAbd al-Rahman b. Ahmad al-Misri. Certainly, something inspired him to place himself under Shaykh Samman in Medina between 1767 and 1772, where he began his studies by reading the *Fath al-rahman*. But whereas Muhammad Arshad, ʿAbd al-Wahhab, and ʿAbd al-Rahman would travel from the Hijaz to the archipelago in 1772, al-Falimbani could only have made a short visit home, if at all, given that he was again active at Mecca and Taʾif from 1773 to 1789. Still, it remains possible that such a sojourn may well have led Kemas Fakhr al-Din to paraphrase the *Fath al-rahman* and inspired the court to go over to the Sammaniyya *in toto*; and at the expense of the Shattariyya.[16]

Another hint to the attentuated religious climate in Palembang may be garnered from a Sufi manual collected by a young William Marsden in Bengkulu between 1771 and 1779. There is the strong likelihood that Marsden had acquired it together with another document, a neatly executed primer (of al-Sanusi) belonging to Sultan Ahmad and copied shortly after he abdicated in 1774. As might be expected, the Sufi manual contained a glossed treatment of the standard admonitions to the student on the necessity of having a shaykh and following him in such matters as reducing sleep and food. There were also Javanese sections containing images related to the Shattari tradition and some badly spelled statements attributed to al-Ghazali. Lying amid this heterogenous material, however, is a note in Malay which, although generic, could almost allude to the loss of authority of a local master who had once owned these texts. It runs: "As he did not know how to interpret the manner of the Companions, he lost his faith by offending them; for the *hadith* of the messenger of God, peace and blessings be upon him, makes it obligatory that we respect and honor them. Know then that this is the true root of belief."[17]

The major part of the Palembang library, shipped to Batavia in 1822, suggests a similar distancing from the Jawi Shattari tradition (see ch. 5). Beyond primers and a scattering of Malay and Javanese materials (including the works of al-Raniri and al-Sinkili), there are key texts representative of a standardizing tradition. These include Ibn ʿAtaʾ Allah al-Iskandari's (d.1309) *Hikam* (The Wisdoms), the works of al-Ghazali, and al-Ansari's *Fath al-rahman*. The writings of al-Fansuri and Shams al-Din, in stark contrast, are nowhere to be seen.[18]

Whereas there is no solid evidence that the Palembangese promoters of the works of Wali Raslan ever invoked him as the Javanese victors had at Kartasura, we might wonder if perhaps this was the case given the tenor of three epistles said to have been sent from Mecca by ʿAbd al-Samad just before his alleged journey to the archipelago. Nearly identical copies of a missive that commended the pursuit of holy war, and which perhaps served as a recommendation for its bearers, went to Hamengkubuwana I and his half-brother, Susuhunan Prabu Jaka. Soon after his return to Mecca, ʿAbd al-Samad furthermore set about writing a treatise on the merits of jihad. Even so, al-Falimbani was much more the "reformer" depicted by Azyumardi Azra, and he is invoked in Indonesian history far more for his translations of Ghazali's works, such as his *Hidayat al-salikin* (The Gift of the Wayfarers, 1778) and *Sayr al-salikin* (The Path of the Wayfarers, 1788).[19]

It was once believed that al-Falimbani was the author of an earlier treatise entitled the *Tuhfat al-raghibin* (The Gift of the Desirous). However, the writer of that work has since been shown to be his fellow traveler, Muhammad Arshad al-Banjari, who most likely dedicated the work to Sultan Tamhid Allah of Banjarmasin (r. 1773–1808).[20] In his youth Muhammad Arshad had been a protégé, and then son-in-law, of Sultan Tahlil Allah (1700–45). This sultan also established a house in Mecca for his pilgrim subjects. Once there, Muhammad Arshad attached himself, much as al-Falimbani had, to such scholars as Muhammad b. Sulayman al-Kurdi (1715–80) before traveling on to Cairo. There he may well have been inspired by its numerous *madrasa*s, for oral history relates that on his return to Banjar he established a complex together with ʿAbd al-Wahhab al-Bugisi. It also appears that he led a campaign against a local Wujudi called ʿAbd al-Hamid Abulung. According to the Banjarese, Abulung was a student of the Mecca-based Muhammad Nafis al-Banjari, who was reported to have proclaimed that "there is nothing in existence except Him . . . He is me and I am Him." And, in a story that should by now be familiar to us, he was ordered executed by Sultan Tamhid Allah.[21]

We are on firmer historiographical ground in 1781 when Muhammad Arshad, acting on royal instruction, would expand al-Raniri's *Sirat al-mustaqim* (The Straight Path) to produce his *Sabil al-muhtadin* (The Path of the Guided). Though Muhammad Arshad placed himself in a lineage of the *muhaqqiqin*, unlike al-Falimbani he made no reference at all to Ibrahim al-Kurani, Shams al-Din, or al-Burhanpuri, and instead advocated a return to the more restrained writings of sober Egyptian scholars such as al-Suyuti and al-Shaʿrani; indeed recent work on the eighteenth century has shown that the works of al-Shaʿrani took increasing pride of place in the Ottoman context.[22] It is also apparent that, rather like al-Raniri, the rising generation abhored "traditional" Malay works and practices. Al-Banjari scorned romances as unverifiable stories and condemned the practice of making propitiatory offerings as was "customary in some of the lands below the winds." A similar attitude seems to have prevailed at Terengganu into the 1830s, some three decades after a local Qadi had issued a directive that all such texts be burnt. [23]

Still, old habits would prove hard to break in the region. In 1837, visiting Western missionaries found the people of Brunei anxiously awaiting the latest romances from Singapore. Rival tariqa affiliations were similarly resilient. Sufi lineages collected in the Southern Philippines suggest that, regardless of the ascent of the Sammaniyya at the Palembang court, the Shattariyya maintained a presence in the surrounding countryside of Sumatra.[24] It also gained in strength up the Malay Peninsula under the influence of al-Falimbani's student Da'ud al-Fatani, who seems to have been more interested in the juridical approach of his master than his tariqa. The partisans of the seven grades were not silenced either. Muhammad Nafis al-Banjari would compose a work, *Durr al-nafis* (The Pearl of the Precious One), expressing this very theosophy in 1786, though this may have been a case of the story of Kamal al-Din repeating itself, as it was most likely written from the relative safety of Mecca or Medina.[25]

We have the explicit statements of ʿAbd al-Samad and Muhammad Arshad to anchor our discussion of events in East Sumatra and Southeast Borneo. Yet when it comes to assessing the intentions of their fellow-travelers in Central and East Java, there is at present less evidence available. It is possible that the Sammaniyya may have spread among the elite troops of Mangkunegara I (1726–96)—to whom one of al-Falimbani's Meccan letters was sent, along with a banner, in 1772—but an eyewitness of the 1780s only reports the frequent performance of dhikr without ascribing to it any tariqa appellation.[26] By contrast, we can point with greater confidence to a hardening of attitudes against the Medinese tradition in West Java, for the royal library of Banten—where the Sammaniyya would find favor alongside the Rifaʿiyya order—contained Arabic works very much like those found at Palembang. Once again a notable proportion of these books are attributable to Egyptian scholars or to authors influenced by Egyptian scholarship. In particular, there were several copies of al-Shaʿrani's *Yawaqit wa-l-jawahir* (The Rubies and Gems) and *Mizan* (The Scales). The first was an eschatological text and contained a description of Judgment Day. The second was a tract composed of the teachings of the four imams, following Khidr, whose opinion al-Shaʿrani claimed to have solicited through his mystic brother.[27]

We should bear in mind that the Egyptian opponents of the Medinese tradition were not opponents of tariqa practices or even of mystical communica-

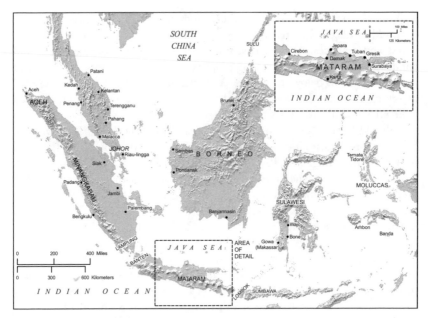

Figure 3. Archipelagic Islam, 1600–1900.

tions in toto. Al-Suyuti may had been famously averse to "Persian" scholarship and al-Sha'rani may have been a critic of the mostly Turkish and Persian Khalwatis and Naqshbandis of Egypt, but both were Sufis.[28] Neither does this mean that all the works popular during earlier times were banished. The primers of Muhammad b. Yusuf al-Sanusi, "the pride of the *muhaqqiqin*," would remain in use, and the Banten archives included numerous copies of the *Dala'il al-khayrat* (Guides to Felicity), a manual of prayers composed in praise of the Prophet by al-Sanusi's fellow Maghribi Muhammad b. Sulayman al-Jazuli (d. 1465). Copies of this text were to be found across the Muslim world, with richly embellished exemplars regularly displaying the powerful images of the grave and pulpit of the Prophet, though it appears that the late eighteenth-century reformist mood saw their replacement with less detailed layouts of the sacred precincts of Mecca and Medina.[29]

As we shall see, these images were chosen for recollection and copying by jihadis in the Padang Highlands in the nineteenth century. Rather than proceeding at length to reconstruct the collections amassed by other centers, such as Brunei (which was developing an appetite for Daghistani illuminated Qur'ans), we should turn back now to nineteenth-century curricula of the *pondok*s, which by this date certainly did exist across the archipelago, and consider how some students might have trodden the path of Muslim learning.

ELEMENTARY BEGINNINGS, MYSTICAL ENDS

Knowledge of the Qur'an is the core of any Muslim education, and the Jawi student would typically begin with the last of its thirty sections.[30] From this point, aided by teacher and peers alike, the student would learn how to recite the text using techniques of enunciation. Throughout the course of studies a strong emphasis was placed on memorization and oral recitation, essential skills for the transmission of Malay literature in general, and highly prized. The blind were among the best-known and most proficient practitioners, as Zayn al-Din of Sumbawa observed in his own textbook of 1888:

> Some 'ulama' say that sight is superior to hearing, because sight allows one to perceive all forms, colors and movement, unlike hearing, which merely registers the traces of all sounds. However this claim is refuted by the fact that there are many things connected to the world that are not perceived by fully-aware people.[31]

By age twelve, the dedicated pupil would often have recited the entire Qur'an and be prepared to move on to study the dogmatic bases of the faith. Available evidence suggests that the most popular texts in the archipelago had once been the *Sittin mas'ala fi l-fiqh* (Sixty Questions on Jurisprudence) of Abu l-'Abbas al-Misri (d.1416); the much older *Alf masa'il* (The Book of a Thousand Questions); and an anonymous compilation called the *Bab ma'rifat al-islam* (Chapter on the Knowledge of Islam). By the mid-nineteenth century, however, these had been largely superseded by two other works. One was the catechism of Abu l-Layth al-Samarqandi (d. 983 or 993). Commonly styled in Java as the *Asmarakandi*, this had itself been excerpted in the *Bab ma'rifat al-islam*. The other was the *Umm al-barahin* of al-Sanusi, known to Malays as the *Sifat dua puluh* (The Twenty Qualities) and to Javanese as the *Durra* (Pearl) or simply as the *Sanusi*.[32]

Most of these books were structured as easily memorized questions and answers, such as this example from the primer of al-Samarqandi:

> Question: If you are asked, "What is faith?" then the answer is: "I believe in God, His angels, His books, His messenger, the Last Day, and that fate—for good or evil—is ordained by God Almighty.
> Question: If you are asked, "How do you believe in the books?" then the answer is: "God Almighty has sent down a book for [each of] his human prophets, from a locus uncreated, eternal and without opposition. And whoever doubts what is in the Suras or the Declaration of Faith has committed unbelief."[33]

In like manner the student would learn of the numbers of books brought by each of the prophets, and how each in turn had superseded those that came before until Muhammad arrived with the Qur'an. Yet even though al-Samarqandi's catechism enjoyed great longevity, it was the *Umm al-barahin* that had the widest currency by the end of the nineteenth century. Zayn al-Din, who provided his own gloss of the work in the 1880s, remarked that it was "the most famous among all the Arabs, Jawis, Turks, Indians and others." Indeed, al-Sanusi's text offered a readily memorizable outline of the attributes of God that could be understood by any believer, as well as listing the qualities of prophets and saints. He also described the angels, the Day of Judgment, and all "secrets" encapsulated by the dhikr.[34]

To gain full understanding, however, one would have needed the active guidance of a teacher learned in all such matters. In his commentary Zayn an-Din went to great lengths to explain the difference between prophets and angels, and to outline how different groups might be classified according to the degree of causality they ascribed to God's will vs. man's acts. Where al-Sanusi spoke of the secrets of dhikr, Zayn al-Din added that while the ordinary 'ulama' should repeat the declaration, "There is no god beside God" three hundred times a day, the Sufi should do so at least twelve thousand times, especially if so instructed by the tariqa.[35]

Despite such mentions of tariqa, inexperienced readers of al-Sanusi's text or even of Zayn al-Din's gloss would by no means have been ready for instruction in the ways of an order at the hands of its shaykh, especially given the premium placed on knowledge of the Shari'a. The student would first need to memorize books on the arts of linguistics and grammar, such as the eponymous *Ajurru-miyya* of Abu 'Abdallah Muhammad b. Da'ud b. Ajurrum (d. 1323). Only then would he or she be able to approach denser juridical works with their commentaries and supercommentaries. These often detailed the same basic duties, from matters of ritual cleanliness, to prayer, the Hajj, inheritance, and even jihad. When it came to all these branches of knowledge, the "approach" or "juridical school" (*madhhab*) of Imam Shafi'i was almost exclusively followed in Southeast Asia, while lip service was paid to the validity of all four Sunni schools.[36]

While the exact array of works encountered by a student would depend on the personal experience of the teacher, it is safe to say that the same core Shafi'i books were read everywhere. Through these, students became aware of how the rulings of *fiqh* depended on the general principles of belief and on validated reports of the actions of the Prophet. More importantly, they would begin to approach the substantive meaning of the Qur'an through the use of exegetical texts. Perhaps the most popular of such among Southeast Asians was that of the "two Jalals." Related to this is the lasting monument of 'Abd al-Ra'uf of Singkel's *Tarjuman al-mustafid*, which would long serve in the Malay reaches of the archipelago, though its usage was usually tied to the "Qushashi" pedigree of the Shattariyya.

Evidence of the subjects mentioned above and of the mnemonic strategies deployed to master them is readily found in many of the manuscripts preserved in collections today. In one early example, transcribed in Java in 1623, we find an abridgement of the juridical text of Ba Fadl al-Hadrami (d. 1512) with an incomplete Javanese interlinear translation.[37] Most students' notebooks are, by contrast, far more crowded. The word-for-word glosses enunciated by the teacher often jostle with longer marginal explanations of the salience of a particular term or idea. Particularly common in such books are statements that Islam is incomplete without attention to the inner dimension, and an admonition that knowledge of the true reality should therefore be sought by all. So too are thoughts attributed to Ibn al-ʿArabi continuing, it would seem at first glance, the tradition popularized by al-Fansuri and Shams al-Din, and then moderated by ʿAbd al-Raʾuf.

Mystical discussions of the relationship between "inner" and "outer" have been a constant in Islamic history, but we need once more to emphasize that ascribing such discourse to the activism of the tariqas is historical conjecture and not based on hard evidence. Mentions of such topics should generally be understood within the wider discourse of ethical learning, commonly glossed as *akhlaq*. While one finds a variety of esoterica in student handbooks, sometimes juxtaposed with quotations from Imam ʿAli or Ibn al-ʿArabi, it is seldom possible to trace this to a verifiable pedigree or even in a general sense to Jawi figures among the ranks of the *muhaqqiqun*.

While this conclusion undermines the common assertion that Indonesian Islam was, by the eighteenth century, essentially tariqa Sufism, the available evidence does allow us to suggest that a prominent minority were at the time pledging their allegiance to one Sufi shaykh or another, depending on the shaykh's perceived claims of orthodoxy and links to Mecca. After all, the point of such knowledge was that it should be accessible only to an elite, and there was naturally contention within tariqa circles for admission to that elite and for the possession of the mantle of the original master. Pakubuwana IV may not have been a witness to a Sammani challenge to the learning of Karang in the late 1780s, but there were more than enough Shattaris to share the legacy of ʿAbd al-Muhyi. After all, debate was often less doctrinal than political.

Current manuscript collections bear witness to the fact that many Javanese would continue to make their pledge to the Shattariyya, and to make use of associated texts like al-Sinkili's *Tarjuman* and the *Tuhfa* of al-Burhanpuri. The older Malay learning of "Karang" would continue to find support on Java for some time to come, through various lineages and in varied forms. Sometimes, however, the multiple interpretations and rivalries could generate new isolates that were more connected to myths of the Nine Walis than to Arabia via ʿAbd al-Muhyi (see ch. 8 below). One example of ʿAbd al-Muhyi's more verifiable pedigrees passed through Bagus Nur Zayn of Cirebon, and thence to his sons. Another line led to the Batavian teachers Anak Tong and Baba Jainan, who would be followed in turn by two other Malay-speaking Shattaris resident in that city during the British interregnum of 1811–16. These were Enci' Baba Salihin and Hazib Saʿid of Matraman, both former students of Hajji Nur Ahmad Awaneh of Tegal.[38]

How exactly did a believer make the pledge to a Shattari teacher like Bagus Anom? For an explanation we can refer to instructions written for a shaykh in a manual printed at Singapore in 1877:

> Call for repentance of one's sins and then take the hand of all present. Then call for the disciple to touch his/her hand to the ground after which the shaykh places his hand on top of that of the disciple. Then the shaykh recites [in Arabic]: *I seek refuge from the Devil, may he be stoned. Verily, those who pledge themselves to you pledge themselves to God, and God's hand is upon their hands. And whoever breaks this pledge breaks it to his own distress, and whoever keeps what he has pledged to God, he shall receive a great reward.* [Q 48:10] Then the shaykh says: *O God, I am content with God as a lord, with Islam as a religion, with Muhammad as a prophet, with the Qur'an as belief, with the Kaʿba as my lodestone, with the Lord Shaykh as our shaykh, teacher and guide, and with the mendicants who follow [him] as brethren. I have the same rights and duties as them. Obedience binds us together, disobedience scatters us.*[39]

The pledge was a powerful act by which the shaykh and disciple became embedded in a continuum of relationships that extended back to the person of Muhammad. It granted the student who pledged total loyalty to the shaykh access to a knowledge of the Divine. In theory, an individual who had attained visions of God that were validated by his shaykh could aspire to lead the ceremony of recollection himself or to stand as his vicegerent (*khalifa*), empowered to give instruction and authorized to take on neophytes by a license for transmission (*ijaza*) that outlined his pedigree. As noted already, authority within an order depended heavily on pedigrees. The nineteenth-century manual cited above, for example, included a "Shaytari" [*sic*] pedigree passed from the prolific Malay author and follower of ʿAbd al-Samad, Daʾud b. ʿAbdallah of Patani, that went back through the Tahir clan of Aceh to al-Qushashi.[40]

For most Sufis, though, participation in a tariqa seldom went beyond learning the rules of the order, joining in communal dhikr, and reciting litanies. Especially popular were festivities known as *mawlid* and *hawl*, commemorating the anniversaries (whether of birth, death, or even both) of the Prophet or of a particular saint. But what did it mean to individuals to make such pledges and to place themselves within a line of transmission? While this is a difficult question, there are hints in the texts as to what individuals were expected to feel. On August 27, 1810, Hazib Saʿid completed his studies under Nur Ahmad of Tegal and was granted a license to transmit his learning to others. Having equated his pledge to the shaykh to a pledge to God—just as prescribed in the Shattari manual quoted above—Hazib Saʿid copied down a statement, first in Arabic and then in similar (but not identical) Malay, affirming the continuing relationship between master and disciple. As the Malay has it:

> I am content with the Lord God and I am content with the prophet Muhammad whose commands I follow from this life to the hereafter. I am content with Islam as my religion, and the Qurʾan whose laws I follow. I am content with the Kaʿba as my lodestone to face with my chest. I am content to direct my heart to God Almighty. I am content for my spirit to praise God, and I am content for my senses to receive permission from God Almighty, and I am content with the one who instructs me, being my teacher.[41]

It is clear from their Malayo-Javanese manuals that Hazib Saʿid and Baba Salihin had completed the same program. Both also had pedigrees invoking Hamza al-Fansuri, if only in the context of remarking that ʿAbd al-Raʾuf of Singkel had belonged to the same "Jawi" people.[42] The question of whether Hazib Saʿid and Baba Salihin considered themselves part of this people is difficult to answer, and it is by no means clear that such teachers, or their constituents, represented the average believer in early nineteenth-century Java. With these caveats in mind, we need now to think about the ways in which the Islamic community was communicated outside the elite contexts of of the tariqa shaykhs and the emergent schools they may sometimes have patronized.

Towards a Muslim Public?

It has been suggested that modern Muslim public spheres have deep roots in earlier social groupings and popular movements, including what would now be called "international" Sufi brotherhoods.[43] There were in fact a great many ways in which Islamic traditions could be shared by the wider population, ranging from communal prayers, meals of thanksgiving, and visits to the tombs of the saints. Common too was an appreciation for the many stories of the prophets and saints, which would be recounted to listeners awake to Qurʾanic exegesis in its mystical forms. With this in mind it has even been suggested that classical Malay literature was suffused with Sufi imagery, and that accounts like the *Hikayat Muhammad Hanafiyya* (The Romance of Muhammad Hanafiyya) should be read as allegorical treatments of Wujudi mysticism.[44]

Though it can be demonstrated that local romances had indeed absorbed many Sufi teachings, it is doubtful whether most listeners would have perceived these recondite messages. While the mystical poetry of al-Fansuri and the tales of the Islamic heroes were certainly enjoyed, it was the life of Muhammad that attracted the greatest interest. Praise poems such as the *Burda* (The Mantle) of al-Busiri (d. ca. 1296), were particularly popular, as were texts concerning the Prophet's birth, such as those of Ibn al-Dayba'i (1461–1537) and Ja'far al-Barzanji (1690–1764). It was often held that Muhammad would join the listeners at recitations of these texts, and while the veracity of this last claim was in itself an issue for theological debate, it is also clear, from requests for fatwas from Mecca, that the generally uncouth behavior of many who attended these sessions was troubling enough to some purists, who complained that many Jawis simply came to smoke, to watch associated performances of *wayang*, or simply to mill about.[45]

Perhaps the most popular text of all was the *Isra' wa-mi'raj al-nabi*, which told of Muhammad's ride on a magical beast up through the seven heavens where he encountered God, who allowed him within "two bowshots" of the throne. But while this was an allusion to the mystical distance cited by al-Burhanpuri, most listeners would have been alive instead to the raw drama of the adventure. Indeed the *Mi'raj* spun off other major works, such as al-Sha'rani's *Yawaqit*, and even the heterodox Javanese *Kitab Usulbiyya*, in which Muhammad asked God if he might sit on the throne. Such excurses would fall out of favor in time as more and more readers would seek out the original. By the early twentieth century a former santri observed that the *Mi'raj* was so popular among his peers because it outlined the basic duties of Islam in dialogues between Muhammad and Moses.[46] Whatever Jawi listeners did make of Sufi odes, the *Mi'raj*, or their own dynastic chronicles, though, it is clear that they were always listening for the latest developments in the wider Muslim world, of which they felt an inalienable part.

Conclusion

Having questioned the antiquity of the pesantren and the ubiquity of the tariqa in earlier periods, this chapter sought signs of just such phenomena in places like Sulawesi, where we found evidence of the Khalwatiyya, and Java, ultimately dominated by Shattari teachers who claimed the heritage of Karangnunggal. We then examined a subsequent eighteenth-century trend; namely a (Cairene) reaction to the popularity of these Medina-oriented *muhaqqiqin* that would lay the groundwork for what would become the standard Islamic curriculum of Southeast Asia. This was particularly clear in the wealthy port of Palembang, where the Sammaniyya order would play its part in developing Sufi scholarship and correctives. Yet again emphasis would be placed on restricting access to abstruse philosophical treatises to an elect and discouraging the dissemination of popular earlier texts and allied romances, which the Malays would nonetheless continue to support. Certainly change was not immediate, far from it, and the latter part of the chapter paused to explain how students might access the array of texts that constituted an increasingly standardized path of Islamic learning, and indeed how many, despite the warnings issued at court, might attach themselves to a tariqa, whether it was of the older speculative tradition, or akin to the newer Sammani mode. Indeed the Sammaniyya was but one alternative, as we shall see in the story surrounding such contentious figures as the Sumatran Imam Bonjol.

Figure 4. Imam Bonjol, ca. 1848. From H.J.J.L. de Stuers, *De vestiging en uitbreiding der Nederlanders ter westkust van Sumatra.*

CHAPTER THREE

Reform and the Widening Muslim Sphere, 1800–1890

We have now seen how, by the late eighteenth century, leading Jawi scholars were tapping into the ascendant "Meccan" discourse reaffirming Ghazalian norms that segregated law and mysticism. Some were in addition enabling orthodox forms of Islam, embodied by the madrasa, for the educated believer, and the tariqa for the elect. Given the dearth of reliable information, we must conclude, at least for the moment, that such forms were either absent or highly restricted in Jawi lands in the preceding centuries. To enact their programs, scholars like al-Falimbani and al-Banjari required the support of potent princes, whether to fund their sojourns abroad or to turn a willing ear to their messages upon their return. But Palembang and Banjarmasin were exceptions rather than the rule. In many other instances, indigenous sovereigns were steadily marginalized by European power, especially on Java. As we shall now see, the implementation of plans to reform Islam on that island soon devolved onto those with alternative sources of wealth and faced a wildfire of interpretations that blazed in the absence of royal supervision. Many writers have viewed the marginalization of the royal elites as a symptom of shock brought on by "modernization" or "globalization," but we should be generally cautious in applying such terms. And they are all the more fraught when applied to nineteenth-century contexts, where some have conflated the rise of puritanical movements with a supposed embryonic form of modernism. This conflation is the anachronistic by-product of allying early twentieth-century reformists with their occasional allies in what is now Saudi Arabia. And it is to Arabia that we shall now return.

WAHHABI SHOCKS

Writing in the 1880s, Ahmad b. Zayni Dahlan (1816–86), who bewailed the unruly behavior of Jawi crowds listening to the odes of al-Dayba'i in a fatwa composed in Mecca, described two disasters that befell the Ottoman Sultan Selim III (r. 1761–1808). The first was the French invasion of Egypt in 1798, which he implied had hastened the second, the final eruption of the great "strife" of the Wahhabi movement begun by Muhammad b. 'Abd al-Wahhab (1703–92). According to Dahlan, war first erupted in 1790–91 after Wahhabi failures to prohibit many of the practices defended by Dahlan's august predecessors. In the following decade the Wahhabiyya succeeded in gaining tribal allegiances and, in 1803, swept down upon Ta'if. Mecca was then occupied at the conclusion of the Hajj, whereupon the people were oppressed and prevented from carrying out such allegedly polytheistic acts as seeking intercession (*tawassul*) from the saints or visiting their tombs (*ziyara*). Dahlan scorned Ibn 'Abd al-Wahhab's attitude, claiming that both practices were attested in Prophetic tradition citing Ibn 'Abd al-Wahhab's own teacher (and al-Falimbani's), Muhammad b. Sulayman al-Kurdi.[1]

Although the Wahhabi garrison was soon expelled from Mecca, this was not to be the last chapter in the story. Following further battles, the city was reoccupied in February of 1806, as was Medina soon after, and both remained under Wahhabi governance for a period of seven years. During this time the Hajj caravans from Syria and Egypt were interdicted, the consumption of tobacco was forbidden, and demolition of the domes over the saintly tombs commenced. Moreover, as Dahlan pointedly recalled, even reading aloud from the *Dala'il al-khayrat* was banned.[2] Dahlan then argued that after glorious Ottoman successes against the Christian powers, the viceroy of Egypt, Muhammad 'Ali Pasha (r. 1805–48), was instructed to reassert Ottoman control, which was achieved with Mecca being retaken in 1813. By this time, news of Wahhabi outrages had spread throughout the Muslim world. One Medinese, who seems to have styled himself a descendant of Ahmad al-Qushashi, regaled the ruler of Bone with tales of how the Wahhabis had ordered all cupolas destroyed, save that of the Prophet in Medina and that of "Muhammad Badawi" of Mecca [*sic*].[3]

All the same, there were Jawis who were perhaps less appalled than emboldened by these events, including members of what is now called the Padri movement, who may even have witnessed the first occupation of Mecca. Though some of the Padris, who declared themselves to be the truly pious "white ones" (*orang putih*) may have been Wahhabi sympathizers, much of what they attempted in West Sumatra, from inderdicting the consumption of alcohol and opium, to banning tooth-filing, matrilineal inheritance, and cockfighting with its attendant gambling, could have been instituted by other pietists. There is, after all, evidence of a similarly stern movement in Sumbawa around this time, which had come into being after the catastrophic eruption of Mt Tambora in 1815. In fact its leader was still revered as a living saint in 1847, a fact that would certainly have offended the sensibilities of any Wahhabis had they been in the area.[4]

Rather than seeing a Wahhabi genesis in West Sumatra, it is more helpful to understand the Padri movement as having grown up around scholars of the Shattari tradition, who rejected the authority of the incumbent masters based in the lowland town of Ulakan. This, we may recall, was the site of Shaykh Burhan al-Din's grave and school, which had been founded within the jurisdiction of the Minangkabau court. That court was by now marginalized and the alluvial gold deposits that had supported it exhausted. The Padri challenge would instead coalesce around Cangking, a highland town that had grown rich from coffee trading. It was there that, after violent confrontations, rebel Shattaris arguably "remade" their teachings to conform to the more globally salient Naqshbandiyya brotherhood.[5]

It is certainly curious that Dutch sources of the 1840s depict the Padris carrying prayer beads, which are accoutrements of Sufis not Wahhabis (see fig. 4).[6] On the other hand, it would be reckless to make much of early Dutch observations, which were so often drawn from the notes of field officers or from conversations with informants whose religious function the Dutch often misunderstood. One key scholar of the 1840s relied on the memoirs of General H.J.J.L. Ridder de Stuers (1788–1861), supplemented by interviews with Tuanku Elok of Kota Lawas, Angku Bendara Panjang of Batipu di Baru, and a couple of "priests." On the strength of such information he wrote of a showdown that had occurred decades before between the most committed Padri propagandist, Tuanku Nan Rinceh (d. 1832), who in his attacks had relied upon "the holy book of *fiqh*," and his former master, the Shattari Tuanku Nan Tua of Kota Tua, Cangking (d. 1824), who for his part is said to have countered with the equally anonymous "book of tariqa."[7]

It is however possible to credit a reconstruction of events that sees a transition from a localized order to one claiming authority rooted in Meccan (if not Wahhabi) praxis. The main account of the wars, written by Shaykh Jalal al-Din Ahmad of Samiang, Kota Tua, also known as Faqih Saghir, supports this scenario.[8] A spokesman of the late Tuanku Nan Tua, Jalal al-Din sketched a contentious history of the reformism launched by his master, whom he presented as a saintly heir to the line of ʿAbd al-Qadir al-Jilani, who had instructed ʿAbd al-Raʾuf to convert Sumatra and spread tariqa knowledge to Ulakan. Interestingly, however, Jalal al-Din made no mention of Burhan al-Din, to whom the Islamization of the region is often attributed.

War first flared up when Nan Tua's strenuous edicts against gambling and drinking were rejected by the traditional elite and Jalal al-Din's mosque and school were burned by way of retribution, which invited similar retaliation by the reformers. Thereafter, Jalal al-Din claimed, he and his master recognized the pointless nature of the violence and made peace with their opponents. Peace was not acceptable, however, to some of the younger Tuankus, who went on burning the villages of their rivals and killing and enslaving their occupants. One notable firebrand was the aforementioned Tuanku Nan Rinceh, who served as protector to one of three pilgrims said to have witnessed the first takeover of Mecca and to have encouraged the campaign against all local deviation. After Tuanku Nan Rincih and his colleagues flouted Nan Tua's order that villages with Muslim inhabitants should not be molested, the eight leading junior rebels set about finding a new Imam to validate their actions.[9]

Until this point in Jalal al-Din's narrative, the unspoken thread seemingly binding the Tuankus of the highlands is the Shattari order of ʿAbd al-Raʾuf. It is the teachings of the Shattari that were ostensibly defended by Nan Tua's partisans when the rebel Tuankus brought forward their rival spokesman, Tuanku Nan Salih. This may be inferred from the fact that Tuanku Nan Salih was the son of a victim of one of Nan Tua's earlier campaigns, known not for his irreligion but for his opposition to the Shattari teaching of the seven grades and most certainly the authority of Ulakan. It would also appear that Tuanku Nan Rincih had been joined in his fiery campaign by a certain Tuanku di Samani, whose name at least hints at older reformist trends that rivalled the Shattariyya.[10] After an inconclusive debate the Eight Tuankus would continue their actions unabated (from around 1815), burning the Shattari center of Paninjauan, murdering Nan Tua's sons, and sending the aged shaykh into hiding. It also sent Jalal al-Din into the arms of the Dutch, for whom he penned his (and thus their) side of the story.[11]

Other allusions to battles between rival Sufi lineages are to be found in the writings of Shaykh Daʾud of Sunur (d. 1858), who penned an attack on the Shattaris after his defeat at the hands of a Shaykh Lubuk Ipoh in the late 1820s. In this tract, probably written following a sojourn in Arabia and while he was a resident of the coastal town of Trumon, he spoke of the superiority of the Islam practiced in Mecca and Medina—by then released from the rigors of Wahhabi writ—noting that the doctrine of seven grades was no longer studied there, much as it was condemned in Cairo. In addition, in keeping with al-Falimbani, whose translations he commended while abhorring traditional Malay romances, he emphasized the works of al-Ghazali and Imam Nawawi.[12]

Given such opposition to the teaching of the seven grades, which is firmly associated with Shattari tradition, is it possible that Tuanku Nan Salih or Shaykh Daʾud had become Naqshbandis? The evidence is only tangentially suggestive of a Naqshbandi presence in West Sumatra, however mentions of the order were certainly becoming increasingly common in Southeast Asia.[13] For example, ʿAbdallah b. ʿAbd al-Qahhar taught its rites alongside those of the Shattariyya in Banten in the 1750s and 1760s, and the appelation was invoked in texts like the *Sajarah Banten* and its Malay equivalent the *Hikayat Hasan al-Din*.[14] We also have a record of the Sufi Sultan of Bone, who had most likely listened in horror to accounts of the Wahhabi outrages in Mecca, commissioning the copying of a Qurʾan in 1804 by a Makassarese who declared himself to be "Naqshbandi by tariqa."[15]

With such instances in mind, it is entirely possible that Tuanku Nan Salih and Shaykh Daʾud represented a new Naqshbandi line that had grown out of local Shattari conflicts. Subsequent Naqshbandi attempts to link to the restored Ottoman order in the 1820s might well account for the impression that Shaykh Daʾud had embraced the "Hanafi" school of juridical interpretation, given that it was dominant under the Ottomans, and was favored by key Naqshbandis in Syria. As we shall see, European observers in the 1880s even claimed that (violent) Hanafis had come to dominate Cangking, though Shaykh Da'ud's own writings make it clear that he regarded himself as a Shafi'i.[16]

Then there is the evidence of Da'ud's students. At Trumon he had been a teacher to the local ruler, Raja Bujang (d. 1832/33), and to the son of Faqih Saghir, Ahmad b. Jalal al-Din, who would return to Cangking as a Naqshbandi in the 1860s.[17] It is moreover probable that Da'ud had been a guide to Isma'il of Simabur (Fort van der Capellen), later known as Isma'il al-Minankabawi. According to B.J.O. Schrieke (1890–1945), Isma'il's first teacher had been killed by "the Padris" and was buried at Solok. In the 1830s, however, Isma'il would edit Da'ud's poem attacking the shaykh of Lubuk Ipoh. By the early 1850s he would be actively recruiting for the Naqshbandiyya in Singapore, perhaps even waving an Ottoman flag that he was said to have brought from Mecca.[18]

Naqshbandi or otherwise, the differences underpinning the conflict in West Sumatra would be resolved with, beginning in 1821, hesitant Dutch involvement on the side of the surviving traditional elite. This set the scene for a highland jihad against the foreigners, but before the Dutch could undertake a campaign, the realization that they could not count on English support caused them to sue for peace in 1824. This did not necessarily bode well for the Padris either, who would lose their north-coast trading outlets. With the recommencement of hostilities after the conclusion of the Java War (1825–30), the Dutch would face the remnants of a movement that had effectively spent its capital. Evidence of such isolation was particularly notable in the case of one of its last leaders, Imam Bonjol (1772–1864), whom the Dutch believed sent gold to Raja Bujang in exchange for arms. Raja Bujang would lose his local support, though, dying in 1831. It is also at this time that Imam Bonjol would back down from his hard-line stance against local deviation. It has been suggested that this was in light of (very stale) news of the defeat of the Wahhabiyya, but one already finds reference in his account to Bonjol's warriors enunciating dhikr in battles that took place before the return of emissaries dispatched to Mecca. With his defeat in 1837, the Dutch would seize at least one volume suggesting that he had maintained an interest in Sufi eschatology all along, for it included excerpts from the *Dala'il al-khayrat* and the writings of al-Yafi'i, as well as al-Qushashi's recommendations on how often a certain dhikr should be enunciated.[19]

The Java War

As far as the Dutch were concerned, mopping up the challenge of the Padris had to be put on hold once Java, the heart of their Asian empire, had come under threat from an Islamic rebellion of far greater scale. In 1825, the son of the former Sultan of Yogykarta, Pangeran Dipanagara (ca.1785–1855), rallied thousands of that island's religiously conscious "white ones" against the Dutch and the juvenile Sultan. There were many factors that led to this conflict, not least the British sacking of Yogyakarta in 1812, the increased incursions of the Dutch state thereafter, and the institutionalization of tax-farming under Chinese clients. It would be inaccurate though to claim that it rested on decades of rural grievances, for it has been observed that the years following the 1755 treaty of Giyanti were largely peaceful. There was, moreover, little disease, and the population grew, as did an independent class of farmers. This prosperity fed the growing number of schools whose masters were most likely eager to have their institutions classified as perdikans.[20]

Prince Dipanagara was marked from the outset for his piety. His great-grandfather had been a religious teacher (*kyai*) from Sragen, and much of his youth was spent in the company of that man's daughter, whose lands at Tegalreja he inherited.[21] Given to periods of meditation, Dipanagara avoided the regular appearances at court that were expected of him and frequented the sacred graves of Imagiri, where he claimed to have had mystical communications with Sunan Kalijaga. This by no means placed the prince beyond the pale of the court. That distancing would only come when he deliberately stood up to Dutch authority by refusing to allow a new road to pass through his lands. After a skirmish, Dipanagara retreated to call ever larger numbers of rebels to his side. His forces ultimately counted in the thousands and included Bugis from Sulawesi. The most noteworthy participants, however, derived from the ranks of perdikan santris. Foremost among these was Kyai Maja of Pajang (ca. 1792–1849), the teacher of Dipanagara's son.[22] After early victories, Dipanagara was slowly ground down. One of the major blows occurred in November of 1828, when Kyai Maja defected to the Dutch and was exiled to Manado. Dipanagara would ultimately be captured in 1830, whereupon he was sent to Makassar.

With Dipanagara's defeat, the royal courts of Central Java were brought more firmly into the orbit of the Dutch and away from explicitly Islamic influence. The rival court of Solo even produced a chronicle that mocked Dipanagara for having associated with such "scum" as the santris, and some subsequent scholarship has at times been guilty of the assumption that palace and pesantren had always been at odds. Kyai Maja may have been dismayed to learn that, having raised the banner of jihad, Dipanagara was in fact more interested in founding a state, but the prince's deep concern with Islam as inculcated by his family, and an early, possibly Sumatran, Sufi mentor, Kyai Taftayani, should not be disregarded.[23] To be sure, one should not assume that jihad is the monopoly of the Wahhabi, or be surprised that Dipanagara's Makassar notebooks contain litanies connected with the Shattariyya and Naqshbandiyya.[24] A descendant of Dipanegara who visited Manado in the twentieth century was apparently more surprised that Kyai Maja had been a Shattari rather than a Naqshbandi or Qadiri.[25] Certainly Dipanagara's book collection did not meet the standards of a Wahhabi library, and Kyai Maja had behaved in a rather un-Wahhabi way, employing pages to hold his white train and golden parasol as he walked.[26]

It seems that Dipanagara embodied what Ricklefs has termed "the mystic synthesis." There are even passages in his notebooks that allude to ecstatic experiences. One may wonder whether he attributed his ultimate failure to a particular moment of heedlessness when, overwhelmed by the manifestation of what he took to be the Divine Presence, "he neglected to pay [Him] honor."[27] Either way, once Dipaganagara had unfurled his banner, there would appear to have been a deliberate appeal to the memories of Sultan Agung as a Sufi king and perhaps even to contemporary impressions of Egypto-Ottoman orthodoxy. His assigning the rank of "Ali Basah" to his field commander may well have been a direct reference to Muhammad ʿAli Pasha, whose forces had recently vanquished the Wahhabiyya. Equally, his taking of the titles of *Kalipat Rasululah* and *Kabirulmukminin*, as well as the name "Ngabdulhamid," can be taken as a claim of parity with ʿAbd al-Hamid I (1774–89), the first Ottoman sultan to have used the title of Caliph.[28]

Like that sultan, however, Dipanagara was destined to fail in war. With his defeat, Peter Carey wrote, "an era in Javanese history closed. The self-confidence of the religious communities was shattered, Europe replaced Arabia as the dominant foreign influence on Java, and the political independence of the central Javanese kingdoms came to an end."[29] Yet, although Dipanagara was the last prince to attempt to cement a grand alliance with the religious "white ones" (*putihan*) of Java, many kyais would continue their dialogue with Mecca in the absence of any reference to their ephemeral sultans or to decrees from The Hague.

Further Expansion of the Pondoks

It is noteworthy how, in the wake of the Padri and Java Wars, the story of the ʿulama' increasingly moves away from the courts. Rather than sending Islamic institutions into decline, the wholesale annexation of Java may actually have proved a blessing to the perdikan villages. Now their protected status would be validated by the colonial state. It is also likely that the independence of some ʿulama' would be enhanced after the inauguration of the Cultivation System in 1830.[30] Though it forced many peasants to grow cash crops such as sugar, indigo, and coffee for the state, it also enabled a minority to become major landholders; including religious teachers and their dependants who were able to maintain (or fabricate) their tax-free status. By 1855 a Dutch observer noted that many perdikan complexes could be counted as "among the best, richest, and most populated" of Java, while another missionary pointed to their growth as the primary cause of the ongoing Islamization of Java.[31] This view is supported by surveys conducted in 1882, which catalogued the existence of some 244 perdikans, whose "sacred territories" often enjoyed unfettered access to the coffee trade.[32]

Another obviously beneficial impact of Dutch rule was the opening up of communications networks. The Great Post Road, completed in 1808, and its feeders would be trodden as much by santris moving between the new pondoks as by Dutch overseers inspecting plantations. By the late 1840s, the pondoks located near the main commercial towns became key nodes of intellectual exchange. From here the more advanced students could move on to the larger ports and take advantage of the presence of greater numbers of Arab scholars. Two major destinations in this network were Surabaya, where the Habshi clan was to be found, and Singapore, the home of ʿAbd al-Rahman al-Saqqaf and Salim b. Sumayr, whose primer, the *Safinat al-najah* (The Vessel of Salvation), was popular in the region.[33]

We also begin now to identify key Jawi figures active at such nodes, of whom perhaps the most famous by mid-century was Kyai ʿUbayda. This teacher claimed descent from Sunan Ampel and presided over a pesantren at Sidosremo, near Surabaya. Many of his contemporaries, meanwhile, were prominent in Mecca. These included Junayd of Batavia and Zahid of Solo (who had shared one of Dipanegara's teachers), as well as another, perhaps older, scholar who seems to have gained universal acclaim; namely, ʿAbd al-Ghani of Bima, Sumbawa. Reputedly a student of ʿAbd al-Samad al-Falimbani, ʿAbd al-Ghani specialized in the teaching of jurisprudence in Malay and was still remembered fondly in the 1880s as a near saint and the pre-eminent teacher to an entire generation of Jawi scholars.[34]

There were many such scholars known for their teaching, yet little survives today of any individual contributions they may have made to the pesantren literature of Java that might rival those translations made for Malay lands by al-Falimbani, Arshad al-Banjari, or Daʾud al-Fatani.[35] Even so, some Javanese contemporaries of Shaykh Daʾud did put pen to paper with similar intentions, including the Javanese rivals Ahmad Rifaʿi of Kalisalak (a.k.a. Ripangi, 1786–1875) and Ashʿari of Kaliwungu, Kendal. The son of the senior mosque official (*penghulu*) of Kendal, Rifaʿi had gone to Mecca at the end of the Java War and, following Acehnese and Meccan models, produced reworkings of Shafiʿi texts from around 1837, before returning to establish his school around 1839.[36] Ashʿari was similarly active, having originally studied in Semarang and Terbaya, before spending seven years in Aceh. It was there that he first read the Malay work that became the basis for his elementary *Masaʾila* (Questions), which would remain in use in Java into the 1890s.[37]

There are also reports from the 1880s of Kyai Hajji Hamim of Gadu Pesing, who specialized in translating Arabic works. His memory, however, has paled in comparison with that of Salih of Darat, Semarang (1820–1904), who promoted his own versions of the *Hikam* of Ibn ʿAtaʾ Allah, as well as sections of the *Ihya' 'ulum al-din* of al-Ghazali.[38] Salih, the son of another supporter of Dipanegara, is also said to have had links to the heritage of al-Falimbani through his grandfather.[39] These Javanese 'ulama' then, while maintaining their distance from the Dutch, were actively engaged in the glossing of fiqh for their local constituents. Their contributions appeared on the presses at a later date than those of their Malay contemporaries, however, and have tended to fade in comparison to the Arabic works produced by some of the Arab scholars in their midst and, as we shall see, by their Mecca-based fellow Jawis. Such a situation is alluded to in the memoirs of a Christian convert, Kartawidjaja of Cirebon (1849–1914), who listed the various works that he had planned to study in the early 1860s at the Pesantren Babakan, near Cirebon. These included Bin Sumayr's *Safina* and titles composed by teachers in Mecca and Semarang, where the best students of West and Central Java would be sent by their often santri and sometimes hajji parents.[40]

FURTHER POPULARIZATION OF THE TARIQAS: CA. 1850–1890

The growth of the pesantrens and the removal of the *priyayi* elite from effective power may well have aided the fragmentation of the old Shattari hegemony of "Karang." The young Kartawidjaja claimed that he had joined a Sufi order at Babakan, even while he mistakenly counted the dogmatic treatises of al-Samarqandi and al-Sanusi as works of mysticism. He also classed mystical poetry as the creation of the Nine Saints, whom he described as deniers of the afterlife. Of course when Kartawidjaja penned his memoirs, the veteran crusader had little time for the santris and hajjis. Still, he respected the Sufis, whose "way of life was better than the others," and asserted that three groupings of them existed in Java: the Naqshbandiyya (which he believed was led at Mecca by 'Abd al-Qadir of Semarang, if not by the saint 'Abd al-Qadir al-Jilani himself [see below]), the Shattariyya, and the "Tarek Moehamaddia" (which he thought had been an invention of the Nine Saints).[41]

Kartawidjaja was right about there being a tripartite rivalry among the Sufis of Java, though it is worth noting that some pesantrens were not open to any of them. The avoidance of tariqa learning was a marked feature of 'Ubayda's pesantren, for instance.[42] Still, there was a blurring of connections at times, as tariqa teachers, especially those recently returned from Mecca, made their pitch to a prospective pesantren constituency by emphasizing the correctness of their methods and claiming sanction from the powers in the Holy City. The Naqshbandiyya was of course not led by 'Abd al-Qadir al-Jilani, as Kartawidjaja mistakenly thought, but some of its shaykhs regularly identified that saint as a primary mediator in their rituals, and those rituals, they emphasized, were practiced more often in Mecca than those of the Shattariyya. There are also hints that some Naqshbandi gurus, boasting pedigrees reaching back to the

Caliph Abu Bakr and evidently quite successful with a wealthy mercantile class, faced opposition from the perdikan-priyayi nexus, much as they had, and would, encounter resistance elsewhere in the archipelago. In 1855, for example, a certain "J.L.V.," the observer who had written of the wealth of the perdikans, described as follows the impact of certain "priests" who had visited Mecca.

> Spread among the people, and above all in a few *desa*s located near each other, a sect is to be found which follows the teaching of ABOE BAKAR, a student of MOHAMMAD, which departs from the normal Mohammedanism in its usages. They are known among the rest of the people by the name of "doel," the meaning of which is unclear to us. One often finds this sect in other parts of Java; they have their own priests and are not very respected by the priests of the real Islam. One notes of them a great underlying cohesion, and the main area in which they differ from the usual Mohammedan is that at certain times and places known only to them, so that they are not troubled or pressured by the Native government, they all come together, men and women, and make themselves busy with singing to the beat of a sort of native drum called a "rebana," with a continual call of "La il Allah Illalah!" and the back and forward motion of the upper body, until a majority of them fall into a state of intoxication or excitement, jumping left and right, on hands and feet, sitting, lying, with strong convulsions and frenetic movements, whereafter they finally fall unconscious. During this time the men or women—even the oldest, who sometimes have difficulty in standing—take turns to dance in the native manner (*tandak*). Those who have fallen unconscious are deemed lucky, as on this occasion they have had a vision of the Overlord. They are laid to the side, and smeared with a sort of yellow water in which turmeric is mixed. Thereafter they slowly come to, in a state of utter exhaustion, and attempt to start again from the beginning.

Having dispensed with their practices, the observer went on to describe how they were perceived by certain "orthodox" parties:

> This sect has spread itself increasingly among the rest of the population under the present administration, though its meetings, as described above, are extremely rare. The hatred, which both the chiefs and the priests of the orthodox Islamic faith nurse for these deviant sectarians, has the result that they are not highly esteemed by the rest of the people ... indeed if they are suspected of doing one thing or another against the current order of things, of which there has been no such incident as yet, then it shall be very swiftly discovered and there shall be no result. In other respects they are unremarkable in their behaviour, and are not very unusual, so that the European government leaves them alone, and needs only stay apprised of their activities. In recent times many have gone over to the orthodox Islamic faith, and in so doing they will slowly die out and cease to exist.[43]

The missionary Samuel Eliza Harthoorn (1831–83) also referred to the existence of a sect at Malang, in East Java, that was known derogatively as *pasek dul* or "the sinful Dul." Such sects have been connected to the antinomian Wong Birai, described in the *Serat Centhini* as participants in orgiastic gatherings, and to an Arab teacher called ʿAbd al-Malik buried at Matingan near Jepara. While the identification with ʿAbd al-Malik seems likely, Harthoorn's colleague, Carel Poensen (1836–1919), explicitly separated the Wong Birai (whom he called the Santri Birai) from the sectarian Dul, though he claimed they were regarded as equally heretical. Either way, the Naqshbandis around Madiun may well have been the first Javanese to begin labelling their abusive neighbours as "the red ones" (*wong abangan*) in contradistinction to themselves, the truly spotless *putihan*.[44]

Despite the obvious hostility and expectations of such observers at mid-century, by its end the Naqshbandiyya would thrive as the ascendant *putihan* of Java. Sometimes they did so in areas where the regents themselves were active in undertaking the pilgrimage and recommending its practice to their charges. But while there is a link to be made between the rising popular interest in Islam and the appearance of the Naqshbandiyya on Java, it is unlikely that this was the same group that had perhaps begun to make inroads in West Sumatra in the 1820s through Shaykh Da'ud of Sunur. Rather, a remaking of the order, pioneered by a long-standing resident of Baghdad and Damascus, Khalid al-Shahrazuri al-Kurdi (1776–1827), was taking on an increasingly populist dimension in the Arab East. It did so in part because it offered a shorter path to enlightenment. Certainly it attracted Da'ud's redactor and pupil, Ismaʿil al-Minankabawi.[45]

Born in Iraqi Kurdistan, Khalid had been on a spiritual quest in Mecca when the city passed into Wahhabi hands for the second time. After having formed a relationship with an Indian preceptor in Medina, he traveled to the subcontinent in 1809. After his return to Iraq in 1811, he offered his disciples his own variant of Naqshbandi teachings. Known as the Khalidiyya, it was distinguished for its claims to be the praxis most faithful to that of the first companions of the Prophet. Accordingly, he sometimes called his path the Siddiqiyya, after Abu Bakr al-Siddiq, a link alluded to in the dismissive Dutch observation above.[46] Ultimately he was to be best known for a number of new techniques adding to the older Mujaddidi practices of concentrating on the *latifa*s, the co-called "subtleties" linked to focal points of the body. Among Mawlana Khalid's innovations was *khalwa* or "withdrawal" (known in Malay as *suluk*), and *rabita*, or the "connection" formed between the hearts of the adept and the shaykh, whose image was to be visualized during the dhikr through intense concentration.[47]

Such practices caused controversies within and beyond Naqshbandi circles, especially when Khalid insisted that his followers were to use his image alone. Still, his methods were undeniably successful in the popularization of the order, helped in part by its link to rising Ottoman claims of patronage over the

wider Muslim world. By the 1840s one of his representatives from Sulayma-
niyya was actively recruiting in Mecca, and in 1867 his foremost Syrian heir
would be invited to establish a permanent lodge there.[48] The obvious location
for a Sufi center was on a hill called Jabal Abi Qubays, already the location of
several lodges. By the 1870s, a visit to such Khalidis as the Daghestan-born
Sulayman Afandi (a.k.a. Sulayman Pasha or Sulayman Zuhdi) would become
an indispensable part of the journey to Mecca for many Jawis and, as a consequence, the Khalidiyya would find a space in pesantren networks and surviving
Jawi courts. Arguably they had become the new Meccan orthodoxy. In the
early 1880s there would be a scare at the court of Surakarta when it was realized that the princes themselves were not immune to its arguments.

The particular agent of this incident was ʿAbd al-Qadir of Semarang, who
had begun his career as a preacher in that town's main mosque, and whom
Kartawidjaja had confused with ʿAbd al-Qadir al-Jilani. He became an active
deputy of the Khalidiyya while in Mecca for his second Hajj, then returned to
Semarang as its foremost imam and began appointing deputies of his own. In
1881 he went to Solo, where he drew the attention of the sons of the Susuhunan. He bestowed a robe of honor on one of these princes as his deputy and
stayed in the home of the other, from which he issued caps and clothing to
other potential disciples. It was only when the Resident became aware of the
matter that the Susuhunan was made to suppress the tariqa. ʿAbd al-Qadir
himself was later arrested in Semarang.[49]

LOCAL RIVALS

As we shall see (in ch. 8), notes taken by Snouck Hurgronje around 1890 suggest that, prior to their ventures abroad, many of Java's Naqshbandis had once
been Shattaris, though, unlike Sumatra's proto-Naqshbandis, on their return
they often transmitted the rituals of the Khalidiyya in tandem with those of
the Shattariyya. Moreover, Shattari and Naqshbandi shaykhs faced a common
rival in the teachings often attributed to the Nine Saints. These were the adherents of what Kartawidjaja called the "Tarek Moehamaddia," though they
often preferred the name "Akmaliyya" as but one rank in an imagined hierarchy
of praxis.[50] By mid-century, and in Central Java in particular, teachers such as
Hasan Mawlani (alias Kyai Lengkong) and his student Nur Hakim had managed to generate substantial followings. The former, whose pesantren lay in the
vicinity of Kedu, in Kuningan, seems to have had particularly harsh methods of
instructing his students. According to Jan Isaäc van Sevenhoven (d. 1841), who
visited his pesantren in 1839, Kyai Lengkong urged the students to eat and
sleep at subsistence levels. They also spent much of their time lying on their
stomachs reading texts by the light that entered through small hatches in the
walls of their communal room.[51]

Kyai Lengkong, whom Van Sevenhoven claimed was a hajji, eventually attracted the sons of elite Javanese from as far as Surabaya, and this raised the hackles of the rival gurus as much as it disturbed uncomprehending Dutch officials. It also seems that some of these gurus, who had priyayi connections, saw to it that accounts of these teachers' activities were cast as an incipient danger to the state; much as "J.L.V.," the Dutch observer quoted above, had predicted would be the fate of the Agama Dul. So it was that Kyai Lengkong was reported to the Dutch authorities in 1842 and sent into life exile in Tondano, North Sulawesi.[52]

Relations between the adherents of such teachers and the followers of their more globally aligned rivals were not always tense; in fact the latter were themselves on occasion under suspicion. Such was the case with Ahmad Rifaʻi, who fell afoul of officials he had mocked as incompetent "padres" in the 1850s, and who was retrospectively counted as a Naqshbandi in Dutch reports of 1881.[53] Much depended on the local context and on personal relations, as is suggested by the diary of one Akmali active in Java in the 1880s.[54] By his own account this Akmali, known as Mas Rahmat, who claimed that his father had been an associate of Dipanagara, was able to move freely in the perdikans of Java and Madura, though it was clear that he was more closely linked to disgruntled priyayis than to the Sufis and jurists whose respect he claimed to have gained. Even if the wealthy Mas Rahmat was esteemed by some, it is hard to give credence to all his claims. Certainly we should doubt that the scholars of Madura requested him to interpret the *Bayan al-sirr* (Explanation of the Secret) and the *Tuhfa*.[55] In their day they were considered to be among the best grammarians of the archipelago, and the learning of the orders was by no means unknown to them. Some must have seen Mas Rahmat as a parvenu. After all, he had never performed the Hajj, increasingly the mark of a fully-committed Muslim teacher in the elite perdikan villages, the independent pondoks, and the wider community beyond.

Hajji Intentions

While aspirant saints like Mas Rahmat could find hospitality in the pondoks much as the newer tariqas had infiltrated the priyayi networks, the links to the Middle East that sustained the teachers of the latter would, as we shall see, generate a degree of anxiety in Dutch society. Metropolitan scholars such as Delft's Salomon Keijzer (1825–68) even pointed to Cairo as the source of the change in the 1860s, perhaps upon learning that pesantren syllabi then included a gloss on the *Umm al-barahin* composed by Ibrahim al-Bajuri, Shaykh of al-Azhar between 1847 and 1860.[56] But while a dedicated lodge seems to have been founded for Jawis in Cairo, it was apparently populated by a mixture of students from South Arabia and "India." Even the six students who had been resident in 1871 had left by 1875, and there would not be a notable Jawi presence again until the 1880s, which is a point to which we shall return.[57]

Even if a faithful few were heading to Cairo in those years—Nawawi of Banten and Ahmad al-Fatani among them (see below)—the crucial center remained Mecca.[58] Ever greater numbers of pilgrims and aspirant scholars were traveling to the Hijaz. Steamship transport was available now, and the route was comparatively secure. During a tour of the north coast pesantrens undertaken in 1885, L.W.C. van den Berg remarked that he had met almost no ʿulamaʾ who had trained in Cairo. Mecca was the true lodestone. Scholars who had spent years there generally spoke fluent Arabic and were, in Van den Berg's estimation, "people of development."[59]

On their return, many of the hajjis would gravitate to the leading Jawi scholars, or even patronize the gatherings of Naqshbandi masters. By way of contrast, in 1899 there was only one hajji among all of Nur Hakim's three thousand estimated followers in Banyumas, and neither he nor any of his representatives had been to Mecca.[60] It was also apparent that the Hajj was enlarging the body of people who set themselves above their peers. In a satirical poem, written in 1867, Raden Muhammad Husayn of Krawang had repeatedly warned the elite sons of "Sunda and Jawa" of the financial burdens of the pilgrimage, of the dangers of being robbed en route, or worse, of ending up as a coolie in Singapore, Japan or Malabar. Meanwhile, he advised the few that made it back to stick to the study of religion and not to lord it over the rest of the community.[61]

Whether they came back learned or respected, it is apparent that significant numbers of the people involved in this new, more intensive, connection to Mecca were knitting the various Islamic schools of the region more closely together.[62] Phenomenal growth was taking place in the pesantrens of Java, bolstered by the presence on nearby Madura of specialists in grammar and prosody, and perhaps even by a number of jurists from Sumbawa.[63] By the 1850s something was certainly drawing greater numbers of students from West Java, who once had favored northwestward journeys to Aceh, Kedah, or even Patani (an important site for scholars from the peninsula until the opening of the twentieth century).

This is not to say that Malay journeys ceased. The Sumatran-Malay nexus remained vital even after the Dutch commenced their three-decade attempt to subdue Aceh in 1873. Where these two circuits intersected, though, was not Dutch Batavia but British Singapore. There the pilgrim, the jurist, and the Sufi could all meet. Much like Sumatra and Java, Singapore had seen its own disputes between the partisans of rival interpretations of law and Sufism. In the early 1850s, Ismaʿil al-Minankbawi was feted in Penang, Singapore, Riau, and Kedah. This enraged Salim b. Sumayr, who believed that the Minangkabau was inducting people into the Naqshbandiyya with no preconditions before taking them back to the holy city. According to his fellow Arab, Sayyid ʿUthman of

Batavia (1822–1914), Bin Sumayr even had a printed refutation of Isma'il circulated at Singapore in 1852–53.[64]

This was not to be the last attempt by a Jawi to gather adepts for the Naqshbandi family of tariqas. In the 1860s, a Bornean living in that city, Ahmad
Khatib of Sambas (1802–72), combined the rituals of the Naqshbandiyya with
the pedigree of the Qadiriyya; both of which he claimed were a progression
from the Sammaniyya.[65] He garnered support from Sumatra to Lombok under
such representatives as Ahmad of Lampung, Muhammad Ma'ruf at Palembang, and Muhammad al-Bali.[66] Following his death, the mantle was passed to
a Bantenese representative, 'Abd al-Karim, who had resided in Singapore in
the early 1870s, and who would win many more adherents from West Java to
Madura. In 1889, for example, the combined towns of Batavia, Tangerang, and
Buitenzorg counted some thirty-eight pesantren teachers, of whom eight were
teaching tariqa Sufism to people of all ranks, including the Commandant of
Manggabesar. Of these eight teachers, four were Naqshbandis connected to
Sulayman Afandi, and each had on average around forty students. While this
number was equalled by two "Qadiris" in Ciomas and Citrap, it was well and
truly dwarfed by another of 'Abd al-Karim's deputies, 'Abd al-Rahim al-
Ash'ari of Buitenzorg, who claimed an astonishing six hundred pupils.[67]

Print Modern

> Kemudian dibacanya: Muhammad^{un} bashar^{un} la kal-bashari bal huwa kal-yaqut
> bayn al-hajari.
> Then read: Muhammad is a man like no other, for he is like the gem found
> among stones.[68] (*Kayfiyyat khatm qur'an*, publ. Bombay 1298)

There was one sort of stone that would prove particularly useful to nineteenth-
century Muslim propagandists as they sought ever-more uniform versions of
Meccan orthodoxy. And that was the limestone used to stamp countless pages
with text by means of the new technique of lithography. By the end of that
century, however, it appears there was no scholarly consensus as to its effects.
Whereas, on a tour made in the mid-1880s, the colonial scholar Van den Berg
would dismiss the printed materials he saw in Java as mere trophies, a few years
later his rival Snouck Hurgronje would attest to their ubiquity and utility,
much as he had noted an upsurge in the use of printed matter in the teaching
circles of Mecca in 1885.[69]

In some sense Van den Berg's dismissive attitude anticipated a common
prejudice of later scholarship against the historical value of Muslim printing
and a consequent lack of interest in examining printed texts as compared with
manuscript materials, an attitude that we will consider further below.[70] Indeed
Muslims did not take up print at the same time as Western Europe, but the

reasons for this were not especially religious, or irrational. Rather, there is evidence that the typographic offerings of the Europeans were deemed barely palatable from an aesthetic point of view. It would be interesting to know just what Southeast Asians made of the first Arabic documents printed in Leiden in 1596, which were requests for safe passage and trade concocted by Frans van Ravelingen (Raphelengius, 1539–97) for ships headed for "the islands far from our borders."[71] It is unlikely that they had much effect. As we shall see, over two centuries later, the missionaries at Singapore would still complain that their offerings were alien and unpalatable.

As in India, the major breakthrough for Southeast Asia came with the adoption of lithography, which allowed for the replication of the calligraphic styles favored for the Qur'anic text.[72] And again on the pattern of India, the technology was handed from missionary pioneers to individuals with both an eye both to profit and the dissemination of their own faith.[73] One such legatee at Singapore was the translator Munshi Abdullah, who printed an edition of the *Sulalat al-salatin* in 1841.[74] Others soon took up printing, if not yet for explicitly Islamic works, then for texts expected to appeal to a Muslim audience. Raja ʿAli Haji of Riau (1809–73) had his *Hikayat Sultan ʿAbd al-Muluk* (The Romance of Sultan ʿAbd al-Muluk) printed at Singapore in 1845.[75] The first religious materials to be mass-produced came from Palembang, where they had been printed by Kemas Hajji Muhammad Azhari, who had spent many years in Mecca and whose name implies some form of connection with Cairo. Having acquired his press at Singapore in 1848 for ƒ500, he recouped his money quickly once his edition of the Qur'an appeared in 1854, despite the high price of ƒ25, which could have secured a professionally copied manuscript.[76]

The Palembang effort was soon emulated at Surabaya, where Husayn al-Habshi (d. 1893) produced a *mawlid* text, the *Sharaf al-anam* (The Highborn of Mankind), which he sold for ƒ15 in 1853.[77] In nearby Riau, too, lithographic printing would begin on Penyengat Island, when Raja ʿAli Haji produced a calendar of propitious dates and a guide to language usage.[78] By this time, the neighborhood of Singapore's Sultan ʿAli Mosque had become the site for a number of print-shops in the hands of north-coast Javanese whose first offerings were primarily from the Malayo-Muslim tradition, produced by scribes from Kelantan and Terengganu. The writings of al-Raniri and his successors were well represented; Arshad al-Banjari's *Sabil al-muhtadin* was printed in 1859; and the *Sirat* itself appeared in 1864.

The labors of al-Falimbani, too, would appear in the 1870s. Yet this was not all about Ghazalian scholarship. Among the first works to be produced in Singapore was the *Bidayat al-mubtadi wa-ʿumdat al-awladi* (The Commencement of the Novice and Support of Sons). Not to be confused with the older *Bidayat al-mubtadi bi-fadl allah al-muhdi* (The Commencement of the Novice by the Grace of God the Guide), which first appeared in 1861 thanks to a subvention by Muhammad Arshad b. Qasim al-Jawi.[79] The colophon of an Istanbul reprint states that the work had first been completed in Mecca in June 1838 by Yusuf al-Ghani al-Sumbawi.[80] Given the existence of even earlier manuscript copies, it is likely that he had been teaching this compilation for some time, and thus became synonymous with it.[81] It further appears that the edition of 1861 had been corrected in Mecca in 1854 by Sayyid ʿAbd al-Rahman b. Saqqaf al-Saqqaf before being sent to the Singaporean print-shop of the Palembangese Anang b. Baqsin b. Hajji Kamal al-Din.[82]

The editor was more than likely the prominent Hadrami shipowner and Java trader ʿAbd al-Rahman al-Saqqaf, who founded Alsagoff and Company in 1848 together with his son Ahmad (d. 1906), who would be involved in transporting thousands of pilgrims to Mecca.[83] It could well be that the text was designed expressly to appeal to their passengers. Befitting its title, the *Bidayat al-mubtadi* is concerned with the principles of belief and the attributes of God and his prophets, in the context of an almanac that includes instructions on ritual cleanliness and dietary proscriptions. In this edition, however, al-Sumbawi was free to augment his translation with passages directed to his Jawi audience, as for example when he mentions that fruit juice and coconut milk were among the sorts of water not deemed acceptable for washing before prayer, or that the consumption or sacrifice of animals unknown to the Arabs was forbidden or at least to be avoided.[84] He also addressed, albeit briefly, local misinterpretations of ritual and the use of the "Jawi" language for prayers of supplication when Arabic was to be preferred.[85]

The *Bidaya* certainly constituted a faithful link to earlier scholarship. It may also have found favor because it offered a connection to the elite Jawi scholars of the day. Were it not for the cultural differences between Sumbawans and Bimawese, who share the one island and the traditions of Malay scholarship, one might link Yusuf al-Ghani al-Sumbawi to the famous ʿAbd al-Ghani of Bima. In any case, we have in the *Bidaya* a distinctly Jawi product. Produced by scholars and scribes from across the archipelago, and supported by Arab patronage, here was an explicitly Islamic text designed to have broad appeal. There were several such printed texts. Another was the *Kayfiyyat khatm qurʾan* (The Ways of Completing the Qurʾan), which first appeared in 1877.[86] Evidently this compendium was a financial success as it was reprinted both in Singapore and, soon after, in Bombay, by some of the same hands involved in the Istanbul printing of the *Bidayat al-mubtadi*.[87] With its diverse sections divided by pages mimicking the ornamented manuscript, the *Kayfiyya* gave appropriate prayers for rituals large and small and included a distillation of the *Umm al-barahin* composed by Ahmad Khatib Sambas's Meccan teacher, Ahmad al-Marzuqi.[88]

Compendia such as these were sometimes bound together with manuals of jurisprudence, or with yet other volumes intended for an expanding pious public. The Bombay edition of the *Kayfiyya* (and probably the original Singaporean one of 1877 as well) was bound with a Hajj guide extracted from the

Ihya' 'ulum al-din by Muhammad Zayn al-Din al-Sumbawi, who would produce a compilation of his own that commenced with sections from the *Umm
al-barahin* (the subject of his own commentary of 1888).[89] Such manuals
played a part in the larger process of conveying an increasingly print-defined
orthodoxy in the region. It is worth noting that the offerings of the Malay
presses were consistent with the earlier shift towards a marked emphasis on
Ghazalian public morality, even if the works of the speculative Sufis were still
to be found in private libraries.[90]

The very mention of Bombay and Istanbul reprints shows that Singapore
was not to remain the only source of such texts. In part this was the market's
doing. As Proudfoot observes, the commercial base of printing in Southeast
Asia was actually to be found in the publication of poems and romances, and
the 1870s also saw a surge in the production of popular tales, including the
poetry of Hamza al-Fansuri and stories of the numerous miraculous episodes
in Muhammad's life.[91] This development did not please everyone, and many
santris had little taste for popular romances.[92] Yet they could take solace in the
increasing amount of explicitly Islamic content being produced further afield,
and even in Mecca itself. It was also from such presses that fresh assaults could
be launched.

One persistent critic long made use of his own press to address the errors of
his opponents and to bombard the public with his correctives. This was Sayyid
'Uthman, who began producing tracts at Batavia in 1875.[93] Born in Batavia in
1822, the grandson of 'Abd al-Rahman al-Misri had studied in Mecca between 1841 and 1847 with both 'Abd al-Ghani of Bima and Ahmad Dahlan
before seeking to make a life and career for himself in Hadramawt. He returned to Batavia in 1862, where it appears that he sought to claim the mantle
of his Jawi predecessor, for a posthumous ode suggests that he had gone there
to replace his ailing teacher 'Abd al-Ghani Bima.[94]

This demonstrates, certainly, a desire to be recognized as the primary juridical authority for Jawi Muslims at large, for whom he produced a constant
stream of writings in which he condemned, in strident terms, anything he saw
as "innovation" (*bid'a*). It was not the case, however, that all innovation was
deemed heretical by Muslim scholars. Arshad al-Banjari, for example, took the
line that while such things as exegesis and linguistic glossing were innovation,
they were necessary. By the same token, discussion of Sufism or the establishment of schools was an accepted practice, and manuscript illumination was
disliked but tolerated.[95] Sayyid 'Uthman must surely have agreed as he produced numerous Malay glosses and discussions mocking the works favored by
his local rivals. He was, moreover, an ardent critic of Malay culture, asserting
that traditional romanceswere the heretical remains of Hindu culture, singling
out the *Hikayat Amir Hamza* (The Romance of Amir Hamza) and *Hikayat
Nabi bercukur* (The Tale of the Prophet's Haircut). He also attacked the use of
talismans "printed in Arab countries," and texts in Arabic, Persian or their

Malay and Javanese translations that relayed unattested litanies, such as those found on the back of copies of Qur'anic verses printed in Singapore. All such were to be burnt, and in their place he commended his own tracts and those of Ahmad Dahlan.[96]

While 'Uthman disliked Malay romances, he spent more time condemning the Naqshbandiyya. He launched his first attacks with his Malayo-Arabic *Nasiha al-aniqa* (Eloquent Advice) of 1883, recycling Ibn Sumayr's attack on Isma'il al-Minankabawi and adding pertinent matter from the writings of Ahmad Dahlan. This he followed, in 1886, with an Arabic tract called *al-Wathiqa al-wafiyya* (The Reliable Document). In both cases, he claimed that he was writing in response to questions from local petitioners. The *Wathiqa* was intended as well to redress criticisms of his first book by offering fuller documentation. Having first paid explicit attention to the names of the true orders and their founders, starting with his fellow 'Alawi sayyids, 'Uthman emphasized that proper tariqa knowledge rested on knowledge of the Shari'a. Here he resorted to the writings of al-Ghazali, al-Haddad, and al-Yafi'i, while citing the living Meccan authorities Abu Bakr Shatta' and Ahmad Dahlan.

There can be no doubt that the Khalidis were Sayyid 'Uthman's primary targets when he echoed Ahmad Dahlan in lambasting their initiations, or when he declared local manuscripts with verses attributed to Abu Bakr al-Siddiq "laughable to Arab and Persian alike." And while he had only heard of nocturnal meetings (of the Khalidis), he claimed to have seen their dancing and their singing, of praise odes to the beat of a drum, practices that led him to mock their local masters, whom he said even claimed that they knew the arts of invulnerability. Sayyid 'Uthman hoped that his readers would realize the error of their ways, and he urged every disciple to engage in serious introspection.[97]

Polemicists like 'Uthman could now use print to engage with the new Meccan orthodoxy, but they still had to monopolize the emerging media. To that end Sayyid 'Uthman was relentless in issuing his own editions of litanies, guides to enunciation, calendars for the calculation of the moon or prayer times, primers on epistolary style, dictionaries, and Hajj guides. As Singaporean romances and poems still out-sold texts on dogma and prosody, he knew that the challenges of the local shaykhs were but one part of the battle. Fortunately for 'Uthman, he could count on friends in a variety of very high places. One of these was Mecca.

MECCAN MASTERS

Sayyid 'Uthman's attacks on the Naqshbandiyya paralleled Ahmad Dahlan's publication of a fatwa against Sulayman Afandi in late 1883 or early 1884. Purporting to answer a formal question put by the Ottoman Governor regarding the soundness of a tract produced by Sulayman, the fatwa condemned Sulayman's teachings and urged that his pamphlets be removed from the face of the earth "by whatever means."[98] This edict was then dispatched to the sultans of Langkat and Deli on the north Sumatran coast, as well as to Sulayman's principal viceroy at Langkat, ʿAbd al-Wahhab "Jawa."[99] For the Khalidiyya had obtained a hold over many of the courts of the Malay world, as is apparent from the increasing prominence of seals bearing the epithet *Khalidi*. It has even been suggested that this may be connected to the ongoing transmission of Daghistani prestige texts to the Borneo-Southern Philippine zone, and perhaps even to the enhanced popularity of stories relating to the Russo-Turkish War of 1877–78.[100]

The entire Sulayman affair was documented in a follow-up pamphlet released by Dahlan on Mecca's newly established state press. Following a preface by the Governor, Dahlan reported that Sulayman had written a tract on the "usages of the Khalidiyya" in which he had derided three rivals: Musa Afandi, Yahya Bey al-Taghistani, and the latter's son Khalil Pasha al-Taghistani. Sulayman had, it was alleged, mocked the exertions they taught, as in the following mordant couplet:

> Like libertines they sway,
> yet like donkeys they bray.
> Thinking themselves on the path of the devout,
> they are more in error than those who doubt.[101]

In his turn Dahlan embarked upon an exposition pointing to the validity of Sufi dances and the likelihood that the Prophet had taught the dhikr accompanied by particular movements. He therefore urged that Sulayman's tracts be destroyed and that the shaykh himself recant. The leading ʿulama' of Mecca backed Dahlan, with the result that Sulayman was forced to cede all authority to Khalil Pasha. This was an outcome gladly embraced in Deli and Langkat, where four of Khalil Pasha's deputies had gained the ears of the sultans.[102]

Certainly there was more to the issue than questions of doctrinal soundness. Sulayman was the ultimate loser in a battle for monopoly over aspirant Naqshbandis from the Ottoman lands and Southeast Asia.[103] In fact both he and Khalil Pasha had already engaged in a war of words by disseminating their own pamphlets, though none of these were produced at Mecca on the press Dahlan claimed would ultimately outdo the world in the production of Arabic, Turkish *and* Malay texts.[104] A sub-branch of this Meccan press even produced Jawi works under the grandson of Da'ud al-Fatani, Ahmad b. Muhammad Zayn al-Fatani (1856–1908).[105] If he had not already gained skills in Singapore, al-Fatani must have adapted quickly to the trade in Cairo where he had ventured in the late 1870s, checking books such as al-Falimbani's *Hidayat al-salikin*, which in 1881 was the first Malay work published on the state press.[106] This work provided the connections that saw him appointed in Mecca, where he ensured that a significant range of Jawi works was released, most especially by himself and his fellow Patanis.[107]

The printing press was the ideal tool for the reproduction of juridical opinions, of which Dahlan's offering on Sulayman was but one released with a Jawi audience in mind. In 1892, a bilingual compilation of fatwas issued by the leading Shafi'is of Mecca was published. Titled *Muhimmat al-nafa'is* (The Precious Gems), it included a marginal commentary by Da'ud al-Fatani. But beyond debates about the commemoration of saintly anniversarys, and a solitary question concerning dhikr formulas, one would be tempted, on the basis of this text, to conclude that little public argument existed about Sufi practice in Southeast Asia, at least compared to the volume of questions concerning inheritance and circumcision.[108] The majority of the works seen to the press by Ahmad al-Fatani were translations of past masters like Ibn 'Ata' Allah, rather than the militant pamphlets of Ibn Sumayr, Ahmad Dahlan or Sayyid 'Uthman. But this particular Meccan press was not issuing the more clumsily presented Sufi guidebooks either, like those still being published in Singapore and Bombay, and this raises the question of what, and where, the Jawi shaykhs might have been publishing themselves.

SUFI PRINT

> Know, O Student, that the books of the tariqa are numerous, clear, and
> well known.[109] (Muhammad al-Khani, *al-Bahja al-saniyya*, Cairo, ca. 1901)

To understand the process by which the Naqshbandiyya gained ascendancy over the Shattariyya in Southeast Asia, we must keep in mind the prominent role played by print, a role complementary to the Naqshbandiyya's more literal prominence on Jabal Abi Qubays. A leading scholar of Malay print once pointed out that much Sufi devotional literature certainly existed in print in Southeast Asia—including litanies, final admonitions, and amuletic texts. This is a picture that we find in other locales as well, and it suggests that print's acceptance may have depended on the sorts of interlinked readerships maintained by Sufi brotherhoods.[110]

The Syrian Naqshbandis were particularly active in propagating the heritage of al-Sha'rani and in seeing their manuals to the press in Istanbul, Beirut, and Cairo. Manuals such as the alphabetically arranged *Jami' al-usul fi l-awliya'* (Compilation of the Origins of the Saints) of Ahmad b. Mustafa al-Kumushkhanawi (ca. 1812–ca.1893) and the *Bahja al-saniyya* (The Radiant Joy) of 'Abd al-Majid b. Muhammad al-Khani, which explained Naqshbandi techniques and terminologies, were widely available and found their way to Southeast Asia in the hands of returning pilgrims.[111] So did the works of Southeast

Asian masters. Ahmad Khatib of Sambas certainly made use of print, and 1870 saw the publication of his short handbook, the *Futuh al-'arifin* (The Victories of the Gnostics). Completed in Mecca, and transcribed by his Palembangese student Muhammad Ma'ruf, this Singaporean imprint presented his interpretation of Naqshbandi rituals coupled with the pedigree of his own Qadiriyya wa-Naqshbandiyya order.[112]

Regardless of the objections that might have been raised about his pedigree and despite the low quality of the lithography, the swelling ranks of the order provided a captive market. A far neater typographic version of the work, transcribed by Muhammad al-Bali, would even find a place on Mecca's Miriyya Press in 1887/88, at which point it was retitled the *Fath al-'arifin* (The Victory of the Gnostics).[113] In the 1870 *Futuh al-'arifin*, the names of the translators and copyists employed in Singapore mention at least one Khalidi. This was perhaps by virtue of the labors of Isma'il al-Minankabawi, whose *Mawahib rabb al-falak* (Gifts of the Lord of the Heavens) appeared at Penang in 1868 with the sponsorship of a shopowner from Palembang.[114] Such patrons were certainly not adverse to profiting personally from disseminating the Khalidi message—as when, for example, they seem to have allowed the impression to remain that the *Syair Mekka dan Madina* was the work of Shaykh Isma'il, rather than his 1834 redaction of the text of Da'ud of Sunur.[115]

This print activity did not mean that the personal bond forged through the transmission of a handwritten text was now a thing of the past. The *Futuh al-'arifin* would reach West Sumatra and West Java in printed copies, but it would also serve there as the basis for copies transcribed by hand.[116] Similarly, a Palembangese bookseller residing in Lampung kept a handwritten pedigree from Ahmad Khatib's emmisary Muhammad al-Bali.[117] Neither did print entail the overnight disappearance of rival orders with fewer international connections. Evidence from the 1890s suggests instead that competing local orders employed similar strategies. Not only are there constant references to the broader Sufi pantheon in the *Kayfiyyat khatm qur'an*, there are also instructions for dhikr and reproductions of two of the most popular pedigrees; one Shattari, the other Sammani.[118]

Such volumes were very cheap compared to the pesantren primers or the reference books from Cairo.[119] In addition there appeared numerous tariqa-oriented odes such as the *Syair hakikat* (1867), which offered pointers for "all the younger and older children of God," and the *Syair Mekah dan Madinah* (1869), repackaged yet again as a Hajj guide.[120] Another example is the once common *Syair syariat dan tarekat*, a twenty-five page tract of rhymed advice reflecting on the process of ageing and the quest for knowledge of the Divine, which first appeared in 1881.[121]

Whereas such material was not necessarily particular to any order, the constant references to rejecting the worldly must have added to the overall impression that tariqa learning remained valid and current. It should be recognized that the Mecca-oriented tariqas played a role in the communication of modernity, with an emphasis on simultaneity, uniformity, and proscriptive accuracy, for there was by no means unanimity as to what day it was in Mecca, Padang, and Batavia. We see this in disputes that arose in West Sumatra, where local Shattaris, committed to the use of the naked eye to calculate the commencement of lunar months, were challenged by Naqshbandis. This time they were likely Khalidis with connections to Shaykh Ahmad Lampung (see fig. 8), touting their "scientific" use of calculation (*hisab*) or the tabulations made available in the bookshops they now frequented.[122]

THE SAYYID AND THE SAINTS

Although we lack much in the way of surviving texts, print certainly played a role in the debates *between* rival shaykhs on the streets of Singapore, Palembang, and Batavia, much as in Mecca, where pamphlets were instrumental in their authors' efforts to scale the heights of Jabal Abi Qubays. Swaying the public was not the sole key to success, however, for regal patronage was crucial in all Ottoman domains. Much was going on in the Netherlands Indies as well, and in additon to the validation he sought from the scholarly heart of the Ottoman Empire, Sayyid 'Uthman was also served by his relationship with the colonial state.

Sayyid 'Uthman's relationship with the Dutch was firmly cemented after a cell of the Qadiriyya wa-Naqshbandiyya tariqa carried out its massacre of Dutch and native officials in the West Javanese town of Cilegon on July 9, 1888.[123] Thereafter Sayyid 'Uthman's books on the tariqas were subsidized by the government. This included the reprinting of his *Nasiha*, his more complete *Manhaj al-istiqama fi l-din bi-l-salama* (Guide to the Faith Making Practice Safe) of 1890, and a simplified Malay reworking of his *Wathiqa*, *Arti tarekat dengan pendek bicaranya* (The Meaning of Tarekat in Short), in 1891. The last offers the clearest indication of his position for a Jawi audience. 'Uthman argues that the true mystics had directed their praise towards God without desire for reward under such masters as Baha' al-Din Naqshband and 'Abd al-Qadir al-Jilani, gathering in houses assigned in perpetuity by pious benefactors. These masters had also composed a great many books, though their dissemination was restricted so as not to confuse the unlearned. Over time, however, various pseudo-Sufis had infiltrated their gatherings, and false teachers had arisen. In fact 'Uthman was quite specific in this regard, claiming that "the last forty-five years" had seen the rise of many greedy charlatans claiming the name of the Naqshbandiyya. They could be defeated, however, just as the many scholars "of Mecca and other places" had defeated false teachers and their ignorant flocks. At this point 'Uthman related the case of "thirty-seven years" before, when a (nameless) Minangkabau had come to Singapore and claimed to be a Naqshbandi only to be exposed by Salim b. Sumayr. 'Uthman was also mindful of the actions "around four years previously" of his similarly unnamed mentor, Ahmad Dahlan.[124]

Though his attacks were eventually supported by state subsidies, Sayyid 'Uthman was no mere tool of the Dutch, for his condemnation of the tariqas predated Western interest in him. What underwrote that earlier criticism? The answer may be found in part in issues of genealogy, for political struggles in the Holy City were often framed as debates over claims to descent from the Prophet.[125] Both Dahlan and 'Uthman were upholders of Sufi ideals as seen through a sayyid lens. Dahlan was a known Khalwati and a transmitter of the Haddadiyya, and he is even named in one famous Hadrami work, the *Taj al-aʿras* (The Crown of Spouses), as a descendent of ʿAbd al-Qadir al-Jilani.[126] Similarly, Sayyid 'Uthman seems to have been a member of the ʿAlawiyya, and his grandfather had been a teacher in Mecca at the time of the Wahhabi occupation.[127]

If Snouck Hurgronje is to be believed, the ʿAlawiyya, while acknowledging the validity of the tariqas, placed themselves at the pinnacle of both the Sufi and the sayyid hierarchy.[128] Indeed ʿAlawis were often invoked in tariqa texts, with men like ʿAbdallah b. ʿAlawi al-Haddad (1634–1720) and ʿAbdallah al-ʿAydarus standing alongside the caliphs and ʿAbd al-Qadir al-Jilani.[129] Sayyid 'Uthman too invoked the sainted ʿAbd al-Qadir in his pamphlets as much as he needed to gain approval for his ideas by quoting Jawi scholars, past and present. These included Muhammad Arshad al-Banjari and the later Nawawi of Banten (1813–97), whom Snouck described in his *magnum opus* as a self-effacing exemplar of "ethical" or even "scientific" Sufism.[130]

By the time that Snouck visited Mecca, Nawawi of Banten was staking a claim as the ultimate authority for many Javanese. In fact his works, written in Mecca and published from Cairo to Surabaya, remain of importance today. Sayyid 'Uthman's pamphlets, by contrast, are now little more than curiosities. Whereas 'Uthman had reached out to his audience in Malay, Nawawi had a less than favorable view of this language as a vehicle of scholarship. This does not mean, however, that Nawawi stressed Arab credentials at the expense of his Jawi roots, for rather than transcending the Jawi fold, he remained a key figure within it, and his style is still held to be more comprehensible to an Indonesian audience.[131] A similar Arabic style seems to have ensured a favorable reception as well for the works of ʿAbd al-Hamid of Kudus, who was also active in Mecca and commenced sending his works to press in Cairo in 1891.[132]

This trend was not universal among the Jawi ʿulama'. The still vital scholarship of Ahmad al-Fatani and Zayn al-Din al-Sumbawi, for example, clearly exhibits pride in the use of Malay.[133] Even so, Nawawi still represents an endpoint of a kind in the wider textual tradition that we have been discussing in these chapters. The tightly packed layout of his books, influenced by the typographic presses of Mecca and Cairo, is demonstrative of this. Space for any interlinear annotation is negligible, and the margins, if clear of commentary or supercommentary, are scarcely wide enough to admit of notes. As such, these are works meant to be comprehended directly, and by the advanced reader.

Still, in 1900 the field was by no fully in the hands of the new "white ones," whether tariqa-inspired or of the so-called "scientific" persuasion. There were ongoing echoes of the clash between the lately self-proclaimed orthodoxy that was tariqa-linked and other localized practices of Islam. The latter would continue in what the Dutch called the "Outer Isles" well into the twentieth century. By this time though, another, far more enduring, fissure had emerged in the societies at the western end of the archipelago. Once again, the question of tariqa Sufism would be linked to the state of Islam among its adherents.

Conclusion

With the increasing economic penetration of the English and Dutch successor states in the wider archipelago in the nineteenth century, we see a final shift in our Jawi story. Indonesian Islam, supported in some instances by a growing native economy, moves away from court-mandated orthodoxy towards a closer connection with Mecca and the Middle East mediated by independent teachers. In some instances, whether by dint of war or peace, these independent religious masters were able to prosper, especially in the locales most closely linked to global trade, and to adapt to new modes of Sufi organization that saw the adoption of the tariqas in favor in the Ottoman Empire. By the century's end, the Naqshbandis in particular were exploring new ways of broadening their constituencies. These included somewhat controversial short-courses of instruction and the dissemination of printed materials that were increasingly available to a pesantren-schooled section of the public. There was of course opposition to this trend, most especially from the Arab elite and their economic partners tied to the Western masters of the archipelago, who it seems were finally beginning to wonder just who exactly it was that they were ruling.

PART TWO

POWER IN QUEST OF KNOWLEDGE

Thus far this book has questioned the oft-posited relationship between tariqa Sufism and conversion to Islam in Southeast Asia. I have suggested that we do not have clear evidence that the one was the necessary engine for the other. Rather, Sufism appears (and then frequently reappears) as a doctrinal issue raised in periods when the orthodoxy of the state needed to be realigned to conform to "Meccan" standards. Such questioning would earn figures like ʿAbd al-Raʾuf, Shaykh Yusuf, and their disciples a role in the sanctioned narrative of conversion and would grant to some of the population avenues of personal exploration in the burgeoning system of residential schools. Once we enter the nineteenth century we begin to have a clearer picture of how particular forms of scholarly tariqa activism operated before their sponsors were reduced—as they so often were—to the status of European clients. This did not spell the end to the old programs of reform. Rather, it seems that certain interpretations of Sufism, and most especially those that could claim a connection to Mecca after its release from the Wahhabiyya, became the primary motors of religious change. This was most clearly evidenced in Java, where there was great uncertainty over which schools and teachers should be the beneficiaries of a policy of non-interference by the successor colonial state. These controversies within scholarly and popular circles furnished consumers for the products of the Muslim presses of Singapore, and raise questions that require us to pay closer attention to the ways in which peoples were familiarized with printed literature. In the course of this process Islam was becoming much more embedded in what might, for want of a better term, be called the Muslim public sphere, with the result that the very policing of tariqa orthodoxy became a colonial problem.

Much of the ongoing process of connection to the Middle East and institutionalization to emulate its structures of learning went unrecognized by the Europeans. The Dutch were not, however, entirely oblivious. The oft-cited dictum that they were solely interested in trade, and thus about as different as possible from their Iberian predecessors, arguably occludes a great many of the competing missions that went into the Dutch colonial endeavor. It did indeed begin as the world's first transnational corporation but, as we shall see in the second half of this book, the Christian heritage has played its role in the shaping notions of the role of religion in a colonial context. For these reasons we

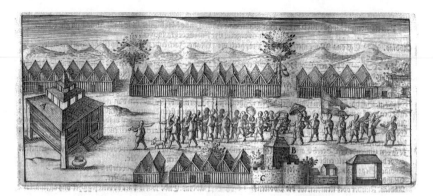

Figure 5. Royal procession to the mosque of Ternate for 'Id al-Adha ca. 1599. From Jacob Cornelisz. van Neck, *Het tvveede boeck.*

shall now turn our attention to the foundational visions of Islam in the era of the trading companies. This will be followed by intersecting treatments of metropolitan framings deployed in colonial classrooms in the nineteenth century and the parallel missiological, field-based writings. In so doing, I hope to show that there was at times a significant disjuncture between what was known on the ground, and what knowledge was propagated for a European audience.

CHAPTER FOUR

Foundational Visions of Indies Islam, 1600–1800

Miskit int Moors een kerck.
Mosque, in Moorish a church.[1] (Frederick de Houtman, "Cort Verhael," 1601)

Dutch interest in the East Indies can be perhaps best understood as a consequence of the subjugation of the Dutch by the Habsburgs, whose trading interests linked the azure waters of the Philippines with the leaden skies of the Low Countries. In the aftermath of the Protestant wars for independence, the eastern spice trade was seen as a potential support for the fledgling republic. This was made plain by the erstwhile clerk to the Portuguese bishop of Goa, Jan Huygen van Linschoten (1562–1611), who returned in 1592 with news of a route to the Indies that he described in his illustrated *Itinerario* of 1595–96.[2]

And so it was that, much like their rivals across the Channel, the Dutch launched expeditions to the fabled spice islands. This was done on a mission-by-mission basis financed by individuals throughout the Netherlands and surrounding principalities, with the not-so-silent partnership of the state. The aim was to divert the costly pick of cloves, mace, and nutmeg from the united crowns of Iberia (1580–1640) that had recently excluded Dutch traders from the Portuguese coast. The return of the much-depleted 1595–97 expedition of Cornelis de Houtman (1565–99) was seen as a sign of good things to come, even though it brought home only a modest cargo of pepper from Banten, having failed to reach the Moluccas. Certainly it resulted in another impressive book, Willem Lodewijckszoon's *Prima pars* (The First Book), or *Descriptionis itineris navalis in Indiam Orientalem* (Description of a Naval Journey in the East Indies), which appeared in 1598 and was filled with accurate depictions of spices, along with stylized images of the populations to be found from the Cape of Good Hope to Bali: Arabs, Persians, even beturbanned Chinese, not to mention the "Governor" of Banten flanked by his "Bishop, or Chief Ceque," apparently sent from Mecca by way of Jeddah.[3]

Getting there was only half the battle. The rulers of the intervening entrepôts, who controlled the Asian spice trade, often listened to advice from such "Bishops," and they were not about to concede space in their markets; even if these latest, somewhat different, "Franks" (*Feringgi*) attempted to curry favor by presenting them with clumsily printed Arabic passes. The sultans of Aceh, who had tried to use their relationship with the Ottomans against the

Portuguese at Malacca, were especially hostile to the founding of yet more European factories, as indeed were the Portuguese themselves.

If we are to trust the account of the English pilot John Davis, when Cornelis de Houtman returned to the region in 1599 on one of dozens of vessels that left Holland and Zeeland around the time of the 1598–1600 expedition undertaken by Jacob van Neck, his tactlessness got him murdered at the court of Ri'ayat Shah al-Mukammal of Aceh (r. 1589–1604).[4] Cornelis's younger brother Frederick (1571–1627), who was also on the voyage, told a different version of the story, placing blame on a plot hatched between the harbormaster and the sultan. Frederick had had more time to find out what had happened, and to build a relationship of sorts with the Acehnese. Incarcerated for nearly two years, he was forced to acquaint himself with Malay, which he later used to draft a basic dictionary, published in 1603, that included Arabic and Turkish words useful for trade in the Indian Ocean.[5]

His was not the first such list to appear in Dutch. Two years previously, the formal account of the Van Neck expedition had appeared, with listings of Malay and Javanese words used in the Moluccas, where the traders had negotiated successfully with the rulers of Ternate and even enjoyed friendly dealings with a Turkish spice procurer at Banda.[6] The Van Neck account also contained drawings of the courts, plants, and mosques of the region that were simpler and more true-to-life that those in Lodewijckszoon's *Prima pars*, as well as two short descriptions of Islam in practice, one of the procession to the royal mosque of Ternate for the Feast of the Sacrifice which graced the book's cover (see fig. 5), and the other of daily prayers at Banda. As the latter had it:

> The inhabitants are in general heathens, having the Mahometish belief, to which they have very great devotion. They shall neither come nor go from the market without first making their prayers in their Temple, which they call Musquita in their language. . . . Once they have done their cleansing and washing, they go into their Church and make their prayers with calls and cries. It is so loud that one can hear it from over 20 houses away and with the following words, which they generally say two or three times: Stofferolla, Stofferolla, Ascehad an la, Ascehed an la, Yll la, Ascehad an la, Yll lol la, Yll lol la, Yll lol la, Machumed die rossulla. And as they say the last word they pass their hands over their faces, by which they evince great devotion. Moreover they say some other prayers, which they do quietly, and mostly in murmurs, which go pretty much as follows: They [first] spread a small rug on the ground, upon which they stand casting their eyes heavenwards two or three times. They then fall firmly upon their knees, placing their head on the ground two or three times. And they do this often together and in their houses, and even in public, in their outrigger vessels, on the roads, and on the beach.[7]

Seen from today's vantagepoint, the book naturally falls well short of satisfy-
ing anyone wanting to know about Islam or about the languages in use. The
cited prayers are rather garbled and the alphabetically arranged wordlists that
were attached to the volume had little specifically religious content. God was
mistakenly glossed in "Malay" with the (Portuguese) word *Dios*, and in "Javanese" with the (Arabic) *Ala*.[8]

The potted dialogues that Frederick de Houtman presented to his backers in
his dictionary meanwhile give insights into Dutch mercantile hopes, but fall
equally short when it it comes to providing details about the religion, though
he claimed that conversion had been proposed to him, both by the inducement
of marriage and by threats to his person.[9] On the other hand his unpublished
account did contain data on social practices and beliefs, such as vigils for the
sighting of the moon and the arrival of the Mahdi, albeit they remained somewhat opaque to the Dutchman who watched his junior colleagues succumb to
the offers of freedom and become renegades one by one. De Houtman also
included his own version of a hearing before some judges in which he outlined
his refusal to renounce Christianity and his arguments as to the superiority of
his Reformed faith over that of the idolatrous Roman Catholic Portuguese.
These he delivered in Malay, basing his argument on the Qur'anic notion that
Jesus was the "spirit of God" (Q 4:171,172).[10] Or at least that is what he had
understood people to have been saying during his captivity. We must be somewhat cautious in accepting his claims of fluency, given that he understood the
Declaration of the Faith to imply that Muhammad was the "beloved" of God,
as opposed to being his "messenger." Either way, it seems that the *Cheech* or
"uppermost advisor to the king," (most-probably *Shaykh* Shams al-Din of
Pasai) thought his Malay good enough that he asked him to translate some
Dutch letters.[11]

It has been suggested that early Dutch travelers like the Houtman brothers
were in a sense immunized against Islam and therefore devoted little effort
to describing that faith as compared to the attention they paid to the more
novel religions of India and China, mentioning only such features as struck
them by their obvious contrast with the Islam they had seen further West.
Long-standing familiarity with Islam is demonstrated, for example, by Van
Neck's inclusion of passages taken from a Portuguese version of the *Alf masa'il*,
which was already in circulation in Europe since its translation from Arabic
into Latin in the twelfth century. This appeared, however, immediately after
the description of the procession to the mosque at Ternate, which suggests that
the text was deliberately reproduced because it was known in the Moluccas
(and thus a century before François Valentijn [1666–1727] would document
the existence of numerous copies there).[12]

Overall it would be fair to say that profit was indeed the overriding impera-
tive of Dutch expansion, and not interfaith encounter. This despite the fact that

the Dutch Reformed Church had its eye on the Indies from the commencement of operations there. At first their concerns were domestic, fearing for the
souls of Dutchmen cast adrift in a sea of unbelief. The *Itinerario* had already
made it plain that the entire Orient was "permeated" by the Mahometish sect
and its "mesquitas," though these were plainly less "horrifying" than what the
Brahmans offered at their "pagodas."[13] At Amsterdam in February of 1603, the
seventeen directors of the (newly formed) United East India Company (VOC),
adopted a resolution calling for the appointment of two "suitable and competent persons to proclaim God's Word and turn the people away from the seduc-
tions of the Moors and Atheists."[14] Soon enough the Moors and Atheists were
themselves the intended targets. In 1606 a contract was even made with a student in Leiden with the intention of training him in "Maleytse or some other
appropriate Indian language" to teach the "blind Heathens God's Word."[15]

Even without such metropolitan trainees (the student was never engaged),
the youth of the castle at Ambon in the Moluccas, seized from the Portuguese
in 1605 (with Muslim aid), would be given instruction using the *Cort Begrip*
(Short Catechism) of Philip Marnix St. Aldegonde (1538–98). This had been
translated into Malay in about 1608 by the new governor, Frederick de Houtman.[16] In 1609, the VOC furthermore instructed its outgoing Governor General to the Indies at large, Pieter Both (in office from 1610 to 1614), to compile
information about the inhabitants and to determine the best means for "the
conversion of the non-Christians."[17] Five years later the church boards of Delff
and Delflant called for the establishment of a training college at Leiden, where
the university's famous theologians could train potential missionaries with the
skills necessary to silence the "Jews, Mahumedists, Bonces, Bremines, and
other seducers." It was also recommended that the youths should learn "the
maleytse tongue" to save time that could be put to better use on their arrival in
India.[18]

Although nothing was done immediately, such calls were briefly given state
encouragement in 1622, when the preamble to the VOC Charter was altered
to stipulate that it would henceforth be concerned with the "maintenance of
the public faith."[19] In the same year, Antoine de Waele (Walaeus, 1573–1639),
would be commissioned to establish a training college at Leiden, the "seventeen" having adopted a resolution to establish such an institution in 1621.[20]
These changes were the result, partially, of domestic pressures that culminated
in the 1618–19 Synod of Dordrecht that affirmed the "five points" of Calvin-
ism as official state doctrine, and partially of the increasing numbers of Luso-
and Malayophone Catholics who fell under Company control after the takeover of Portugese bases in Asia. Naturally "Heathens and Moors" were still
regarded as fair game, even if, as we shall see, some of the missionaries in the
field began to doubt their effectiveness against the latter.

Still, the Netherlands was not a place for religious doubts. Even those members of society who were out of favor with officialdom were well disposed to

the eradication of Islam once the Papists had been dealt with. During his 1619–21 incarceration at Loevestein castle, Hugo de Groot (Grotius, 1583–1645) devoted several rhymed verses to bemoaning the historic spread of "Mahumetisterije" in Asia Minor and Africa. India and the further Indies, however, remained unmentioned by Grotius, despite his having written his first treatise justifying the VOC seizure of an Iberian vessel in the Strait of Malacca in 1603.[21]

In the long run, the Dortian stipulations would fall into abeyance as the VOC developed, for the company was licensed to act as a power unto itself, to establish bases and factories from the Cape of Good Hope (the base there was founded in 1652) to Nagasaki (1641) and to raise armies to defend those bases and discourage any rivals. Indeed, in the seventeenth century the VOC was far and away the largest trading power in the world.[22]

THE CONFUSIONS OF SCHOLARS AND MISSIONARIES

Although private dealing was forbidden to employees of the companies, a few of them—Calvinist ministers included—made fortunes trading in the products of the archipelago. Some—a small number—came back to Europe carrying texts, including fragments of the Qur'an, the *Burda* of al-Busiri, the anonymous *Idah fi l-fiqh* (The Elucidation on Jurisprudence), and the *'Aqa'id* of 'Umar b. Muhammad al-Nasafi (d. 1142).[23] Especially interesting are a group of texts that came ultimately to rest at Leiden University. Though the Dutch Republic had had its Academy since 1575, it long had no resident expertise on the Indies per se. Among the long-term victims of this lack of knowledge was a palm-leaf manuscript that had come into the hands of a professor of Greek, Bonaventura Vulcanius (1538–1614), after the return of the first or second Dutch fleet. This tract, containing a series of Islamic teachings attributed to Seh Bari, was long identified as being Japanese.[24]

This is not to say that all of the material brought back from the Indies landed in the wrong basket, though some texts were evidently shelved as too obscure to tackle. For example, while one Sufi tract was correctly identified as being Javanese in 1597, it would have to wait until 1881 to be published in scholarly form.[25] There was, moreover, no guarantee that such works would even remain in Holland. Six Malay texts belonging to Thomas van Erpe (Erpenius, 1584–1624), hired to a Leiden Chair of "Arabic and other Oriental languages" in 1613, would be sold upon his death to the Duke of Buckingham, George Villiers (1592–1628), while a Malay dictionary owned by Erpenius's successor, Jacob Gool (Golius, 1596–1667), would be purchased for the English Archbishop Narcissus Marsh (1638–1713). And of course the fact that something was in a collection did not mean that it had been read. In 1613 it took a visiting Morisco, Ahmad b. Qasim al-Hajari, to identify an Arabic tract brought from the Indies as being concerned with the subject of philosophical Sufism. The very fact that advanced Arabic was known in the Indies seems to have been equally surprising to the Morisco and to his learned hosts, Erpenius included.[26]

In the wider East, though, there was a deepening understanding of the cultures and religions of the Indies based on hard experience. More can be gleaned from letters sent home than from the print record, a fact that we may probably attribute more to the perception that information on such subjects was of limited utility in the metropole than to a lack of knowledge per se.[27] After all, there simply had to be people on the ground with the skills to learn about Islam via the languages of its expression. Ahmad b. al-Hajari had already met one such Dutchman, Pieter Maertensz. Coy, dispatched to Marakesh in 1607 by virtue of his having learned enough Arabic when he was in the Moluccas.[28]

Given his experience, it is highly likely that Coy knew some Malay too, for the Dutch had certainly not sailed into the archipelago without charts or some degree of linguistic help. Malay was already in the public domain well before Frederick de Houtman presented his hard-earned *Spraeck ende Woord-boeck* to the VOC. One of the survivors of the Magellan expedition, Antonio Pigafetta (c. 1491–1534), had published wordlists for the Moluccas in the 1520s (the mission included a Malay interpreter taken from Malacca in 1511) and one list naturally commenced with such Islamicate terms as "God" (*Alla*), "Christian" (*Naceran*), "Turk" (*Rumno*), "Moor" (*Musulman/Isilam*), "Heathen" (*Caphre*), "Their mosques" (*Mischit*), and "Their priests" (*Maulana catip mudin*).[29]

As we have also seen, the reports of the first two Dutch fleets had included Malay and Javanese appendices too. Yet De Houtman may have wanted to go further still and outdo such Catholic predecessors as Francis Xavier (1506–52), who had translated some catechisms into Malay in 1548. As we have seen, by 1608 it is clear that De Houtman had translated Aldegonde's *Cort Begrip* for use in the schools he had opened on Ambon.[30] Then, in 1612, a trader at Ambon, Albert Cornelisz. Ruyl, completed a translation of Matthew's gospel into Malay, alongside a primer and revised version of De Houtman's lexicon; though there was already some resistance to their use.[31] One missionary declared that teaching religion in anything other than one's own tongue—by which he meant using Malay with the Ambonese—smacked of Papism.[32]

The equally negative Caspar Wiltens (active 1615–19) further held that locals had a hard time understanding De Houtman's "Acehnese" Malay.[33] Even so, they persisted in their efforts at Christianizing the islanders, and Wiltens collaborated with Sebastiaan Danckaerts, who arrived in 1618 and expanded De Houtman's dictionary yet again. Danckaerts also worked on an improved version of the Aldegonde catechism, and both books were published at the order of the Amsterdam Chamber in 1623 to the optimistic tune of a thousand copies.[34] It seemed that there was cause for optimism in VOC circles, especially once the crucial isles of the Banda archipelago had come under Dutch rule during the tenure of Governor General Jan Pietersz. Coen (in office from

1618 to 1623 and again from 1624 to 1629), a zealot of the Dortian mold who entertained hopes for the conversion of all the "Indians."[35]

This is not to say that the Dutch had everything their way. Letters from Ambon often bewailed the hospitality shown to Bandanese "popes," who established schools among the local populations to teach the "Moorish law."[36] In response the Dutch would burn newly established mosques in places over which they claimed jurisdiction and would station soldiers to prevent the return of any Muslim missionaries.[37] As one senior trader closed his letter of August 1619, in which he had written of various new mosques: "This then, is the inheritance of the land, to know well that the Moors are our sworn enemies, seemingly fine on the outside, yet false at heart."[38]

Such falseness was also attributed to converts within the Dutch orbit, especially to those who had submitted to circumcision at the hands of Bandanese or Gujaratis. Having sent out an expedition to burn a mosque and a school established by local renegades at "Rossonive" in June 1619, the Governor of Ambon, Herman van Speult (in office 1618–24), attempted to have Danckaerts convince "two Moorish *moodens* or popes" within the castle bounds to desist from all further activities. Van Speult then threatened all the local Christians with the loss of their property and expulsion for backsliding and death should they engage in such Moorish "superstitions" as wearing turbans, and expressed the firm hope that those with Christian names and Moorish hearts would soon die out.[39]

There were certainly hopeful moments for the Dutch, as with the apparently successful conversion of some of the inhabitants of the tiny isle of Rozengain, in the Banda archipelago, in August of 1622.[40] Having given instruction in the Ten Commandments and the Lord's Prayer, with the assistance of a local aristocrat who explained them in Malay, the missionaries were met by a large crowd asking exactly when Christ had come, why he had come as a man, and what would be the punishment meted out for the crimes of this life. They were furthermore curious as to what the Dutch knew of Muhammad and his teachings.

> Whereupon we taught them to know that he was an Arab trader, and also the leader of a number of thieves, robbers and murderers, and that he had in his company a Jewish magician and other blasphemers and seducers who had made a book, called the Alcoran, well known to you people, which is used by some of the Moorish nabis or popes.... [Then] they asked us what we knew of its content, upon which we answered that, indeed, that was not hidden from us.[41]

Despite their confidence, what the missionaries proclaimed showed that their knowledge of Islam reflected social praxis rather than the text of the Qu'ran. They believed that the Qur'an taught that (1) everyone should be circumcised, (2) that believers should forswear alcohol and pork, (3) that Muslim men could marry as many women as they wished, and (4) that a paradise had been promised by Muhammad, whose miracles and "foul deeds" they would explain.[42]

Throughout this time, the church councils of Amsterdam and Delft remained conscious of the need to train suitably qualified missionaries, preferably at Leiden, for dispatching to the Indies. They also knew full well that Malay would be a key skill in their arsenal against the Muslims, who, reports indicated, were still expanding their networks of mosque-schools and circumcising the islanders. Even so, when Walaeus had been engaged at Leiden, an education in what he vaguely called "the most usual language of these lands," was considered subsidiary to the students' proper moral upbringing in what remained a very dangerous town. Walaeus all the same proposed that some language training be provided prior to their departure by some recently returned and "orthodox" man with experience in that tongue.[43]

To be sure, lofty hopes had led to the establishment of the Collegium Indicum. One agitator for its establishment, the physician Justus Heurnius (1587–1652), declared that God had "laid bare the riches of India for us in order that the Kingdom of Christ ... [would] be spread en route to and in the immense lands of the East."[44] Heurnius would practice what he preached. Between 1622 and 1638 he journeyed to the Indies himself, and he later published various Christian tracts in Malay. He also helped to bring Ruyl's Dutch-Malay Gospel to the metropolitan press in 1629, and was involved, after his return in 1639, in its expansion. In a related endeavor Heurnius would later turn his hand to Malay lexicography, updating the work of Wiltens and Danckaerts at the behest of the VOC in 1650.[45]

Compared with the rigors of Heurnius's labors, and despite his allegations that great success had been achieved by Walaeus, results among the student body in Leiden were meager. The Collegium trained only two dozen preachers, who were sent to posts in Ceylon, Ambon, and Formosa, before it was closed by the VOC in 1632. At this time, too, Heurnius was clashing with the authorities at Batavia over the degree of independence to be allowed the missions whether by the Company or the competing metropolitan councils. Regardless of its official statements, the VOC certainly cooled in its stated commitment by the 1630s. Despite outright denials about the planned closure of the Collegium Indicum, and faint promises to support missionary training, the "seventeen" deemed it more efficient to train the local sons of Dutch employees at a seminary in the Indies, though in fact they did not establish any such body for some time to come. As of December 1638, a missionary writing from Batavia bewailed the fact that none of their reports, sent over the previous several years, had received any response.[46]

What Malay or Javanese *might* have been acquired in Holland clearly remained of secondary importance, in some minds, to the more critical task of dealing with Papism, and only then with whatever Muslims were closest to hand. The enlightened denizens of Leiden University long saw the comparative study of Semitic languages as being of far more value to a modern college than instruction in Malay. The Arabist Golius possessed a Malay dictionary when he died in 1667, but it would seem unlikely that he was its compiler, given numerous lapses in spelling and the mistaken definitions of Arabic terms, not to mention the fact that the Malay columns were drafted in Roman rather than Arabic script.[47]

At first sight this document may be suggestive of the work of Heurnius's orthodox teacher. However this possibility can be excluded on codicological grounds, and it is possible that Heurnius himself was the compiler.[48] Whoever he may have been, he was apparently ignorant of the theology underlying some of the technical terms he had transcribed. Consider, for example, his curious explanation of the "Aijaan thabida" (i.e., the *a'yan thabita*) as being "visible and demonstrable."[49] This is certainly the opposite of the correct meaning of the phrase, which denotes, roughly, the unfathomable and immutable aspects of divinity. The definition might thus be suggestive of an entry written from memory or yet of a Malay scholar having attempted to explain the concept of "realization" and its application to the study of the seven grades of being.

To be sure, there are clues in this dictionary that give us a sense of how unprepared the Dutch were to understand elite Islam, and perhaps as well a sense of how far Islamization had gone among the wider Indonesian population. Accepting the definitions of the Golian dictionary at face value, one comes away with the understanding that texts (*kitab*) were valued as much for their power as amulets as for their written content and that the verbal form of *hajj* was understood to mean "reading something of the scriptures in the Arabic language" rather than performance of the pilgrimage. Whereas the terms *fakir*, *faqih*, *haram* and *kafir* were included for glossing, we find no mention of *pondok*, *dhikr*, or even *tariqa*.[50]

Deeper and Further

As a certain Snouck Hurgronje would observe in 1886, early Dutch views of Islam were shaped less by historical knowledge than by what he called "sound conviction."[51] As the seventeenth century wore on, that conviction would come to rest on the Protestant notion of a return to the text. This followed on an initial period of relative openness signified, for example, by scholars like Erpenius, who engaged in cordial discussions in Leiden with the visiting Morisco Ibn al-Hajari on the subject of theology, or the occasional humanist who survived in the tropics, like Jacob de Bondt (Bontius, 1592–1631), who resided at Batavia from 1627 to 1631.[52]

What the Muslims of Southeast Asia actually did as Muslims, beyond being circumcised, maintaining calendrical rituals, and building rival mosques and attached schools, was usually of little interest to the more religiously minded scholars at home. This was the attitude of a professor at the University of Utrecht, Gisbertus Voetius (1589–1676), who in 1655 issued a guide for outgoing ministers. Voetius's manual was laid out in the Socratic style and was itself based on a fifteenth-century work composed by a Muslim convert to Christianity, Johannes Andrea of Valencia, which Voetius had reissued in 1646.[53] For despite having learned some Arabic from Erpenius, Voetius habitually relied on secondary works rather than consulting what texts had been brought back from the East.

Though some of the savants of the Low Countries were kept in the dark, or perhaps preferred to stay there, it is nonetheless clear that more and more people were to be found on the ground who could mediate for the VOC in the languages of the local populations. What such mediators, who were often the children of mixed marriages, could not explain, however, were the religious proclivities that, theoretically, were shared by the client rulers of the Dutch and their diverse Jawi subjects who were now spread from Malacca (taken from the Portuguese in 1641) to Makassar (conquered in 1669) and the Moluccas (fully overwhelmed by the late 1650s).

The same was true of the representatives of the Reformed Church, which, with its ever-increasing stock of Malay bibles, preferred to shepherd the once Catholic congregations under the charge of Malay-speaking pastors. One such missionary was the young François Valentijn, who would be impressed on his arrival at Batavia in 1686 by the Malay of Isaäc Hellenius, and at Jepara soon after by a military officer, Maurits van Happel, who could also handle Jawi, and who claimed a rather dubious hand in the capture of Shaykh Yusuf.[54] Evidence of even more linguistic expertise can be gleaned from notes on the estate of the commandant of the Batavian Garrison, Isaac de Saint Martin (1629–96), whose extensive library included some eighty-nine Malay and Javanese manuscripts.[55] These would form the backbone of the collection of Batavia's General Secretariat, and were described at the time of their accession by Melchior Leijdecker (1645–1701), whose appointed task it was, from 1691, to produce a definitive Malay dictionary and bible.

To restate the broader point: knowledge of language was one thing, knowledge of religion was another. While Isaac de Saint Martin was known locally as an authority on the languages and culture of the people of Banten, he deferred in matters of religion to the Leiden-trained herbalist and merchant, Herbert de Jager (ca. 1636–97).[56] De Jager—reputed to know Sanskrit, Persian, and Singhalese—had been employed at Batavia in 1683 to provide training in Arabic and Malay for "furthering the Malay religion"—meaning, in this case, Protestant Christianity.[57]

One final example of a learned Westerner is a farther-flung merchant and naturalist who corresponded with both De Jager and Saint Martin on matters botanical. This was the German-born Georg Rumph (Rumphius, 1627–1702).

Yet another VOC soldier, Rumphius had arrived in the Moluccas in 1652, and was there employed as a junior merchant, being gifted with a very useful command of both Malay and Portuguese. Outside his official work he devoted as much time as he could to a series of natural histories based on the previous writings of Bontius and his observations at Ambon. It is clear that throughout the project Rumphius relied on a great deal of information provided by his local wife and by informants who were people of influence in their own societies. These included the exiled raja of a Timorese kingdom, Solomon Speelman (restored by the VOC in 1680), and one "Iman Reti," a "Moorish Priest" from the island of Buru, whom Rumphius described as his "master" in botanical matters.[58] Another valuable source was "Patti Cuhu" (Pati Kuhu), a notable from the village of "Ely" on the Hitu Peninsula.[59]

It was doubtless through such relationships transcending confessional boundaries that Rumphius would compile his own (now lost) dictionary of Malay in the late 1660s and early 1670s. We must wonder, too, whether educated Muslims knowledgeable in such matters as the *a'yan thabita* or the rules of *fiqh* may have shared, or informed, his distaste for "superstitions." At one point he ridiculed the Lord of Giri as a "false holyman" who had long deceived all manner of people by handing out special soil, buoyant arm-bands, and blessed Indian iron taken from his "temple," that he declared would render the wearer invulnerable.[60]

Proof to the contrary, as Rumphius scoffingly noted, came in 1680 and took the form of a Dutch musketball and the dagger of a Madurese.[61] At another point he made sport of the traditional practice of ascetic withdrawal (*tapa*) current on the island of Bima, declaring it "a Godless relique of their Heathendom, which the Moors perform against their law, and, therefore, in secret."

> When they desire something from a *Djing*, that is, *Daemon* (which they distinguish from Satan or the Devil) or when they want to learn a new trick, or want riches, or how to be lucky and invulnerable in warfare, how to rob, steal, or commit thievery, gamble, or love, etc., they go to such distant places and high mountains, stay for a while, day and night, and bring some offerings to the *Djing* . . . [who] finally gives them a small piece of wood or a little stone, which they are supposed to wear in order to get the things they prayed for, and so they even think that they are Religious in their fashion.[62]

Whereas Rumphius was content to explain such practices as heathen survivals, the *Djing* here could just as easily be identified as Jinn, who are attested in the Qur'an, or at least of a willingness on the part of the locals to play into Muslim belief in those beings and in the efficacy of amulets. Whatever the case, such amulets as the floating arm-bands of the lord of Giri were worthy enough of depiction in Rumphius's *Rariteiten-kammer* (Cabinet of Rarities).[63]

It is worth remembering that De Jager, Saint Martin, and Rumphius were themselves erudite rarities who had drifted far from home. Even Rumphius's asides reporting on local Islamic practices were not to appear until the 1740s, once the VOC had determined that none of its commercially valuable secrets were at risk through the publication of the larger works of natural history in which they sat. In fact, so little new about Islam was available in print in the Netherlands during their lifetimes that a former student of both Leijdecker and Voetius, Adriaan Reland (Relandus, 1676–1718), issued a call for greater knowledge of that faith in his *Religione Mohammedica* (Mohammedan Religion) of 1705.[64]

Relandus was no apologist for Islam. His arguments were primarily designed to arm his Protestant co-religionists against Catholic polemicists who accused them of being Muslims. As Relandus rebutted, the Catholic Church's teachings on such matters as prayers for the dead, the intercession of saints, and numerous pilgrimages were more akin to "Mohammedanism" than their own reformed faith.[65] Thereafter though he urged those with contact with the Turkish empire and with Muslims in their distant colonies to invest more time in coming to terms with Arabic and the Qur'an in order to engage intelligently in disputes with them. He even joked about the potential for a shift in attitude among his countrymen if the State were to offer bounties to anyone who could successfully convert a Muslim by such efforts.[66]

Despite Relandus's calls, there were few who thought that texts on Islam would find a readership. François Valentijn, who had supplied Relandus with some of his manuscripts, is said to have been persuaded that his notes on the religion were unlikely to find a receptive audience.[67] He had certainly had good opportunity to form an opinion, having been posted to Ambon, Banda, East Java, and Batavia from 1686 to 1694 and 1706 to 1713. During the first period he was educated at the hands of Rumphius, whose notes and engravings he freely incorporated into his *Oud en Nieuw Oost-Indiën* (Old and New East Indies) of 1724–26. Certainly Valentijn was accused of many infelicities during his ventures in the Indies, in addition to having an imperfect grasp of Malay. Apparently on the defensive, he was in the habit of slighting other scholars with at least some pretensions of knowing Malay, or even Arabic, such as Saint Martin, whom he cast as ponderously slow.[68] He also crossed quills with Leijdecker at Batavia and with local detractors like Pieter Worm (Petrus van der Vorm, 1664–1731) on the issue of what form of Malay was appropriate for delivering the gospel. Whereas Van der Vorm and Leijdecker preferred to have the scriptures in a universal "High Malay," Valentijn championed the use of local dialects, arguing that Malay was really the preserve of an Islamicate culture.[69] His assessment was well founded. We may recall that De Houtman's translations were deemed unsuitable by some early vicars, and Heurnius had complained that un-Islamized populations had little comprehension of the Malay that they were using.[70]

In the end Valentijn's bible disappeared in much the same way as the notes he had assembled on a series of Malayo-Arabic manuscripts in his possession. Based on an obituary of 1727, these included "A Description of the Religion of the Muhhamedans" that was presented with the *Vitae* of the Prophets Moses and Joseph in "High Malay."[71] It is furthermore clear from the sale catalogue of his library that he had at least two copies of the *Ma'rifat al-islam*, which more than likely provided the foundation for his own guide.[72]

Valentijn was not the only one to have attempted such a work. Leijdecker made a partial translation of the beginning of the *Idah fi l-fiqh*, while Van der Vorm translated Shams al-Din's *Mir'at al-mu'min* (The Mirror of the Believer).[73] In spite of setbacks, Valentijn did present information on Islam in his *Oud en Nieuw Oost-Indiën* that pertained to Ambon, Makassar, and Java. For Ambon he turned to Portuguese and Malay sources to relate the coming of the religion as largely the work of "Pati Toeban" (i.e., Sunan Bonang, buried at Tuban) after the conversion of the Moluccas. He also was able to differentiate sufficiently between Sunnis and Shi'as to propose that those "Moors" who had brought the religion there had been Sunnis like the Arabs who had presumably Islamized Java. That said, he had little respect for most Ambonese Muslims, whom he regarded as generally ignorant of their own texts, though he told of his having observed men at prayer in a mosque on Hila once, as well as of having been in the presence of a priest who had offered prayers for his conversion. For other summary details on fasting, marriage, and oaths he relied upon another "priest" from Hila called Hasan Sulayman, and he opined that the Muslims were generally more religious than the Dutch in the Indies. He also held that they were more competent Malay speakers than were the Christians by virtue of their extensive and varied literature, and as evidence gave an outline of various texts in his possession.[74]

In the case of Makassar, he noted that he has derived his information from "one of the most learned Mohamedans" of his acquaintance, a captain based at Batavia called "Dain Matàra."[75] What Valentijn apparently heard was an account of the legend of the kingdom's Islamization at the hands of the founder "Dato Bendang." Although he relayed this information, he noted that he found the date problematic. Valentijn was clearly more interested in Islamic history than in Islamic practice, and he actively avoided speaking of it. As he declared in his section "Macassarese Matters":

> We shall speak no more of the content of this Religion, as is done under the rubric of Java; but we shall merely add here that this Religion is very widespread among these blind Heathens, such that the major part of this island [i.e. Sulawesi] is Mohhammedan, a Religion that is extremely easy and unusually light for them to take on, which is also the reason why we can gain so little fruit. . . . [76]

Valentijn hardly regarded Islam as a religion, relegating it to a poor third place in his section on "Religious Matters," after Heathenism and the "Romish" Religion. Much as he had promised, his explicitly titled subsection on the "religion on Java" held scant information beyond the fleeting mention of the conversion of that island at the hands of Shaykh "Ibn Moelana" (i.e. Mawlana Maghribi) and then Pati Tuban. Valentijn also reasserted that, compared with Heathenism, Judaism, and Christianity, the "Muhammedan religion" was not actually a "primary religion" at all. Instead, he repeated the ancient fiction that Islam had been invented by merging the "dregs" of Judaism with elements of early Sabean and Saracen religion.[77]

In a century, the Dutch had not made much progress compared to their Muslim rivals. As Valentijn reflected, the Qur'an, which "anybody" could read for themselves, was read from Patani to Java. It had spread so vigorously, he admitted, that "with very few exceptions," almost the whole island was Mohammedan, and he begrudgingly added that they had "not so far spread themselves by use of violence" but rather had secured only voluntary converts, with the exception of a few who had "carelessly married a Mohammedan female, or uttered the words of their creed."[78]

Having dispensed with the regrettable faith of most Javanese, Valentijn wrote about the topics that he knew would interest his own public: he tracked the progress of Protestantism in the archipelago while detailing its attendant geography and history. Valentijn's work served as the primary reference for Dutch scholars and visitors for over a century, and was reprinted until the 1860s. That said, he was not the only eighteenth-century figure to write about the religion of the Javanese and the Malays, if only in a tangential way. Another was the Swiss-born bible translator, George Henrik Werndly (1694–1744), who was posted to Makassar (1719–23), and then to Batavia (until 1730), where he helped Pieter Worm bring Leijdecker's bible to press in 1723. It was also in this period that he compiled his *Maleische Spraakkunst* (The Malay Art of Speech), in which he suggested that the bible Valentijn had offered was really the work of another missionary, Simon De Larges (d. 1677).[79]

Like Valentijn's *Oud en Nieuw Oost-Indiën*, Werndly's grammar enjoyed extraordinary longevity in official circles, seeing editions well into the nineteenth century. And yet again the scholar's concern was the promulgation of Christianity. It was only subsequent to a bibliography of the works published by his fellow Europeans, all of which were assumedly on the shelves of the General Secretariat, that Werndly listed sixty-nine books that he felt approximated an ideal Malay library, most likely on a separate shelf nearby in his case. These included several titles that can be associated with Islamic learning, for Werndly's list begins not with a royal chronicle like the *Sulalat al-salatin*, although he certainly had high regard for that work, but with a dogmatic tract called the *Usul Agama Islam* (The Roots of the Islamic Religion). This he followed with eight titles which, apart from the *Bustan al-salatin* (The Garden of Sultans) and the *Taj al-salatin* (The Crown of Sultans), are vaguely identified as being

about jurisprudence or exegesis. After a long diversion into the realms of romances and poetics, Werndly ended his list with fourteen works that might
well have been used in the pondoks. These included the *Ma'rifat al-islam* as
well as Shams al-Din's *Mir'at al-mu'min*.[80]

The titles only give a general sense of the books' contents, but we note
straight away a number of striking absences when we compare the lists of Valentijn and Werndly with the Banten inventory that would be made a century
later. Whereas there were evidently books on basic jurisprudence and dogma in
circulation in the early eighteenth century, along with the eschatological *Kanz
al-khafi* (The Hidden Treasure) of al-Raniri and the *Kashf al-sirr* (The Revelation of the Secret) attributed to Hamza al-Fansuri, one finds no evidence of
the kinds of direct Ghazalian glosses that al-Falimbani would produce half a
century later. Nor yet is there any obvious sign of the odes of al-Jazuli or the
treatises of al-Sha'rani, which would be popularized by the reformers discussed
in chapter 2 above.[81]

For his part Werndly expressed the belief that "many and varied" books were
still to be found among the Malays. In fact some were to be found almost immediately, for an appendix lists eight more, including translations of the canonical traditions concerning the utterances and deeds of the Prophet, and a
copy of al-Samarqandi's catechism. But while Werndly had used Shams al-
Din's *Mir'at* for his introduction, he felt its value was as a source of knowledge
about "the religious technical terms of the Mohammedan clergy."[82] Indeed it
seems that the Dutch were now at last becoming better acquainted with these
clergy, if a much-edited draft of Leijdecker's dictionary is any guide. Copied
around 1750, it bears witness to an evolving Dutch awareness of Islamicate
terms, which were perhaps coming into more general use in the region. These
included *bid'at* for heresy, *chalwa* for seclusion, and *santrij* for *santri*, though
these were already known by the late seventeenth century (in 1684, for instance, Shaykh Yusuf had been consigned to exile with twelve "santrijs," described as "temple popes"). More curious though is mention of the enigmatic
ahl al-tahqiq (even if the scribe wrote *tahfiq*) and the curiously garbled *tariyaka*
and *tirricat* which, glossed as "meekness" and "compliant," point to a tentative
notion of the tariqas as quietist organizations.[83]

If notions of tariqa and Sufism would remain foggy, matters to do with marriage and inheritance could not, especially when issues of taxation were at
stake. In December of 1754, Governor General Jacob Mossel (in office 1750–
61) commissioned a compendium of "the most important Mahomedan laws
and customs concerning inheritance, marriage, and divorce," composed after
consultations with "some Mahomedan priests and *kampong* officials." A committee then presented a draft for discussion in February of 1756, which was
checked by Dutch and local "priests" alike before promulgation in 1760.[84]

It also appears from the correspondence logs of the Governors General that
the effective conquest of Java, formalized by the 1755 Treaty of Giyanti, saw

the Dutch consider the training and examination of their officials in Arabic and Malay.[85] Perhaps they would have preferred to dispense with the need for foreign intermediaries like an Ottoman adventurer, Sayyid Ibrahim (known variously as Bapak Sarif Besar or Padre Grande), who had negotiated on their behalf in 1753–54.[86] It is also clear that they preferred to deal with Muslim states on Java, given that Batavia encouraged the Islamization of the Eastern Salient from the 1760s at the expense of the neighboring powers on Bali.[87]

It even appears that some ministers felt they were winning a Muslim audience at last. In 1759, J. M. Mohr (1716–75), a Batavian minister who had recently completed a four-volume bible in Portuguese and Jawi editions, in 1753 and 1756 respectively, would inform the Leiden Orientalist Jan Jacob Schultens (1716–88), that he was preparing to disseminate some 3,500 copies among the Muslims of the region. Yet he could only regret that while he had sent the King of Terengganu, on the Malay Peninsula, some fifty copies in the hands of a linguistically gifted supercargo, he had been unable to send along with them a teacher knowledgeable in the "Alkoranic" religion, who might lend to the work "the living voice of a humane and wise teacher."[88]

To return to Werndly, though: His text was certainly deemed useful by officials and preachers throughout the Indies, and well into the nineteenth century, but there is little of a specific nature to be learned from it about Islam in daily life. Beyond brief mention of certain texts being useful, and a recommendation of al-Raniri's *Kanz al-khafi* as (to quote Valentijn) "a very fine book treating the creation of men, of death, the grave, the Antichrist, Gog and Magog, and the last day," Werndly expressed only the prejudices that we might expect of an eighteenth-century cleric. He remarked that the popular story of the *Night Journey* told how the "false prophet" was conveyed to Jerusalem on the back of "the fictitious creature Burâk," and thence to heaven where he was shown the throne of God.[89]

Obviously men like Werndly and his immediate successors were much farther than two bowshots from full Islamic knowledge. But then, many churchmen felt that the Malay language, with which they were more concerned than Arabic, was not really equipped to deal with Christian theology either.[90] So it was that the orthodox scholar in the colonial scriptorium might scale the terminological heights of Islamic theology in manuscript while remaining but little aware of how a Muslim a few dozen meters away from him might say his or her prayers. (Despite earlier prohibitions issued at Batavia against any gathering of Muslims for the purposes of worship or study, such had continued to occur.[91]) Hence, for contemporary observations of Muslim practices in the eighteenth century we must often rely on occasional asides in letters written by learned travelers. Some, such as the drawings of the Lutheran pastor Jan Brandes (1743–1808), have now been published. Many more likely languish in dank repositories.[92]

Certainly Brandes was not the only enlightened European to visit Indonesia. Indeed Batavia had served as a field site for European scholars on several occasions. The bible translator and minister Mohr famously built an observatory on the roof of his house, though he later complained that there was "no science" in Batavia other than that geared to "getting money and becoming rich quickly."[93] After the death of Governor General Mossel, who had sponsored the publication of Mohr's Malay bible and who perhaps admired his observatory, the next two Governors General were certainly opposed to any scientific endeavors. 1777 saw the death of the last nay-sayer, however, and in the following year the Batavian Society for Arts and Sciences (Bataviaasch Genootschap van Kunsten en Wetenschappen) was born.

The driving force behind the society was the freemason, and member of the Haarlem Society for Sciences, J.C.M. Radermacher. Even more handily, he was the son-in-law of his co-founder, Governor General Reinier de Klerk (in office 1777–80). An enlightenment of sorts had come to the East Indies, and while members of the Batavian Society directed the bulk of their attention to matters agricultural, botanical, and historical, it would not be quite true to say that there was no interest in Islam and its success in the region. At a meeting convened on June 30, 1782, it was resolved to offer a monetary prize to anybody who could produce a paper explaining how "Muhamed, the Imams, and the successor teachers and missionaries of the Muselmans" had managed to convert the heathens of the various regions and islands of the archipelago. The intent was clearly to produce a model for the future Christianization of the population but, interestingly, it was recommended that an answer be sought from learned Muslims, and that the answer of a Muslim would be rewarded just as fully as that of a European.[94]

It has been suggested that this competition may well have inspired Brandes to sketch turbaned santris and "priests" at prayer in Batavia.[95] We may never know though, for as with almost every contest sponsored by the committee, no one ever stepped forward to formally claim the 100-ducat prize.[96] It was also clear that while consulting a learned Muslim was recommended, one should not consult too closely, as the Resident of Surakarta, Andries Hartsinck (1755–1811), learned in 1790 when he came under suspicion for donning Javanese dress and frequenting the palace of Pakubuwana IV for the purposes of religious instruction.[97]

Although later Dutch scholars (and some Indonesian Islamists) wondered whether Pakubuwana IV was supporting a Wahhabi faction at court, Ricklefs is inclined to accept the contemporary suggestion that he simply followed a less orthodox, anti-Karang, interpretation of the Shattariyya.[98] Pakubuwana's clique was not the only new religious force on Javanese soil. Following, once again, on the heels of their English fellow-travelers, metropolitan Christian interests saw the establishment of the Dutch Missionary Society (Nederlandsch Zendeling Genootschap) at Rotterdam in 1797, with eyes firmly fixed on the still unwon prize to the East.

Conclusion

The brief treatment above has suggested that we need to consider the long history of competition between Protestant Christianity and Islam in the archipelago in relation to accepted ideas about what the latter faith signified to Europeans in the context of trade and empire. Islam, it seems, was indeed a familiar enemy encountered now in a new part of the world. Its presence (and notable expansion) did not necessarily generate much printed material. Nonetheless, some Dutch scholars, many of them churchmen, did gain new ideas about Islam in the process of acquiring Malay texts that were intended as grist for the bible translations of the future. As we shall see, such tangential experiences and analyses—haphazard and ideologically charged though they were—would color many of the interactions to come.

CHAPTER FIVE

New Regimes of Knowledge, 1800–1865

Leiden University is rightly famous today for its holdings of Islamic manuscripts. Its Indonesian collection has had an uneven history, however, rather like that of the Dutch tropical venture at large. One leading Dutch historian has argued that efforts to provide colonial officials with a working knowledge of local languages and cultures proceded by fits and starts and really began in earnest only after the British interregnum of 1811–16. For much of the nineteenth century, Dutch scholarship followed the British lead, spurred on by the need to compete with the only real power that ruled over the waves lapping as much at the docks of Rotterdam and Batavia as at those of London and Calcutta.[1]

That said, the British had not reached Batavia without opposition and had arguably built on Dutch foundations. After the birth of the Batavian Republic in the Netherlands in 1795, the subsequent scrapping of the VOC, and then incorporation under Louis Bonaparte in 1806, governors had been be dispatched to the Indies with very different ideas geared to the maintenance of their Asian winnings. Under Marshall Herman Daendels (in office 1808–11), a great Post Road would cut the length of Java, and inventories would be taken in preparation for more direct rule over the tens of millions of Asian subjects, for it had become clear that their corporate predecessors had had only the vaguest notions of the numbers of people over whom they were ruling.[2]

It also seems that Daendels ordered that preparations be made to assess the state of Javanese education and to supply something of a European alternative.[3] Such efforts were soon curtailed by the wars in Europe and, by extension, in the Indian Ocean. In the aftermath of the many battles that followed, yet another set of adventurer-imperialists set out to stake their claim on the Indonesian archipelago. Among these were the future Lieutenant Governor of Java (in office 1811–1816), Thomas Stamford Raffles (1781–1826) and the Surveyor General of India, Colonel Colin Mackenzie (1753–1821). Both set to work acquiring what texts they could, often by looting libraries of courts that had seen their chance to reassert independence.[4] Unfortunately, a portion of Raffles' collection was destroyed in a fire aboard the *Fame* in 1824, but a great deal of other material, as well as much of the Mackenzie collection, made it back to London at the same time as the Islamic remains of the Palembang library was being shipped to once-more Dutch Batavia.[5]

Even before the arrival of Raffles, British interest in matters beyond "their"

India had been growing, most notably in the person of Raffles's patron, the Bencoolen veteran William Marsden (1754–1836). When he published his *History of Sumatra* in 1783, Marsden expressed some surprise at the lack of interest in history shown by the Portuguese and their North Atlantic rivals. Not having seen the proceedings of the Batavian Society, Marsden suggested that the Netherlandic disinclination to record the history of their possessions had been due to their penchant for commercial secrecy. He went so far as to ascribe it to "the supposed hebitude of the[ir] national character . . . [and] their attachment to gain, which is apt to divert the mind from all liberal pursuits."[6]

Compared to Raffles, who had no qualms about both using and occluding the contributions of Dutch scholars, Marsden repaired such overstatements in later editions of his work, doffing his cap to Valentijn.[7] Moreover he recognized the failings of his own English predecessors at Bencoolen. Yet even as he collected and collated a body of Islamic texts that now sits in the library of London's School of Oriental and African Studies, Marsden believed that Islam was a foreign accretion that deprived the peoples of the archipelago of their original culture. He disdained the use of the term "Malay" as a Muslim coverall resting on nothing more than circumcision and an ability to read Arabic script, and bemoaned the process by which the Minangkabau people had thus "lost in a great degree their genuine Sumatran character."[8] By extension he alleged that the Acehnese, because they had so thoroughly adopted Arabic ways and the Arabic script, had even less claim to originality. For even as he remarked that Malay might be celebrated as "the Italian of the East," he regretted that Arabic made its "daily encroachments" in the form of the Qur'an and other books on paper that contained "legendary tales" that he felt had little merit as compositions.[9]

In his disdain for legendary tales, Marsden would have been in sympathy, at least on some level, with al-Falimbani, whose colleagues he had more than likely met. But there would be others in the Java expedition of 1811 who would embrace exactly these works. Among them was John Leyden (1775–1811), a Scot famous for his claims to mastery of Oriental languages, including Malay, which he seems to have first looked into in 1802 when he copied down Werndly's sixty-nine titles. After a visit to Penang in 1805, where he befriended Raffles, Leyden set to work on a translation of the *Sulalat al-salatin*, marked by Werndly as being "the most prized" of Malay books.[10]

Doubtless Leyden was itching to do some literary ransacking of his own. However, the expedition to Java would be but the briefest of adventures, for Leyden contracted typhus soon after landing and inspecting a local library (possibly that of the Batavian Society). With the loss of his favorite Orientalist, Raffles formed a working relationship with key Dutch officials and oversaw a revival of the Batavian Society. The Indies became a zone to be explored and exploited anew, albeit in the name of progress for its indigenous inhabitants; whereas the Batavian Society slogan had proclaimed that its efforts were "for the common good," Raffles made explicit claims that English rule was designed for native uplift. Setting his sincerity aside, the honeymoon was brief for Raffles too, and he was obliged to return Java to the Dutch in 1818 and to take himself off to Bencoolen (Bengkulu). There he plotted the creation of British Singapore in 1819 and saw Leyden's translation of the *Sulalat al-salatin* to press as the "Malay Annals."[11]

The Dutch Revival

Once the Dutch returned to power, they made a fresh effort to collect information about indigenous education with an eye to substituting something of their own devising. Following instructions issued by Governor General G.A.G.P. van der Capellen (in office 1816–26) in December of 1818, local officials were requested the following March to look into: (1) what education was provided to the natives of Java, (2) who provided it, (3) where it took place and who paid for it, and (4) what part of the population it affected.[12] Only a dozen administrative heads appear to have complied, and, even allowing for the usual bias and incomprehension, the picture that they painted of the pesantrens was dismal.[13] Whereas the "priests" and teachers supplied students—sometimes significant numbers of students—with a passive knowledge of the Qur'an and the associated techniques required for reading, few graduates were deemed functionally literate in Malay, let alone Arabic or Javanese. Even at centers like Surabaya it was alleged that religious education was limited to memorizing passages from the Qur'an and the rudiments of reading and writing Arabic.

Even so, the reports provided some details that appeared now for the very first time in Dutch records. A report from Rembang provided a list of the texts taught in various "langgars" and "mesigits" by some thirty-two priests. Despite following the Javanese practice of listing books by their topics rather than their formal titles, this list confirms the information in the contemporary *Serat Centhini* about the scholarly diet of the time.[14] It also becomes apparent that the leading households preferred to educate their sons on the family estate under the tutelage of their chief administrators and scribes. On occasion a promising student might be sent further afield, most often to the ports of Surabaya and Semarang, where the use of Malay was allegedly limited to the upper echelons, and then, perhaps, on to the more advanced inland schools of Madiun, Ponorogo, and Yogyakarta.

All this information was collected for naught, it seems, as the responses were simply filed away and no further action taken. The same fate befell another survey conducted in 1831, which effectively repeated the 1819 exercise; though this time fourteen administrators replied with data covering a dizzying number of places of instruction.[15] Once again the education was described as poor, providing only a purely passive knowledge of texts, even if some graduates were able to enunciate those texts very well indeed. And it was again alleged that the elite preferred to educate their sons (and daughters) within the precincts of their regional palaces. It is worth noting that one of the native commissions that sent in a report affixed to it numerous proposals for the introduction of Western-style schooling and the supervision of all teachers and schools, pesantrens included, under a body headed by locally appointed Muslim officials.[16]

What is really striking in the reports, at least in the form in which they were digested, is that there is no explicit mention, let alone fear, of Mecca as a scholarly destination. The pesantrens were assumed to cater to interested members of society below the level of the increasingly Westernizing (and expanding) priyayi elite. There is little suggestion of students going much further afield, nor of sums of money in circulation other than as voluntary recompense for the teacher's ministrations.[17] Despite this, we now know that, beginning at about this time, increasing numbers of people were able to make the Hajj and to seek out just such an alternate destination for study. This was also the moment when more teachers, including Arabs, were venturing to the Eastern Salient to offer classes conducted in Malay. It was a development that few would have predicted. The Sultan of Madura, for example, deemed a basic *langgar* education adequate to develop the minds of all but the "most brutish" of his subjects.[18]

With the benefit of hindsight, it appears that there was a growing divergence between the Dutch and Javanese perception of the place of the priyayi elite vis-à-vis Islam. An analogous disjunction between the literary and the religious is also manifested in the activities of the Batavian Society. Perhaps mindful of Raffles having issued Leyden's *Malay Annals*, the Dutch steering committee offered a prize in 1823 for the translation of the same work into their own language. Their aim was to recognize its merits as a history and its polished literary style.[19] Any contribution it might make to an understanding of Islam was of no concern, just as the details of Islam were still being ignored in analyses of the polities being brought back under the Dutch flag. In a long report on Palembang, Commissioner J.I. van Sevenhoven may well have documented the ranks of the clerisy and teachers there, but he concluded that the court that had appointed them was not properly religious. He even averred that it had earned the hatred of the local Arab population, isolated among a generally superstitious and blasphemous populace.[20]

Not so far away at Bencoolen, a former Resident of Central Java, Lt. Col. H. G. Nahuijs, would confer with Raffles and give voice to their shared vision for the future of the Javanese unbelievers:

One ought, in order to avoid giving any offence to the world, never to discuss subjects contrary to the prejudices or religious beliefs of the older ones or which would clash with the Mohammedan religion, and this should in no way prevent leading the youth through selected moral tales to a sense of duty and to a feeling of honour and virtue. It is a particularly fortunate circumstance, of which by good generalship much assistance can be derived, that the Javanese are very fond of stories, so much so that the princes give up hours of their time to those of their subjects who can hold their attention by one or another story; and it is a no less fortunate thing that the native of Java, much more than any other follower of Mohammed is closer to the Christians and with less difficulty changes his manners to those of Europeans, which opens to me the gratifying prospect that under the guidance of an understanding and fatherly government the time is not far distant that the Javanese, if not Christians in name, will be Christians in practice, which latter, to my way of thinking, is of more value than the former.[21]

Nahuijs's letters were published in Breda in 1826. Despite what he bemoaned as a "concatenation of unfortunate circumstances" that had forced the Dutch to fight for almost every former territory so that the "blood of their natives ... flowed over all these possessions," the Netherlandic order was well on its way to full restoration.[22] Moreover, the British and the Dutch, though in active competition with one another, would together bring the power of science and the rhetoric of religion to bear on their imagined task, described by one later missionary as "introducing Civilisation among the Millions."[23]

REPRINTING CHRISTIAN KNOWLEDGE

For some, the British interregnum was about more than surveying a newly-won possession for the enhancement of their personal reputation. Among the members of the expeditionary forces, there were also those who saw the archipelago as a potential missionary field, regardless of their historic failures in the region. What this generation had now that earlier comers lacked was the portable printing press. It was as important for them as the cannon was for their protectors.

Of course printed works were by no means unknown. Ruyl's sections of Matthew's gospel had been sent from Enkhuizen as early as 1629, followed by copies of his New Testament as repaired by Heurnius in the 1650s. The VOC had even overseen the publication of religious texts, beginning in 1659, as it maintained its ambiguous relationship with the reformed churches. Still, it was the British interregnum and the invention of lithography that allowed an explosion of print activity in the region. Soon after the arrival of agents of the London Missionary Society, printing took off; in Malacca in 1817, the Straits Settlements and Batavia in 1822, and Padang in 1834.[24] And the British would again be followed by their Dutch kin, after the establishment of the Netherlands Bible Society in 1814, which would work to make sure that scripture was

available in both Jawi and Roman scripts. The first project was a reworking of
the Leijdecker bible, printed in 1820.[25]

The medium offered promise, but the missionaries recognized that major
cultural hurdles still had to be overcome. In July of 1828, W. H. Medhurst
(1796–1857) reported from Singapore on both the difficulties and a possible
solution:

> The Malays have few or no printed books; and when they are presented
> with one executed by a letter press, they find it altogether so unlike their
> own, and so foreign in its appearance, that they are inclined to reject it on
> this ground alone. Besides, the natives here have been accustomed to read
> books with points, which it is difficult to put to every word on a letter-
> press. All this is easily remedied in lithographic printing: books printed in
> this mode, have every appearance of manuscript; and with a Moham-
> medan inscription at the beginning, our publications find as ready an ad-
> mittance among the people as their own.[26]

It took more than a mere "Mohammedan" inscription at the beginning,
however. The men who operated the new presses depended upon local interpreters, and these men took more away from their employers than a knowledge
of Christian theology. Perhaps the most famous example is Munshi Abdullah,
who had assisted Leyden in Penang, and then Raffles, Medhurst, and various
other missionaries in Singapore. Through working with these men over the
course of two decades, Munshi Abdullah gained an appreciation for typographic printing. It is even possible that memories of the fire aboard the *Fame*
set him on the path of preserving Malay literature and history in the 1840s,
establishing a precedent for both Kemas Azhari at Palembang and Husayn al-
Habshi at Surabaya.[27]

This is not to say that the pastors never gained converts, or that they had no
understanding of the religion of those they intended to harvest. While Arabic
was beyond the ken of most missionaries, there is strong evidence that in Batavia at least they gained the active assistance of one convert who had more than
a little knowledge of that language. The relevant text is a manuscript copy of a
tract, the *Hikayat Maryam wa-'Isa* (The Tale of Mary and Jesus). Completed in
1826, it contains ample quotations from the Bible in Arabic with a Malay
gloss. As such it goes far beyond Medhurst's initial inscription. It mimicks a
traditional work of exegesis replete with the rubrication of scripture. The declaration of faith is even reworked as the mystically tinged, "I testify that there
is no god but God and that Jesus is the spirit of God."[28]

Once again, such concepts were by no means new. We may recall how, during his captivity at Aceh, Frederick de Houtman had built his defense of
Christianity on the Qur'anic designation of Jesus as the spirit of God, and it is
known that Isaac St. Martin owned copies of the Psalms in Arabic.[29] Now,
though, such texts were being printed in large numbers, as was a series of
hymns composed by a Baptist Minister active in Java, William Robinson

Figure 6. Tomb of Malik Ibrahim, from Van Hoëvell, *Reis over Java*, I, 156–57.

(1784–1853).[30] Still, form was one thing, content another. And that was a key problem, one that would plague colonial understandings of a seminal period in the history of Islam in Southeast Asia. Fear now arrived on stage.

THE PRIESTS OF WAR

> Thereupon he drew his watch from his pocket and said to the priests: "If you value your lives, then you will not waste time with chit chat."[31] (Le Bron de Vexela to Kyai Maja's followers, November 1828)

The Dutch and English alike assumed that their foes were supported by a class of priests, much like their own. At Bengkulu, the harbingers of the newest trend stemming from Mecca quickly came to be called (slightingly) the "Padries," being an old reworking of the Iberian term for "priest." The British had already used the term in India, and the Dutch had referred to the pseudo-Ottoman mediator of 1753–54 as the "Padre Grande." It was readily adopted by cynical Indonesians, too. By the 1850s, the missionaries in West Java were termed *padri* by suspicious Sundanese, and Ahmad Rifa'i would attack his Dutch-allied Muslim rivals as such.[32]

For the most part, Europeans saw hajjis and imams as troublesome priests, but they could also ascribe laudable principles to them. Colonel Nahuijs shared Raffles's view of the "Padres" as righteous activists seeking "the improvement of the morals of the Malays, which had wholly degenerated and were very divergent from the Mohammedan or Islamic precepts," even suspecting (perhaps by their nomenclature) that they were originally "a company of Christian Malays."[33] For his part Raffles had already written to Marsden in 1820 that they seemed "to resemble the Wahabees of the desert" and had proven themselves "most unrelenting and tyrannical," though their rule seemed "calculated to reform and improve." Even so, Raffles confessed to his churchman cousin that he would have much preferred to see hundreds of Christian missionaries dispatched to the highlands than men with "the Koran in one hand, and the sword in the other," bringing the "desolating influence of the false prophet of Mecca."[34]

West Sumatra had certainly been racked by violence for some nineteen years before the first Dutch interventions, as Tuankus of varying hues campaigned for the destruction of the lavishly decorated cock-fighting arenas and the traditional halls that were the pride of so many of the villages of their rivals. With their return to power, the Dutch established themselves at Padang and began to engage the Padris in 1821. This first campaign stalled once it became clear that the British would not support them, and a treaty was signed with the Tuankus of Bonjol and Alahan Panjang in March of 1824.[35] When events turned against the Dutch for a time in Java, a broader peace treaty was concluded in November of 1825. It was at this moment of inertia that the Dutch asked Shaykh Jalal al-Din of Samiang to provide his outline of the history of wars among the people he obligingly referred to as "Paderi."[36] Yet this mention would be no more than a fleeting reference in his coda to what he called the "war of religion," that the Tuankus waged against the regal Adat party before they turned to fighting among themselves.[37] By the time that Jalal al-Din, whom the Dutch thought to be a son of Tuanku Nan Tua, wrote his account, the internal wars were largely over. With independent trade to the north cut off by British withdrawal (and their cooperation with the Dutch), there was a commensurate decrease in the religious fervor that Padri agriculture had sustained. This was not quite the case in the redoubt of Bonjol, whose master would reopen conflict in the 1830s, having reconciled with the Adat faction. He was finally defeated in 1837.

There is no small irony in the fact that one of the Javanese sent to fight the Padris had been the grandiously titled "Ali Basa" who had defected from Dipanagara in October of 1829. It has been declared that with Dipanagara vanquished, "not only Javanese, but henceforth also European colonial rulers, cared what sort of Muslims Javanese were or became."[38] Much the same (and perhaps more) might be said of Sumatra, where (now) Commissioner General Van Sevenhoven even made a direct appeal to the peoples of the Padang Highlands in 1833, declaring them to be fellow monotheists who had been led astray by some of their teachers.[39] Still, even if the colonial state might now entertain vague thoughts of transforming or redirecting the educations of Javanese and Sumatrans, it did not yet care enough to disseminate the information it already had about the existing educational system. Collecting information seemed like a better thing to do than sharing it. Perhaps the explanation of this lies in the fact that colonial experts were simply overwhelmed with information. It was a daunting task to make some kind of sense of the large swathes of material that had recently been added to their libraries in the wake of so many conquests.

MAKING CHRISTIAN SENSE OF CAPTURED LIBRARIES

The Dutch and the English enjoyed their share of military victories, but despite fervent hopes and printed prayers, conversions of local Muslims were few and far between. Even the region's "heathens" were unenthused. (And the luck of the Americans was no better. After seven years of operation, the American mission at Singapore could only claim five Chinese converts, and it closed down in 1843.) Over time more and more officials probably came to the same conclusion: the native Muslims were intractable, devoted to the many scholarly visitors active among them. As we have already seen, such visitors (and increasing numbers of Jawi returnees) were having an ever greater effect on the courts of the archipelago. This may be seen in a sampling of texts from several royal libraries that were taken as trophies of war, from Selangor (1784), Yogyakarta (1812), Bone (1814), and Palembang, first looted by the English in 1812, and then retaken by the Dutch in 1821.[40] Yet even these collections and additional non-courtly gleanings, such as the Sufi manual taken at the fall of Bonjol, failed to convince some Europeans of the commitment of Southeast Asia's Muslims to their faith. Raffles had only taken away some poetic odes and Javanese texts belonging to Sultan Badr al-Din of Palembang, leaving the substantial Arabic and Malay collections alone. These were similarly ignored by Van Sevenhoven in his treatment of the court, which he regarded as having nothing in common with the Arab community in residence there.[41]

Raffles and Van Sevenhoven were even more disparaging while John Crawfurd (1783–1868) maintained that the Malays were known for being "exemplary" if tolerant Muslims, and pronounced the Javanese to be "the most lax in their principles and practice," due to "their little intercourse with foreign Mohamedans."[42] How much he really knew about such intercourse is in doubt, however, for it often took place outside the archipelago, beyond the ken of Europeans. The evidence before them, though, was of a renewal of a text-based approach to Islam. This is perhaps best demonstrated by the most interesting prize collection, that of Banten, whose Sultanate was abolished by Raffles in 1813. Its contents would only be described in 1833–35 by B. Schaap. The same Schaap, who later served as the Adjunct Secretary of the Government at Batavia, also happens to have been a member of the Dutch dictionary committee and the possessor of the *Hikayat Maryam wa-'Isa*, coincidences that provide us one more instance of how an interest in linguistics and the propagation of Christianity overlapped at the official level. And yet again, students of Islam can only be disappointed with Schaap's brief definitions, that betray limited interest in (or perhaps simply time for) the finer details of Islamic knowledge.

He categorized some of the Banten collection as being concerned with "language," "duties," and "religion" (and, in one instance, "religious songs or zikir-zikir"), but it is clear that many of the works before him were advanced Sufi works in Arabic. This perhaps explains why the first description of the Batavian Society's collection, undertaken by its custodian, R. Friederich (1817–75), dealt with the Arabic material. As we shall see, this prioritization matched the scholarly imperatives of the Delft training school.

From Batavia and Surakarta to Breda, Delft, and Leiden

With the return to Dutch independence under Willem II (r. 1813–40), various attempts would be launched to equip colonial officers with a knowledge of Malay and Javanese. Where the VOC had once sent out officials and their families and trusted that they would get a footing and learn what tongues they needed once on the ground, the new state would, ultimately, dispatch a generation of young, single, men, who were expected to speak at least the major languages of the archipelago before commencing their official labors.

That at least was the plan. Among the pioneering individuals whom we would today term Indonesianists was P. P. Roorda van Eijsinga (1796–1856). Sent to Java as a soldier in 1819, he would be engaged to teach Malay in Batavia, where he compiled a grammar of that language. His Javanist counterpart, in the meantime, was the short-lived A. D. Cornets de Groot (1804–29), for Malay was not necessarily the language of choice for those setting out for service in the Indies. The first formal school for officials, modeled on the College of Fort William at Calcutta and given impetus by Dipanegara's revolt, would be founded at Surakarta in 1832 under the German J.F.C. Gericke (1799–1857), who had been hired to the Indies by the Netherlands Bible Society.[43] After an ambitious start, Gericke would depart the scene to be replaced by the Eurasian translator to the Solonese court, C. F. Winter (1799–1859), whose notes would color the later grammar of Taco Roorda (1801–79). Even then the Institute struggled with a tightening budget and limited official interest. It was wound up in 1843 in favor of the official metropolitan training school just established at Delft in 1842.

Some would argue that, in the wake of the wars to reassert and expand Dutch control of the Indies, such efforts were too little and too late. But Delft had not been the first locus of training in the Netherlands. There had been thoughts of establishing a dedicated school in Leiden, and Roorda van Eijsinga had been recruited to the Military College at Breda in October of 1836, where he would commence work on a multi-volume guide to the Indies, in which a mere six pages related to the practice of Islam on Java.[44]

The Dutch historian Cees Fasseur once quipped that the recruitment of

Roorda van Eijsinga was a case of Mars trumping Minerva.[45] Yet Mars was not well served by the veteran and he was soon joined by the young P. J. Veth (1814–95), whose life work demonstrates the interconnectedness of religious faith, Orientalism, and a sometimes uncomfortable colonial utilitarianism. Departing from an avowed inclination to take a clerical vocation, Veth took advantage of an offer from Roorda van Eijsinga in 1838 to work as a teacher of both English and Malay (despite never having been to the Indies). Even though he never traveled to the East, he certainly recognized the need to demonstrate a knowledge of Arabic and Islam, producing a text edition of al-Suyuti's *Lubb al-lubab* (The Heart of Hearts) prefaced by claims that the Malays had had no literature prior to their adoption of Islam.[46] He would remain at Breda for three years before moving to teach at the doomed Atheneum at Franeker. With its impending closure and the appointment of Taco Roorda at Delft, Veth shifted to the Amsterdam Atheneum in 1843, where he gave his opening oration on "The Importance of the Practice of Islamology and its History for the Christian Theologian."[47]

Yet Veth remained something of an (outspoken) exception at Amsterdam once the real business of training officials for the Indies began at Delft in 1842. There young men were to be equipped for placements at mines, plantations, and in clerical offices. And whereas the Java Institute had focused on Javanese literature as the key tool of the modern official, at Delft it became an ancillary subject to the more practical subjects of mineralogy, agronomy, and fragmental readings of Roman and Islamic law, the latter in Arabic and Malay. In 1844, one of Delft's new staff members, Albert Meursinge (1812–50), who had defended a thesis at Leiden on al-Suyuti's *Tabaqat al-mufassirin* (Generations of Exegetes), produced a handbook on Islamic law intended for use by European officials and "developed" natives. In essence that was an edition of ʿAbd al-Raʾuf's *Mirʾat al-tullab* derived from a Leiden manuscript brought from Gorontalo, Sulawesi. Such an emphasis was paralleled at Breda. A year later, J. J. de Hollander (1817–86), who had succeeded Roorda van Eijsinga in 1843, would produce his own guide to Malay language and literature, followed by a reference list of Malay works in 1856. He also issued a series of readers, including the *Hikayat Jalal al-Din* based on a fragmentary edition produced by Meursinge in 1847.[48]

Even so, Malay remained poorly esteemed. De Hollander's edition of the *Hikayat Jalal al-Din* contained numerous erroneous emendations, as for example when the perfectly spelled Arabic word for "alms" (*zakat*), was twisted to become something like "ritual prostrations" (*rakʿat*).[49] The assumption was that the Malays were not as familiar with formal Arabic as studied in the Dutch Academy, and that Malay was in any case not equipped to deal with complicated concepts. Jan Pijnappel Gzn. (1822–1901), recruited to Delft in 1850, regarded it a simple tongue for simple minds. Still he offered a perfunctory grammar of the language for second and third year students, given that "High" Malay was included in their curriculum.[50]

Given that Dutch officials would be placed in judgment over Muslim subjects, there was a pronounced concern for teaching Islamic law, as may be seen with the Javanese translation of al-Haytami's *Tuhfat al-muhtaj* (Gift of the Needy), issued in 1853.[51] This time the editor in question was Salomon Keijzer, who had arrived at Delft after Meursinge's early death in 1850. Keijzer's guide was based on texts held in Holland and England. They included a Bantenese version owned by Taco Roorda, as well as one from the papers of the former governor of Java's Northeast Coast, Nicolaus Engelhard (1761–1831 or 1750–1832) bequeathed to the newly founded Royal Institute for Linguistics and Anthropology of Netherlands India (KITLV).[52] With the early passing of Keijzer, Taco Roorda retitled the manual "A Javanese Handbook for Mohammedan Law."[53]

This manual was destined to remain in use in official circles in Java for the next four decades, alongside another of Keijzer's guides produced in 1853 in emulation of French efforts in Algeria. In his *Handboek voor het Mohammedaansch regt* (Handbook for Mohammedan Law) Keijzer offered an explicit argument that "pure" Islamic law—which the student would find exemplified in his translation of the *Tanbih fi l-fiqh* (The Reminding of Jurisprudence) of Ibrahim b. 'Ali al-Firuzabadi (d. 1083)—should be studied before turning to look at whatever "deviations" had been effected in the various local codes in the Netherlands Indies.[54] Perhaps the best work for gaining a sense of what Keijzer thought of, or feared from, Islam in the Indies, is to be found in a collection of essays he released in 1860. Herein he drew on his knowledge of Islamic law in general, and of the corpus of Javanese and Malay texts copied in Batavia in particular, to argue that the peoples of the Indies were at bottom as much Muslim as any others, and that a reading of Islamic texts and an understanding of the Hajj were therefore key if one was to come to grips with them. Keijzer's study can be seen in the wake of the War of 1857 in India, and the more recent Jeddah massacre of 1858, as raising a large question mark over the academy and the colonial interests it so explicitly served.[55] At the heart of this was his allegation regarding a lack of knowledge of Mecca and how precisely that city's influence was exerted. As he wrote:

> [W]herever the [juridical] books are excerpted, edited and translated in the general interest, Islam shall require a new stimulus for the blood to quicken throughout all of its arteries. Such a stimulus is to be found in the pilgrimage to Mekka, from whence new life-force is sent to the most removed lands of the east. In this sense the Holy Land is not merely the birthplace of Islam, where it was born and bred. Rather, by means of the pilgrimage, it becomes the ground from which, for almost every Mohammedan land, the teaching of Mohammed is spread and magnified. This

thus demonstrates that, as far as the Indian Archipelago is concerned, it is fitting that one should assess what importance the pilgrimage has for our territories.[56]

In his subsequent discussion, Keijzer followed a theoretical pilgrim to Jeddah before attempting to reconstruct the remainder of the journey from the works of jurisprudence he knew so well, providing translations of the requisite prayers uttered at each stage and rite. Still, Keijzer knew that his charges had to rely on people as much as on a knowledge of texts. He therefore argued for the creation of something akin to a Muslim church, using the very Arabic titulature he believed was alienating the people from their "national" identities. Indeed Keijzer was no advocate of the Hajj, supporting the draconian pass regulations of 1858 as a check againt Meccan fanaticism. He saw Islam as a faith that had left its "blackness" upon the people, and the Hajjis as clergy charged with filling the chests of war.

Despite his bigotry, Keijzer was nonetheless prophetic. In his history of Mecca he sketched a tripartite struggle between the interests of the Sharifan clans, the Ottoman Porte, and the movement of Ibn ʿAbd al-Wahhab, and predicted that if either the Sharifs or the Wahhabiyya were to regain ground, the aftershocks were sure to be felt in "our India." What is perhaps more surprising to the modern reader, however, is the position taken by Keijzer in regard to these factions. While he had nothing but contempt for the "heretical" Turks and the Sharifs that "the treacherous" Muhammad ʿAli had installed, he expressed a measure of approval for Ibn ʿAbd al-Wahhab, declaring him a learned man who had brought the people to a closer understanding of God and done away with many "inhuman practices," transforming the city of Dirʿiyya into "the Geneva of Protestant Mohammedanism." He also wondered if there was anything to the apparently commonplace claims that Sumatra's Padris had been inspired by the movement.[57]

Keijzer was not the only Orientalist to hold such views. The French scholar, Garcin de Tassy (1794–1878) had regretfully come to the same conclusion in the 1830s.[58] Even so, when G. K. Niemann (1823–1905), the sub-director of the training institute of the Dutch Bible Society in Rotterdam, issued a guide on Islam in which he repeated much of what Keijzer had offered, he did so with a less emphatic treatment of the Wahhabis as reformers. He also raised doubts as to the "usual story" about the Padris having come under Wahhabi influence, asserting that their origins were far more obscure.[59]

All this was moot in the 1860s, however, when the Wahhabi and Padri movements were both so clearly disabled, and Keijzer had to content himself with urging that the Dutch state emulate the British by establishing a consular presence in the Hijaz to find out exactly how the "priests," who wore the clothes of the "victorious Arab" on Java, could live off the backs of the rest of the population. Even though he bemoaned the ignorance and inability of so many previous Dutch observers of Islam in the archipelago, he contented himself two years later with reissuing Valentijn's *magnum opus* with little or no editorial comment.[60]

The various training schools were not the only metropolitan sites with an interest in the expanding Netherlands Indies. The year 1851 saw the establishment at Delft of the KITLV. From 1853, it would publish its own journal, the *Bijdragen tot de Taal-, Land- en Volkenkunde van Nederlandsch-Indië* (*BKI*). But while this periodical was a mouthpiece first aligned to Delft and the conservative regime responsible for the maintenance of the Cultivation System, its academic offerings on Islam were not all that different from the more avowedly liberal contents of the *Tijdschrift voor Nederlandsch Indië* (*TNI*), founded at Batavia by W.R. van Hoëvell; or yet the prestigious *Tijdschrift voor Indische Taal-, Land- en Volkenkunde* (*TBG*) over which he had also had influence.

It has been claimed that the product of a Delft education at the hands of masters such as Roorda and Keijzer, who had neither hands-on experience of the Indies nor any regard for the horizons below "high" Javanese literature and "pure" Arabic law, was generally a graduate ill-equipped with practical knowledge of his future field. It would also seem that graduates were about as prepared to use Javanese and Malay in daily discussion with Indonesians as the latter would have been to use Arabic on the Hajj. Delft certainly had its detractors, both at home and in the Indies. And the academy was regularly under threat of closure as the decades wore on. In time too there would be rival outlets for the training of students for the official Indies exams. In 1864, a new Liberal regime would move the KITLV to the Hague and demote Delft to an ancillary preparatory school, founding a new State Institute for the training of Indies officials at Leiden. This would live alongside, but not within, the hallowed University, which would only start offering Indonesian languages in 1871, at which date its own library collection would be built around the manuscripts gathered by Cornets de Groot.

The committee that had argued for the establishment of this institute at Leiden had included Roorda and the now famous savant, Veth, who would join its staff. Veth's teaching abilities and his sometimes patchy linguistic skills were not held in uniformly high regard by the Leiden establishment, however, as he discovered when the rising Arabist Reinhardt Dozy (1820–83) criticized his oration on Islamic education given at Franeker. Undaunted, Veth had persisted. And with numerous articles in *De Gids* he managed to emerge as the major Dutch encyclopedist of the Indies. He had, moreover, been a founding member of the KITLV, though he moved to found the more liberal Indies Society (IG) in 1854. He was also behind the publication of accounts of all kinds written by Indies officials, such as that of Ridder de Stuers on Sumatra, together with Van Hoëvell's translation of Jalal al-Din's text. In the preface Veth even seems to have been the first to enlarge upon Raffles' speculations of 1822 concerning a Wahhabi-Padri commonality.[61]

Veth would become known for bringing to press all manner of contributions from some of the men who had had their training at the hands of Delftians like Roorda and the Malayist Pijnappel, who would both join him at Leiden. Left behind was a bemused Keijzer, who succeeded as director in Delft under the aegis of the city council. For what Delft had lost to Leiden was the over-paid director Roorda. Even with his avowedly humanist approach, few would prove eager to take up Veth's lectures on Islam and Indies ethnography, or the Malay classes of the dismissive Pijnappel.

Regardless of the intertown rivalries, though, the scholarly differences be-tween the respective staffs of these institutions were not necessarily deep in this period. It might even be said that, with respect to Islam, there was some-thing of a metropolitan consensus stretching from the academy to the training schools and back. For example, by 1863 Dozy would produce the first mono-graph of a series on "the principal religions" that agreed in many respects with Keijzer and Niemann. This work even made use of Keijzer's plates, with occa-sional adjustments (as when the already unflattering head of a "Javanese" pil-grim was replaced by an even less flattering "Arab" one).[62] With somewhat greater subtlety he drew on what Veth had said of the Indies in the 1840s. Thus the Sufis of their day were cast as degenerate tricksters and the Wahhabis as principled reformers who may even have influenced the Padris. But while Dozy happily cribbed Veth's notes on the term "Padri," like Niemann he was more cautious in equating the movement to the Wahhabi struggle.[63]

CONCLUSION

Our chapter opened with the story of rivalry between a former power and an emergant one, facing off across Southeast Asia in the wake of the collapse of the VOC. Yet such shifts of hegemony and influence were by no means simple, as many local sultans tried to take advantage of changes in oversight to extri-cate themselves from old treaties. In the wars and ransackings that followed, the Dutch would find themselves in need of officials able to administer to Muslims who were now more formally within their imperial grasp. To this end the previously ignored troves of captured texts would form the basis for the training manuals used by teachers who had often never been to the Indies, and whose natural inclination might be to contrast them with the materials that were already available from the Middle East.

As we shall see, metropolitan views of what Islam was were shared by certain activists in Java. Where they differed though, and quite profoundly, was in recognizing that what obtained on that island was really Islam in the first place. But although the academies of Holland differed in political temperament, they shared one aim: that of turning out competent servants for the colonial ven-ture. The results from Leiden were disappointing, so the enterprise was badly in need of the fresh start that it received in 1867. It came in the form of yet another training school: namely, the "B-section" of the Willem III Gymnasium, opened at Batavia in 1860. It would emulate the Delft curriculum but obviate the need for sending the foreign-born sons of so many Indies hands to a cold and uncertain experience in the metropole. After all, the future surely lay before them in an ever-expanding (but still regrettably Muslim) Netherlands India.

CHAPTER SIX

Seeking the Counterweight Church, 1837–1889

> We were solicited night and day for every thing they saw about us; and finding themselves not altogether successful—for it was impossible to satisfy the demands of such unblushing suitors—they began to ask us for books, which we promised to give them on our return to the vessel. We told them that we had no romances or pretty sonnets to give, nothing but Bibles and Testaments. "Well," said they, "give us them."[1] (G. Tradescant Lay, Brunei, 1837)

While the state was founding its training schools for aspiring colonial officials, travel writing and book collecting by churchmen-scientists continued, whose disdain for Islam was all too apparent even when they did communicate something new. This may be gathered from the accounts of the American James T. Dickinson (1806-?) and his English companion, the naturalist G. Tradescant Lay (c. 1805–45), who together journeyed from Malacca to Sulawesi, Magindanao, and Borneo in 1837.[2] Both men were concerned with mapping out opportunities for future Christianization, and whenever possible they handed out printed propaganda in Malay and Makassarese. Their tracts were apparently well received by the people of still-independent Brunei, if only as substitutes for the "romances" they apparently craved. Their reading tastes must have been frustrating to Lay and Dickinson, who were affronted as well by the way in which the Dutch seemed to be inhibiting missionary activity wherever they held sway. Lay even had it that while "the Prince of Darkness" had long had possession of Borneo, "the Hollanders" had "lately guaranteed the sole ownership thereof to him in perpetuity."[3]

Sometimes, though, the two missionaries were surprised by the openness of the Muslims of the archipelago. The chief "priest" of Brunei—who had resided in Mecca for twenty-five years—claimed to be on good terms with one of their brethren in Singapore, and had sanctioned local access to the Malay gospels, which Lay and Dickinson had mistakenly imagined to be off-limits to pious Muslims.[4] They were witness to communal dhikr at the court of Brunei's Sultan 'Umar 'Ali Sayf al-Din II (r. 1829–52), but it would appear that they were unable to absorb its import. The obviously hostile Lay described it as follows:

> On the Thursday evening . . . the members of the household assemble, sit down in a circle with a book and a light in the centre, and chant a few score of verses; while each beats a small tambour as an accompaniment. This choral entertainment occupies between two and three hours, and is

often associated with a good deal of waggery, as if the performers were laboring to render the whole as great a jest as possible. . . . When this part is finished, they pass into a kind of minor mode of a dull and lamentable character, which prepares the way for the finale, wherein all stand up and repeat the faith of the Mahommedan creed in three words. The repetition is simultaneous, and is delivered with a deep bow; at first in the tones of a rational creature, but as the celebrity of utterance is continually increased, it partakes more and more of the brute, till at last it resembles that sudden ejaculation made up of something between a bark and a grunt, which a herd of swine gives out when unexpectedly aroused from their slumbers, while the motion of the head in cadence with the noise is ludicrous in the highest degree. This mad work lasts till the whole party is quite exhausted; but such adepts are they at it, from long practice, that they are in full vigor a long time after we should expect to see their heads fairly shaken from their bodies.[5]

Dickinson, for his part, recounted the episode as follows:

In the evening, it being the eve of their holy day . . . we had an opportunity of witnessing their *sambayang* (worship). It commenced in the sultan's verandah about 9 o'clock, with singing, accompanied by tamborines. The music was the best I have yet heard among the natives of the east. After an hour or two of rather monotonous singing, they became more animated, and commenced a very singular chanting, and bowing at the same time in a manner equally singular, to keep time with the tune. The chanting was occasionally varied, and with it the motions of the body. The excitement went on increasing until they were exhausted by this chanting and bowing. A young pangeran [prince, M. L.] who took part in it said that, it made his head ache. There were two priests present, and the sultan was a part of the time among the worshippers. When asked what was the meaning of all this, they said it was "praising Tuhan Allah." The language used was Arabic. The name of Mohammed was occasionally to be distinguished. The worship, if worship it might be called, was continued until midnight.[6]

Although it is hard to know what precise mode of dhikr was being practised at Brunei, recent studies of the style of Qur'an illumination and Malay seals in the nineteenth century point to the strong likelihood that a connection had been formed between an elite within the community and teachers and scribes of Daghestani origin. Such teachers were already well known for their popularity in Mecca and for their long-standing affiliation with the Naqshbandi family of tariqas.[7] At the same time, however, we should keep in mind that people of all ranks were journeying to and from Mecca. The courts might not always have been able control the dissemination of such ideally privileged knowledge.

We can say with certainty, though, that the Sultan of Brunei was a practitioner of the dhikr of some form of tariqa in 1837. About three years later (according to Spenser St. John [1825–1910], who was British Consul at Brunei from 1856 to 1858 [and no friend to the missionaries]), the return from Mecca of a Hajji Muhammad led to a schism that separated the court, along with the other Hajjis who supported it, from wider society. This dispute would rage into the following decade, outliving its instigators. By the end of the 1850s, rival missions had been sent to Mecca to either justify or refute Hajji Muhammad's particular philosophy (that God could not be assigned a personality), and his supporters in the countryside had set up mosques beyond the pale of what the confused British Consul deemed to be the court-sanctioned "orthodoxy."[8]

The Consul's report does not allow us to decide whether Hajji Muhammad represented the intrusion of a rival tariqa (or sub-tariqa), as was probably the case with the Agama Dul at Madiun. Even so, it would seem to fit a general mid-nineteenth-century pattern that saw indigenous sovereigns losing the last vestiges of their monopolies over Mecca-oriented mystical practice at about the same time as Europeans were being given authority over them. Another pointer in this direction is that the two Bruneian factions argued over the duration of the month of Ramadan, which echoes contemporary debates in Sumatra and Banten. There ultimately print-oriented and pro-Ottoman Naqshbandis, who favored dates derived by means of calculation, were at odds with the local Shattaris, who trusted the results of traditional observation and thereby gave the impression that they were Hanafis.[9]

Past Islam as Safe Islam

A similar blend of distaste for and confusion regarding Islamic practices is also evident in a travel account written by the director of the Indies Bible Society, Wolter Robert van Hoëvell (1812–79). Van Hoëvell, the well-heeled nephew of former Governor-General Van der Capellen, had arrived to minister to his Batavian congregation in 1837. Ten years later, in 1847, he spent two months touring Java, Madura, and Bali. His description, threatened with censorship in Batavia, was published in Amsterdam by Veth, who had joined the board of the Dutch Bible Society in 1843. Van Hoëvell saw in Veth a perfect partner who would share his proselytizing ambitions. He would undoubtedly have agreed with the tenor of Veth's lengthy 1845 article on "Mohammad and the Koran," which outlined the influence of Islam on and, implicitly, its threat to the colony. They also shared the quixotic view, expressed by Van Hoëvell in his *Nederland en Bali* of 1846, that the Indonesians might still prove amenable to Christianization.[10]

Van Hoëvell told his readers in 1849 that his journey had been designed "to garner a treasure of linguistic knowledge and science" and to study the Javanese, Madurese, and Balinese in their daily lives.[11] But while he did accumulate a wealth of observations (and the odd manuscript) between parochial visits, much of what he saw he compared to what he had read in Valentijn's *Oud en Nieuw Oost-Indiën* and Raffles's *History of Java*. Hence he was more than a little discomfited by the strange spectacle of "the *kedeboes* performance" he witnessed in Cianjur, which neither predecessor had mentioned. This was, in fact, the *debus* ritual of the Rifa'i tariqa, once practiced at the court of Banten.[12] For Van Hoëvell though it was merely one of the means by which the cunning "priests" brought their influence to bear upon the people:

> On a mat sat two lines of fifty or sixty locals, including many young lads of twelve to sixteen years, each with a tamborine in hand. Hung at the end of the rows was a red square sheet of linen, on which, in white letters, bad Arabic was printed, filled with adulations of God, Mohammed, the Angels and the Saints of Islam, of which we attach a copy here for those who have interest in deciphering such nonsense. Behind this hanging sat a priest who had been to Mekka on the pilgrimage (*hhadji*) [*sic*]. On a piece of white linen in front of him lay a few of the so-called *soelthans*, iron awls, some a foot long, some a little longer or shorter, with a sharp point on one end, and a broad wooden head, to which iron chains were attached and joined to the other end. Besides this he had a pair of round heavy stones, roughly a foot in diameter, and a few other objects in front of him. On his lap was a cushion on which lay an opened manuscript, from which he read in the usual singing manner of the Mohammedans. At the end of each verse all the others in the choir repeated the last words, with a deafening shriek accompanied by the striking of the tamborines and an "Amin! Amin!" Once this, with increasing feeling, had lasted about an hour, the passion seemed to have reached its peak, and one of the group stood up and, dancing, approached the hanging, knelt before the objects, made peculiar shakings with his upper body and head and then grasped the iron awl which the priest proffered him . . . .

From here the youth, and all those after him, proceeded to stab at their bodies and faces with the awls, appearing to pierce themselves and yet remaining uninjured. For the dubious churchman this just meant one thing:

> I say it again, priest-fraud. That all who bring a few prayers to the Prophet, and on these occasions, to this Sjech 'Abdoe'l-Kadier Djilani, can in such a manner make themselves invulnerable! For the priest makes sure that nobody is touched by the awls . . . and if they are, then it is a sign of insufficient faith or weak prayers. You will see that such a feast is very instructive. [You have] . . . the chiefs of the Preanger Regencies who are very rich, and have many treasures, and occupy a higher rank of civilization than the others of Java; and then you have met the priests as cunning

fraudsters who attempt to maintain their influence by stirring up and keeping vital the superstition of the population. Then you will complain that the people have sunk into a sad state of stupidity and ignorance. And if you but cast your eye across the whole of the land, and follow their situation there, too, then you will come to the same conclusion.[13]

It was obviously, all of it, well beyond the limits of Van Hoëvell's patience, and the information he supplied was apparently beyond the limits of Veth's knowledge, at least at times, for in his marginal notations on Van Hoëvell's manuscript Veth could not untangle some of the allegedly unclear names on the banner and pronounced them pointless "twaddle."[14]

By comparison Veth was more than happy to complete an analysis of the skillfully executed epigraphy on a saintly grave such as that of Malik Ibrahim (see fig. 6), which had clearly impressed Van Hoëvell. The minister-scientist author read this as a testament to Islam's peaceful birth that had laid the groundwork for the very "mild" faith he believed he saw on Java.[15] In fact Van Hoëvell was frankly bamboozled by the accommodatory manner of one of the keepers of Sunan Giri's by now dilapidated mausoleum. As he recalled:

He treated us with the greatest kindness, telling us what he knew. The *missighit* and *langgar*, which stood close by the grave, the hut in which the tomb was shut, the grave itself, the iron chest, the kris, the document—everything was to be trodden, experienced, tried. And on our parting, he kissed me, the Christian-teacher whom he knew as the *toean pandito* [i.e. Master Priest], on the hand with great sincerity. These fanatical Javanese![16]

Less surprise was evident in the case of Van Hoëvell's translation of a vita concerning the Islamic education of the Europhile ruler of Sumenep, Adipati Natakusuma II (r. 1825–54). Here Van Hoëvell relayed a list the various works that the sultan, named as such by Batavia for his loyalty in the Java War, had mastered in his youth. The topics ranged from linguistics and exegesis, to jurisprudence, astronomy and poetics. Veth could only hazard a couple of guesses as to the titles based on the seventeenth-century dictionary of the Ottoman Katib Celebi (1609–57) and J. von Hammer-Purgstall's *Encyklopädische Uebersicht der Wissenschaften* of 1804, which borrowed heavily from it. Otherwise he simply pointed to the paginated fields of knowledge schematized by the Austrian.[17]

Van Hoëvell and Veth were clearly more impressed by the sultan's claim to have been Raffles's leading informant on Arabic, Javanese literature, and antiquities.[18] He was, moreover, a regular contributor to the *TNI* (established by Van Hoëvell in 1838), and had been recognized by the Royal Dutch Institute itself.[19] The sultan was indeed a most agreeable host for Van Hoëvell, who could only regret that, despite his possession of the gospel, he was not disposed to its contents. As the sultan apparently put it on one occasion when the topic of Islam and Christianity arose: "Oh, my dear sir, I understand both as two different paths which will bring us, if we but travel them respectfully and properly, to the same destination."[20]

The path of Islam was certainly the road less traveled in Van Hoëvell's book—in contrast, for example, to the paths of local agriculture, archaeology, architecture, and above all, to the issue of the still-to-be-Christianizied population. In regard to the latter, the Batavian minister felt that there were two main enemies over and above the lassitude of these not-so-fanatical Muslims: the censorious regime in Batavia, and the insidious threat of the domestic Catholics whom, like Relandus before him, he adjudged to be more similar to Muslims than Christians.[21] Hence much of what he offered in between his observations and services came in the form of an oft-repeated lament addressed to the homeland, that there be "more remaining from your conquest and rule over these lands than ruins and rubble, something better than a feeble shadow of artistry and artisanship!"[22]

At first sight it might seem that few shared Van Hoëvell's concerns, any more than they had shared Relandus's in 1705. The Batavian Society of Arts and Sciences, over which Van Hoëvell had also presided since 1845, was scarcely on a good footing as far as its collection of Islamica went. Or at least this was the impression of the half-willing bible translator, H. Neubronner van der Tuuk (1824–94), who arrived for preparatory work in 1849 after some of its best sources had been sent out for copying as materials for the Academy in Delft.[23] Nevertheless, information was seeping out. In its first two years the *TNI* had featured contributions on the Padri wars and the Meccan importation of "fanaticism," and Van Hoëvell also translated Meursinge's edition of the *Hikayat Jalal al-Din* for General De Stuers.[24] But while Van Hoëvell had been happy enough to feature articles on the life of Muhammad, Arabic literature, and sacred graves, his contributions were really an excuse to argue that, in contrast to the Sumatrans, the Javanese barely knew their Prophet.[25] He also eagerly cited the observations of supporters like the Chairman of the Raad van Indië, Van Sevenhoven, who in 1839 had described the pesantren of Lengkong, near Cirebon, as a foul-smelling collection of bamboo huts full of half-starved and listless students.[26]

> And what do these unfortunate youths gain at the cost of so many sacrifices? Are their minds developed and civilized to a degree commensurate with the level to which their bodies have been undermined? We can give but an unsatisfactory answer to this question. First, in the *pendoppo* [pavilion], they are taught reading and writing in a somewhat mechanical fashion . . . they all drone the text selected for their lesson together. This makes for a screeching and howling to the uninitiated; nonetheless the Priests or *Santrie*s, who wander among them at the time, can clearly determine who has uttered the lesson incorrectly. The students understand almost noth-

ing of what they read; now and then the *Hadji* explains the meaning, by which they gain some comprehension, but it is very defective, insufficient, and undetailed.[27]

In the years thereafter other snippets came to hand, which proved equally defective, insufficient, and undetailed. In 1844, there was a brief contribution on the various ranks of cleric in Surakarta, in which Mounier and Winter claimed that the term *perdikan* was a rank, rather than a place.[28] Figures such as Kyai Lengkong were usually buried within larger statistical overviews. Such was the case concerning two of the leading scholars of the Priangan highlands of West Java in 1846, Kyai Nawawi of Limbangan and his late peer at Sumedang, Kyai ʿAbd al-Jalil. Although the number of students taught by each man was reported, nothing was said of what they learned beyond "the mechanical reading of various *kitab*s and the learning of a number of prayers," a phrase which itself became a mechanical mantra for Dutch observers.[29]

Perhaps the best example of contextual brevity was the statistical waltz through Java offered by P. Bleeker over the course of 1849–50, which only occasionally featured the reported numbers of clerics by residency. It would seem that this information was sometimes collected and sometimes not. When it did appear, it was quickly overwhelmed by data on crops and population, and, naturally, by references to Van Hoëvell's own journey of 1847.[30] And then there were features that made a point of how tolerant the Javanese supposedly were. In one instance, an account was given of a dispute in Banten between the local native official and a number of "priests" who tried to commence the Ramadan fast a day early. This was resolved by the resident, who waited for the next full moon to determine who was in the right, and sentenced the guilty party to the less-than-odious punishment of a day's contemplation in the mosque.[31]

On the whole it can be said that observers like Van Sevenhoven, Van Hoëvell and Bleeker wanted to find in Islam a fixed institution that resembled their own church. Java must have a representative church full of clerics who could be unpacked, counted, and categorized. Hence they were eager to exhume long-neglected reports that seemed to relay exactly such information, as for example that submitted by Cornets de Groot in 1823.[32] Living teachers, meanwhile, were scarcely questioned about their precise beliefs or even as to their assumed enmity for Christianity. Had there been deeper and more respectful engagement than a day's visit to Kyai Lengkong or Kyai Nawawi, the mission-positive officials might have been given more information. They might have gained a more nuanced understanding of the different categories of "*phakir*s." Indeed, had they voiced it, they would most surely have been corrected in their misapprehension that a Hajji was a pilgrim to the grave of the Prophet.

Islam was a religion that they were determined to understand through the limited textual offerings available to them from Holland rather than through their experience of the field itself. Consider a brief article on the distribution of assets according to the Shafi'i school, written in 1850 by the incoming chair of the Raad van Indië, J. van Nes. Derived from a text edition rather than from a living teacher, it was intended to aid Dutch officials in cases where subordinate regents had insufficient knowledge of Islamic Law; and indeed its operative assumption was that indigenous knowledge of religion was defective.[33]

Nevertheless, building on such modest information as they could glean from Van Hoëvell (who was forced to relocate to the Netherlands in 1849 for his criticism of Batavia), far more optimistic missionaries than Van der Tuuk were becoming active both in engaging with their intended converts and in coming to terms with the challenges before them. As Ricklefs has shown, it was the missionaries Harthoorn and W. Hoezoo (d. 1896), both active in East Java in the 1850s, who first observed the apparently novel tendency on the part of the self-declared "white ones" to label their allegedly less-religious fellows as "the red ones." Their lengthy reports, reproduced in such journals as the *Mededeelingen van wege het Nederlandsche Zendelinggenootschap* (*MNZG*), are among the most valuable published sources for tracking social change on Java in the nineteenth century, even though the authors were clearly the captives of their elite informants. An uncomprehending Harthoorn, for example, who was anxious that Javanese society might be overwhelmed by some sort of puritanical Mohammedan "despotism," placed the "Doel" to the side of the more sober santris as a class. Taking things further, his colleague Poensen claimed that they equated God and Muhammad and sought rebirth as Dutch officials! Certainly any santris who had engaged in Naqshbandi gatherings had to make a case for their practice. In one dialogue collected by Poensen, a Dul teacher reacted angrily to one aristocrat's charge that his followers believed that the spirit of the Prophet entered them during dhikr.[34]

Other travelers bound to the colonial state were becoming interested in tracking the details of daily life and in puzzling out what exactly it was that was being taught in the pesantrens—even though, like Lay and Dickenson, they might have trouble seeing what lay before their eyes. Such was the case in 1855, when "J.L.V." published his contribution on the "priests and seminaries" of Madiun. As we have already seen, J.L.V.—perhaps an official who used his initials to avoid the official repercussions of associating with Van Hoëvell— was vocally opposed to the furtive members of the sect also known to him as "Doel." Yet as much as he took the side of local "orthodoxy" against the sectarians, he still derided the state of education among the orthodox he championed, claiming that what was offered in their perdikans consisted of "the rote-learning of a few sections of the koran and prayers in Arabic, without the student understanding a single word of Arabic, and without the teacher being able to give him any notion of its sense and meaning, for he seldom understands more than the student." And he went on:

> If one now considers that these seminaries in the residency of Madioen are among the most famous on the whole island; that youngsters come

here from near and far to hear the lessons of the teachers, or better, to stay some time in order to be able to say that they were here; and thinks that these institutions are the sources from which the Mohammedan faith spreads its sap through the population; then one can well imagine that the Javanese are very poor Mohammedans. And so it is indeed. Apart from a little ritual, the spirit of Islam exerts but little force among them. It is little more than the form [of Islam], supplemented and varnished with all sorts of superstitious traditions, part drawn from the previous Hinduism, part from the play of their own fantasy.[35]

So much for orthodoxy. One wonders too what it was in J.L.V. that Van Hoëvell might have objected to, for he remarked in a footnote that he did not necessarily agree with what the author had to say on the subject of the perdikans.[36]

A good sense of the sort of study Van Hoëvell might have preferred came two years later, when his fellow minister Jan Brumund (1814–63) published an assessment of the state of education among the Javanese and with it won a prize offered by the Society for Promotion of the General Good in the East Indies. Much like the entrance requirements in the 1819 competition, this one required that contestants conduct an investigation into the nature of indigenous education in order that it might be improved by the state. Brumund attacked his subject with great zeal, juxtaposing Van Sevenhoven's earlier account of Lengkong with his own of Tegalsari and Sumenep.[37] Indeed, "attacked" is the best description of what he did. Having concluded that the common village langgars were nothing more than factories for "lorikeets and cockatoos" that turned the children into a class of beggars, his prodding and prying at the declining pesantren of the octogenarian Hasan Besari II of Tegalsari (fl. 1820–62) provided him with little information on the works that were studied there.

Brumund's shortcomings as an ethnologist must have been a function, at least in part, of his admitted inability to converse with the Kyai, not to mention his insistence on keeping his shoes on in the latter's "sanctuary"![38] He badgered some of the students into naming Raniri's *Sirat al-mustaqim* as their primary training manual, and his demands that they produce some work other than the Qur'an saw them fetch a copy of Roorda van Eijsinga's *Taj al-muluk* (The Crown of Kings). A triumphant Brumund then claims to have taken great pleasure in reading the work of his fellow-countryman to an incredulous audience.[39]

Brumund's work was printed in far fewer quantities than Roorda van Eijsinga's Malay text, but he seems nonetheless to have brought his clerical supporters back home firmly around to his view that Indies Muslims were but surface Muslims and scroungers. While Niemann would crib Brumund's work on the poor quality of pesantren education, Van Hoëvell, who had since become a strong voice for the Liberals in the Dutch parliament, moved to an even more radical position.[40] By the early 1860s his journal could sneer at "so-called scholars" who dared to pronounce Javanese society "Mohammedan," while he himself bemoaned the training of officials in Islamic law at Delft as a ridiculous waste of energy and an embodiment of all that was wrong with the Dutch system.

Certainly Van Hoëvell had received criticism from Delft, as for example when Keijzer had taken his writings on Java to task in 1859, repeating once again his argument that the study of "pure" Islamic law should precede any assessment of local traditional laws as "Polynesian."[41] A stung Van Hoëvell must have had the stay-at-home Keijzer in mind when he wrote that a Delftian would find on his arrival in the Indies that everything was quite unlike the "dreams and invented conclusions of [his] Mohammedan professor." Moreover:

> If the Javanese are truly Mohammedans, and Javanese society is a real Mohammedan one, then there should be organs through which Islam remains vital in this society, and there should be means by which the spirit of Islam lives from generation to generation. . . . Are there such organs? Are there such means? Are there Mohammedan schools, where the youth obtains education in Islam? Are there Mohammedan priests who awaken the spirit of Islam in the youth and keep it vital in the adults? It is true that in every village there is a mosque or prayer house and a priest. But the prayer houses are only used on certain occasions and stand empty. And the priests! Who are the priests? [42]

The editors then announced that they would not answer such questions by citing Van Hoëvell, Brumund, or other such "opponents of the Islam-theory." Instead, the 1839 article of Van Sevenhoven was dredged up once more in order that the dimness, dirt, and ignorance of Lengkong might stand for Islam in Java as a whole. For his part Veth seems to have recycled the same conclusions in an article of 1858.[43] With the rise of Christian-backed Liberals like Van Hoëvell to power, and the removal of the state training school to Leiden (and the KITLV to the Hague), this point was made amply clear to Keijzer. It was deemed pointless to fund a post teaching Islamic law given that Java was "no pure Mahommedan society," nor yet "run by Mahommedan laws."[44]

Despite negative assessments such as those found in the *TNI*, and despite the ascent to power of the Liberals, it is apparent from contemporary reports written by other figures in the Indies that things were changing. Books other than the *Taj al-muluk* were in circulation, and in increasing numbers and forms, though these did not yet find their way into Western hands. In 1857, Hermann von de Wall (1807–73), a German and the latest to be charged with producing the definitive Dutch-Malay dictionary, had solicited copies or inventories of any holdings of Malay, Javanese, Sundanese, and Arabic manuscripts from the various Residents of the Indies.[45] The results were mixed. In some cases the officials (or their juniors) ignored his request, disavowed the existence of such manuscripts, or even replied that they did not have enough contacts among the right sort of natives (Von de Wall had suggested that "native heads or priests" be consulted in the matter).[46] At Solo, A. B. Cohen Stuart (1825–76) even expressed the opinion that, compounding such factors as the maintenance of secrecy and a fear of losing manuscripts lent out for duplication, there were few to be had in the first place. He even advised his Resident that he doubted the very existence at court of any Malay, Arabic, or certainly Sundanese, materials.[47]

A proportion of Von de Wall's order was filled, however, by Residencies in West Sumatra, Palembang, West Java, and Madura. He received a fair assortment of the desired texts, from al-Sanusi's primer to the *Ratib* of Shaykh Samman.[48] The port town of Surabaya, with its prominent Arab minority, also delivered numerous Malay romances copied from the personal collection of one Shaykh ʿAli (al-Habshi?), who also made available eighteen works of history, jurisprudence, and linguistics.[49] The precise array of texts and their practical deployment was probably not foremost in Von de Wall's mind as he set to work on his dictionary (yet another that would never see the light of day). But unlike so many of his peers, he seems to have engaged actively with his principle informant, Raja ʿAli Haji of Riau, and most likely thought of Islam as something more than a tattered mantle worn by a people who had lost touch with their "original" literature. Such would however remain the entrenched judgment for some decades to come, as would Brumund's caustic verdict on the pesantrens, even though there were some who would publically denounce it.

Whereas Harthoorn had briefly treated the curriculum of a pesantren in an internal report of 1857, and Carel Poensen happily echoed Brumund in another, written in 1863, two notices in the newly established *Bataviaasch Zendingsblad* offer comparatively open-minded observations of a pesantren in West Java, and of the books in use there.[50] These were written in 1864 by the journal's youthful editor, a protégé of Taco Roorda called Gerhardus Jan Grashuis (1835–1920). Grashuis was a former trainee of the NZV in Rotterdam and a teacher at the Free Scots Church Seminary in Amsterdam. He had first been sent to Bandung in 1863 to study under K. F. Holle (1822–96) as preparation for translating the Bible into Sundanese, and to await permission from the government to commence missionizing.[51] It was to be a two-year wait, and having failed to gain permission the frustrated missionary sailed for the Netherlands in late 1865.

Although he resumed teaching at the seminary he was soon to depart again, complaining that his efforts (such as his translation of Luke's gospel) were not properly appreciated by his employers.[52] In 1868 he took the exam for officials and entered the Government Service on Java. In 1873, he took up a post as lecturer in Sundanese at Leiden's State Institute, and in 1877 transferred to the University itself along with Veth and Pijnappel.[53] Over this period he issued a series of texts on Sundanese and Malay, in which he reprised his articles of

1864 and translated a sampling of Islamic texts for consumption by aspiring officials.[54]

Back in 1864, though, on his first visit to the east, Grashuis had been far more theologically oriented. He claimed that he had long been attracted to the missionary endeavor in the Indies and was thus disquieted by the limited resources and information at his disposal.[55] The impetus for his first short piece on Islam was his dissatisfaction with available information about what was taught at Java's pesantrens. It struck him that, after years of experience in the Indies, the Dutch seemed none the wiser. It was all the more frustrating that the new training school at Delft was more concerned with commissioning a study of how, or indeed whether, the Javanese paid a tithe, than with what they learned of Islam.

As he observed, the usual answer to that question was little more than a repetition of the claim that there remained far more of the old pre-Islamic religion in the Javanese than of Islam, and that the institutions meant to inculcate Islam in fact offered very little of anything they considered "education." Of course that view was not universal, but even those who did not share it would gladly have seen a reduction in the number of such institutions, in which one could count far more enemies than friends of the Dutch government. Grashuis suggested that finding out about these schools would be no simple task, especially as the subjects of one's inquiry tended to avoid Christian unbelievers. But in 1864 he had made an effort at just such an institution. This pesantren, probably located in Garut, had been set up in 1857 under the leadership of a scholar who had trained elsewhere in Java. By Grashuis's account, the teacher was quite open in explaining his faith and the methods he used. Grashuis was thus able to offer some important correctives regarding the distinctions between pesantren teachers and the very idea of a clerisy in Islam, likening the difference to that between the ministry and the members of the theological colleges.

In the introduction to his second notice, he complained once more that Dutch missionaries had long paid "far too little attention to the nature of the people that they were in the business of evangelizing."[56] It is also clear from comments in his later *Soendanesche Bloemlezing* that he had by then come to realize that, regardless of Holle's teaching on the subject, the Sundanese possessed a written literature thoroughly grounded in Islam.[57] Indeed Grashuis also recognized that, through their emphasis on literacy, the pesantrens offered access to education in a broader sense. He was therefore intent on providing missionaries and officials alike with better access to that civilization through a preliminary analysis of the texts he had seen, commencing with a work on ritual cleanliness and al-Samarqandi's catechism.[58] Grashuis also demonstrated that the student would learn how many prophets there had been, how many books each had brought, and that Muhammad was the very last Prophet with the final message and the final law—a message Grashuis felt should not be underestimated. Grashuis also related details of "knowledge of religion and belief" and outlined the contents of another primer (Sanusi's *Umm al-barahin*) on the attributes of God, "a topic greatly favored by Mohammedan theologians."[59]

For a mission-minded officer, Grashuis offered an admirably fair assessment of the pesantren system, even if he still believed that there was a profound gap between the Dutch and their Muslim charges. In 1881 he wrote:

> On occasion I have had a native say to me that "Your religion and mine are two ways; God knows the correct one, and we cannot discern it," and also "You have your prophet, we have ours. The names may differ, but in principle our religions are one." This is a liberal Mohammedan opinion, and less representative than one might think. It is offered in an effort not to bother the outsider. The santris learn otherwise, in which respect we should have no illusions. It runs: "MOHAMMED is the last prophet, the seal of the prophets, the prince of the prophets." Thus their teaching is the only truth, their religion the only way pleasing unto God.[60]

Leaving books aside, and his own convictions as well, Grashuis could not help but comment in 1864 on the process underpinning the public's ever-increasing attachment to such an exclusive Islam:

> The pilgrimage makes up for whatever is lacking in the dissemination of Islam among Heathen tribes and nations. The proselyte is not as a rule deeply immersed in the new religion which he is preached, taught and into which he is pressed by sly Arab traders; but the pilgrimage is the bond which encompasses all Musulmans, and even the most distantly removed people come into contact with the holy orders where Islam was founded. Each year there is a reminder for and an admonition to the believer; each year one sees them coming and going, who have given much, and sometimes all, for their religion, and in similar fashion are thus rewarded with honor and respect. Even if no inspiration and enthusiasm were to emanate from Mecca, still this city would remain the heart of the Mohammedan world, from which each year new religious life flows through every artery.[61]

And flow it did, eventually leading other officials either to follow Grashuis's lead in seeking deeper insight into the teachings of the religious schools in their districts or, at least, to ask what information might be already available. In 1864, the school inspector J. A. van der Chijs was even able to dredge up the information on Java's pesantrens that had been gathering dust in the archives ever since the questionnaires of 1819 and 1831.[62] Another interested party, the freshly minted Delftian A.W.P. Verkerk Pistorius (1838–93), attempted to survey the works in use in the *suraus* of West Sumatra for the *TNI*.[63] As far as he was concerned, next to nothing was known of Dutch possessions beyond Java. Belying Grashuis's assertion that Dutch Christians and local Muslims were inherently incapable of communicating, he was able to build up a good relationship with a local scholar, Shaykh Muhammad of Silungkang over the three years he was in West Sumatra (c.1866–68), even alluding to the shaykh being quite prepared to have a glass of wine with the local Dutchmen on festive occasions.

Verkerk Pistorius was also welcome to wander among the school's students at all hours of the day and was consequently able to provide a valuable image of a living institution founded by a teacher who had studied in Mecca for a decade. He characterized its curriculum as flexible, with an emphasis on moral education and on building personal bonds between Sumatrans more normally divided by clan loyalties, and he suggested that Dutch educationalists seeking to make lasting changes in Indies society might do well to follow Shaykh Muhammad's model.[64] Verkerk Pistorius's work was a big advance over the catalogue of guesses made by Van Hoëvell and Veth, but his listing of the texts explained by the living shaykh remained a breakdown of fields of knowledge listed by their local designations.[65]

Perhaps his inability to go deeper was due the great discrepancy between the texts he was seeing and the texts that Delft had taught him he should have been seeing. Similarly, little of what he had learned under such men as Keijzer, to whose work on the Hajj he referred, would have prepared him to properly understand the "twaddle" people spoke about the Hajj, let alone to connect the practices he witnessed to the expanding Naqshbandiyya order, of which Shaykh Muhammad of Silungkang appears to have been an exponent.[66] In this last respect, however, his own ears apparently misled him. On the one hand he wrote that the students had told him that the communal dhikr that they practiced to the accompaniment of frame drums introduced by Indians resident at Aceh had first been composed by the ascetic "Baroedah."[67] At the end of his article, however, he referred to the new teachings of Tuanku Shaykh "Baroelah" of Tanah Datar, who had returned from Mecca and was spreading the teachings of the school of "Abu Hanifa," whose recognition Verkerk Pistorius believed was conditional upon the practice of *suluk* and commencing the Ramadan fast a day earlier.[68]

This aligned with Naqshbandi-Shattari debates, and Arnold Snackey dutifully reported in the 1880s that the Cangking-allied "Hanifi" Tuankus from Pasir, Silungkang, Kersik, and Bonjol gathered under Shaykh "Beroelak" at Padang Genting in 1858.[69] Observers like Verkerk Pistorius may have missed the precise import of the differences between teachings, but they knew well enough that arguments over sightings of the moon had the potential to disrupt the Dutch administration's dealings with its Shafi'ite subjects, whose school Verkerk Pistorius believed was notable for its "tolerance" in contrast to the official Ottoman juridical school.[70] "Be watchful," he urged readers of the *TNI*, reminding them of Van Hoëvell's tour and the hostile example of the last Padri, Tuanku Imam Bonjol, "for we stand on volcanic ground" and the embers of fanaticism could wreak no greater disaster than on "glowing Java."[71]

Verkerk Pistorius's rather florid articles, and indeed his call for further investigations and watchfulness, were to be gathered up and republished in 1871, but the next significant breakthrough did not come until June of 1883, when Poensen—who had since taken to training officials at the Willem III gymnasium—began sending letters to the *Soerabaiasche Handelsblad* that drew on his many years of observations of village life. Poensen urged that the Dutch need look no further than their own backyards to see peoples going about their business as fully aware Muslims. He also criticized the late custodian of the Batavian Society, Friederich, who had once written that the Javanese Hajjis were "little inspired by the fanaticism of the Western Asiatics," and remained "quiet, peaceful people."[72]

To counter this description, Poensen drew on the very latest writings from a young Snouck Hurgronje on the "international" character of Islam as reinforced by the Hajj. Poensen also pronounced upon the general contempt for the Dutch "Kapir-sétan," who fooled themselves with the naïve notion that people were truly satisfied by their provision of education and the building of a few mosques, taking a very Grashuisian line on what Muslims really thought.

> Indeed, the indolence, syncretism and good-natured character of our natives—to the great sorrow of the zealotry of the Bongso-poetihan [white ones]—certainly helps enforce this impression. But it is, and remains, a great error! ... At the very moment, as occurs here daily, when a Muslim says to a Christian, "Oh, it is all the same! Allah has given everyone their own religion (more correctly *sarèngat*); all have their own *Panoetan* [Prophet]; indeed whoever follows Allah's *parentah*s [instructions] shall be saved!" he adds in his heart: "But Islām is actually the only true *igama* [religion], and my Panoetan Mohammed is the last of the Prophets."[73]

Having delivered his version of the Javanese apologist, Poensen immediately contrasted the work of his Christian peers with that of others active in the field, linking the very phenomena first observed in the 1850s with the Naqshbandiyya (if only for rhetorical purposes).

> If an Arab or Arabic-speaking *goeroe* or *kjaï* makes known some *dzikir* or another, or some unusual religious practices, then he [the Javanese] receives them with interest, and will even attend their gatherings; as, for example, that of the Napsjibendiyah Darwîsj [*sic*] order. The *desaman* [villager], not so apprised of the fine differences between the sects, simply calls all this "Doel" or "Pasèq," yet he treats it completely differently from the "new *ngelmoe* [knowledge]" of the Christians, who have no Arabic etiquette.[74]

Poensen's letters, which were tempered versions of his earlier, zealous articles in the *MNZG*, covered a wide range of subjects, from calendrical matters and marriage to the Hajj and fasting. They soon drew the attention of the inexhaustible Veth, who released them as a monograph in 1886. For it was Veth, finally recruited to Leiden University in 1877, who now dominated the Indological field. His was a loud voice on the geography, botany, history and ethnography of Sumatra and Java, much of this knowledge compiled from the reports of retired officials and missionaries or from those for whom publication would have been an impolitic act.[75] It was also Veth who identified the quagmire in which the Dutch then sat in Aceh as being the direct result of their failure to collect accurate intelligence prior to 1873. Much of what did become known of Sumatran ground was contributed not by the desk-bound Veth, however, but by his entrepreneurial son, Daniël (1850–85). The elder Veth remained best known for his writings on Java, on which he gave a presentation at the Colonial Exhibition of 1883.[76]

Another scholar to develop a great interest in the Indies and the laws obtaining there was a former Delftian, A.W.T. Juynboll (1834-87). Hired to Leiden along with Veth and Pijnappel, he published in 1881 two short treatments of al-Samarqandi's primer intended to help colonial officials better understand what his colleague Grashuis laid out in his Sundanese textbooks.[77] Juynboll's efforts would be eclipsed in 1887, when Roorda and Veth's former student, Van den Berg, issued a survey of the Arabic books used in the pesantrens of Java. This marked a major advance for the field of Indies research, it came from one of its most prominent exponents, for by this time Van den Berg had emerged as the principal scholar in Batavia of Arabic, and, it was assumed, of Islam.[78] Soon enough events would cause him to direct his attention beyond the security of the scriptorium to consider the place of the Arabs in local society. It was a shift that could not take place, however, before the entire entire colonial administration had experienced something of a shock. The very shock, in fact, that Verkerk Pistorius had predicted.

THE SLUMBERING VOLCANO AWAKES

> His Highness, our Prophet Muhammad, gave this text of command to the ruler of Mekka, who has further made it known to the Mohammedans in all cities and towns . . . [that] the rulers and *panghoeloe*s shall call the fakirs together, and read to them the instructions of this letter; that they shall call their kin, etc., living in the cities, towns, villages, and hamlets, together—great and small, young and old, men and women—and instruct them of this *hadis* [*hadith*]. See to it that this *hadis* is obeyed![79] (Anonymous tract circulating in Sumatra and Java ca. 1865)

So read part of a letter, allegedly sent from Mecca in 1865, that circulated from the coastal hubs of Padang, Batavia, and Semarang. The missive called for a renewed commitment to the practice of Islam and repeatedly commended the reading of a particular tract of "hadith": although it was actually the *Tanbih al-*

ghafilin (The Reminding of the Forgetful) of al-Samarqandi, and not one of the attested traditions of the Prophet. Such letters had appeared before, and many more would come well into the 1880s. They would occasion understandable bouts of colonial anxiety. The translator however, in this instance Poensen, writing in early 1888 about something that had circulated among the *putihan* twenty-three years earlier, may have felt himself at something of a distance from such concerns when he wondered why such tracts "of purely religious content" had always seemed to have "a political tenor."[80]

Back in early 1880s, however, officials had been particularly worried given the fact that the fourteenth Muslim century was due to commence on November 1, 1882 and that the advent of a new century is often associated by many Muslims with the appearance of a renovator of the faith. In West Java in particular some officials were concerned over rumors that a plot was afoot to wipe them off the colonial map. Matters would soon become worse, for many Bantenese began to suspect that the 1883 eruption of Krakatau and ensuing agricultural blights were some form of divine punishment for their laxity in religious observance. Hence, when a revolt did break out in the town of Cilegon on July 9, 1888 (and thus after Poensen had finished preparing his article on the "Meccan" letter of 1865), colonial officials with far less open perspectives would look back to these events and see a logical connection between them and indeed two decades of the comings and goings of "fakirs" from Mecca. One such official was R. A. van Sandick (1855–1933), a senior colonial engineer who had been a witness to the eruption of Krakatau. He would write two books on the subject, the geophysical *In het rijk van de vulkaan* (In the Kingdom of the Volcano) and the more impassioned and polemical *Leed en lief uit Bantam* (Suffering and Love from Banten), which linked the events to Mecca.[81]

There had indeed been a greater mobilization of West Javanese Muslims headed to and from Mecca beginning in the late 1870s, and Van Sandick's narrative of disaster, written in the late 1880s, readily fused this story with the later rumors of massacres and the all-too-real eruptions that followed. The vectors of the Indies plot had also seemed clear enough to the amateur Islamologist and honorary adviser to the colonial state, Holle, who was informed by the Penghulu of Garut, Raden Hajji Muhammad Musa. Though he associated with Muslim scholars (and was a Muslim himself for the purpose of his marriage), Holle nonetheless wished to turn the Sundanese away from what he saw as an infatuation with Islam. (He in fact even wanted to discourage the use of Islamic script, as Grashuis had learned when he studied with him in the 1860s.) After a trip to Singapore in 1873 to gather information about regional sympathies for the Acehnese, Holle had decided that the signs pointed to an intensifying influx of fanaticism from Mecca. He therefore urged that government appointees be removed from office if they proved too zealous in their religion; whether by expressing an interest in leading Friday prayers, by performing the Hajj, or by correcting local practices (for example, some native officials now favored a call to prayer over the traditional beating of a drum to summon the faithful to the mosque). He even recommended the adoption of uniforms for Hajjis.

All of Holle's proposals were ignored. Later however, when rumors spread of the plot of 1881, he made use of his contacts with the then consuls at Jeddah and Singapore to revive some of his earlier suggestions for the suppression of Islamism, including the institution of formal uniforms for Hajjis, the close surveillance of Arabs and of materials printed in Arabic, and even the dispatching of a spy to Mecca. His proposals once again fell on deaf ears, especially after it became known that some of the panic could be sourced to correspondence between Holle and the consuls.

Also crucial to this setback had been the advice of the colonial Advisor for Mohammedan Law, whose teachers had originally destined him for a chair at Leiden. The financially troubled Van den Berg surprised his professors by sitting the civil-servants' exam instead. After arriving in Batavia in 1870, he had been appointed as a clerk for a time in Semarang. After several unhappy years with the Council of Justice at Batavia, he transferred to the Department of Education, where he assumed the aforementioned rank of Advisor for Mohammedan Law in 1879. In 1880 he toured Aceh with T. H. der Kinderen, then secretary of the Raad van Indië. Such duties allowed him to devote more attention to his primary interest; namely the Arabs of the Indies and their language. For having completed Friederich's catalogue of Arabic manuscripts in 1873, and then of part of a catalogue the Batavian Society's Malay, Javanese, and other Arabic holdings in 1877, he remained ever the frustrated Arabist.[82]

Regardless of his Leiden training, Van den Berg's scholarly interest had a decidedly Delftian feel, and he remained focused on translating core works of Sunni jurisprudence for an official audience, including Nawawi's *Minhaj al-talibin*.[83] However, as his necessarily part-time concentration was on texts rather than people, Van den Berg was caught out by the panic of the early 1880s. Once it became apparent in subsequent official reports that the Naqshbandiyya had, contrary to his previous assertions, long been active in the archipelago, he set to work on his own updated article on the subject.[84]

In the beginning of this article he was less than forthcoming in describing how exactly he had become aware of the order. He claimed that recent discoveries of manuscripts, and indeed his own trip to Aceh, had convinced him that his earlier pronouncements that there was no such order in the Indies were somewhat hasty. It was but a partial *mea culpa*, however. Using the already classic work on Egypt by Edward William Lane (1801–76), who had associated with an ecstatic descendant of ʿAbd al-Wahhab al-Shaʿrani, Van den Berg remarked that what *remained* of the Naqshbandiyya in Aceh was merely leftover bits of dhikr now performed solely for public entertainment—as in such forms as the *sadati* dance, in which rows of young men would clasp arms and chant while another youth danced in front of them.

Like Lane and Dozy before him, Van den Berg saw modern expressions of popular Sufism as mere superstition. While he had also heard vague press reports of a Naqshbandi presence at Padang, he apparently knew little of the details. In Batavia, meanwhile, there was only the Qadiriyya, which seemed to resemble the Naqshbandiyya. Van den Berg believed that all such orders were only of interest to some particular (presumably low-caste) Arabs, for his own (sayyid) informants seem to have assured him that the pursuit of financial gain was the only aim for their meetings.

By contrast in Buitenzorg the Naqshbandiyya appeared to be in full swing. Local officials were even leading scandalous mixed assemblies at the mosque of an evening, with all manner of indiscretions occurring as soon as the lamps dimmed. Naturally Van den Berg could no longer neglect the 1881 affair of ʿAbd al-Qadir of Semarang (see ch. 3), whom he cast as a rather unsophisticated guru who had even managed to lose the printed license issued to him by Sulayman Afandi of Mecca. He also observed that ʿAbd al-Qadir had had some success among the lower classes around Yogyakarta and Kedu before being chased off by local religious officials, and that his deputies in Semarang, Kendal, and Salatiga oversaw similarly mixed, and potentially fatal, assemblies of men and women of all ages.

So it was then that Holle, when in 1882 he encouraged Sayyid ʿUthman to publish his tracts warning against the Naqshbandiyya, gained the support of his erstwhile opponent Van den Berg. Matters had certainly taken taken a turn, and Van den Berg must have had quite a red face when he was shown the various reports about the Naqshbandiyya in Java. Indeed much of what he had earlier said had clearly come through an official filter of one kind or another. Like the old stories of the *agama dul* or *santri birai*, the accounts he repeated were naturally biased, even to the point of alleging that rival groups indulged in illicit sexual activities. The possibility of bias seems to have eluded Van den Berg, though, who, while assuring his readers of the trustworthiness of his informant as "a respectable lord" from Tangerang, could go on to report that one Naqshbandi gathering in Serpong consisted of the teacher sitting in a square with his fellows while each grabbed the pudenda of his neighbor. "If this report is true," Van den Berg concluded, "then we see in abundance how the Polynesian phallus-religion manifests in today's form of Islam."[85]

For all his experience, then, Van den Berg was captive to his elite interlocutors. It is also clear that he believed that it would be impossible to mingle fully with the subjects of his inquiries. Even when he did try to go deeper, undertaking a study tour of Java in 1885 (while Holle was penning an article of his own on the Naqshbandiyya for the *TBG*[86]), his assessment of the quality of the education provided remained shaped by elitist Arabo-centric views. The primary result of his exertions was actually a monograph in French on the Arab communities of the Netherlands Indies.[87] And while he noted the increasingly widespread appearance of numerous printed Arabic books coming in from the ports of Java, he felt that these were little more than trophies; though he did concede that they might ultimately displace the manuscripts they emulated.[88]

It is also clear that Van den Berg held a low, and pseudo-ʿAlawi, opinion of the tariqas in general, seeing them as an accretion on authentic Islam or even as a bridge to unbelief. He claimed in this regard that the activities of so many "Persians, Turks, and Bengalis" in the tariqas headquartered at Mecca were sidelining the noble Arabs from their proper place at the head of Islamic education in Java. Near the end of his 1887 report on education, he spoke very much to this effect, stating that when the Arabs of the archipelago spoke of Sulayman Afandi and his associates, they felt themselves "not in their element."[89]

It also seemed to him that they were losing their rightful hold over some of the pesantrens, as more and more Javanese were assuming leading roles in the teaching of Islamic law. Perhaps the reason for this was that some Arabs felt shut out because much of the activity was occurring in Javanese, rather than Malay. Indeed Van den Berg, who noted that Sulayman Afandi was savvy enough to have had his works printed in Javanese at Cairo, belittled many of the pesantren teachers for not knowing Malay.[90]

Whatever his failings, Van den Berg did signal that a sea change was in process in the pesantrens of Java. By the time he wrote his article, however, his eyes were set more on Holland than the Indies. He departed for Delft in 1887, where he arrived some ten months before the "Qadiris" of Cilegon seemingly wiped out all that he had worked for. Indeed, with the Cilegon affair, the pesantrens and the tariqas alike were again drawn into the spotlight as being either the source of anti-government agitation or the means for its effectuation by disgruntled priyayis—past and present. The Resident of Surakarta would conclude his report of October 1888 by noting that Java was awash with many sacked and disgruntled officials and their relatives, as well as increasing numbers of "wound-up fanatics from Mecca." In his view the local gurus served as the intermediaries between such officials and these Meccan-influenced fanatics, and their pesantrens could become a danger to the security of the state "at any given moment," especially as local conditions made it possible that the average Javanese might be drawn into the mix by the practice of the so-called "dikir." What was needed to preserve Dutch rule, therefore, was the highest possible level of surveillance and control of such groups.[91]

A similar case was made in a pamphlet initialed at Banten by the retired official K. F. van Swieten. Having read of the activities of the Sanusiyya in North Africa, and having seen the resistance in Aceh, he urged the Dutch to find out why it was that Islam was becoming less and less a "loosely worn robe" over the "old popular practices and superstitions." It seemed to Van Swieten that his colleagues needed fresh lessons both in Islamic history and in the practical details of the tariqas: their rituals, and most especially their principle of absolute loyalty to the shaykh. These he gladly supplied, drawing on the work of A. Le Chatelier and L. Rinn (1838–1905) on the Marabouts of North Africa.[92]

There were other officials who had a more finely tuned perspective. One was

J. J. Verwijk, who conducted an investigation of the Islamic "sects" in the Residency of Banyumas and submitted his report in January of 1889. Based on his observations of four groups—the Akmaliyya, the Khalwatiyya, the Shattariyya, and the Naqshbandiyya—Verwijk argued against the all-too-common view that the Javanese were really believers in some form of syncretic religion, pointing out that if the same standards were applied to the Christians of Southern Europe, then they too would be cast as syncretists.[93]

More importantly, he argued that there was little to fear from the many local movements and little to be gained by restricting the Hajj, or indeed from placing Islamic schools under the direct administration of the state. While it was advisable that teachers should request permission to establish a new school, excessive interference by local officials should in all cases be avoided. As we shall see in the following chapter, Verwijk's argument was also made by Snouck, much as Poensen cited Snouck's earliest publications as the stimulus for his letters to the *Soerabaiasch Handelsblad*. But while Poensen would be recruited to the municipal school at Delft in 1891, and Verwijk ultimately went on to become the Governor of Bandung (1910–12), it is Snouck's name that has occluded all—officials and Islamologists, allies and enemies.

CONCLUSION

This chapter has focused on the activities of missionaries in the field and on the backing they received from prominent scholar-polemicists, such as P. J. Veth. In many instances they saw a chance for Christianizing the natives given what appeared to them as the natives' weak understanding and practice of Islam, arguing that the Javanese could not be adjudged Muslims for their "Islam" fell far short of the Islam they knew from the texts edited by their teachers in Delft. More crucially, however, we can see in their writings tangential and certainly unintended evidence of an active engagement with new modes of thinking, with printing, and with Sufi practices imported from the Middle East—practices that were leading some Javanese to label their neighbours ruddy *abangan* while they themselves identified as spotless *putihan*. Missionaries and some local officials tended to underplay the sincerity of the latter, and especially of the undifferentiated Arabs and hajjis behind them, but they were in full earnest when faced with the potential threat of the tariqas that burst onto the scene with the Cilegon massacre. If anything was clear by 1888, it was that Dutch knowledge of Islam was outdated and far too oriented towards texts above contexts. Islam had to be understood, Mecca had to be known. It was fortunate then, that the firm of E. J. Brill was just now offering precisely the work that colonial officials most desperately needed.

PART THREE

ORIENTALISM ENGAGED

Certainly evolutionary theory has had a much stronger influence on our practice of religious studies than it has had on the scholarly labors of our jurists.[1]
(C. Snouck Hurgronje, "Mohammedaansch recht en rechtswetenschap," 1885)

The last three chapters provided a general overview of the early encounter between Dutch interlopers in the archipelago and their Muslim rivals, showing
how metropolitan scholarship and observation on the ground were neither of
one accord nor yet reliably apprised of the ways in which the so-called "Mohammedan church" differed from their own, "reformed" faith. More specifically
we saw how, in the nineteenth century and in the wake of two intense wars in
Sumatra and Java, scholars hired to train future administrators would differ
with their missionary kinsmen on the ways in which Javanese and Malays were
not proper Muslims. While, on the one hand, a legist like Keijzer saw it as a
matter of degrees (i.e., that the Javanese and Malays deviated to a greater or
lesser extent from the proper juridical understanding of normative Islam),
some Indies-based missionaries could declare that the Javanese in particular
failed to meet even the most rudimentary tests of Islamic belief. Over time
perceptions would change, and they changed largely due to the work of one
scholar whose early career in Europe, Arabia, and the Indies is the subject of
the next three chapters and the pivot on which this book turns.

CHAPTER SEVEN

Distant Musings on a Crucial Colony, 1882–1888

Among the papers bequeathed to Leiden University after Snouck Hurgronje's death is a file now designated Or. 7935. Like other such folders its contents are diverse, ranging from a prayer for Queen Wilhelmina (r. 1890–1948) written for the regents of Pasuruan and Malang by Isma'il b. 'Abdallah al-'Attas, to a Malay romance about Egypt and Syria written around 1844. It also contains two documents emblematic of Snouck's historical tasks and influence. One is a tract written in Arabic on three sheafs of paper. Collected in Aceh, it was most likely the property of an opponent of the Dutch taken during the long war of resistance. It consists of a basic manual of the "Qadiriyya" order, complete with the final admonition (*wasiyya*) of 'Abd al-Qadir al-Jilani and invested with amuletic power. It also bears a pedigree that situates it within a continuous Southeast Asian blood lineage of master-pupil relationships. In it Ibrahim al-Kurani (whom we met already in the Shattari pedigree of Da'ud al-Fatani [see ch.3]) is cast both as past master and ancestor to the Tahir clan. It begins:

> [The possessor of this document] took the tattered robe of the Qadiriyya from the poor one belonging to God Almighty, Muhammad As'ad Tahir. He took it from the hand of his father and shaykh, the late Shaykh Muhammad Sa'id Tahir, who took it from the hand of his shaykh, the famous Shaykh Mansur al-Bediri, who took it from the hand of his shaykh, Shaykh Muhammad As'ad Tahir, who took it from his father and shaykh, the late Shaykh Muhammad Sa'id Tahir, who took it from the hand of his father and shaykh, Shaykh Ibrahim Tahir, who took it from the hand of his father and shaykh, Shaykh Muhammad Tahir. And he took it from the hand[s] of his father and ancestor [lit. "his grandfather"], the Divine Axis, the Knower of God, Mulla Ibrahim al-Kurani. And he took it from the hand of his shaykh, the Divine Axis and Praiseworthy Sanctum, Shaykh Safi al-Din, known as Sayyid Ahmad al-Madani al-Qushashi ....[1]

And on it runs, passing through the hands of the jurists al-Ansari and al-'Asqalani, and then on to the sainted 'Abd al-Qadir al-Jilani and blessed 'Ali, until finally it reaches the Prophet, "the lord of messengers," Gabriel and God.

The other document of interest in Or. 7935 is somewhat smaller. Consisting of three pages written in Cairo on July 28, 1925, it is infused with a very different mix of blessings. Here Professor Mansur Fahmi of Cairo University, a scholar known for his controversial thesis on the rights of women (defended at

the Sorbonne in 1913), recalls his time with Snouck in Europe, thanks him for
his ongoing interest and advice, and tells of his hopes for the future:

> I have now obtained, by God's good fortune, a learned post among my
> people, making me hopeful that I can obtain what I desire from a position
> and realize ... the general good and reform. ... I am inspired by the cur-
> rent situation, and remain resolute and filled with hopes, just as you found
> me in my youth, for I hope that I can say that I have done my share on the
> path of renewal and reform and, moreover, that I have done no violence to
> the advice you sent me in all of your letters.

As he continues:

> I have passed on your thanks to my friend Shaykh ʿAli ʿAbd al-Raziq,
> who was greatly pleased. I should also tell you in this regard, my esteemed
> professor, that his book has raised a great storm. A group of renewers has
> formed around him while others of the hardliners have opposed him, to
> the extent that the ʿulama' of al-Azhar gathered to strip him of the learned
> title he had obtained from their institution. The journals have been dis-
> cussing this for weeks and the movement it has generated resembles that
> which formed as a result of the treatise that I wrote for you for my
> doctorate.[2]

Obviously Fahmi saw himself in the vanguard of major intellectual change
in his own country. Certainly the book by ʿAbd al-Raziq, which Fahmi had
sent to Snouck with a card noting that it offered "a new viewpoint on the matter of the caliphate and Islamic government," did cause a storm. Its thesis denied the necessity of twinning the caliphate to religion. It is curious, though, to
ponder what role Snouck's scholarship on the caliphate, widely published in
French, might have had in shaping such an argument. The author, who had apparently asked Fahmi to send his book to Snouck, was another of the many
recent graduates of al-Azhar who had also studied in France, so he must surely
have been aware of the Dutchman's writings.[3]

On the face of it both of these documents, separated by three decades and
concerned with very different matters, are only related by dint of having landed
in the hands of Snouck Hurgronje. But this is no mere coincidence. For
Snouck's life and teachings bridged these two apparently very different Muslim worlds: the world of Aceh's anti-colonial jihad infused with the very traditional aspirations of believers who sought refuge in the saints; and the world of
reformers who sought, with the aid of printed journals and a Western education, to maintain their faith and strengthen their countries.

In order to link these themes, it is necessary to accompany Snouck on his
journeys and to attempt to read how he balanced what today seem to be the
contradictions of his colonial and scholarly endeavors. Only then will we be
able to assess the impact he may have had upon the people he studied and, in

turn, upon the people he taught. For while Snouck seems to have been tangentially involved in at least one Egyptian's plans for the renewal of his country,
his impact in the Indies was far, far greater.

Eyes on Indië, 1880–1884

> By a colonial power such as ours, Islâm, that great INTERNATIONALE with the
> green banner, must be studied with seriousness and handled with great wis-
> dom.[4] (C. Snouck Hurgronje, "De laatste vermanning van Mohammed," 1884)

The son of a Protestant Minister, Snouck Hurgronje entered Leiden University as a student of theology in 1874. His initial training was the standard
course of Classics and Hebrew. He soon became disenchanted, however, and
moved on to study Arabic, defending a dissertation on the origins of the Hajj
in 1880, which he wrote under the guidance of M. J. de Goeje (1836–1909). In
the process Snouck challenged many of Dozy's conclusions in the latter's 1864
De Israëlieten te Mekka (The Israelites at Mecca). His career, however, was not
destined to keep him focussed on the textual history of the Middle East. He
was then employed by Leiden's municipal institute for the training of colonial
officials. It was from there that he made his debut on the very public scholarly
scene with a series of articles that would have a profound bearing on his future.
Among them were blistering reviews of the work of the official he would ultimately replace.

The first article of 1882 was essentially a corrective of the works of T.W.J.
Juynboll (1802–61), P. A. van der Lith (1840–1901) and, to a lesser extent, the
official in question, L.W.C. van den Berg. Though there was little in the way of
directly Indies-related content in this article, Snouck deliberately published it
in the *BKI*, claiming that before anyone could even hope to increase their understanding of Islam on Java, writers on Indies matters needed to become "acquainted with a knowledge of the elementary principles of this world religion
and its history." The Dutch, he argued, were "still very far removed" from that
goal.[5] Snouck, it seems, had little time for the offerings of the late Keijzer, or
for the republished observations of Grashuis, as he turned the full force of his
criticism on Van den Berg in ever more acrimonious instalments over the
course of 1883.

The initial site of battle was the first volume of Van den Berg's edition of the
Minhaj al-talibin, published under the auspices of the colonial government
with a French translation. Having noted that only Europeans seemed interested in reading Islamic jurisprudence as a vehicle for understanding Islam,
Snouck next drew attention to numerous inconsistencies and errors in the
translation, beginning with the title. He also wondered who might be the intended audience of such a work, for it could be of no real utility either to the

public or to colonial administrators or to Orientalists who would certainly do better to purchase a cheaper version from a Cairene publisher.[6]

The message was clear on another level as well. There was no place for the colonial jurist at the high table of European scholarship. For it was in that very year (1883) that the guild of Orientalists was coming to Leiden for its sixth international congress under the chairmanship of Snouck's teacher, the theologian Abraham Kuenen (1828–91). This was an event timed to coincide with the Great Colonial Exhibition in Amsterdam, where, after a short trip on the Royal Train, the assembled (mostly) Western experts could marvel at the riches of the Indies, spread out for their viewing. One viewer was Amin b. Hasan al-Madani (d. 1898), a visiting Arab bookseller and pamphleteer against the excesses of the Sufi orders. What he saw may have had a formative impact on the young Orientalist.[7]

Then again, neither the Amsterdam spectacular, which drew throngs from across the nation through its temporary Moorish gates, nor the Leiden Congress, which would have hoped to keep them outside its well-worn iron portals, paid much attention to the reality of Islam in the context of the Christianizable Indies. The very use of pseudo-Islamic architecture at the exposition, approved by the mission-friendly Veth on the grounds that the Indonesians had not developed a style of their own, was controversial.[8] In Leiden a famous British missionizer, R. N. Cust (1821–1909), could happily remark that Holland, the "Cradle of Liberty" and "Nursery of Scholars," was "the fellow-labourer" of his own country in the work of "introducing Civilization among the Millions."[9] The region was, moreover, specifically marked as a domain for the study of its *Indic* heritage and as a site of recent tragedy. It was an especially poignant moment for al-Madani when the delegates paused in memory of the great eruption of Krakatau that had occurred only ten days before.[10]

Given these circumstances, Snouck's Amsterdam offering was nothing less than an intervention on behalf of Islam in the archipelago. After presenting his thesis that Gujarat was the likely source of Islam in the Indies, his paper became an appeal, urging that the believers of the archipelago be regarded as no less Muslim than those of any other place and that his readers should not to be blinded by the demeaning views of them commonly expressed in the writings of those with limited experience there. He was particularly biting when it came to those who claimed that Islam found in the Far East was a threadbare garb "through which "the half-Hinduized Polynesian" could be seen "in his true, heathen, form."[11]

Views akin to this were also to be found in the writings of many who (like Snouck) had never been to the Indies, but claimed to know pretty much everything about its peoples. For even as he noted the ubiquity of "priests," schools, and mosques in the archipelago, and acknowledged that Islam's rules were "more-or-less" followed throughout, Veth nonetheless shared the common view of the natives as superficial Muslims and gave voice to that view in his discussion of "Religion and Religious Usages," written for the catalogue of the Colonial Exhibition.[12] His ambivalence is underlined by his approval of the faux-Moorish gates. It was also demonstrated by the leading theologians Cornelis Tiele (1830–1902) and by Kuenen himself. While Tiele accepted that Islam was a "world religion," Kuenen, who had first formulated that notion, later changed gears and decided that as a system it was indeed a world religion, but in some of its regional praxes it would be more accurately characterized as a "folk religion."[13]

For his own part Snouck—whom Kuenen had invited to read the drafts of his 1882 Hibbert Lectures—pointed out that the allegedly threadbare dress adopted by the peoples of the Indies had been less a mantle than a complete uniform. Moreover, one could just as easily find the same sorts of folk-traditions in the Middle East. Snouck was eager to show how Lane's work on Egypt could be read alongside some contributions to the *MNZG* (largely those of Poensen) to demonstrate that the "most developed," and juridically minded Muslims had always formed a self-conscious minority in their own societies in face of the "dervishes and other religious parasites." Still, with such knowledge as they gained in their religious schools, the Javanese and the Malays were shown the "true path." Their industry in pursuing this path was to be seen in their interlinear translations, which bore witness to their determination to attain "true knowledge." For there was false learning as well. Such was known in Java in the form of the so-called *ngelmu pasik*, identified by some of the same missionaries who saw the Javanese in tattered foreign dress, and on whose scholarly shoulders Snouck himself stood. As he reported, even the "heretical delusions" of an "opium-addicted Javanese mystic," (published by Poensen) betrayed "a Muslim tint."[14]

Regardless of such opiate dreams and the challenges they posed to Dutch order, Snouck urged that those who had been Muslim for a mere five centuries should not be regarded as inferior to those who had accepted Islam for twelve, and he cited yet another article of Poensen's, from 1864, in which he stated that, regardless of what exactly the Javanese did, they did it as "good Mohammedans." Snouck even suggested that were a Javanese to go to Europe, he would find that Christianity was a similarly tattered robe bedecking the underlying heathen.[15]

None of this is to say that Snouck held a totally positive view of his country's very distant Muslim subjects. At his thesis defense, he had impetuously suggested that the Hajj should be curtailed, and he ended his Amsterdam paper with a warning that the potential power of the Hajjis was like "gunpowder" within the Netherlands Indies and that it was urgent to investigate what precisely it was that they brought back from their Indian Ocean sojourns. For they must surely be bringing back more than what Van den Berg had joked of as consisting of little more than "an empty wallet, a handful of holy earth, and the memory of many unpleasantries."[16] Indeed Van den Berg had laughed off suggestions that someone should be dispatched to Mecca, but it was already clear that Snouck had for some time been pondering a future engagement with the Indies by way of the Holy City where so many of its peoples congregated. He was well aware that a knowledge of Malay was crucial for this endeavor, just as Van der Tuuk had argued in the previous decade that a bible translator really should "stand on the shoulders of a linguist."[17]

At first the missionaries greeted Snouck as a kindred spirit. In a warm review of his Amsterdam lecture, whose missionary sources were duly observed, J. C. Neurdenburg (1815–95) claimed the distinction of having anticipated Snouck's thinking regarding the recognition due to Indies Muslims as Muslims. Even so, he still doubted that Islam was as deeply rooted in much of the Indies as Snouck believed and suggested that fear of a loss of social position was likely what stood in the way of the average person's conversion.[18]

Snouck now had gone beyond merely calling for serious engagement with the Islam of the Indies. Even before his overseas ventures, Snouck had already begun learning Malay and engaging with its primary sources, as can be seen from an article on some of the Islamic texts in use in the Padang Highlands, which he presented to the *BKI* for a volume marking the Orientalist Congress. The particular texts he discussed had been acquired from a colonial administrator who was back in Holland on leave: K.F.H. van Langen (1848–1915), whose dictionary of Acehnese Snouck helped bring to the press in 1889 once Van Langen was appointed resident at Bengkulu.[19] But whereas such texts had long been collected as souvenirs, rarely had their contents been subjected to a study close enough to determine how representative they were of their particular locale or of how the interlinear translation related to the Arabic source.[20]

A near exception might be Niemann's analyses of Malay and Javanese manuscripts, though Snouck seems to have ignored his work of 1861. He certainly ignored Keijzer's use of Hajj guides copied in Batavia. He credited Grashuis's work on the pesantrens of West Java (probably because the latter had started to teach him some Malay and had lent him some manuscripts), but dismissed the efforts of Verkerk Pistorius on the schools of Sumatra. Instead Snouck gave a detailed outline of the contents of the books, commencing with the works devoted to the study of Arabic. He also made the point (à la Grashuis) that while such a method of instruction had its drawbacks, given that it depended on the ability of the shaykh to explain the contents, it was highly serviceable and would ultimately equip the student with enough knowledge to read even the canonical *Minhaj*, the translation of which Van den Berg had recently "begun."[21]

Perhaps in light of his earlier observations about Cairene editions and Van den Berg's apparent dismissal of them, Snouck noted that manuscript copies were in use alongside such imprints. Yet even as the organization and value of the work was respected, it was generally only the practical chapters on purification, prayer, alms, the Hajj, and fasting that would be read. Whereas an *imam* might find some utility in learning the regulations pertaining to marriage, the rest would have been seen as a merely theoretical conception of how God's *imam* had ruled prior to the advent of the "Olanda Sétan."[22]

This was the turn of phrase that would be used by Poensen in his *Brieven*, the first of which opened with praise of Snouck's article. As we might already have gathered, though, Snouck was concerned that there was another Sétan bedevilling the Malays and Javanese. In his analysis of mystical learning he reported the excessive devotions of practitioners of dhikr who believed that "their eyes were open and yours closed." Here though he was quick to compartmentalize the meaning of dhikr in terms of class. "Naturally," wrote Snouck, "for the most educated," dhikr was "incidental," not central to their worship. By contrast, for "the great mass of the brethren," the "screaming and howling, dancing and spinning" was merely "physical exercise done in God's honor," and those who placed themselves above the law were to be labelled "sinners" (at which point Snouck referred to Harthoorn's article of 1860).[23] Still, there were to be found "orthodox" Sufis—those who acknowledged that the study of the Shariʿa was a prerequisite for the highest learning. Here Snouck explained how any student engaged in the pursuit of gnosis was named a traveler, *salik*, while his path was that of *suluk*. In so doing he was making an intervention for the Indies context. Beyond adjudging previous explanations given by Verkerk Pistorius as wanting, he declared that J.G.H. Gunning's 1881 thesis on the subject, which followed Keijzer's mistranslation of *suluk* as "threads," was "beneath all criticism."[24]

The remainder of Snouck's discussion was devoted to a text collected by Van Langen in the Padang Highlands that emphasized Sunni orthodoxy while delving into Ibn al-ʿArabi's *Futuhat* and the later *Tuhfa* of al-Burhanpuri. This text was completed by the writings of the "Acehnese Sufi" Hamza al-Fansuri, in which "the most daring and pantheistically tinted expressions are quoted and apparently treated as the highest truth."[25] In the end, Snouck averred that the consumers of such higher learning were indeed not necessarily to be found among the aficionados of dhikr, and that what he had outlined was an idealized version of Muslim education, an education that would in the future have to conform to Dutch guidelines.

MECCA

> Anyone who visits a foreign land for the purpose of study leaves off a part of his personality in order to accommodate himself to the country's practices. How far one goes in this is a matter for one's own conscience to reconcile.[26]
> (Snouck to Van der Chijs, December 1885)

Van den Berg had once mocked Holle's notion of sending a scholar to Arabia, but it was for just such a mission that Snouck obtained a subvention from the Dutch government in 1884, following the debacle of the rumored massacres of

1882–83. 1884 was also the year in which another of his articles appeared, this one discussing the widespread dissemination of testaments said to have been written in Mecca following dream-communications with the Prophet.[27]

His writings no doubt played a large role in convincing the government that he was the ideal man for the appointment, which was arranged after a meeting with the Jeddah Consul who was then on leave in Holland. Snouck was no doubt anxious to experience Islam as a lived faith, wishing perhaps to emulate Lane's study of Egypt and to conform to the wishes of his teacher De Goeje, who had argued that a trip to Mecca need not be dangerous if the doors to the Holy City were opened by prominent Arabs of good family.[28] And it was in fact through just such personal connections that Snouck was able to gain access to the Holy City after several weeks in Jeddah. The Arabs in question though were not necessarily of Meccan origin, or even of what Snouck would have subsequently regarded as "good" families. One unfortunate early contact was an Algerian with murky connections to the French Consulate whose offers of assistance and housing in Mecca Snouck would eschew in favor of deepening an ongoing friendship with the ever "amenable" Bantenese, Raden Aboe Bakar Djajadiningrat.[29]

Aboe Bakar was but one of several crucial mediators who aided Snouck during his sojourn in Arabia, and indeed assisted him in his formal conversion to Islam. Recently published correspondence shows how two sayyids from Borneo, Salim and Ja'far al-Qadri, also had a strong hand to play. Both had been introduced to Snouck through contact with Habib 'Abd al-Rahman al-Zahir (1833–96), a Hadrami adventurer who had been pensioned off to Mecca by the Dutch in exchange for his surrender at Aceh. Even so, the Habib was still hoping to play a role in securing a resolution to the conflict that might involve a significant title and emolument for himself. Salim and Ja'far, by contrast, came from a family that had ruled over Pontianak in appreciative partnership with the Dutch since 1770.

Before he traveled to Mecca, Snouck busied himself at Jeddah interviewing and photographing pilgrims while engaging in close consultations with Aboe Bakar. It would also appear that better social and scholarly connections were secured through Aboe Bakar's networks, as at least one scholar of note, the young 'Abdallah al-Zawawi, numbers among Snouck's preceptors. Moreover, 'Abdallah and his father, the distinguished Muhammad Salih al-Zawawi, were closely connected to the al-Qadris (Ja'far even shared a house with 'Abdallah), and ministered to a Jawi community deemed by Ja'far to have "no real 'ulama."[30]

Born in Mecca in 1850, the precocious 'Abdallah was educated at home. But even as he ascended by this non-standard path, his scholarly excellence had been acknowledged when, in the 1870s, he was awarded a teaching position in the Holy Mosque.[31] 'Abdallah also had links to the Pontianak dynasty, which so clearly favored Dutch rule and reaped the benefits of same, as well as links to the Sultanate of Riau, which was in the last throes of attempting to ward off

Dutch annexation. Muhammad Salih had even visited Riau around 1883 and had penned there a short work of Sufi instruction for the Mujaddidiyya.[32] It seems that while he was in Riau he reoriented the court away from the Khalidi teachings that Isma'il al-Minankabawi had introduced in the 1850s.

In Mecca in 1885, however, the younger Zawawi was busy training students up to the level that was required of them before his father would take them on as his disciples. Snouck, whose collection of Western text-editions he admired, would be unready for such an internal step that year.[33] Doubtless he was held back to some extent by his cynicism toward the many groups he had so recently described as parasites. He would likely have kept to the fringes of Sufi ceremonies, observing the behavior of the participants while remaining as unobtrusive as possible. We see a hint of this in his diary entry concerning a public prayer for rain in Jeddah in December 1884. As Snouck recalled, "I could witness all this from very close by, where I was accompanied by Ra[den] Aboe Bakar with a friend and servant. Nobody took the slightest notice of me, not even the school children, who sang and yelled during the çalāt [prayers], and even amidst the rows of the holy ones."[34]

Snouck's journey to Mecca commenced in a camel-borne pannier on the 21st of January. Under his adopted Muslim name of "'Abd al-Ghaffar," Snouck arrived in the Holy City a day later, and it seems that he was immediately accepted for the believer he claimed, at least outwardly, to be. No less an authority than Ahmad Dahlan invited him to partake of his lessons both within the sacred precinct and at his home. But it was the Jawi community itself that opened the most doors, providing intimate insights into Meccan life. The aunt of one Jawi guide even opened her door far wider than Lane had witnessed of any lady in Egypt. On taking Snouck to his uncle's home, an accidental encounter was contrived with the lady in question, who alluded to the possibility of being able to obtain far more for him than accommodation and bedding.[35] Such offers were rebuffed by Snouck, who was still learning how to judge people in the Hijaz. We may be certain that he did not rebuff the alleged procuress out of prudishness. His letters to P. N. van der Chijs show that he plunged into Meccan society in ways that would have left the infamous Richard "Dirty Dick" Burton (1821–90) gasping. This included purchasing and marrying an Abyssinian slave in order to maintain a degree of respectability (certainly Lane's status as a single man had bemused many of his Egyptian interlocuters). The encounter with the guide's aunt was merged into Snouck's narrative, much as other events were incorporated, to create the impression of total immersion in a "Medieval" society.[36]

When not engaged in observing daily life or training a "very liberal" Meccan physician in the art of photography (out of the public gaze), Snouck made his way through yet other doors that Ahmad Dahlan had opened wide for him. He was granted access to the teaching circles of scholars such as Nawawi of Banten, and had the chance to discuss world affairs with Sufi shaykhs like 'Abd

Figure 7. Snouck Hurgronje, alias ʿAbd al-Ghaffar, Mecca, 1885. In
LOr. 8952, Nagekomen Papieren 1980—foto's.

al-Karim of Banten and Ahmad of Lampung. All three expressed views hostile
to Dutch rule but tempered by the recognition that resistance to that authority
was then impractical (and against the occasional interjections of Sayyid Jaʿfar).
It was also here that Snouck was able to gauge the relative status of the various
scholars of the Holy City, especially those of the Shafiʿis who placed themselves
under the authority of Dahlan. Of particular note was the Egyptian Abu Bakr
Shatta', the author of the widely used *Iʿanat al-talibin* (Seekers' Aid), whose Sufi
father had been served and succeeded by ʿAbd al-Shakur of Surabaya.

Figure 8. Ahmad Lampung and another Jawi shaykh, Mecca, ca. 1885. LOr. 18097 s67 no.17.

Snouck formed good relations also with another of the Indies-based ʿAlawis then studying in the Hijaz. This was the young ʿAbdallah al-ʿAttas (d. 1928), whom he had first met in Jeddah with Mujtaba of Batavia and Arshad of Banten.[37] The Jawi ʿulamaʾ, as Snouck observed and learned from additional notes supplied by Aboe Bakar, included many Bantenese like Arshad, along with teachers from other parts of the archipelago. They ranged from exponents of jurisprudence, such as Junayd, Nawawi, and Zayn al-Din, to tariqa gurus like ʿAbd al-Shakur, Muhammad of Garut and Ahmad of Lampung. Clearly

Snouck favored the former group, members of which even called on him at times, and who preferred the authority of sober Arab tariqa masters like al-Zawawi to the departed Ahmad Khatib Sambas and Isma'il al-Minankabawi.

Of course this division between jurists and mystics was not without some overlap. There were many prominent Sufis, such as the highly regarded Meccan printer Ahmad al-Fatani, who had an eye on the juridical needs of his fellow Jawis as much as on the unseen world. But al-Fatani's being a Malay from lands beyond Dutch reach who was engaged in embracing the modern did not fit so well in Snouck's Meccan narrative, for he was more excited by the echoes of antiquity. He certainly paid attention to the very contemporary nature of the political discussions in which he shared, and he took note of the elite setting their fob watches by the time of the gun and expressing pride in the city's new press, but evidence of modern strivings was toned down in his later account of his experiences. Sometime this was accidental. Snouck later recalled how he had commissioned a professional scribe to hand-copy Dahlan's history *Khula-sat al-kalam fi bayan umara' al-balad al-haram* (Summary of the Words at Hand Concerning the Rulers of the Holy Land), which was crucial to his history of the city—and his letters show how eagerly he had awaited deliveries of the various sections of the manuscript. It was not until 1889, and while en route for the Indies, that he discovered that the book was in print and commercially available in Cairo.[38]

Had he stayed longer in the Hijaz (and in fact he entertained hopes at one point of being appointed Jeddah Consul), he might have seen the work in print locally. Such was not to be, however. His alleged interest in antiquities, combined with the malefactions of the French Consul, led to his expulsion from Mecca once it became known to the Ottoman authorities in Istanbul that a Western dealer, perhaps posing as a Muslim, was on the loose in the Hijaz.

The Question of Islamic Reform

On his return from Arabia, Snouck went back to his work enraged at having been exposed by the French Consul, whom he continued to attack until the latter got the upper hand by threatening to expose Snouck's conversion and even his covert marriage. Forced ultimately to back down, he continued to send reports to scholarly forums while weaving the material he had gathered, and which was still being sent to him, into a master narrative encompassing the Holy City's past history, the lives of its contemporary denizens, and the impact that they would likely have on the future of the Netherlands Indies.

Much of the energy that went into Snouck's work was aimed, still, on deconstructing what was known about Islam. He took to task anyone who believed that they fully understood the threat posed by the continued journeying to Arabia by so many Javanese: for a potential threat he *did* still publicly claim to see.[39] In pointing it out, he was staking his claim to a position of influence within Dutch society. Of course that society already had its pundits, and they were soon to feel even more threatened, for Snouck was about to direct contemptuous ire at any who dared to defend Van den Berg.[40]

In May of 1886, for example, he used an article to target what he saw as largely a corps of elitists, ignorant lawyers, and ne'er-do-wells who plied their trade in the Indies. One was a knighted member of the Indies High Court, M. C. Piepers (1835–1919), who had called Snouck a troublemaker who pranced with "apes and vagabonds." While Snouck did not respond to the charges of keeping company with degenerates, he eagerly refuted any aspersions cast at his knowledge in the field or at his fitness for to making public statements. He also took the opportunity in passing of drubbing Van den Berg once more as "the so-called scientific official" who was "still unacquainted with the tools of his trade."[41]

Snouck freely admitted that he had studied theology rather than law. This lay at the core of his questioning of the disciplinary divisions in the academy that he believed had let the Netherlands down in practice. The newspapers of metropole and colony alike had been the bearers of his message in January of 1886 when he used a review of two works on jurisprudence by a German scholar to call for a shift in the universities away from the study of juridical theory toward what he called "scientific investigation." In so doing the jurist could, he suggested, engage the help of "the ethnographer and the philologist" to understand more accurately how written laws interacted with the unwritten laws of Muslim societies. For just as one should not use Roman Law as the yardstick for judging the lives of the Dutch, so too Islamic Law, which he preferred to call "the teaching of duties," should not be the measure against which Muslim daily life was judged. After all, history had shown that the people had long had their ways of interpreting the law so as to arrive at a compromise between spiritual and worldly interests.[42]

This approach also informed his much broader assault on received wisdom, which came in a series of articles in *De Gids*. Here he let loose on notions of Islamic "reform" in newly colonized Egypt as espoused by the Englishman Wilfred Scawen Blunt (1840–1922) and a Dutch lawyer working on the mixed tribunals under the Khedives, P. van Bemmelen (1828–92). Both saw themselves as allies of the Egyptian people, and their opinions were well-regarded by Snouck's peers. Snouck argued that they were nothing less than deluded to imagine that they could really assess how Islamic a society was by comparing classical legal texts to living people. It was absurd to suppose that Islam could be "reformed" by a simple "return to the Qur'an" or by the updating of (a single work of) jurisprudence. For Snouck, Islam was not merely revelation coupled with prophetic example. It was an organic system that had evolved to take into account extant practices and the general consensus (*ijmaʿ*) of the community. It was also a system that had taken four centuries to achieve the tripartite, but mutually reinforcing, elements of Tradition, Law, and Mysticism. For Snouck, any reform movement that claimed to return to a pure source denied history. A real reformer—if one were to arise in a Muslim country—would have to deal with the issues of jihad and *ijtihad*, with the infallible consensus of the ʿulama', and with the structure of the juridical schools; all of which were deeply ingrained in Islam by virtue of what he alleged was its "catholic" and "conservative" character. [43]

We should not neglect the fact that underlying Snouck's thinking there was always a colonial focus. He called for greater knowledge of Muslim societies on the grounds that they could be more tactfully administered if they were understood. This was, once more, an argument for his future employment, as he clearly implied that there was an urgent need for a learned Orientalist in the pay of the state who could anticipate the greatest threat to the security of Dutch rule: namely unruly tariqa Sufism. He made sure to point out that it was an error to equate, as most did, Muslim mysticism with this form of Sufism alone, a form that, he alleged, was an elitist fashion born of contact with the Indo-Persian world. With their loose structures and methods that were largely derived from intuition or inspiration, the tariqas provided an escape route for individuals who wanted to transcend the every-day demands of religion. Yet, as this system of learning developed, it had opened the door to theosophical departures from "true" belief, and it had fostered all manner of local superstitions and misuses ostensibly based on scripture. Once so many of these practices had come into common use beyond India and Persia, "compromise" was the only available way forward for what he termed "Muslim Catholicism."[44] Snouck even claimed—much as Dozy had—that Muslims had forgotten that the respect for the saints had originally been a concession.[45] Slowly the requirements for mastering Islamic literature became a puzzle reserved for jurists, while Sufism was left in the hands of the holy men who had to find ways to differentiate themselves from the expanding ranks of fakes and pretenders. It was therefore fortunate that the great al-Ghazali had provided a solution with his *Ihya' ʿulum al-din*, a work that united all the fields of knowledge and "animated all of the sacred sciences," taking "a special place in a good upbringing."

> Whether he joins a recognized mystical brotherhood or not, every believer ... will, after studying the duties of belief, move on to study mysticism. This is always taught in the spirit, and mostly in the actual words of Ghazzali. This ... is even popular in the East Indies; and many Malay and Javanese students use three books bound as one as their guide, of which the first subject concerns the *fiqh* (the teaching of duties), the second the *tawhied* or the *oeçoel* (teaching of belief), and the third the *tasawwoef* (mysticism).[46]

The tripartite edifice of Islam had thus been completed with the capstone text of al-Ghazali complementing the keystone life of Muhammad. And yet there was more to come. Snouck urged readers to be wary of the Wahhabis for theirs was no "reformist" movement, despite what some (Keijzer, Dozy, and Poensen) had suggested. Rather, what the Wahhabis sought was the "repristinization" of Islam, and thus a falsification of history. Following the lead of Kuenen, Snouck even deemed Wahhabism an "incomplete" Islam that futilely aimed to return to an earlier Arab time and place that would invalidate any claim to be a World or Universal Religion.

Snouck may have been influenced by Ahmad Dahlan's published views on the matter, tempered somewhat by al-Madani's pragmatic observation that the peoples of Medina and Dir'iyya had moved beyond their sectarian differences. The potential reformers admired by Blunt and Van Bemmelen seemed, by contrast, to come from the class of libertines least likely to be respected by their fellow Muslims, while the Hajj remained the fount of a "medieval belief."[47] In that respect at least Snouck thought Van Bemmelen correct in asserting that the Eastern Question was crucial for the West. For the Dutch it had to become *the question*, and it was high time that better-informed officials were to be sent to the Indies.

This is not to say that Snouck damned any and all who dared to write on Islam. He did have some regard for the interventions of Poensen, even if he took the latter to task for his writing style. Poensen had done a good job of detailing the rituals of people he knew full well placed Islam at the center of their lives. What Snouck could not forgive was that so much of Poensen's account was taken from European works—including those of Van den Berg and Keijzer—and that he stuck to the opinion that the Javanese were less Muslim than the Dutch were Christian. Poesen had, all the same, done a far better service to the public, both in the Netherlands and the Indies, than so many hacks with all their so-called "practical experience."[48]

Forging a Common Front for Indië

Snouck had stood on the shoulders of the Java missionaries to exorcise the jurists of Delft and Batavia. He had attained field experience and a measure of notoriety. And now he saw before him yet another path to future influence and authority. He would form an alliance with Sayyid 'Uthman. When Snouck began to correspond with the Arab printer in October of 1886, 'Uthman's scholarship and industry had already caught his peers' eyes, through his relationships with Holle and Van den Berg, and his atlas of Hadramawt, which was reprinted by the firm of E. J. Brill in that year. Snouck had also heard of him during his sojourn in Mecca, and saw fit to mention his polemics against the populist tariqas.[49]

In preparing the way for his discussion of 'Uthman's pamphlets in the *Nieuwe Rotterdamsche Courant* in October 1886, Snouck made their shared

Ghazalian concerns plain by announcing that "every well-educated Mohammedan treats them [the Sufi orders] as heretical, or even as a survival of old
Heathendom . . . with their magic, spells, snake-oaths and what-not."[50] Snouck
moreover saw the orders as institutions in constant search of financial gain,
with the shaykhs dispatching their agents to the four corners while excusing
themselves from the rituals they prescribed for their followers. What little
knowledge they did possess was "dribbled out" to students who were "from the
uneducated classes" and ignorant of the very basics of Islamic law, wrongly
believing that dhikrs, litanies, and absolute obedience to the shaykh would
guarantee them salvation.[51] Thus, much as the French had heeded the "regrettably facile" work of Louis Rinn on the dangers of the Sanusis, so too the
Dutch should pay more attention to what little had been written of the various
orders in the Indies. And they should pay heed as well to Snouck's forthcoming *Mekka*, which he hoped would open the eyes of many.[52]

But what would the average Javanese make of such a scholarly work? Far
better that the damning message come from one of their own authorities—and
who better than Sayyid ʿUthman? ʿUthman possessed the perfect combination
of education, lineage, and attitude—and he would defer to the highest authorities in Mecca, including the new mufti of the Shafiʿites, Muhammad Saʿid Ba
Busayl, and such Ghazalian exemplars among the Jawa as Nawawi and Junayd.
Here was a man who understood full well how eager the average Javanese was
for "magic cures" that would grant him happiness on earth and in heaven, and
thus how slippery the tariqa gurus were with their false promises. Snouck and
ʿUthman also agreed that the Khalidis were exemplary in their unworthiness,
and that while the rest of the orders might teach something of outward piety,
most used the Shariʿa "as a Shibboleth." There were others, too, who were
awaiting the moment when they would be unleashed on their enemies. "We
are not working with hypotheses here," intoned Snouck, mindful of what he
had heard from ʿAbd al-Karim of Banten; though he would save the details for
Mekka.[53]

Snouck also put his most sincere seal of approval on ʿUthman's views that
true miracles were a thing of the past and that proper instructon could not
come from the hands of fakes and carpet-baggers. But, he insisted, "this Arab,"
was different:

> deserving of the regard of all right-thinking people by virtue of the moral
> spirit which he has dedicated to combating the heresy-teachers of Java.
> He thus places himself in no small danger; for cunning demagogues pres-
> ent him as an assailant on sanctity, and an ignorant, agitated mass readily
> place their trust in such allegations. Nevertheless he has courage in his
> conviction, and will not give up the fight. We hope for this above all be-
> cause the sjêchs and their followers are the most dangerous enemies of
> Dutch authority in the East Indies, at least as dangerous as the Senousis

are for the authority of France in Algeria. It is fit, therefore, that our scholar from Hadramaut is deserving of the gratitude and sympathy of all who wish the Netherlands Indies well, above all our Government. Such allies are as jewels deserving of being set in gold. To fail to recognize their value is to give a blow to one's own face. We have repeatedly indicated that it is only through delicate tact and great discretion that we shall be able to maintain authority over a land such as ours with its millions of Mohamedans. . . . For the present let it be noted here that one Arab like Othmân ibn Jahja is more valuable to us than any number of "liberal" wine-drinking regents.[54]

For his part, Sayyid 'Uthman was fully apprised of Snouck's growing interest in him. In 1886 Holle and J. A. van der Chijs told him that Snouck had read the validation he had garnered from Nawawi Banten and Junayd Batavia for his *Nasiha al-'aniqa*. This impelled the Batavian scholar to write to Snouck about his *Wathiqa al-wafiya*. He pointed out his desire to protect the public from those who encouraged all sorts of potential corruption among the ignorant, but would not, in order to avoid trouble, name any particular shaykh. He sought Snouck's support in reaching out to the authorities against these tariqa gurus and "jealous men" who sought his destruction, going so far as to claim that "Were it not for the justice of Holland in the land of Java and other places, there would be no possibility of my living in Batavia!"[55]

'Uthman saw clearly that Snouck was his means to a secure career in the Indies. In subsequent letters he included lists of his works and of concerns that he hoped Snouck would advertize among the Dutch political elite. In the end his strategy paid off. He and Snouck became ever more closely bound together, and Snouck sought, at 'Uthman's request, a position for the scholar as an Honorary Adviser on Arab Affairs, which he would be granted in 1891.[56]

Snouck meanwhile was doing more than battling the established order and identifying the weaknesses of Dutch colonial policy vis-à-vis Islam. He was at work on his *magnum opus* and keeping up correspondence with his Hijazi informants. Aboe Bakar was particularly active, sending regular answers to Snouck's questions and books he had ordered. Most prominent in one early list are the works of Dahlan and Nawawi, with those of the Bantenese easily outstripping the Meccan.[57]

Throughout the period Souck also kept his eyes set on the Indies. As we have seen, his first substantial article had been an analysis of the books read in the Padang Highlands as collected by Van Langen, and this was followed by a piece on millenarian testaments. In 1885 he had obtained a report on works available in Java prepared by the Regent of Lebak, S. Soerianataningrat, and in 1886 he corresponded with the retired official W. E. Bergsma, who forwarded reports from Kendal and Tegalsari.

Soerianataningrat's report, resting on information supplied by the Penghulu of the Landraad of Lebak, Mas Hajji Muhammad Isma'il, listed eight works used in the pesantrens of the Priangan. Study commenced with the elementary *Alif-alifan*, which explained the Arabic alphabet; then the *Turutan* and the Qur'an were read for the purpose of learning pronunciation; and five "advanced" works followed. These last were enumerated as the *Sittin, Tasripan, Amil, Ajurrumiyya*, and *Sharh al-sittin*. Most of the books cost from *f*1 to *f*1.50, but the *Sharh al-Sittin*—probably al-Sharqawi's gloss on the *Masa'il al-sittin*—which was said to make a student competent to read and understand "all the books of religion," sold for *f*5. The Regent of Ponorogo, Tjokroamidjojo, would declare that, having studied at pesantrens like Tegalsari, the student could go on to buy whatever books he liked.[58]

The material available was still limited, certainly, but it was richer than the pesantren offerings described by Van Sevenhoven, Van Hoëvell, or even Brumund, who had worked under governments with as little interest in the pesantrens as some of the older kyais evinced in collaborating with the state. By way of contrast, it is well worth noting that the masters who taught the texts listed by Soerianataningrat were not merely linked to Meccan networks of scholarship through their teachers; those of the younger generation were affiliating to the newly constituted Landraads, most likely by virtue of the patronage of those same men. For example, leading the list of the recognized 'ulama' of the district of Lebak was Kyai Samaun of Muntare, described as having studied in Batavia under "Habib Shaykh" (Sayyid 'Uthman?). He taught in "the language of Serang" like another of his former teachers, Kyai Lopang. The list went on to name office holders, whether on Dutch-appointed councils or as penghulus, who were the direct students of Kyai Samaun, Kyai Lopang, or both, with the exceptions of Kyai Hajji Seram of Karawangi, who had studied at Tegalsari, and Kyai Hajji Hasan, residing at Citandun.

Such information confirmed Snouck's inference that the study of Islamic texts did not necessarily create a corps of men hostile to the colonial state. Some may have had anticolonial proclivities inculcated in pesantrens linked to the memory of Dipanagara, but many others now hoped that the skills they gained would earn them semi-official posts within, or at least adjacent to, the colonial bureaucracy. Such patronage must have played its part too in the appointments of men known to Snouck, such as Hasan Mustafa of Garut (who may well be the same person as the Citandun-based scholar mentioned by Soerianataningrat) and Arshad b. 'Alwan of Serang, a friend from the Hijaz who would fall victim to the Cilegon panic of 1888.[59]

Elementary learning and pesantren patronage opened a path to the lower echelons of the Dutch administration but, as Snouck would learn, more advanced scholarly itineraries led away from Batavia toward the north coast, where students would be offered a richer and more varied diet of works printed at Singapore. In another Malay report, sent from Kendal in March of 1886, a native official who had collected copies of the *Sittin, Safina*, and *Asmarakandi*, reported that there were four sorts of books used in the pesantrens, each of about 300 pages. These were (a) the works of exegesis, for "understanding high Arabic written in the *koorän*"; (b) works of grammar, for "understanding the sense of the Arabic stories used by the people written of in the *koorän*"; (c) works of *fiqh*, for "understanding and memorizing the actions of a good heart"; and, perhaps most important, there were (d) the books of *tasawwuf*:

> for remembering the doings of the Prophets accepted by the Lord God, or those people who never committed sins, or to guard Islam from forbidden things, such as lying, offending others, taking other people's possessions or stealing, or using magic spells against the living.[60]

Snouck wanted to get beyond such broad subject-based descriptions, and it is clear that he was able to obtain more detailed information from other officials. His notes on the Residency of Demak, for example, record the widespread use of the *Safina, Sittin,* and *Fath al-qarib* (The Victory of the One at Hand) of Ibn Qasim al-Ghazzi (d. 1512), as well as more advanced texts by al-Ghazali and the *Sullam al-tawfiq* (The Stairs of God-Granted Success) of ʿAbdallah Ba ʿAlawi (d. 1855). While most teachers had had their training within the residency, the leading kyais had been to Jepara, Madiun, Surabaya, and Mecca. Such connections were vital in the communication of the most recent works of scholarship, as with the text compiled by Dahlan's successor, Ba Busayl, which was used by a follower of Sulayman Afandi in the village of Kauman Kadilangu. In Rejoso, meanwhile, teachers like Hajji Yusuf of Jelak taught using printed editions of the *Fath al-muʿin* (The Victory of the Provider of Aid) of Zayn al-Din al-Malibari (fl. 1567) and the *Minhaj al-qawim* (The Straight Path) of Ibn Hajar al-Haytami.[61]

Similar works could be found in the larger towns, and the strong generational, and increasingly institutional, character of the pesantrens was clear. Many of the kyais occupied the places held by their fathers and grandfathers before them, some of whom had composed their own works. Snouck's notes confirm that these local glossings were now being displaced by the standardized international fare. It was not all a story of the local being overwhelmed by the global, however. Many kyais were claiming a relationship with Sulayman Afandi in Mecca, but the Khalidiyya had by no means won the day. Shattari teachers like Muhammad ʿUmar in Watuagun, Salatiga, were still to be found, as were other interpretations of tariqa learning, leading to Snouck's quizzical notations next to such appelations as the "Sadririah" or "Djawahir."[62]

Snouck had some mysteries to unravel. Before he set out for the Indies he prepared himself by pouncing upon any erroneous interpretations regarding the tariqas in the journals that crossed his desk. Responding in one instance to admiring missionary requests for information on the fanaticism of the "satarijjah-secte," he asserted that he had never even heard of people who were Shattaris per se (forgetting Muhammad ʿUmar of Salatiga). A tariqa, he explained was more usually but a stage in a series of practices acquired by the elite over time. He recalled once having met "a very learned" grandson of a retired regent from Semarang, who was given to reciting certain formulas, formulas which Snouck adjudged "entirely unimportant."[63]

CILEGON

The spectre of the crazed dervish leaps to the fore with the Cilegon massacre of July 1888. But for all the planning that went into the revolt, it was no more than a small disaster for the Dutch, for the rebels had neither the princely appeal of Dipanagara nor the iconoclastic fervor of Tuanku Nan Rinceh. Cilegon is in fact more realistically seen as a localized uprising than as a popular jihad, though the Indies press was naturally obsessed with its tariqa agents and many a finger pointed to Mecca. This is not to say, however, that all officials, while anxious about a pandemic of Islamic activism, were of one mind about the mechanisms underlying social unrest in Java. The Resident of Surakarta saw disgruntled former officials and grandees manipulating the santris as much as fanatical teachers manipulating priyayis, but all the same, he still pointed to a Meccan connection embodied by many lurking hajjis who led their charges to madness through excessive dhikr. And dhikr supposedly led to "an intoxification," in which one blindly followed the leader, even to the point of "voluntarily killing one's self." Perhaps more worryingly for the Resident, the railways had made the visiting of pesantrens where such techniques were taught "almost commonplace":

> No youngster who wishes to represent himself as having some learning or knowledge of the world would wish to deny that he has spent some time, however short, at a pêsantrèn. The pêsantrèns are now visited by youngsters from the poorest classes, who live in the manner of beggar-monks at the cost of the wealthier people. At these pêsantrèns, and at an age when one is most susceptible to forming enduring bonds of friendship, connections are formed between persons of the most different social ranks, and from all parts of Java. Thereby the propagation of one idea or another is made all the easier, and therein lies a great danger, which at a given moment can grow from the prevailing malaise and poverty when the masses harken to a better time, and are thus all the more amenable to the prophecies of their so-called religious leaders . . . no matter how nonsensical the prophecies may be.[64]

One figure who would be vindicated in the aftermath of the Cilegon affair was Holle, who was able to report to the Governor General about the much-suspected ʿAbd al-Karim of Banten, said to be the primary teacher to "nearly all" district and subdistrict penghulus in the *afdeeling* of Serang and a person who could do much harm from Mecca.[65] After communicating with Snouck, Holle was able to relay his opinion:

> Abdulkarim Banten is well known to me, the successor to Chatib Sambas and the most respected tareqat-sjech of the Jawa in Mecca (after Abdel-Sjakoer of Surabaya), he has lived in Mecca for more than forty years. I have all sorts of anecdotes about him and I have visited him often. He told me himself how, during his stay in Bantam, there was a certain ferment and that his murids [disciples] then asked him if it was not yet the time to carry out the teaching, but he, through lack of inspiration, responded in the negative. I do not believe that he would himself play a leading role in a battle even if he could take pleasure in the defeat of the kâpir hôlanda. Yet his influence is great, even among the moderates, and all the more as he leads truly quite holy lessons, and even the representatives of the official learning respect him; e,g., Sjech Nawawie of Tanara and even the Arab authorities, who cannot hold him to be a learned man. By virtue of our intercourse I have gained a certain respect for him, yet from a political perspective I regard his activities as dangerous. If the opportunity arises I suspect that the Government will not do itself a disservice if an appropriate person is found to follow the steps of Abdel Karim at Mekka. For I am of the conviction that religious intolerance is stoked from Mecca.[66]

Even if his intent differed from that of so many of his predecessors, Snouck echoed them when he later pronounced that Mecca, with its "blooming Jâwah colony" was the veritable "heart of the religious life of the East-Indian Archipelago," from which "numerous arteries" pumped "fresh blood in ever accelerating tempo to the entire body of the Moslim populace of Indonesia." Where he differed from Keijzer and Grashuis, though, was that he had been to that heart, and that he knew far better how there "the threads of all mystic societies of the Jâwah" ran together:

> Just as no dam can be set against the pilgrim stream, so now nobody can do anything to prevent every flow backwards and forwards from bringing to Arabia seeds which there develop, return to the East-Indies as cultivated plants, and multiply themselves again. It is thus important to the Government to know what goes on in Mekka, what elements are exported from there every year, and how by skilful handling these can be won over to support the Government or at least made harmless.[67]

It has been rightly observed that the entire final chapter of *Mekka*, completed late in 1888, was Snouck's clinching argument for his employment in the Indies.[68] Certainly the salaried post he craved in Europe was not yet open to him, and even a post he had half wished for at Delft had been handed to Van den Berg in May of 1887.[69] So, following a request from the Minister of

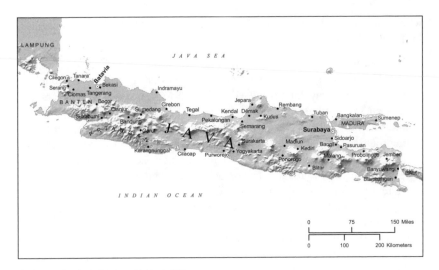

Figure 9. Java in the late Colonial Era.

Colonies on 26 September 1888, Snouck was hired to provide advice regarding the training and dispatch of Indies officials to Jeddah, where Aboe Bakar would be employed in an ongoing capacity.[70] So it was, too, that the harbinger Snouck would finally be called upon to travel to the Indies to carry out an investigation of Islam there. He sailed from Brindisi on April Fool's Day, 1889.

CONCLUSION

The first we hear of young Snouck are words spoken in a caustic tone. They are the interventions of a scholarly skeptic eager to chart the ways in which religion was experienced in colonies whose connection to the metropole would not to be sundered in his lifetime. Trained in the field of religious studies, Snouck had a decided aversion to legalistic scholarship that prioritized text over context. He urged instead that the observations of his academic and churchmen forebears should be twinned to a more professionally developed Orientalism, such as would more effectively service an empire contending with Islam as its primary threat. But he had yet to prove himself in the field. That he did by bearing witness to Mecca and the tariqas as a potential source of danger to his people's colonial wealth, thereby staking a claim to prominence in his chosen field. With the publication of *Mekka* and the shock of Cilegon, Snouck's personal future was all but guaranteed.

CHAPTER EIGHT

Collaborative Encounters, 1889–1892

It has been argued that in the process of inventing the category of World Religions, and of including Buddhism within that framework, the European textual archive came to supplant indigenous self-representation, leaving the field to the missionaries.[1] But while a similar course of events can be followed in the field of Netherlands Indies Islamology, this is true only until 1889, for in that year the most energetic critic of Orientalists and churchmen alike landed on Java, ready to reprise his role as ʿAbd al-Ghaffar.

Among Manuscripts, Printed Texts, and Sufi Masters

> It will become clear only after I have been there a couple of days whether I shall be left in peace as a European Muslim wearing a fez, or if I shall be [harrassed] without mercy in a hat.[2] (Snouck to Van der Chijs, December 1888)

When Snouck arrived in Batavia on May 11, 1889, he was certainly juggling two hats, for his Meccan sojourn marked him as a fully accomplished Orientalist for his peers, while for his future subjects, he was a Muslim of apparently deep learning. Some were even prepared to designate him as a hajji or mufti (he was neither), which half explains the enthusiasm expressed in *Bintang Barat* in late May, when a correspondent described how the arrival of a "Mr Dr C. Snouck Hurgronje *alias* Moefti Hadji Abdoel Gafar, a man very learned in Arab language and religion" had caused some excitement, with some wondering whether he would also be going to Solo, in Central Java, to examine the practice of Islam among the Chinese.[3]

Snouck would in fact be going to Solo, as a part of a study-tour shuttling between Batavia, the Priangan, and Ponorogo from mid-July 1889 to early February 1891. At the end of this phase of his career he would pass up an opportunity to return to a chair in Leiden and commence negotiations for a tenured post as the foremost "Advisor for Native and Arab Affairs." This should have come as no surprise. Snouck had long favored employment where he could pass on what "useful knowledge" he could generate to the state. As he informed his theologian friend Herman Bavinck (1854–1921) in July of 1890, "knowledge of the situation in the Mohammedan region here, of the spirit and influence of Mohammedan education, of the scope of the so-called mystical societies, etc. etc. is as necessary for government and legislation as one's daily bread."[4] Although he was not especially interested in the Muslim Chinese as a separate category of observation, he was intensely methodical in the way he set about seeing how Islam was practiced in daily life. This was in part simply his customary way of working, and in part due to the nature of his assignment, which was to assess the ways in which Islam was organized so that the state could formalize a "Mohammedan" church and coordinate the collection and allocation of its funds.

In stark contrast to his Meccan venture, which took place far from the comforts and protection of European power, Snouck was able now to fill some two dozen notebooks with observations, working in surroundings that were frequently nothing short of palatial.[5] Beyond this he was able both to aquire manuscripts and to draw on the services of copyists, in contrast to predecessors like Grashuis, who sometimes had to wait years to secure particular works.[6] As may be expected, a sizeable proportion of Snouck's notes are given over to placing the various 'ulama' participating in the new religious councils, mapping out how they connected to the colonial hierarchy, to each other by marriage, and to the networks of learning that crisscrossed Java and the wider Muslim world. Interspersed within the pages of his notebooks are fragments of other texts: reports by learned informants, fatwas inscribed on doilies, and copperplate transcripts of pre-Islamic legends.

For our purposes, we will concentrate on his observations of the networks of knowledge and of the tariqas in particular. This remained his primary colonial directive, as was clear in a report he submitted to the Governor General four weeks after his arrival, in which he reiterated that the shaykhs of the "lower mystical orders," who were opposed by such respectable teachers as Junayd, Mujtaba Batavia, and Sayyid 'Uthman, had the potential to be the greatest enemies of the colonial government. He further scoffed at suggestions that the "orthodox" Nawawi would approve of "such shows" as that of Cilegon, having condemned the same sort of "vulgar mystics" in a fatwa, whose issuance earned him death threats according to one junior official at Serang.[7]

And so it was that Snouck set off in search of the vulgar enemies of Islamic orthodoxy and colonial security alike. It was a journey that began sedately. At Sukabumi, in mid-July, he stayed with the son-in-law of the former penghulu, with whom he toured local schools and found the teachers using the *Sullam al-tawfiq* as commented upon by Nawawi, as well as a recent printing of al-Sanusi's primer. He also noted that teachers could not hold their jobs without the permission of the Dutch-supervised clerisy, and that any new books were to be examined before being used. Snouck furthermore observed that while the texts were all in Arabic, their explanations were delivered in Sundanese. It was also here that he jotted something regarding his search for a mysterious book, the *Martabat tujuh* (The Seven Grades), disseminated by a Batavian teacher called Wirta or Merta. Nobody he met in the Priangan seemed to have heard of it, or to have met its author, who was said to make his appearances in the capital just after the house servants had received their pay.[8]

These notes would long serve Snouck for his recommendations on Islam in the Indies. They would serve others too, for they were the product of an engagement with informants who stood to gain from a relationship with the young Dutchman. Principal among these was Hasan Mustafa, whom he claimed he had met in the Holy City. Hasan Mustafa made his appearance on page two when Snouck, who had traveled to Garut with Holle, recorded that he had been a student of Muhammad Garut (followed by Nawawi Banten, Muhammad Hasab Allah, Mustafa ʿAfifi and ʿAbdallah al-Zawawi) in Mecca, but returned home when his father could no longer continue to support him. Having linked himself to the Chief Penghulu, he was allotted a school and residence near the town's misaligned mosque.[9]

Such cursory notes have led to suggestions that they had never met before this point. The corresponence of Hasan Mustafa is elusive on this point, and Snouck himself never gave details of their meeting in Mecca.[10] But though their Meccan encounter may had been fleeting, they were surely destined to meet, for Hasan Mustafa had been a protégé of both Holle and ʿAbdallah al-Zawawi. Their Indies futures would be inextricably linked, for Hasan Mustafa became Snouck's informant, paid ƒ50 per month. It is from this time on that Snouck's working method becomes evident to readers of his notes, as he documents his visits to local mosques and pondoks, jotting down the titles taught, the names of teachers, and the orders that they claim to represent. In some cases he did not even need to ask such questions. Hasan Mustafa, for example, had already compiled a list of the Arabic works in use in the Priangan for the government in November of 1889, differentiating between those that were deemed "old" (perhaps in the sense of "classical") and a slew of more recent kitabs, such as those of Nawawi and his own verse treatise on the famous *Waraqat* (Leaves) of al-Juwayni (d. 1085). In an echo of the official who had reported on the books used in Kendal in 1886, Hasan Mustafa described the works on Sufism as being intended to "preserve the good actions of [the] body and heart" of the reader.[11]

Old and new was the dominant theme of Snouck's work, and in his interviews he often began by asking about the structuring of time and about key rituals, and would then move on to questions about the nature of the teachings in the nearby pesantrens, and finally—but not always—to the tariqa being taught there. It is also evident that, throughout this process, materials were gladly given him by the shaykhs by virtue of his connections to the Meccan community and the belief that he still manifested. Many of these were Shattari texts, and the shaykhs' willingness to part with them in some places reflected the declining popularity of that order in the face of Naqshbandi encroachments. Yet even if there was little apparent hesitation to offload Shattari manuscripts in some towns, the Shattaris remained entrenched in parts of Java.

Or at least, Snouck could find teachers who went by that name, including Imam Prabu and Adi Kusuma (Raden Muhammad Nur Allah Habib al-Din, d. 1903). But while both teachers, based in Cirebon, claimed the name Shattari, Imam Prabu emphasized that few of their ilk really went beyond explaining the dhikr.[12] Adi Kusuma, who claimed descent from Sunan Gunung Jati, and who preferred the dress of a Javanese official to that of a kyai, seemed to offer markedly less to his following. Despite never having studied the Qur'an, he led numerous students through what he called Shattari teachings; though not in the dhikr itself. He owned a copy of al-Sinkili's *Tanbih al-mashi* (Direction for the Adept), but his pedigree bore no resemblance to the line of 'Abd al-Ra'uf and Muhyi al-Din Karang. Adi Kusuma was also sheepish in regard to his own abilities, recognizing that his precious manuscript was more akin to a magical "heirloom" than a functioning guide. It seems that Snouck agreed, for he went back to his pages on Cirebon and noted that it and Pekalangon maintained the teachings of the "principles of the old sciences."[13]

Recognizing the moment of transition for what it was, Snouck later recalled how he had gained possession of many of the bark-paper manuals that had belonged to the fathers and grandfathers of sometimes embarrassed "orthodox" teachers. One such instance occurred at Cikalong in August of 1889, when Kyai Sahwi gave him pieces of his grandfather's manual that contained the Shattari pedigree of 'Abd al-Muhyi. The pedigree aside, all of the texts (*'Awamil, Ajurrumiyya, Sittin, Samarqandi, Miftah* and *Mufid*) were works that remained in favor. Hence, it was perhaps the sad state of the manuscript that may have contributed to Kyai Sahwi's willingness to hand over his hierloom. For there were many new printed works to be had, and cheaply too.[14]

By and large, though, students of all traditions headed on to the famous schools of the north coast, such as that of Salih Darat of Semarang, whose regulations Snouck was given. Such references paled in comparison to Surabaya as a scholarly destination. Wherever Snouck went in West Java—and he spent more time there than anywhere else after he married the daughter of the Chief Penghulu of Ciamis—the more it became clear that most roads led to Surabaya. Apparently some students would even return home satisfied to be known as *santri Surabaya*. That city was, moreover, synonymous with 'Ubayda, for an entire generation of Garut's kyais had studied under him at Sidosremo. Snouck did not learn a great deal about him, however, beyond his reputed descent from Sunan Ampel, and that he had been succeeded by a certain Zubayr at his death, probably around 1874. Van den Berg had asserted that the institution had passed into the hands of one 'Abd al-Qahhar, who led it until a disastrous fire consumed its dilapidated buildings soon after his visit of 1885.[15]

At any rate, it became clear to Snouck that pesantrens like Sidosremo were, for some, staging posts on the way to Mecca, where they would spend on average a period of six years, and perhaps after that a further period studying grammar in Madura. It would become clearer on his journeys, too, that the new

Figure 10. Title page of the *Majmuʿat mawlud* (Bombay:
Muhammadiyya, 1324), a compilation of texts printed in India for
the Southeast Asian market, ca. 1900.

print editions were important to those Javanese who advocated the use of advanced Arabic works rather than the Malay primers favored by the Shattaris. Still, Malay remained important in West Java and in some schools on the north coast. The late ʿAbd al-Ghani of Cikohkol, who had claimed descent from ʿAbd al-Muhyi Pamijahan, was said to have studied in Aceh, Kedah, and Palembang, and the works of ʿAbd al-Samad al-Falimbani and Daʾud al-Fatani alike were still debated in Cianjur and Kendal.[16] Many of the kyais of

Cianjur had studied in Mecca under the very vital Zayn al-Din al-Sumbawi. Similarly, two sons of Raden Hajji Yahya by his Minangkabau wife had studied under the Sumbawan, and they had taught his works in Cilegon before the outbreak of what Snouck referred to as the *khawf* or "terror."[17]

So it would seem that after all, the Meccan experience—though it frightened the Dutch—played its role in fashioning an enduring sense of Jawi communality. Zayn al-Din was by no means the first Sumbawa-born scholar of interest to Malays, Sundanese, and Javanese. Snouck's Leiden notes mention several kyais in the vicinity of Surabaya who had studied under ʿAbd al-Ghani Bima, still remembered as the shaykh to the Jawa at large. The scholarly trajectories Snouck noted were not merely recountings of scholarly pedigrees. These were ties of blood as well. As one further example of such relationships we can return again to Snouck's notes from Garut. When he passed through that town, Snouck met with Kyai Mulabaruk, who had studied at Tegalsari under Hasan Besari, the teacher so dismissively treated by Jan Brumund. Clearly Mulabaruk had found more at Tegalsari than Brumund was shown, for as Hasan Mustafa and others had told Snouck, Mulabaruk specialized in the Qurʾanic exegesis of al-Baydawi (d. 1286), as well as key works by Imam Nawawi and al-Firuzabadi. Snouck's listings also show that Mulabaruk was able to place his former students across the Priangan after they had completed further periods of study from Mecca to Madura.[18]

Many more such lists would fill the pages of Snouck's diaries as he traveled eastward, and they give incredibly detailed insight into the ties of marriage and sojourning that made up the pesantren network. But while these lists also confirm that the Khalidiyya was casting deep roots in Java, there were other tariqas in evidence as well. One finds the mention of kyais having studied the Khalwatiyya under ʿAbd al-Shakur Surabaya in Mecca, or Muhammad Maghribi in Medina. There were also indications of challenges launched by such figures as Imampura of Bagelan, who was propagating his particular version of the Shattariyya for thousands of visitors after ca. 1885. Beyond this, there was evidence of new fusions. Two texts copied for Snouck in West Java (of which one was owned by the Patih of Menes) seemingly bring elements of the Naqshbandiyya and Khalwatiyya together, but they deploy non-standard lineages straight from Ahmad al-Qushashi to Muhammad Tahir of Bogor and are, in truth, more compilations of techniques than coherent programs fusing the two methods of tariqa practice.[19]

Such an equivocal assessment does not, however, fit a tariqa that was rapidly gaining ground. It was consistently identified by Snouck as the Qadiriyya, but its more correct identification was the "Qadiriyya wa-Naqshbandiyya" of Ahmad Khatib Sambas. One of its better-known representatives in the Priangan was Muhammad Garut, one of Hasan Mustafa's teachers and a son of Mulabaruk's student Hasan Basri by his Javanese wife in Mecca. Snouck had certainly heard of the fluent Arabic-speaker, whose name was often given by

Snouck's informants in tandem with that of 'Ubayda.[20] Muhammad Garut had his early education from his father in Kiara Kareng, after which he went to Mecca, aged around twenty, where he stayed for seven years under Shaykh Zahid of Solo, 'Ali Rahbani al-Misri, Muhammad Salih al-Zawawi, and Muhammad Hasab Allah, ultimately linking himself with Ahmad Khatib Sambas. He then came to Garut in 1879, before returning to Mecca around 1882. He traveled back and forth to the Holy City thereafter, appointing his own deputies, such as Muhammad Salih in Sukabumi.[21]

More interesting though is the deeper connection between Muhammad Garut and Hasan Mustafa through Muhammad Garut's nominated successor Adra'i. Adra'i had been one of Hasan Mustafa's teachers at Garut. They had journeyed to Mecca together and, after a six-year stay, returned together, whereupon Hasan Mustafa married Muhammad Garut's niece. Hasan Mustafa was thus the ideal informant on many levels of learning, from the grammatical to the mystical. Their personal contact may well have opened Snouck's eyes anew to the practitioners of the tariqas, and may have given him reason to rethink, or at least to temper, his previous prognostications of public danger.

That said, there were other teachers who could have had the same influence on Snouck, and he was perhaps most impressed by yet another "Qadiri" in Cirebon. This was Muhammad Talha of Kalisapu. The son of the Chief Penghulu of Cianjur, Talha had studied locally under Muhammad Sahih (d. 1886)—a student of both Mulabaruk and 'Ubayda—and then under Hasan Mustafa in Mecca, before returning to his hometown as a master of the Qadiriyya wa-Naqshbandiyya. Talha's background must have influenced the direction he took, for it would appear that his father may well have been instrumental in the slandering and exiling of Kyai Lengkong, whose pesantren Van Sevenhoven had mocked in 1839. Even though the sons of Kyai Lengkong had since found favor with the colonial government, Snouck was disparaging of Hasan Absari of Cianjur and others of their ilk. He was equally dismissive of the many Akmalis of Cilacap, noting that the town had "no scholars."[22]

When juxtaposed with such teachers, Talha did seem to set a higher standard. Snouck was clearly impressed when he first met him at Kalisapu on August 24, 1889. His pesantren was no mean assembly of bamboo huts. It boasted a stone house, a prayer hall, a Friday mosque, and a dormitory for visiting students. From what Snouck could glean, Talha often advised local officials on questions of Islamic law (he was apparently known for his "useful" fatwas on brandy and polygamy). He was also the product of a very diverse tariqa education. During his nine-year stay in Mecca, where he had studied with Hasan Mustafa, he chose to affiliate directly with the Khalidiyya through the father-in-law of Sulayman Afandi. Talha also pledged himself to the Haddadiyya via Ahmad Dahlan and to the Qadiriyya wa-Naqshbandiyya of Ahmad Khatib Sambas. It is the last for which he would be best remembered, and Snouck seems to have come away with the impression that he had inducted the Regent into that tariqa. This despite others insisting that the Regent and his family were loyal to the Shattari ʿAbd al-ʿAziz of Cirebon, who was also said to have taken the Khalwatiyya from ʿAbd al-Shakur Surabaya in Mecca.[23]

They were by no means the only such multi-tariqa gurus. Muhammad Ilyas of Sukapura, a veteran of twenty years in Mecca, taught *both* Shattari and Naqshbandi dhikrs to his students. In Tegal there was similar evidence of a transition in progress, as previously Shattariyya gurus began teaching Naqsh-bandiyya rites on the grounds that the Shattariyya was in fact the basis for the Naqshbandiyya.[24] Moreover, the multi-tariqa approach of Talha and his colleagues flies in the face of scholarly presumptions about the nature of "neo-Sufi" reformism in the nineteenth century, and his scholarly credentials demonstrate an equally varied assortment. Among his manuscripts were texts gifted by the son of the Sultan of Cirebon, including a copy of the *Tuhfa* of Burhanpuri. He had some prestigious printed works too, such as a two-volume edition of Ibrahim al-Jaylani's *Insan al-kamil*, published in Cairo in 1876, and an edition of epistles by Sulayman Afandi lithographed in Istanbul in 1883–84—most likely the same ones ordered burned in Mecca. This was by no means strange. Ilyas Sukapura also owned works by Sulayman Afandi in manuscript and print. What really marked Talha out was that while he taught the Shafiʿi approach to fiqh, he presented himself as a trained Hanafi and argued that the fatwas of all the schools should be taken into consideration. What connection he might have had with Southeast Asia's earlier "Hanafis," such as Daʾud of Sunur and Muhammad of Silungkang, remains for now an open question. For Snouck, however, the problem was to communicate his findings to a still worried public.[25]

SNOUCK AS WEDONO

Snouck, it seems, emulated his erstwhile source Poensen in newspaper articles aimed at the colonial public but in another series, in which he assumed the persona of a junior official or *wedono*, and placed himself above Poensen's "villager" *desaman*. These articles started appearing as instalments in the progressive paper *De Locomotief* in early January of 1891 and would continue until December of the following year, by which time Snouck was conducting his first-hand investigations into the Aceh insurgency. In letters supposedly inspired by the loving care of an unusually knowledgable inspector, Snouck gave his readers a vivid picture of Javanese life from cradle to pondok, and beyond. It was also a story, told in a self-deprecating tone, of an encounter between a spiritual East and a rational West, where the intuitive wisdom of the locals who lived in a world brimming with spirits were too often neglected by their blustering and frequently drunk European overseers.

But while Snouck's wedono set about describing the various rites surrounding pregnancy, birth, and other life events, he also noted that times were changing. Strict santris were now omitting many of the older ritual meals, prayers were more often heard in Arabic than Javanese, there were more and more Arabs and hajjis in evidence, and even the priyayi elite were choosing Arabic names for their children. The hajji and the Arab were still bugbears for the common child (alongside the Dutchman and the priyayi), but most people now aspired to send their children to a pondok where they would submit to the guidance of the guru as a surrogate parent. Here they they would engage in intensive peer learning, their completed texts being personally certified by a teacher whose license would allow the student to travel on to the next pesantren, where they would often be expected to engage in agricultural work, most often coffee-growing. Echoing Verkerk Pistorius's remarks on Sumatra, Snouck observed that such travels gave the Javanese santris practical geographical knowledge of the island far superior to that of the officials who were supposed to oversee them.

The problem went further than this though. Snouck's wedono not only bemoaned the ignorance of Dutch officials minted in Holland, but regretted as well the general attitude they held towards Islam. It went so far that a priyayi who refused to drink alcohol was suspected of fanaticism, and one who wished to pray had to do so in secret. As a result the priyayi officials, forced away from their own religion, were useless to the Dutch when they needed advice on developments within the pondoks, where the guru's word was law.

Technically speaking, such law was even more strongly enforced if the shaykh in question was a tariqa master. To illustrate this point, Snouck had his wedono recall an incident from his youth when his whole family became "Satariah":

First I had to recite the Fatihah in front of the teacher, being the first chapter of the Koer'an that is reeled off in every division of every sembahjang [prayer]; and then another formula, called tasjahoed, which is also said in the sembahjang, and which contains our profession of faith, among other things. Thereafter the goeroe impressed upon me that it was not good to skip the five daily prayers, and that I was not to neglect them during the holy fasting month, above all else because I was learning the tarèkat. Eventually he taught me to say, after each of the afternoon sembahjangs, being after magrib [sunset prayers] and ngiso [evening prayers], to say one hundred times: *la iláha illa 'lláh* "there is no god but God," during which I had to sit in a manner specified very precisely by the goeroe. Once I had practiced with the goeroe for three days, each day for an hour, I was allowed to do the *bé'at* or *bèngat* [oath]. What this entailed was not clear to me at the time. Having first bathed and perfumed myself, I had to sit before the teacher in the instructed posture. He held a white cloth by one corner while I took the other in my right hand. He then said a few

Arabic formulas, which I repeated. The cloth was dropped, a prayer said, and the matter was thus at an end. Only in later years did I learn that this *bèngat* was actually a sacred pact between moerid (student) and goeroe, whereby the student promises thereafter to treat the goeroe as a representative of Allah, and not to disobey any of his commands.[26]

Of course Snouck pointed out the objections of the orthodox to such teachers, claiming that while the leading 'ulama' averred that the Nine Saints had been holy men, the majority of the new tariqa gurus were cheats, and, further, that the teachers of Javanese myticism had no valid pedigrees at all.[27]

Leaving aside the obvious skepticism that underlies Snouck's narrative, one might ask whether Snouck's earlier metropolitan, and somewhat "orthodox," view of tariqa Sufis had been to some degree moderated by his contact with diverse practitioners on Java. Based on what followed in his article, the conclusion has to be yes, for Snouck placed words in the mouth of the wedono that he himself could not say so easily:

> I have often been asked if these tarèkats could cooperate in order to alienate the population from the administration or stir up hatred in them against people of a different orienation. My answer remains thus: that in all cases it depends upon the goeroe. If he is stupid and bad, then he teaches the superstitious villager not so much to be a good and religious person as to do his every bidding; indeed there are even some who teach thieves the arts of invisibility or invulnerability for missions that they have planned against others. If he is ignorant without malicious intentions, then he teaches false magical arts, or such things that his students will not understand, and about which he himself has little idea. A clever and good tarèkat teacher, meanwhile, directs the people, to the best of his knowledge, on the path of religion, such that they will have a greater influence upon the hearts [of the people] than the [normal] kitab teacher. Here in Java he will only become mistrustful of the administration if he observes that he is mistrusted. And clever teachers with less good intentions are dangerous, while the population treats their instructions almost as if they were divine.[28]

Here then Snouck advocates judging gurus on an individual basis. And he would do so for the rest of his official career. In fact he at times served as an advocate for hapless gurus persecuted by the more "orthodox Natives," who used their relationship with the Dutch to claim that the teachers were a public danger. He would even warn in 1892 that if the state allowed itself to be turned into the persecutor of pantheism and mysticism, then it would actually turn the village teacher into a far more important person than he really was.[29]

It is furthermore clear that Snouck regarded the circumstances leading up to the Cilegon massacre as symptoms of an institutional problem. Rather than blaming the killings on the international connections of the orders, as one might have expected, he argued that the fault lay more in the confluence of internal movements to the Priangan of "fanatical" immigrants from North Banten, combined with the regrettable incompetence and ignorance of local officials. Certainly Snouck would adopt a negative attitude, sometimes volubly so, towards officials such as the colonial engineer, Van Sandick, who used an account serialised in July 1891—as well as information from Van den Berg and his old ally Piepers—to identify ʿAbd al-Karim as the inspiration for Cilegon in his *Leed en lief uit Bantam*. In an article concluding that strong Civil Service oversight would always be required to guard the ever-smouldering fire of Islam, Van Sandick claimed that Cilegon would be but the first of any number of future events of the same kind. Whereas Snouck had himself been taking the same position in practice, Van Sandick's efforts earned him a patronising review from the Advisor, writing under the guise of a pensioned official. The mask (and gloves) came off, however, when Van Sandick dared ask how many Acehnese "religious leaders" had submitted to the state since Snouck's classic report of 1894 (see below). For since 1892 Snouck had been playing his most controversial role on the very front-line of Dutch colonialism.[30]

Sketches from Aceh and Lombok

> The Acehnese, a few accompanied by dancing boys (*sedati's*), sat down forming a wide circle on the ground and commenced loud calls of "la Kaoula oula Kouata bi Allah," [*sic*] that is: "only in God is the power and might," whereupon heads were rolled forward and back in time, which became faster and faster, until they degenerated into a vaulting of the trunk. Having done this a certain number of times, the Acehnese stretched out their arms and laid them upon the shoulders of their neighbours left and right. With the salutation of the "la illaha ill' Allah" they threw their whole upper bodies to the ground as one, and performed the movement as a single man, but in the opposite direction, thus backwards. These gymnastics were carried out with ever increasing speed and continuous calls. It was a fantastic spectacle. In the torchlight dark forms were illuminated with naked upper bodies, unkempt hair and faces rendered wild through nervous exhaustion.[31] (V.S., "Mohammedaansche-godsdienstige broederschappen," 1891)

Aceh was without doubt an exciting place in 1891, and not a safe one for the Dutch. It was now eighteen years since the first expedition against this so-called pirate state. With so many famous military failures behind them and the parliament back home vacillating over what to do about a people that simply refused to surrender, the best that the Dutch could do was create a "line of concentration" encircling the coastal areas they controlled. A wide swathe of land was cleared and a tramline laid that linked a series of armed posts along the way. Beyond lay a hinterland in which a patchwork of traditional heads and religious leaders vied for influence and arms. While a visitor within the line of control might encounter Sufi practice in the form of public entertainments, in the land beyond matters were more serious: amulets and Sufi pedigrees were believed to grant their possessors invulnerability to Dutch bullets and Ambonese and Javanese machetes.

Ever on the look out for an opportunity, Snouck—who had had limited dealings with the former Acehnese mediator Habib ʿAbd al-Rahman al-Zahir in Mecca—first offered to reprise his role as ʿAbd al-Ghaffar while en route for Java in 1889. His offer was rebuffed, as it was felt that his services could be better employed in Java. Later, with his surveys of ʿulama' and pesantrens under his belt, Snouck remained willing to turn his attention to Aceh, and he reported to Kota Raja in July of 1891. Even though he later described the actions of some of his countrymen with some irony, it is clear from his letters to his mentor, Theodor Nöldeke (1836–1930), that he enjoyed his experiences moving among the soldiers; and above all his friendship with then Major J. B. van Heutsz (1851–1924).

Snouck's official assignment was to document a society for the purposes of its suppression, but one can readily see in his book *The Achehnese*, which resulted from his visit, that he was ever the historian and ethnographer looking to understand the ways in which a people had embraced Islam, how Sufi philosophy had become the concern of its scholars, and how its sultans had sought to monopolize the esoteria of the tariqas. The book also enabled him to trace the Shattari lineages of West Java back to ʿAbd al-Ra'uf and to see many of the observations he had made in Java to the press, if only in the form of footnotes where Javanese practice served as a control against which other forms could be measured for deviation. Much of what Snouck found—or had brought to him—in Aceh was disappointing. Prosperity and scholarship had fallen from the levels attained under Iskandar Muda. Aceh, in Snouck's eyes was very much a land in decline. The court had lost the last vestiges of its wealth and authority, and the Sultan had been reduced to the status of a regional warlord, one among many.

Snouck devoted some space in his study to what was known of Sufi praxis, which he believed had been brought to Aceh from India. Then he considered the "pantheistic" Hamza Fansuri, the "heretical" Shams al-Din, and the echoes of the teachings of the "heterodox" Ahmad al-Qushashi that followed on the heels of the famous disputes initiated by Nur al-Din al-Raniri. Reflecting his experiences on Java, he painted this Shattari "corruption" as having come under challenge from the newer "Qadirite and Naqshbandite" tariqas of Mecca, though he held their Acehnese representatives of "no account" compared to those in West Java, or Deli and Langkat. Rather, he reprised earlier arguments echoing Lane's observations in Egypt and Sayyid ʿUthman indicting his enemies, and intimated that tariqa ritual had sometimes degenerated into public entertainment or, worse, that it gave an opportunity to some to indulge a penchant for pederasty; though he was by no means firm that this was always the case, and he gleefully mocked Van den Berg's linking of the *sadati* dance to Naqshbandi dhikr.[32]

As we have noted, Snouck's assessments of the state of Aceh were as much founded on his observations on Java as on what came across his path in the field or across his desk in Batavia. One finds in his footnotes frequent reference to experiences or conclusions drawn on that island, perhaps abstracted from a book he intended one day to write. The difference now, though, was that he had other, more pressing tasks to perform, and there have been suggestions that, when it came to Java, Snouck preferred to defer to his good friend, J.L.A. Brandes (1857–1905).[33] Whether this is true of not, Aceh, like Java, presented a rich seam of texts to be collected, and lineages to be traced as fuel for future studies of the inception and inflection of Islam in the Archipelago.

And of course Snouck's studies of Aceh and the Gayo Highlands, as well as his ongoing advice to the colonial state, would not have been possible without the mediation of key informants. Hasan Mustafa would prove crucial once more, sending a constant stream of reports from Kota Raja, where he was installed as Chief Penghulu in January of 1893.[34] These included details of the movements of their temporary ally Teuku Uma (1854–99), reports on threats made against Van Langen (now Resident for Acehnese Affairs, and still gathering material for Snouck) and news of the internal affairs of the Dutch themselves. There were also details of culture and religious praxis, such as a description of a *ratib* described by an Acehnese representative of a tariqa in May 1893.[35]

Much of the material would be processed by Snouck for his own reports. Beyond this, though, Hasan Mustafa played the role of willing intermediary between the Dutch and the Acehnese. One letter reported Hasan Mustafa's conversations with Acehnese leaders about possibilities for the safe practice of religion under Dutch rule. Matters of marriage, divorce, and prayer seemed to rank highest among local concerns, while Hasan Mustafa, for his part, wanted to know how the principle of sultanic rule figured in the Acehnese imagination. When asked how long the Sultan of Java had lived under the "Company," about conditions for the ʿulamaʾ, and the possibilty of there being a "Just Ruler," Hasan Mustafa obligingly noted that the Dutch had a longstanding policy of allowing the free practice of religion, provided that it did not endanger the public welfare.[36]

Such willingness to engage the ʿulamaʾ seems to have made some of his superiors suspicious, and Hasan Mustafa was placed under investigation. The aggrieved Sundanese would nonetheless compose a long tract that included a fatwa on the duty of loyalty to the state and, in December 1894, a short guide instructing his peers on how to deal with their European overseers. Along with other sage advice he recommended that they not change the substance of any document that they were required to translate.[37]

Also active was the rather idiosyncratic Teungku Kota Karang (d. 1895). Once one of the most aggressive of the Acehnese polemicists, he had withdrawn from public life after the submission of Teuku Uma. He appeared now pacified and eager to see the renewal of trade at the port and even seems to have convinced Hasan Mustafa that he was interested in the wider dissemination of printed works, including books on astronomy, geography, and natural science, not to mention his own edition of the *Taj al-muluk* (The Crown of Kings).[38] But while he advocated the resumption of trade, as did quite a few of the sayyids of the region—among them ʿAbdallah al-ʿAttas, who visited in April 1893, and perhaps even a Sayyid Qasim, whose sketches ended up in Snouck's files—many of the Acehnese leaders of the interior "war party" remained staunchly opposed to a truce or indeed any form of cooperation.[39]

In July 1887, Shaykh Samman (d. 1891), acting as the Teungku di Tiro since December 1885, had sent a letter to the Arabs of Kampung Jawa condemning any who dared to work with the Dutch. He also called them to a meeting at the tomb of Teungku di Anjong (Sayyid Abu Bakr, d. 1782), a monument that, Snouck would observe, had come to outshine even the tomb of ʿAbd al-Raʿuf.[40] In 1891, another Acehnese commander would complain that the Acehnese leaders were being incorporated one by one, and that while the Ottoman Consul at Singapore was unable to intervene on their behalf, the Meccan shaykhs seemed only interested in coming to the area to find "Dutch" wives.[41]

Even apparent Acehnese collaborators, such as Teuku Uma, would turn against the Dutch when the moment seemed ripe. Nonetheless, armed with the information assembled by men like Hasan Mustafa and processed in turn by Snouck, the Dutch would ultimately turn the tide in their favor, though at the cost of thousands more Acehnese lives. Their strategy involved incorporation of the remaining hereditary warlords, ruthless pursuit of the surviving bands of ʿulamaʾ insurgents, and the wholesale destruction of enemy support bases. The entire dirty affair would be declared at an end by Van Heutsz in 1903, when he accepted the surrender of the pretender to the Acehnese throne. But this was a show for the press. Fighting—and atrocities—would continue into the years before the First World War.

Setting aside the problems inherent in the nationalist historiography that has presented the Aceh war as a template for the story of the clash of Islam and colonialism in the whole archipelago, there are further problems with the specific modern valorizations of local Sufi, and indeed even Arab, resistance. In one key case at the other end of the archipelago, the Dutch government was actually seen as the saviour of Muslims against their other enemies: the 1894 East Sasak Muslim revolt against the Hindu Balinese lords of Lombok was used to justify an invasion that restored a measure of Dutch military pride. The revolt had been precipitated, in part, by the Balinese execution of an Arab in

1892. The man, Sayyid 'Abdallah, had served both the king and, more quietly, as a Dutch trading agent. It is also apparent that he was esteemed by the elite Sasaks, who were almost all members of the Sufi network headed by 'Abd al-Karim of Banten.

Given what we know of the Qadiriyya wa-Naqshbandiyya at Cilegon, and even allowing for the mitigating advice of Snouck, it is ironic that this deputy of 'Abd al-Karim, Guru Bangkol, was the very man who called for Dutch intervention. For their part the Dutch were more than happy for a humanitarian excuse to further their plans for acquiring Lombok, and few concerns (if any) were voiced about the Naqshbandiyya. It has previously been argued that the order had appeared among the Sasaks in the 1880s and had melted away just as quickly after annexation, when many of its leaders became the client landlords of Lombok.[42] It is however possible that the issue of the tariqa was not of much concern to either party. Rather than disappearing, it simply slipped from official view. All that was ever sent to Snouck from that island appears to have been some drawings of the mosque and palace of Kelayar, as well as the sketch of a spear-bearing saint (see frontispiece).[43] These had apparently been done by the Qadi of that town, who, perhaps like Sayyid Qasim in Aceh, had arranged for his sketches to be sent to a man known as the famous "Mufti" of Batavia, 'Abd al-Ghaffar.

Conclusion

Building on his field-defining venture in Mecca, Snouck took advantage of both the connections he had formed there and the political storm of Cilegon to tour the pesantrens of Java. He did this as a conscious servant of empire, albeit one who believed that he could play a part in the elevation of its subjects. It was also in the course of this journey, and the ones to come in Aceh's troubled borderlands, that he threw off the mantle of doomsayer and began to counsel greater patience with, attention to, and even respect for Islam as the faith of a distressed people. Islam, he argued, needed to be modernized. Muslims had to be weened from their faith in jihad and from the mystical teachers whom Snouck either belittled or respected, depending on his personal encounters with them. Indeed, these various 'ulama' and their manuscripts (especially on Java) were now more a source of antiquarian interest than of counterinsurgency intelligence to Snouck as he trod the fields in the person of 'Abd al-Ghaffar or broadcast his message under the guise of a pensioned minor official. Over the course of these journeyings, however, Snouck's Muslim identity and his quasi-colonial authority would be exploited as much by others as by himself. They would also be challenged by yet others, who feared that their own particular interests in the Indies were under threat.

CHAPTER NINE

Shadow Muftis, Christian Modern, 1892–1906

THE MUFTIS OF BATAVIA

Writing on the very eve of the Cilegon uprising, Sayyid ʿUthman asked Snouck to supply copies of the papers in which his polemics on the tariqas had been praised. He had just put himself forward as the potential (pro-Dutch) mufti who could potentially advise local Muslims on questions of family law. This was not the first time that he had positioned himself at the side of the government. His anti-Naqshbandi tracts had by now won him respect in high places, and in 1881 he had even compiled a manual of jurisprudence intended for the new religious courts. Of course there had been guides printed before, from Taco Roorda's *Tuhfa* to Van den Berg's *Minhaj*, which Snouck could not help belittling as he leant his support to Sayyid ʿUthman's cause. In fact Snouck and ʿUthman became two faces of one coin. ʿUthman's biographer has observed that the Arab scholar clearly regarded his new position as Batavia's quasi-offical mufti as analagous to that of a Western "Advisor," and one might well suppose that Snouck would now accept the Muslim designation.[1]

The numerous letters sent to Snouck over the course of his incumbency in Batavia tell that story. In October 1893, the Imam of Tanjung Beringin, in Deli, addressed his requests for fatwas to "the office of his excellency, our noble master, shaykh of Islam," which he specified as the *two* Shaykhs ʿUthman and ʿAbd al-Ghaffar. In March of 1898, one Pangeran ʿAbd al-Majid addressed him as "Mufti of the Land of Netherlands India," while a group of Arabs from Cirebon hailed him as "the esteemed Shaykh of Islam for the Jawi sector, Hajji ʿAbd al-Ghaffar."[2]

While Snouck was clearly addressed as a mufti both with and without Sayyid ʿUthman, and from a range of parties across the region, it seems that he never replied as such or provided fatwas to his supplicants. Rather such tasks would fall to his Hadrami henchman, who would often produce a pamphlet on the subject in order to create a precedent for the wider sphere of Dutch control. One incident, a dispute over the Friday mosque in Palembang, provides us with a particularly good example of how such matters were handled.

As we saw in chapter 2, Palembang was the birthplace of ʿAbd al-Samad, whose affiliation with the Sammaniyya order arguably enhanced the prestige of that tariqa in courtly circles of the late eighteenth century. The Sammaniyya became so important in fact that its members were at the forefront of the resistance when the sultanate was attacked by the British and the Dutch in turn, actions that culminated in the deposition of Sultan Badr al-Din in 1822 and the final ransacking of the court's library. Events of that nature engendered strong memories of the central role played by the sultans in the propagation and defense of Islam, and the abiding symbol of their sultans' courage was the town's principle mosque. Known as the Sultan Mosque, it served as the primary site for the reading of the Friday sermon to a unified community. It was the locus for a staff of prayer leaders, preachers, and jurists, whose authority was recognized by the custodians of smaller sites of prayer. Like their brother functionaries in Java, these officials were now effectively clients of the Dutch state, which kept a close eye on the collection and dispersal of mosque finances. (In fact it was the Dutch who had restored the large windows and bejewelled cupola of the mosque in 1823.) Hence the officials were gravely concerned about the threat to their authority and security when a new site of prayers, established by one Mas Agus Hajji ʿAbd al-Hamid, began to function as a rival Friday mosque. A group of the aggrieved wrote in July of 1893 to Snouck, alias ʿAbd al-Ghaffar, as "the Great Mufti of Batavia and trustee of the Government," complaining of a major schism erupting on account of the ignorant Chief Penghulu's having granted permission for the construction of the new mosque, which permission was no doubt due to ʿAbd al-Hamid's being his own (probably Sufi) teacher.[3]

While ʿAbd al-Hamid enjoyed the support of many of the indigenous (perhaps Khalidi?) Hajjis of Palembang, the names of Snouck's petitioners suggest strong connections to ʿAlawi concerns. They were led by Hajji ʿAbd al-Rahman b. Ahmad b. Jamal al-Layl, a preacher and jurist of Arab descent and a member of the Dutch appointed Raad Agama. He was supported by two sayyids, ʿAbdallah b. ʿAydarus b. Shahab and ʿAlwi b. ʿAqil b. Marzuq, as well as Kemas Hajji ʿAbdallah b. Azhari, who was perhaps a relative of the pioneering printer, Hajji Muhammad Azhari. According to their first letter to Snouck they had already written to Sayyid ʿUthman who had composed a fatwa and two pamphlets on the subject. Yet such interventions had not been looked on kindly by the local mufti, who claimed that Batavia was a separate jurisdiction and promptly commenced actions to expell them from their posts. This resulted in appeals to both the pretender to the throne of Palembang and to the Governor General, with the specific request that he send Snouck himself to Palembang. A despairing ʿAbd al-Rahman insisted that he needed something beyond the printed works of Sayyid ʿUthman, and hoped that through Snouck's "rational interpretation," right and truth would be made "manifestly clear."[4]

Clearly the plaintiffs played to the notion that, juridically speaking, Batavia was Palembang's capital. Even so, their letter did not receive an immediate reply, let alone a visitation from Snouck. Thus another would follow, repeating the story in more anxious terms. Although the record is incomplete, it would appear from Snouck's official recommendations that matters were ultimately resolved in favor of the plaintiffs after the further dissemination of yet more tracts written by Sayyid 'Uthman. The opposing faction had not gone down without a fight, however. They attempted to fund Snouck's visit to Palembang themselves and they sent letters to someone whose authority they felt might outweigh anything coming from Batavia. This was Ahmad Khatib al-Minankabawi (1860–1916), a leading jurist whose star was just then rising in Mecca. He would test the mettle of Sayyid 'Uthman during exchanges that would take place over the course of the next five years.[5]

A decade later we find more relaxed, even assertive, correspondence from the once embattled 'Abd al-Rahman who was eager now to secure a promotion to the rank of Chief Penghulu after seventeen years of loyal service. By this time Snouck's position at the apex of Dutch-sanctioned Islamic juridical authority in the Indies was unquestionable. In May of 1905, the well-known journalist Dja Endar Moeda (1861-?) asked Snouck to adjudicate a matter dividing the 'ulama' of Padang after his own press had produced a primer by a local shaykh that contradicted Sayyid 'Uthman.[6]

Yet all was not well. The Palembang mosque issue would flare up again in 1906 and, as we shall see, storm clouds were gathering for Snouck and 'Uthman in circles where state and Christianity were seen as indivisible. This despite the fact that Snouck had already so often acted behind the scenes against the publishers of articles impugning Islam, as when Semarang's *Selompret Malajoe* published "servants tales" in 1896 claiming that Muhammad had been the illegitimate son of a teacher whose mother Khadija [*sic*] had fled to Egypt where she had taken up with a Christian priest.[7]

The missionaries' initially positive attitude toward Snouck was changing too. Much as some Christians still had little understanding of Islam, it is clear that many now had little appreciation for Snouck's intentions, most especially once rumors of his conversion to Islam did the rounds. When such doubts were voiced Snouck would respond both privately and in the press. Soon after his 1890 marriage in the Priangan, for example, he had *De Locomotief* quash rumors of it and he outright denied the fact of the marriage to his theologian friend Herman Bavinck. In February of 1897, having written to Aboe Bakar to ensure that his Meccan secrets were safe, he also got the *Soerabaiasch Handelsblad* to redress statements that implied he was a desk-bound scholar with little appreciation for the dangers of Islam. Indeed he was always able to find column-space for his rebuffs, especially those directed at such critics as Van Sandick.[8]

Despite the questions that were being raised, as of 1900 Snouck's networks remained largely unthreatened. With the death of Nawawi in Mecca in 1896, another Jawi scholar, 'Abd al-Hamid of Kudus, had taken on the task of collecting books for Snouck to be passed on by Aboe Bakar.[9] Like Nawawi, 'Abd al-Hamid would become famous for his Arabic works. Some see him as an important link to the development of the new Islamic movements on Java in the twentieth century, or even as a conduit for reformism and nationalism. On the other hand, he is excluded from the story of the modern, for this distinction was claimed by rather different people, some of whom were looking at "Mufti" ʿAbd al-Ghaffar with ever narrowing eyes.

FROM QUR'AN TO BIBLE

One more element of the story needs to be emphasized before we turn to examine the entangled futures of Sufis, reformers, and scholars in the early twentieth century: namely, the prospect (or spectre) of Christianization. The epithet "Nasrani" had been part of the Southeast Asian vernacular far longer than "Padri," but it would seem that by the late 1800s the missionaries were finally making hard-won gains in the hinterlands of Sumatra, along the south coast of Java, and among the farther-flung isles to which they were granted admittance. In some cases the activities of missionaries reaped unintended harvests. At Bagelan in 1882, a santri turned priest claimed that belief in Jesus placed the Javanese on a par with white Christians and absolved them of their labor obligations to the colonial state. Local officials and their missionary kin were not amused.[10]

In West Java, meanwhile, there was greater resistance to Christianity as an element of colonialism. This is apparent from the story of Kartawidjaja, at least as he presented it in his autobiography, *Van Koran tot Bijbel*, written at the behest of A. Vermeer of the Djoentikebon Mission. Although Kartawidjaja commenced with an account of his early years in a pesantren, these chapters were removed by the editors, who did not wish to confuse readers with notes on so many "strange words and names." In a further effort at simplification, many of the opponents of Kartawidjaja were given initials, which of course only complicates their identification today. Despite these obfuscatory touches, Kartawidjaja's story provides insights into intercommunal relations on the border of West and Central Java at the turn of the century.[11]

Kartawidjaja was born around 1850 and died at Djoentikebon on October 4, 1914. His grandfather, Hajji Patih Mas Muhammad Salih, had been an official and religious teacher in Indramayu, where he had instructed two future regents, one of whom was perhaps Raden Tumenggong Soerianataningrat of Lebak, whose reports on the pesantrens Snouck had used in 1885. Muhammad Salih had remained a member of the local Landraad well into old age, a position that secured him valuable contacts in Dutch society. Even so, while the young Kartawidjaja's friends were sent to the new European schools for the native elite, he commenced his education at the Pesantren Babakan in Cirebon, where he was taught by another of his father's students. Three months later, however, Kartawidjaja was taken ill and went home, never to return. By this time his father had decided that he was sufficiently schooled to seek service in the colonial bureaucracy.

Kartawidjaja claims that he felt his knowledge of the Arabic-script was not at all useful for this service, and although he remained a santri at heart, he nonetheless took it upon himself to learn both "Hollandse" and Javanese letters.[12] The years between 1872 and 1891 saw him occupy numerous posts, apparently rising to that of Demang of Luwung Malang. Despite these advances, Kartawidjaja's total dedication to his work apparently led to a spiritual crisis, and he withdrew to Indramayu. There he turned his attention to the canonical works of exegesis he had collected, became absorbed by prayer, and made regular visits to the nearby pesantrens of Wot Bogor and "Kak Sepoeh" (probably that of Shaykh Talha), where he claims that he took the rites of the Naqshbandiyya.

Living in the Arabic precinct of a largely Chinese town, Kartawidjaja began preparing for the pilgrimage to Mecca under the guidance of two sayyids, whom he soon forsook, having decided that the knowledge found in his books should suffice.[13] One day, though, he received his friend Raden Wira Adibrata, the son of the sub-Regent. Muhammad was no Prophet, claimed Adibrata, who had apparently been converted to Christianity by J. L. Zegers (1845–1919) of the Dutch Mission Organization (NZV). Kartawidjaja drove Adibrata from his house, but upon reflection began to wonder how Muslims were supposed to accept the Old and New Testaments without actually having read them. So, after gaining his Sufi master's blessing, he was given exerpts of the testaments by two local Chinese. His reading led him to stop praying and to attend the services of another missionary, O. van der Brug. This brought visits from his teacher, the two sayyids, and many of their "Arab" followers, all of whom argued that he was betraying his scholar-grandfather and father.

To his own mind, however, Kartawidjaja remained a Muslim, for he had not been baptized. This was despite his playing the role of an avid proselyte and playing it in fact with some alacrity. He engaged in debates with scholars using a Javanese translation of the Qur'an produced by Lange and Co. (Batavia 1858), a work he averred had been "adjudged correct by Javanese and Meccan scholars."[14] It seems that Kartawidjaja felt he was entrusted with a mission within his own intellectual community, that of the 'ulama' of Java. It was a community from which he formally parted with his baptism on Christmas day of 1899. His wife then fled to the house of an Arab shaykh, and a hostile crowd gathered outside his home for a time. Prayers and veiling were subsequently emphasized in a community whose leaders wanted to draw a sharp line around the Christians, and rumors were broadcast that the corpses of apostates would be denied prayers.

After further travails, Kartawidjaja moved to Pekalongan. In his account he notes the conversions of other prominent Javanese in Cirebon, and finally he moved to Bangodua, in 1902. Muslims tried to bring him back to the fold. Their summons were rejected and answered with sermons on the absurdity of the Prophet's alleged ascent to Heaven in a single night. The final pages of

Kartawidjaja's account (which may well be a coda added by the missionary translators) supposedly present his rationale for the necessity of conversion. What is key, apparently, is the confluence of Christianity and the modern:

> The Javanese are Mohammedans, santris and Islamic scholars. Following the Arabs they hate the Hollanders because they are Christians, calling them Nazarine unbelievers. In the Mohammedan book on religious teaching, entitled *al-Mufid*, Mohammedans are forbidden to adopt the clothing and habits of the Hollanders such as jackets, hats, ties, spoons, forks etc. Yet isn't it odd? Nowadays all Mohammedans, even scholars and teachers, wear clothing according to the Dutch model: a hat, coat, tie, etc., and they use forks and spoons. Everyone thus disobeys the injunctions of this book. Through this God will teach the Mohammedans that what is in their books is not His will but has been placed there by men who have not been inspired by the Holy Spirit. Provisions have been made for the Mohammedans to obtain some knowledge; the Hollanders teach them some mathematics and writing in Javanese and Dutch letters. The Government has appointed educators in the whole of the Netherlands Indies for native children. One can obtain beautiful clothes, all sorts of furniture and decorations for the home, various pieces of equipment. One has machines; the telegraph; steamships; railways; gold, silver, and copper, as well as paper money; one can make the pilgrimage to Mecca with ease. The Government does all of this. It is thus aid from Christians to the Mohammedans and other peoples who live in the Netherlands Indies. God willing, the Mohammedans will . . . understand that there is no blessing . . . other than through the Hollanders.[15]

Writing in March of 1900, the newly arrived missionary C. J. Hoekendijk (1873–1948) joyfully reported that Kartawidjaja, "a man proficient in the scriptures, in the Koran, in Javanese, Sundanese, and Malay," was urging the 'ulama' to proclaim the salvation of the New Testament. A month later he noted that Kartawidjaja and another individual of high rank had been the first natives to have ever been converted by Van der Brug.[16] Hoekendijk seems to have been rather impressed by this and to have enjoyed the consequent discomfort his own presence caused at Indramayu:

> When I come into the Arab *kampoeng* I hear voices from afar: "The missionary! The missionary!" People get out of the way so as not to be infected by me, and others spit on the ground in order to make their feelings known. They have tried to make KARTA WIDJAJA's wife unfaithful to him. He has become a kafir (unbeliever) and they may thus treat him as they will. They have threatened his life many times, at which time he has answered: "To die for Jesus is bliss; I remain a witness to Him." At Djati Barang people have threatened to burn down Christian homes, so that

few will openly dare proclaim themselves for Jesus. KARTA WIDJAJA is scorned, DOEKAT is humiliated, and MAKDOER has been disowned by his brothers.[17]

Kartawidjaja is also mentioned in some issues of the metropolitan paper that later relayed Hoekendijk's dispatches. In June 1900 his presence was reported at a public debate with the Wedono of Jati Barang.[18] The debate failed to convince the latter, and indeed Indramayu would prove in the end a great disappointment to the Dutch Mission. Although conversions of the Chinese continued, letters sent home spoke more and more of the impossibility of converting natives. The missionaries, local Arabs, and members of the pesantren effectively agreed about who could be Christian and who could be Muslim. And soon enough they would agree on what a proper Muslim was.

THE DEVIL OF BANDUNG

Kartawidjaja's story is added evidence of increasing social polarization in Java at the end of the nineteenth century, showing how the spectre of Christianization, with its link to colonial modernity, became more and more a source of anxiety. It was this very spectre that would be evoked when Snouck's sincerity as a Muslim was openly challenged outside Dutch circles. In 1902, reports reached Cairo's *Misbah al-sharq* about a "treacherous Qadi" of Bandung, Hasan Mustafa, who had "spread his modern ideas rejecting the resurrection and Judgment Day, calling on Muslims to abandon the obligatory prayers":

> He has taken recourse to tricking the ignorant Muslims of high status in Islamic matters to the extent that they are inclined towards his teaching and follow him in his apostasy as a group. . . . He has sent his epistles and disciples to all the villages around Bandung to lead the people astray from the path of guidance. He has been prepared and set upon this path by the Dutchman Dr. Snouck who claimed to be a Muslim called ʿAbd al-Ghaffar in order to trick the Muslims and deceive the unitarians. He is a man whose words are accorded great import with the Dutch government and among its great men. And he has explained his new stratagem to them to achieve the long cherished aim of converting the people of the Priangan . . . to the religion of the Christians.[19]

According to the writer, Hasan Mustafa had aided Snouck in Mecca until he had been discovered and expelled, having learnt but "a little" of linguistics and law. He had then been rewarded with a government job in keeping with the policy of using well-paid traitors to pervert local Muslims. After qadiships in Aceh and Bandung, Hasan Mustafa had steadfastly advanced Snouck's plans for Christianization. Efforts had been made to remove him from his post, and some of the notables had even approached Sayyid 'Uthman to secure his aid. This to no avail for Sayyid 'Uthman declared himself unable to help on account "of the strength of trust that the Dutch government had in this Qadi."

There are some grains of truth to this story. Following his unhappy service in Aceh and his return as Chief Penghulu of Bandung, something had happened to Hasan Mustafa. While Kartawidjaja was embracing the Christian faith in nearby Cirebon, Snouck's Sundanese ally appears to have gone back to his Sufi roots (and those of Kartawidjaja's guru), and to have commenced teaching speculative philosophy in his mother tongue. Given that Mustafa's language is still regarded as extremely dense, it is no wonder that local 'Alawis were disquieted and sent their complaint to the Egyptian Press.

A second letter was promised to *Misbah al-sharq*, but this seems not to have been published. It wound up instead with Hasan Mustafa, along with some vituperative corresponce. This second missive, "the Rejection of the Devil of Bandung in Affirmation of the Living and Everlasting One," detailed a panoply of charges. Among other missteps, Hasan Mustafa had rejected Ghazalian orthodoxy in favor of a Wujudi philosophy that denied God's attributes. He was even accused of being a "turbanned devil" misleading a crowd of mystics. But while the Sufis could be saved if they confined their seeking to questions of the stations of the Divine and accepted the immutable laws that underwrote His Creation, Hasan Mustafa's heretical (pseudo-Christian) "materialists" were of another ilk. He claimed that matter was formed and animated by innumerable random events and that creation had come into being through something called "natural selection" (*al-intikhab al-tabi'i*).[20]

It appears that Darwin's ideas had been baptised by association! An obviously stung Hasan Mustafa wrote a point-by-point refutation in which he mocked the anonymous writer as a callow youth filled with the arrogant confidence provided by a village school education. He gave a detailed explanation of true belief and the nature of God and creation and then went on to react to what he felt was a racist attack, claiming that the writer had the termerity to suggest that there was a hierachy of languages "such that he thinks that Arabic is closer to God than Malay, and that Malay is closer than Javanese, and that Javanese is closer than Sundanese." He concluded that what the writer really objected to was the cultural differences separating Muslims in such matters as tariqa practices and death rites, and opined that, when all was said and done, such distinctions would never be overcome. "Javanese are Javanese, and Sundanese are Sundanese."[21]

Snouck and Hasan Mustafa were apparently of the opinion that Sayyid 'Uthman was behind the whole affair. On being pressed by his Sundanese colleague, however, the sayyid denied all knowledge, and urged Hasan Mustafa to send him his refutation for publication.[22] Had this actually occured, it still would not have been enough for Hasan Mustafa's most committed detractors. One who sent a particularly nasty letter some six months after the first article appeared, even claimed to have compared what Hasan Mustafa had written with what was revealed in the books of Judaism, Christianity and "Magianism," and naturally to have found nothing of value in the writings of the qadi he addressed as "the ugly, the despicable, the accursed, the criminal."[23]

If tempers were fraying in West Java with debates over God, creation, and the modern, they would truly explode in East Java. Snouck never seems to have visited any of the famous pesantrens of Sidoarjo. The region, or rather the small hamlet of Gedangan, was the scene, in May of 1904 of a botched uprising. On the face of it, the revolt was very much like Cilegon some sixteen years before. It lead to panicked calls to action among the Dutch and yet more excited declarations from Cairo.

On Gedangan

Jihad, O Muslims! Jihad, O Muslims! . . . [it is] the Jawi revolution![24] (*al-Liwa'*, August 1904)

I have enough of firearms and weapons of every description. Should the natives attempt another rise as the last one at Gedangan, I can supply a good many of my friends with them.[25] (*Engelsch Maleisch-Hollandsch . . . Samenspraken en Woordenlijst*, ca. 1910)

On Friday the 27th of May, 1904—the Prophet's birthday—a crowd of several dozen Javanese men clad in white shrouds and brandishing picks, machetes, and lances, advanced on a group of Dutch soldiers guarding a bridge, who were backed up by a posse from the nearby sugar factory of Sroeni. After the soldiers discharged two volleys, the first ranks of the Javanese lay dead and dying. Numerous prisoners were taken on the spot and their leaders apprehended at the house of a kyai who was killed nearby soon after.[26]

Unlike the circumstances at Cilegon, this attack had not been a complete surprise. Suspicions had been aroused when the Dutch discovered several letters supposedly sent by the "Imam Sultan Mahdi." These called upon the Javanese to kill the Europeans, to institute the laws of Islam, and to await such signs as the appearance of white flags and banana leaves in the fields. They had also pointed to the now fallen kyai, Hasan Mu'min (1854–1904). Visits were made to the pesantrens, the names of teachers and students were checked against the registers, and spies were dispatched to nocturnal gatherings of the ringleaders. All this, and the purported murder of one such spy, guaranteed that Dutch troops and their enthusiastic auxilliaries would be ready and waiting.

As events unfolded, more troops were sent to keep an eye on skittish factory workers and incensed villagers. Matters would remain unclear for some time.

There was a question as to who had ordered the first salvo, and just how is happened that the Assistant Resident ended up in the creek with an assailant. Snouck, for his part, advised the new Governor General, Van Heutsz—whom he had disparaged privately as being a disciplinarian with little interest in any policies that smelt of Christianity or yet the "Ethical" principles Snouck proposed for the advancement of Indonesians through Dutch education—that Cilegon had taught him that little could be determined until the dust had settled.[27]

Speaking through the Cairene press, on the other hand, an Arab correspondent attempted to link the latest affair on Java to everything from the rise of Japan to the tricks of Snouck and Hasan Mustafa, who were decried once again as Christianizers and advocates of "Naturist" materialism. Meanwhile, the alleged chief materialist had come to view the events at Gedangan as having little plausible connection to the international Sufi orders, despite the local sugar factory having issued a publication that accused him of links both to Cairo and the "Qadiriyya." In Snouck's view, based on a report submitted by his deputy G.A.J. Hazeu (1870–1929), Hasan Mu'min had been impelled less by the teachings of any tariqa than by Javanese millenarian prophesies. The Hasan Mu'min described by locals had started out as a trader in woven mats who dabbled in healing. Born in Magelang, he had traveled first to Semarang and Pekalongan, where he met Kyai Krapyak. Given that the pesantren of Sidosremo had just burned down, Hasan Mu'min had then gone for a time to a pondok in Tirim, and then to a pesantren in the Sidoarjo area led by the then penghulu. His brief marriage to that teacher's cousin and successor established him as a santri of note. He did not teach any texts or tariqa learning in the formal sense, but his amulets were increasingly prized by farmers, small traders, and fishermen. As time went on, his fame rendered him the logical focal point for people with grievances. In 1903 Kyai Krapyak informed him that he would have a role in a state soon to be established by the Mahdi, and he began to look forward to a place in history.[28]

As Hazeu noted, there were indeed local grievances aplenty. They ranged from family disputes and complaints against a former village headman (known derisively as "Pak Padri"), to burdensome taxation, pollution of the wells due to public works for Surabaya, and even the laying of train-tracks over Muslim graves. Hazeu declared that, "in as far as real teachers of religion are concerned," or even people who, like Hasan Mu'min, were "simple village doekoens [healers] who can gather a certain circle of adepts around themselves in exceptional circumstances," oversight was to be left in the hands of the regular police, and the military need not be called in. Times were changing under the global impact of capital upon a people sorely in need of intellectual and societal development.[29]

But if Hazeu saw the events as but one response to the onslaught of capital, others saw in Hasan Mu'min a prescient warning about the possible conse-

quences of the ill treatment of Muslims. One letter sent to Snouck from Singapore invoked Sidoarjo in relation to rising tensions in Riau. Having visited
Tanjung Pinang in June of 1904, Hajji ʿAbd al-Jabbar of Sambas claimed to be
"most shocked" by the behavior of the government there:

> The Dutch very much abuse people and disrespect Islam. . . . One kam-
> pung head called Hajji Muhammad Tayyib was sacked from his post be-
> cause he held a *mawlid* in his home until 2 in the morning, even though
> his home is in a Malay kampung nowhere near the Dutch. Meanwhile,
> the Dutch can do whatever they like if they want to hold a party, whether
> in their homes or at a ballroom, with band music or drums and violins,
> dancing and making other noises while letting off firecrackers until late at
> night, even though they are close to the mosque in which people are pray-
> ing. Even more [shocking] is that they force Muslims to plant crops on
> graves, such that these are effaced, which is done by people who have been
> punished by the Dutch government which governs this *negeri*. Thus all
> the Muslims of this *negeri*, and the *negeri*s nearby, are extremely upset.
> They want to complain, but they fear to go against the power. So they just
> nurse vengeance in their hearts. Hence there is the potential for turmoil
> whereby the population will rebel against the government. People always
> blame the Hajjis, saying that they stir up the people. Because of this, I
> write to Sir in the hope that Your Excellency will help discuss the behav-
> ior and inappropriate actions of the Dutch people, so that the Great Men
> of Batavia can enact policy and give better guidance, lest there occur the
> sort of unrest and uprising as just recently occurred in the *negeri* of Java,
> Sidoarjo. For Your Excellency is most knowledgeable of the Muslims,
> even if there are many who do not carry out all that is necessitated by
> their religion.[30]

With Van Heutsz as Governor General, however, Snouck found himself up
against a corps of officials with little liking for his "liberal" views. His advice on
Gedangan was rejected, and he perhaps came to the opinion that he would
have to return to the Netherlands to have any hope of changing the institutional culture operating in the field. For ʿAbd al-Jabbar's worries about Dutch
insensitivity when it came to Muslim religious practice were justified. Many of
the officials likely to make such blunders were yet to be convinced that the last
word had been said on the matter of religion. One was the Jeddah Consul,
C.C.M. Henny (b. 1856). Henny was no fan of Snouck and judged the Gedangan Affair to be but the latest manifestation of an ancient archipelagic roy-
alist movement tied and a "national" identity that had been imprinted by "the
Sufi guru."[31]

Having concluded that the sugar factory would be unfairly blamed for the
events in Sidoarjo, Henny argued that Southeast Asian Sufis would continue
to use their links with local aristocrats to encourage resistance to any occupier.

Moreover, he worried about the potential "national" (i.e. pan-Jawi) influence of a Patani leadership of the Shattariyya with links to Mecca (there had been a rebellion in Siam in 1902), citing the parallel examples of chauvinistic Buddhism in Siam and Japan.

> Here we find an order which is primarily, though not exclusively, confined to the Malay race, and is thus specifically NATIONAL, with its seat in a vassal state far from Mecca located on the borders of a Buddhist kingdom, inhabited by a people related to the exemplary Japanese who are looked upon with sympathetic wonderment by all Oriental people; an order which ultimately has the sympathy of the world of native officialdom.

Henny went on to claim that the Dutch had done "absolutely nothing" in the way of studying local sects in their overseas territories. "Nothing shall give me greater pleasure," the unread consul opined, "than having the opportunity to carry out this study for a few months in the libraries of The Hague."[32]

While Henny never got the sabbatical he was fishing for, his letter does bring us to a new phase in the story: that of Snouck's return to Holland in 1906 and a new role overseeing the training of a new generation of scholar-officials. Even if these new officials would still be mainly concerned with issues of law and legislation in their daily work among Muslims, their philological teeth would be cut on the often mystical manuscripts in his collection. In this process of training, tariqa Sufism was effectively marked as a past concern for official classrooms and as an antique form of religion to be redirected to a privatized faith in closer conformity to the needs of the modern age. In this venture, Dutch scholar-officials, Churchmen, and Muslim reformists often agreed far more than modern nationalist historiography would admit.

Conclusion

In his role as unofficial mufti of the undeniably Muslim Netherlands Indies, Snouck was, it seems, perceived as servant to state and Islam alike. Such services (and the favoritism he was assumed to enjoy) would irritate the missionaries who had originally provided the scholar with his ethnographic data and a warm welcome. And certainly they also rankled those Muslims who were not the direct benificiaries of his policies, most especially those with an interest in connecting with the Ottoman Empire and its periodicals. To that end it is ironic that their globally oriented attacks on the Dutchman were framed in terms of policing the boundaries of Sufi practice supposedly transgressed by Hasan Mustafa. Moreover, while the missionaries thought Snouck was Islamizing Java, some Arabs feared that his projects were geared to easing a path for Christianity. Whatever the various viewpoints in play, all and sundry would be put on notice once again by the unwelcome surprise of Gedangan.

PART FOUR

SUFI PASTS, MODERN FUTURES

> On the basis of intimate relations with the Javanese and their kin, I am firmly convinced that a compromise is possible between Islam and humanism in Indonesië and, based on my most recent observations, I would not dare deny such a possibility for Turkey and Egypt.[1] (Snouck to Nöldeke, June 1909)

The last three chapters observed Snouck at work in the Netherlands, in Arabia, and in the Indies, and provided an overview of his critiques and interventions. On the basis of his reading of missionary reports, he began to question the value of texts produced by his juridically oriented metropolitan rivals, and he determined to lead by example, from the field, an effort to reorient Islamology so that it might become of direct benefit to the state. Henceforth the colonial authorities would have at their disposal a scholar who could provide a bridge to places and people once imagined off-limits to detailed inquiry. Of critical importance was his recasting of the place of the Sufi orders in Indies society, for it gave him valuable contacts with like-minded critics of folk practice among elite Muslims, who now saw the utility in collaborating with a state that recognized them as a force for effective governance. Yet there would not always be smooth sailing for the famed Orientalist. By the end of his Indies tenure he would face criticism from a youthful corps of Muslims oriented to new intellectual capitals, and, perhaps worse for him at the time, from an expanding body of Dutch officials with little liking for what they saw as his indulgent policies which, they feared, had the potential to create social equality between Europeans and Natives.

CHAPTER TEN

From Sufism to Salafism, 1905–11

When Snouck Hurgronje left the Netherlands Indies in 1906, there was as yet nothing known in this land of Reformism or Modernism, the newer religious movements within Islam. During his seventeen-year Indonesian stay, Snouck Hurgronje knew Islam as the religion transmitted by the ancestors. In none of his writings of this period is there a trace to be found of the religious phenomena of the newer times.[1]

So wrote G. F. Pijper (1893–1988), one of the last colonial administrators to be trained by Snouck Hurgronje, and a scholar now known (much as he had hoped) for his apparently novel interest in reformism and its impact on the Indies. But although the Salafi reformism of Cairo's Muhammad ʿAbduh (1849–1905) and Muhammad Rashid Rida (1865–1935)—so known because of their claims that it emulated the attested practices of the "pious ancestors" (*al-salaf al-salih*)—had yet to penetrate Indies society when ʿAbd al-Ghaffar turned his back on Batavia, we should now recognize that when it did reach the archipelago, it found common cause with an impulse already well under-way in Southeast Asia. Snouck may not have referred to the modernism of Cairo in so many words but, as the following chapters will show, he and his acolytes had opened the door for modernist interpretations of Islam. To reach this point in our understanding, we will need to step back again in time and space to view a broader perspective of the Jawi lands.

Ahmad al-Fatani and Ahmad Khatib al-Minankabawi on Tariqa

By the beginning of the twentieth century, printed works had already for some decades provided affordable access to Islamic learning. That much is clear. The Muslim public, however, still lacked the means to participate in the ongoing religious debates. This would not become possible until an audience grown used to the printer's art had developed a taste for journals. Until that time, and even though they had themselves played a role in the creation of a reading public, the Sufis of popular tariqas were targeted by their elite enemies as victims of foolishness, potential enemies of public safety, and lust-maddened rural simpletons.

It remains questionable whether these critiques worried the Sufi shaykhs who were still busy imparting their knowledge in person and granting their all-important licenses for the further transmission of tariqa knowledge with the nibs of their pens. The policing of Sufi orthodoxy was an internal matter, and the shaykhs of Mecca remained the final arbiters for kings and commoners alike. One such authority was the Meccan printer Ahmad al-Fatani (1856–1908), as famous on the Southeast Asian mainland as Nawawi Banten had been for the isles. In 1905, al-Fatani received a request from Raja Muhammad IV of Kelantan, a Malay state then under Siamese control. In his letter the Kelantanese sovereign asked for his opinion on the purported practices of a Sufi order whose teacher had just arrived in the area and had gathered some disciples at Kota Bharu.[2]

The teacher in question was a Peninsular Minangkabau called Muhammad Sa'id b. Jamal al-Din al-Linggi (a.k.a. Cik 'Id, 1875–1926). Cik 'Id had been a student of the Egyptian Muhammad al-Dandarawi (1839–1911), a disciple in turn of the Sundanese Ibrahim al-Duwayhi (1813–74), who followed the tradition established by the Moroccan Ahmad b. Idris (1750–1837). Indeed al-Duwayhi had established himself in Egypt before moving to Mecca in 1855 to build his own lodge at Jabal Abi Qubays, where he would draw on the flow of aspirant Sufis incoming from all corners, including the Malay world.[3]

As it happens, the Ahmadiyya, as the order was known, had already been introduced into Kelantan in 1870 by 'Abd al-Samad b. Muhammad Salih (a.k.a. Tuan Tabal, 1850–91), who represented a sober interpretation of Idrisid teachings. Matters were somewhat different with Cik 'Id, who favored al-Dandarawi's ecstatic and populist interpretation, despite his having studied in Mecca under the restrained Zayn al-Din Sumbawa, Nawawi Banten, Ahmad Khatib al-Minankabawi, and Ahmad al-Fatani himself.

In his request, Muhammad IV asked Ahmad al-Fatani about the legitimacy of assemblies where males and females of all ages came together. More especially the ruler was concerned about the ecstatic visions reported by youthful participants who had been drawn into a state of heedless "rapture" or "attraction" to the divine presence (*jadhba*). In the preamble to his fatwa, most likely completed in 1906, al-Fatani admitted that he had once been "received" into the Ahmadiyya, but confessed that his experiences of "attraction" had differed from what the raja was describing. Hence what followed would be derived from his extensive reading of "the words of the Sufis" from an insider's perspective.[4]

The resultant, somewhat lengthy, fatwa did not condemn the order, but offered an explanation of the possible sorts of "attraction" based in part on the writings of Muhammad Abi 1-Wahhab al-Shadhili and al-Sha'rani's mentor, 'Ali al-Khawass. These ranged from a state of error to genuine moments of ecstasy experienced by a true "strider" on the path of gnosis. This was a classic explanation, but al-Fatani's images could also be very modern, as when he likened the experience of divine attraction to travel on a speeding train. To be sure, the primary criterion for a true experience remained, as may be expected, knowledge of the law as communicated by the example of the shaykh. Indeed al-Fatani conceded that some people falsely claimed visions in order to undermine their teachers, and he emphasized that access to true esoteric experiences should be restricted and never communicated to the ignorant.[5]

Al-Fatani also noted that he had fielded requests for fatwas on Sufi praxis from other parts of Siam and Perak, where the ignorant had allegedly introduced pre-Islamic practices into the rituals. Such criticism would seem to align him with Sayyid ʿUthman, but on the other hand al-Fatani was also critical of unnamed Hadrami shaykhs who encouraged "shifting about" and "hand waving" by "ignorant Javanese and Malay commoners" attending the ode recitations that the shaykhs led. Ultimately al-Fatani implied that the order in question in Kelantan could be adjudged sound, given that its teacher claimed a connection to Sidi Muhammad Salih and Ahmad al-Dandarawi. He was clearly of the school of thought that the tariqas could be accepted as conforming to orthodoxy. In closing he affirmed that knowledge of both the crucial inner and outer sciences of Islam was to be sought in addition to (modern) knowledge of the world, for it was by this combination of learning that all Muslims could "defend and elevate the sovereignty of Islam."[6]

There were, however, other Jawi voices at Mecca who were far less indulgent of the ecstatics of Southeast Asia. Perhaps the loudest, Ahmad Khatib al-Minankabawi, who was appealed to in the 1893 case of the Palembang mosque, excoriated the shaykhs of West Sumatra. Born at Kota Gadang, he is reputed to have been a troublemaker in his youth. But he was gifted and ambitious, and a sojourn in Mecca, accompanied by his younger cousin Muhammad Tahir Jalal al-Din (1869–1956), was to be the beginning of a famous career. According to the Jeddan historian ʿAbd al-Jabbar, Ahmad Khatib's grandfather had been a Salafi sojourner from the Hijaz during the first Wahhabi occupation, and was appointed as preacher in the mosque of Kota Gadang.[7] Ahmad Khatib's own rise to prominence as a scholar most likely dates to the late 1880s, following an advantageous marriage to the daughter of an intimate of Sharif ʿAwn al-Rafiq, for he did not attract Snouck's attention until 1893, when he was appealed to in the case of the Palembang mosque. Ahmad Khatib busied himself with condemning the traditional system of inheritance in West Sumatra, but he is perhaps best known for his polemics against the Khalidiyya, which he began to write around the same time as al-Fatani was responding to Muhammad IV; perhaps even within a few hundred yards of him.

Like al-Fatani, al-Minankabawi was writing in response to a question from one of his students about a tariqa active in the student's particular "Jawi" homeland. Unlike the fatwa of al-Fatani, Ahmad Khatib's far lengthier response was not kept close to the bosom of a court.[8] Rather, his *Izhar zaghl al-kadhibin* (Exposition of the Adulteration of the Liars) was printed at Padang in June of 1906, accompanied by a fatwa issued by the Meccan muftis Ba Busayl, ʿAbd al-Karim Daghistani, and Shuʿayb b. ʿAbd al-Karim al-Maghribi, and with the backing of a consortium of local ʿulama'.[9]

The book caused a storm among the local Khalidis. In it Ahmad Khatib took Mawlana Khalid to task for introducing heretical innovations, most especially that of the *rabita*. For support, he drew on canonical collections of Prophetic tradition and Qur'anic exegesis, including that of Shihab al-Din Mahmud al-Alusi (ca. 1802–ca. 1853). He also made good use of the authoritative texts of earlier Sufis and the newer manuals of the Naqshbandis. These included the books of al-Suhrawardi and al-Kumushkhanawi, and a text that he called the *Fath al-rahman pada tarekat Naqshbandiyya dan Qadiriyya*, which was actually the *Fath al-ʿarifin* of Ahmad Khatib of Sambas. This Ahmad Khatib, however, argued that while the manuals presented some correct notions, alongside those were other statements that confused the innovations of recent masters with ritual practice, appropriated the authority of the juridical schools, and claimed for their own order the right to be emulated without question.[10]

Ahmad Khatib used these texts as rhetorical sticks to beat the shaykhs whom (he was at pains to emphasize) he had seen in Mecca. For it was there that aspirant Sufi deputies about to travel to the Jawi lands would gather to *buy* the licenses that they would need to suck whatever advantage they could from Southeast Asia's credulous and wealthy peoples; even if, as far as he could tell, neither their licenses nor their deportment were in accordance with their own manuals. Such men were in no way to be compared to the true masters of Sufism, including the original Naqshbandis, whose tariqa had been so sullied by shaykhs like Sulayman Afandi who misinterpreted the Qur'an and the works of respectable Sufis, such as al-Shaʿrani.[11]

Thus it seems that Ahmad Khatib was also receptive to the notion of a properly respectable Sufi tariqa, provided that it accorded with attested practice, and that the attributes of God were not to be imputed to the Prophet or the saints. He also made it clear that he did not reject the language of the Sufis, but merely sought to answer the questions put to him and to clarify which acts and which pedigrees truly reached back to the Prophet. Indeed he repeated his general view towards the end of the work, when he explicitly denied having any objections to the tariqas of Sufis who were in full accord with the Shariʿa.[12] As such Ahmad Khatib's approach should be seen as yet another elite critique that respects the great names of the past and by no means embraces the Wahhabiyya. In this respect he is to be placed in the company of those scholars in Baghdad and Damascus who also bridged the divide between Sufi reformism and rationalist "modernism" retrospectively labelled as Wahhabism.[13]

Similarly miracles, while obviously beyond the reach of the snake-oil salesmen who were allowed to prosper under Sultan ʿAbd al-Hamid, were not to be denied. They just belonged to past and better times, much as reliance was to be placed upon the truth of the Night Journey and the existence of Angels. In fact very similar ideas were expressed by Zayn al-Din al-Sumbawi some two decades beforehand when he had defended the legitimacy of the *Night Journey* as an argument against the claims of (unnamed) Sufis who alleged that they had seen God.[14]

On the other hand, there were also very respectable figures who had affirmed such Naqshbandi innovations as the belief in *latifa*s, or focal points of the body. They included Muhammad Salih al-Zawawi, who had penned a short guide to the Mazhariyya when he visited Riau in the 1880s; and which was printed there by the Ahmadiyya Press in 1895.[15] But Muhammad Salih was now dead, and his son remained in Jawi exile following a dispute with Ahmad Khatib's patron, ʿAwn al-Rafiq, in 1893. But either way, the Khalidis of Sumatra were not going to take Ahmad Khatib's treatise lying down. Declarations were issued accusing the Mecca-based Jawi of apostasy, and Muhammad Saʿd Mungka of Payakumbuh (1857–1912) alleged that he had insulted the saints in his *Irgham unuf al-mutaʿanitin* (Spiting the Noses of the Vexatious).[16] Then another Khalidi, ʿAbdallah b. ʿAbdallah of Tanah Darat, addressed a personal letter of admonition to Ahmad Khatib.

The arrival of tract and taunt alike in 1907 merely had the effect of stimulating the "Imam of the Shafiʿi School" into further action. In September he drafted a refutation of Muhammad Saʿd, *al-Ayat al-bayyinat lil-munsifin* (Clear Signs for the Righteous), followed in December by a shorter, but equally caustic, tract called *al-Sayf al-battar* (The Sharp Sword). Both were published in Cairo in 1908, along with a reprint of the *Izhar zaghl al-kadhibin*, funded by the estate of Ahmad al-Saqqaf, the late Singaporean philanthropist and Meccan mufti, whose patronage obtained a degree of legitimacy for their author designed to trump all possible refutations from the Indies.[17]

Perhaps the sheer weight of the argument coupled with the volume of the qotations cited were calculated to overwhelm his intended audience, whom Ahmad Khatib decreed were effectively powerless in the grip of their teachers and stubbornly unwilling to abandon the cherished traditions of their forebears. After restating his position in the *Ayat al-bayyinat* on the subject of innovations introduced by such trickster Khalidis as Sulayman Afandi and Khalil Pasha, Ahmad Khatib announced that the world had been deprived of mystics with true insight since the fourth Muslim century. In his *Sayf al-battar*, he offered reflections on the dangers of excessive accusations of apostasy among the ʿulamaʾ, clearly mindful of the wars that had brought the Dutch into the Padang Highlands, and he addressed his Khalidi opponent as a representative of an idolotrous movement geared to personal gain.[18]

And there was more. In the last pages of the *Sayf al-battar*, Ahmad Khatib gave personal grounds for the strength of his feelings, claiming that "for years" he had sought out the people of gnosis, making himself "their slave" as he followed their programs. But he had found them to be no more than "tricksters who sold religion to the world, seeking a livelihood by using the name tariqa."[19] And he had yet another surprise in store for the tricksters of Padang:

[Had I found the matter to be] in keeping with your base passions, you would have praised my response day and night, bearing it above your heads. [But it was not], so a group of you went to ask for aid from the learned Habib 'Uthman of Batavia to respond to the *Izhar*, for you wanted to gain a powerful aid for your innovations. And so Sayyid 'Uthman answered by saying that the truth which is in accord with the Shari'a cannot be faulted. And he also said that you should not think that our committing wrong in the matter of the Shari'a would become a cause of enmity. For our aim is nothing other than to state the truth. . . . It is not our intention to engage in competition and conflict for base passions, as you seem to think. The respected Habib 'Uthman's answer reached me, and it was the words of a man whose heart God has cleansed of base passions.[20]

As it happens, a group of Naqshbandis from Bukit Tinggi had indeed written to ask Sayyid 'Uthman to write a rebuttal of the polemic of a man they claimed was animated purely by jealousy and to send that rebuttal to the Dutch "commanders" on Sumatra's West Coast.[21] They must have been disappointed when he answered in very diplomatic terms confessing his awareness of Ahmad Khatib's book and referring to his *Wathiqa*, which he sent to them. Having acknowledged the principles of brotherhood in Islam and the need to seek advice, he got down to business, referring constantly to his own work to argue that the real Naqshbandiyya was a respectable order and that it was nothing less than sinful to abuse its members if they truly followed its original precepts. Yet such emulation was difficult, perhaps too difficult for many people who sought to "contain their lower passions." And, he went on:

> . . . for this reason, centuries have passed in which nobody in Malaya or Java has been brave enough to claim to be of the Naqshbandiyya, even if the people of past times were more learned and stricter in their adherence to Islam and more respectful of religious practices than the people of today. Only recently have people of the current day, that is about fifty years ago, begun to claim to be people of the Naqshbandiyya without complete adherence to its conditions. If the brethren are able to comply with all the Sufi conditions mentioned in the first section of the *Wathiqa al-wafiya*, then thanks and praise be to God for his support, for given these conditions then the bretheren are bretheren of renunciation with little attachment to the world nor any desire for praise or rank over people, nor the desire to create trouble, disturbance or disorder in the land. All this is a blessing gained through enacting the tariqa as laid out in the first section of the *Wathiqa al-wafiya*. We therefore present this book to the bretheren so that it can be studied and the conditions of the tariqa as mentioned therein can be followed in accordance with the texts of the 'ulama' of Shari'a and tariqa. . . . It is [only] the Naqshbandiyya that is not complete in its conditions, as stated in the third section of the *Wathiqa*

al-wafiya, that is rejected by the ʿulamaʾ of Shariʿa and tariqa, especially those gurus of this day who have inserted all sorts of additions in the form of innovation as mentioned in the fourth section of the *Wathiqa al-wafiya*. Hence, Ahmad Khatib's rejection of all this is the same as the rejection of the ʿulamaʾ of Shariʿa, haqiqa, and tariqa, which thus cannot be regarded as offensive or slanderous. Indeed to give dhikr to God Almighty and to gain a license for dhikr in accordance with Sunna cannot be condemned.[22]

It thus appears that the Khalidis of Padang, who must have been naïve to have expected help from their ancient adversary, unintentionally connected the aged sayyid in Batavia with the younger Minang in Mecca. Indeed the younger man arguably gained in prestige. Whereas multiple copies of ʿUthman's response were soon returned by a local official with the request that it be rewritten in plainer language for his constituents, it is clear that regardless of the sayyid's approval, Ahmad Khatib's works would prove to have a decisive impact in West Sumatra.[23]

The Appearance and Significance of *al-Imam*

So it was then that, regardless of what they might have said in print, the claimants to the latest Meccan orthodoxy were linked to a long tradition of criticism of ecstatic Sufism. We hear this in their responses to requests for their opinions, but we still do not hear the voice of a modern Muslim public. That day was at hand, however, for readers were beginning to engage with a new crop of Muslim journals being published at Singapore. Even if Ahmad Khatib is said to have permitted his students to read Muhammad ʿAbduh's writings as published in Cairo, the first Malay mouthpiece of "modernist" ideas is held to have been a short-lived but profoundly influential monthly paper called *al-Imam*, which appeared in Singapore from July 1906 to December 1908.[24]

The majority of its two thousand reported copies were sent to subscribers on the Malay Peninsula, Sumatra, Java, and Borneo. Compiled under the editorship of several figures of mixed background, and offering articles translated from the Egyptian press, together with commentary on local affairs, *al-Imam* bridged the local Arab and Jawi communities of a world that they sometimes referred to as "our Jawi side." Even if some principals, such as the journal's Shihr-born first director, Muhammad Salim al-Kalali, let it be known that they were from another side, the first nominated editor had a very local history. This was Shaykh Tahir, a lineal descendant of the Naqshbandi master of Cangking and Faqih Saghir. He was, moreover, the younger cousin to Ahmad Khatib, with whom he had traveled to Mecca. Both reportedly studied under Ahmad al-Fatani. But unlike the two older Jawis, Shaykh Tahir appears to have embraced the Salafi ideas of Muhammad ʿAbduh, traveling to Cairo to meet him. Indeed in some ways his family trajectory symbolized the shift in elite Jawi Islam from the once regally sponsored Shattariyya to the reformist Naqshbandiyya and, ultimately, to the rationalist Cairene Salafiyya.

There have been several treatments of the importance of *al-Imam* in disseminating the message of the Cairene reformists (and nationalists).[25] Here, though, I wish to highlight aspects of the journal's treatment of tariqa Sufism and the tensions it seems to have caused in the relationship between the Arab and Malay members of the board. While the exact cause will probably remain a mystery, two significant changes that occurred in 1908 must have contributed to the journal's sudden demise. One was a move to take control of the press made in February by board members who identified with Arab concerns. These included Sayyid Shaykh b. Ahmad al-Hadi, al-Kalali, Muhammad b. 'Aqil (1863–1931, a son-in-law of Sayyid 'Uthman), and Hasan b. 'Alwi b. Shahab; though the journal was still edited by the Malay Hajji 'Abbas b. Muhammad Taha. The other shift was a striking upsurge in debate about the place of tariqa Sufism in the religious life of the Malays.

This began with a relatively innocuous question about withdrawal (*suluk*) sent to the journal from Penang in January, and then a second inquiry about the matter of a tariqa in Siamese territory sent in February. The first question produced little reaction, other than the standard condemnation of withdrawal from productive life and a recommendation that the inquirer consult the extant body of manuals on the subject. By contrast the question from Siamese territory created a stir. In part this was due to its relatively lurid descriptions of mixed assemblies of believers seeking visions of the divine while stamping their feet and disturbing the peace, images that clearly resonated with the Raja of Kelantan's letter to Ahmad al-Fatani.

The questioner then asked about the authenticity of such practices and whether the ruler should intervene. In March the journal's correspondence section featured the remaining paragraphs of the response left hanging in the previous issue, along with further testimony regarding the profane practices of the tariqa in question, almost certainly that of Cik 'Id, which was condemned as "the fraud of the deceivers of our time," if with subtle qualifications:

> All who enter into this tariqa must be ignorant of religion and their task in their world, which they have left by reason of it being a tariqa that contravenes the Shari'a .... For they have moved away [from this world] with their dhikr dances and their twirling and their killing of the self with their jumping and stamping and such things that are nothing other than a danger to this life and that to come.[26]

While *al-Imam* may have condemned such misguided killing of the self, its editors seem to have been unable to kill the story. Ever more letters were received regarding tariqa practices, most especially in Sumatra and Malaya. It soon became clear that the targets of these stories were most often local Khalidi shaykhs, as it was the practices of *khalwa* and *rabita* in particular that were attacked. In response *al-Imam* offered the all-too-standard line familiar from internal debates among Ghazalian reformers, arguing that, much as the Prophet had foretold, "the sickness of people of past times" had grown, leading people astray from "the true Sufism ... the proper path of the Prophet ... and all his companions and the leaders of learning":

> The greats among the people of Sufism of former days were the pick of all men, such as the men of erudition, the greats of the ʿAlawi sayyids, and those who followed in their path by following the words of the Book and the Sunna of the Prophet. Yet [now there are] those who have made a god of their selfish passions and have corrupted their religion by adding to it and misrepresenting it, composing all sorts of works of deviation .... Indeed those of this ilk are mostly peddlers of religion who drink the blood of all the poor and destitute.... Let all people guard themselves against them ... [for] one of these people is more dangerous to all Muslims together than a multitude of devils![27]

Reaction was not long in coming, but it appeared in another journal, the *Utusan Melayu*, where a troubled correspondent from Penang asked for Qur'anic justification of *al-Imam*'s positions on *rabita* practices, Hadith, or indeed al-Falimbani's *Sayr al-salikin*. The writer from Penang further urged the community to consult a learned Meccan shaykh visiting Singapore called ʿAbdallah al-Zawawi.[28]

The response of *al-Imam*—which had by now fielded a further question from Tengku Muhammad Jamil of Serdang asking whether the Qur'an justified the *rabita*—was more indignant than ever, asserting that the Qur'an more commonly condemned such practices. The writer in fact claimed to be astonished at the very mention of the shaykhs al-Falimbani and al-Zawawi:

> [F]or these two are accounted ʿulama' whose work states and elucidates matters brought down from God and His Prophet without either of them [taking] the right to fiddle with or add anything to religion that is not of it. However, as we believe that S.A. will prove unable to bring forth any such proof, could [we ask] kindly that Habib [al-Zawawi] help him? Still, we suspect that he will rather keep things to himself, for Sayyid ʿAbdallah al-Zawawi is one of the foundations of *al-Imam* ... and we have absorbed his teachings and directions in our breasts.[29]

There must have been much that al-Zawawi may have wanted to keep to himself. The friend to Muhammad b. ʿAqil and Snouck Hurgronje alike, he had been able, after his expulsion from the Hijaz, to make use of his previous connections to obtain refuge in the Indies, moving regularly between Riau, Pontianak, and Batavia, where he had often visited Snouck Hurgronje, though not without occasional hindrance from officialdom.[30]

It remains unclear whether all this was known to all the editors of *al-Imam*, whose undertaking had initially been pronounced a worthy endeavor by Sayyid 'Uthman. The fact that an earlier feature in the journal concerning Western scholars who had infiltrated the sacred colonnades of Mecca made no reference to Snouck Hurgronje or his alter ego 'Abd al-Ghaffar suggests a positive relationship of some kind.[31] Similarly unclear is al-Zawawi's position on tariqa Sufism. The fact that his 1893–94 visit to Riau stimulated the publication of his late father's manual, however, is suggestive of an ongoing commitment to the more elitist interpretation of the Naqshbandiyya than to the interpretation offered by the shaykhs of the Khalidiyya or the Qadiriyya wa-Naqshbandiyya.

To be sure the issue was by no means resolved, and further exchanges between the readers of *al-Imam* and the *Utusan Melayu* show that the local gurus were far from impressed by the whole affair. Some went so far as to defend their teachings, citing the pedigree of Sulayman Afandi or urging that such issues should not be discussed in the press, while their opponents began citing the by-now infamous *Izhar zaghl al-kadhibin* of Ahmad Khatib and the appended fatwa of the Meccan 'ulama'.

It should be noted that it was not *al-Imam* that raised the spectre of Ahmad Khatib, though their sources and quotations were remarkably similar. In fact the reference to the *Izhar* came in a letter sent by "Masbuq" to the *Utusan Melayu*, whose editors clearly hoped that the matter would be settled by some sort of authoritative statement from Mecca.[32] In *al-Imam*, though, the controversy would eat away ever more print, for the journal claimed to offer space to adepts and detractors alike. The apparently penitent Murid al-Haqq of Perak, for example, claimed to have narrowly avoided induction into the tariqa of Sulayman Afandi because he read someone's copy of *al-Imam*, which confirmed the doubts already in his mind.[33] The similarly pseudonymic Murid al-Yaqin of Pahang defended the learning and authority of the Khalidiyya as compared with "some of the tariqas of today," and urged Murid al-Haqq to examine the writings of Ahmad Khatib Sambas, not to mention the works of Isma'il al-Minankabawi and the prominent Syrian Khalidi, 'Abd al-Majid al-Khani, a Cairene imprint of whose *Bahja al-saniyya* could be ordered from the catalogue of Muhammad Siraj in Singapore.[34]

Other gurus had obviously had enough of this commotion too. If we are to believe reports sent to *al-Manar* from Singapore and Kuala Lumpur in August of 1908, tariqa masters began to prohibit the reading and circulation of *al-Imam* among their disciples and among the common people in general. If we accept the possibility that much of *al-Imam*'s readership was to be found in tariqa circles, and then in the communities that supported them, then such a boycott must surely have affected the paper's viability as yet more ink would be spent on tariqa questions in 1908.[35]

Once the Cairene edition of Ahmad Khatib's further assaults became available, the conflation of his teachings with those voiced by *al-Imam* would become more common. They would be more closely identified with the pronouncements of Rashid Rida as well, prompting subsequent Western observers to annoint the journal as the harbinger of Salafi "modernism" in the archipelago. *Al-Imam* was not merely about translating the message of Muhammad ʿAbduh, however, and there were significant tensions between Cairo and Singapore. Rida's criticism of the perquisites of the ʿAlawiyya, particularly his stand on legal parity between sayyid and non-sayyid, must have been especially problematic for some of the more ʿAlawi-oriented backers and editors of *al-Imam*, who would never problematize the matter of legal parity or the assumption that it had been their elite Arab ancestors who had brought Islam to the Jawi lands.

Then again, some Malay contributers and readers probably disagreed, and strongly. It seems quite likely that, by the end of 1908, the backers and remaining readers of *al-Imam* would have begun to wonder what their constituency was. The fact that in years to come we find *al-Imam*'s actors on different sides of several ideological divides would suggest there were indeed internal fissures during the journal's final days. By January of 1909 *al-Imam* was no more, and al-Zawawi would sail back to the Hijaz to take up the post once held by Ahmad Dahlan. This was by no means the end of the Arabic-script periodical in Singapore, however, let alone the end of disputes over the leadership of the Muslim community. At least four papers emerged in the following months, each declaring its own particular path for reform. The difference was that they now offered reforms to two discrete communities, and in two tongues.

Two of the Arabic papers are clearly derivatives of *al-Imam*. One, *al-Islah*, featured articles by al-Kalali, and, after initiating production elsewhere, soon occupied the premises of *al-Imam*. Quite unlike its forebear, however, it adopted an openly pro-sayyid platform. Meanwhile the original press of *al-Islah* would be used for a second paper, *al-Husam*, that claimed as its readership the Arabs of Riau and Johore. Yet a third, *al-Watan*, was under the editorial guidance of another sayyid, Muhammad b. ʿAbd al-Rahman al-Mashhur, who has been linked to the early days of Jamʿiyyat al-Khayr, an Arab welfare organization founded at Batavia around 1905.[36]

Of the three, *al-Watan* was the most exclusively Arab paper, promoting the modern while guarding the privileges of the sayyids. It was also the paper that took the clearest stand on the Cairene reformers, alleging that *al-Manar* and its editors were in fact poorly concealed frontmen for the Wahhabiyya. Sayyid ʿUthman too would become disgusted with the tone of *al-Manar*. While his grandson Muhammad b. Hashim b. Tahir (1882–1960) had initially been a regular correspondent, Sayyid ʿUthman was now finding himself and his writings on the receiving end of criticism from the self-hating sayyid Rashid Rida, who had been spurred on by other letters from the region deriding his collaborations with Snouck. When in 1909 Rida began to feature articles condemning him as a misguided "anti-Christ," the octogenarian hit back with a work that accused Jamal al-Din al-Afghani, "the Copt" Muhammad 'Abduh, and "the master of *al-Manar*" Rashid Rida as the real antichrists besetting modern Muslims. Rida might have extolled 'Uthman's son-in-law for his work in spreading *al-Manar*'s message in Asia, but Bin 'Aqil resented the Syrian's position on sayyid prestige and came to worry that he had embraced the writings of Ibn Taymiyya, by now the primary source for Wahhabi authors.[37]

While the Arabic papers that emerged in the wake of *al-Imam* may be grouped together as mouthpieces of a pro-'Alawi position foisted upon them by their colonial milieu, and then distinguished one from the other by the degree to which they rejected the Salafiyya, it is also fair to say that their respective claims to greater authenticity in the transmission of reform of any stripe may have engendered a reaction among their local collaborators of supposedly less noble birth. This can readily be seen in the pages of *Neracha*, the earliest Malay successor to *al-Imam*. *Neracha* was edited by 'Abbas b. Muhammad Taha. While it would soon welcome the birth of another Malay paper printed in Cairo, *al-Ittihad*, it saw the struggle of "the Jawi" people as separate from other Muslim struggles, including those of Turks and Egyptians.[38]

Arguably Jawiness can be seen as underlying the even more polemical West Sumatran successor to *al-Imam*, *al-Munir*. Founded by a consortium of Ahmad Khatib al-Minankabawi's students in 1911, *al-Munir* seems to have moved even further towards adopting a policy of exclusion towards *both* the tariqas and the 'Alawi sayyids. Padang was likely one of the very few places in the archipelago where this could occur. Whereas West Sumatra had seen its share of campaigning on behalf of the Naqshbandiyya, it had one of the smallest Hadrami communities in the archipelago, doubtless because they had made few inroads into its matrilineal communities. Ahmad Khatib's own grandfather was clearly not a sayyid, and while he respected the Sharifs of Mecca who supported him, in his conversations he also reflected upon the unequal lot of the Jawi in Arabia.[39]

Whether the leaders behind *al-Munir*—'Abdallah Ahmad, Hajji Rasul, and Shaykh Jamil of Jambek—had also made a full transition from the elitist Sufism of Sayyid 'Uthman and Ahmad Khatib to the Salafism of Muhammad 'Abduh and Rashid Rida is not immediately clear. What is clear is that they were seen by their opponents as the new Wahhabis and direct heirs to the Padris. For their part, they were effectively turning their backs on what seems to have been six centuries of conscious emulation of Meccan orthodoxy under Jawi rulers who had invested in the complimentary poles of the foreign sayyid and the local saint. As we shall see, some Dutch scholars could not but agree with their position and joined them in looking forward to a seemingly brighter future.

CONCLUSION

In this brief chapter we have directed our gaze out beyond the Dutch sphere once again to track the transmission of Islamic reformism into the archipelago. It is a story shaped by Malay voices but ultimately linked to Cairo, where printing and public activism were becoming a hallmark of the new Salafi movement of Muhammad ʿAbduh and Muhammad Rashid Rida. As a part of their platform to reorder Muslim society, this movement called upon Muslims to break with the older patronage networks organized around the tariqa and the sayyid. But, as we saw in the case of *al-Imam* and its genesis, such ideas were actually launched by thinkers with precisely such connections. Still, their goals could be harmonized for a time: both wanted to restrict Sufism to the elite once more and promoted extending a proper understanding of Shariʿa to a widening circle of readers. There were tensions inherent in this "harmony," however, and they led inevitably to the collapse of the sayyid-led reforms and to the genesis, as we shall now see, of an increasingly bifurcated public sphere in the Netherlands Indies. Going forward the various strands of the "modernist" Muslim movement will seek to take the lead under the aegis of the Office for Native (but no longer Arab) Affairs.

CHAPTER ELEVEN

Advisors to Indonesië, 1906–1919

In his pseudonymous letters of a pensioned wedono, Snouck Hurgronje had insisted, as any respectable Muslim scholar would, that a genuine Sufi was to be known by his pedigree. The wedono, however, said nothing about that same individual's representing a danger to the state. It is also clear from the outset that Snouck's personal concern was with untangling the various pedigrees he found in the field, with an eye to exposing the genuine pedigree of Indies history. In January of 1890 he had written to his mentor Nöldeke that he was looking forward to spending the rainy season with his newly collected bundles of material. For despite "all manner of unfinished government work," which he anticipated would revolve around his ethnographic data and trump the misunderstandings engendered by Van den Berg, he was particularly excited by the prospects of the material he had collected on "the earliest spread of the mystical brotherhoods in these territories," which he claimed afforded "an insight into the earliest spread of Islam here, and the manner by which Islam and Hinduism engaged and interacted." Later that year he wrote to the Director for Education, whom he informed, in similar terms, that he possessed "a rich collection" of indigenous literature which he hoped to exploit at some stage "in order to present the history of the introduction of Islam and its present character in a clearer light."[1]

Most Dutch officials had very different priorities. They wanted to know what to make of the manifestations of Islam that they saw before them daily. In their eyes, Snouck's primary duty was to explain matters of jurisprudence, or yet of materials brought in from rebellious suspects. In the wake of the *Selompret Malajoe* affair of 1896, for example, he corresponded with the Assistant Resident of Police at Semarang, G. Hogenraad, whose spies had reported that local teachers were making use of Cairene imprints of the *Jami' al-usul fi l-awliya'* in quest of invulnerability. In response Snouck advised (yet again) that such orders as the Naqshbandiyya were pantheistic movements "completely free of political aspirations," and that the books gave no specific instruction on such matters.[2]

Much like Van den Berg before him, Snouck would find that his historical interests had to come a distant second to his official tasks, most especially once he was engaged in frequent expeditions to Aceh. So long as his advice was heeded by attentive officials like Hogenraad, however, this was probably not too bitter a pill to swallow. His desk was often crowded with the gleanings of some raid or other, and he could readily designate interesting documents to be copied or simply added to his collection. But as it became increasingly clear that what he had to say was falling on deaf ears or that it would have to be repeated for yet another green official, he began to yearn for new horizons.[3]

With the 1904 ascent to the Governor Generalship of Van Heutsz, the now disgruntled advisor saw his window of opportunity in the Indies mist over. In April of 1906, Snouck set sail for Europe, where the doors of the Leiden Academy would open much as those of Mecca's Sacred Precinct would for al-Zawawi in late 1908. Snouck would be formally appointed to the faculty at the end of October 1906, though he would remain a senior advisor to the Dutch crown, overseeing the examinations of aspiring colonial administrators until his retirement in 1927. Certainly the training of officials of quality was now a great priority for him. Reprising his early tilt at the status quo he would dispatch a series of letters to leading papers in which he bemoaned the state of education for overseas service, noting that most instructors seemed more interested in demonstrating the supposed superiority of Western civilization than in imparting information about the cultures and languages their students might encounter. He argued that the British, by contrast, had long understood the educational needs of their colonial officials.[4]

In Batavia, meanwhile, the first of several scholars of similar inclination would occupy his seat, though as the Advisor for "Native" rather than for "Native and Arab" Affairs. This was G.A.J. Hazeu, a Javanist who had defended a thesis on classical *wayang* theater at Leiden in 1897, and whose assessment of the cause of the Gedangan uprising Van Heutsz would reject.[5] When Hazeu became Snouck's direct subordinate after his arrival at Batavia in 1898, the latter's impact had already been felt in the field. P. S. van Ronkel (1870–1954), the son of the well-known preacher of the same name, had already been inspired to trace the origins of the *Hikayat Amir Hamza*, drawing on Snouck's observations about popular literature and its links to the history of Islam in the archipelago. He had even preceded Hazeu in 1895 as Temporary Advisor for Indies Languages.[6]

Van Ronkel soon left Snouck's side to move to the Willem III school, but this did not mean that he had forgotten Snouck's message. He ended his classes for 1900 with the declaration that Muslims had to learn to do away with the doctrine of jihad and recognize that their faith was merely "another ritual for attaining eternal salvation." But before it goal could be achieved, "all the less civilized Mohamedan peoples would have learn to bow to a powerful European government."[7] Snouck however did not always think well of the stars who gravitated to him, no matter how eagerly they shared his opinions and set about disseminating his message. Whereas, in 1900, he rated Hazeu as a promising Javanist, and the missionary N. Adriani (1865–1926) a fine comparative linguist, he dismissed Van Ronkel, claiming, furthermore, that the "thought-worlds" of all three were merely incidental to his own.[8] In 1904 T. W. Juynboll (1866–1948) apparently surprised him with the quality of his manual on Shafiʿi law, for Snouck deemed the spirit of his generation of Orientalists to be "poorer" than that of the two previous.[9]

Perhaps the new generation was simply too prudent to question the conclusions of their outspoken master in the way that he had dared to challenged his forebears and chose safer paths in related but distinct subfields, especially after he returned to Leiden and set to work charting the first *Encyclopedia of Islam* (1908–36). Still, it was not impossible for those working under Snouck's direct supervision to achieve safety and to win his regard. Hazeu had certainly garnered praise for his help in preparing Snouck's work on the Gayo Highlands for publication.[10] Those who worked closely with Snouck soon found that it was wise to make good use of the materials offered them by the man who was too much occupied with administrative tasks to devote his personal attention to them, and wise as well to listen carefully to what he had to say. The substance of Juynboll's manual, for example, came directly from Snouck's own lectures, and thus from his experiences in Mecca.[11]

An advisor to the colonial state on matters of Islamic law would of course need to understand the principles underlying trust and inheritance, and this became especially critical after the Guru Ordinance went into effect in 1905. Another attempt to get a tighter grip of Islam as an institution, the ordinance decreed that teachers were henceforth to register both their teachings and their pesantrens. The same teachers looked upon the Advisor as an advocate in such matters, as we see in the case of three gurus from Kediri who were deprived of the right to conduct Friday prayers at their pondoks in 1909. One in particular attracted Hazeu's eye, for it appeared that this man, Muhammad Minhad, in the Afdeeling of Trenggalek, had lost this privilege by reason of not having declared that he was a teacher of the Naqshbandiyya and its books.[12] Hazeu protested the move and the thinking behind it in strong terms:

> This instance illustrates once more the undesirable consequences of the frequent, yet all too apparent, mistrust fostered by the Administration (also the Native Administration) against the tarekat-teachers in general. Such mistrust makes these people in their turn mistrustful of the Administration and induces them to make up lies and falsehoods in order to have the opportunity to offer education in secret, which in any case is greatly esteemed by the ordinary Javanese, and which the eyes of the Administration, in general, cannot detect. Thus in the Register of Kjahis and Gurus in the Residency of Kediri for the year 1903, one finds a mere handful of the teachers of religion listed as giving tarekat-instruction, which is a flagrant contradiction of the reality! There have indeed been tarekat-gurus from times immemorial in Kediri, and they are there today. It goes without saying that this method of taking action against the tarekat-gurus should definitely be avoided, both from ethical and political

considerations. After all, the supervision of the teachers of religion intended by the Guru Ordinance can not attain its objective if the tarekat-gurus are not listed in the registers.[13]

Hazeu went on to point out that, among the (assumedly ancient) tariqas practiced in the Indies, no more than a handful had been found to promote teachings that ran against the prevailing order. There could thus be "no question" of forbidding tariqa practices, as had occurred in some regencies. This is not to say that Hazeu favored the tariqas by virtue of their assumedly ancestral presence. Despite the apparently pan-Islamic sentiment that sometimes informed its articles, and which justified ongoing monitoring, he looked with cautious interest at *al-Imam* and its respectable editors who sought to carry out their program within legal bounds, requesting the advice (and contributions) of no less an ally than Sayyid 'Uthman.[14]

We have noted *al-Imam*'s stand on the tariqas and seen how questioning the mystical origins of the orders would become a primary task for many of Snouck's chosen students, not all of whom would feel particularly blessed by their mentor. One who was less than devoted to Snouck was D. A. Rinkes (1878–1954). Originally sent to the Botanical Gardens at Bogor in 1899, he enrolled at the Willem III Academy in search of broader career prospects and was posted to Korinci, West Sumatra, in 1903. He returned to Holland and enrolled at Leiden in 1906 in order to follow interests developed under Hazeu and Van Ronkel. There he was to make extensive use of the manuscripts that Snouck had collected in the field, and no doubt impressed him with his desire to link personal observation to archival sources. He defended his resulting history of 'Abd al-Ra'uf al-Sinkili and the Shattariyya in 1909, extending Snouck's observations on the influence of the latter over 'Abd al-Muhyi Pamijahan. This was followed by a series of articles devoted to the Nine Saints in the *TBG*, the flagship journal of Indies research. A final decision as to their number became moot when he abandoned the project after having written installments concentrating on only four of the saints, on the nature of the miraculous, and on the power of graves.[15]

Not all of Snouck's Leiden students were devoted to the study of mystical pedigrees, saints, and magic, but it would still be fair to say that the most of them would be obsessed with the question of origins. In a way what they were doing was not so different from what some Muslim scholars were seeking to achieve. To a point. For while they all wanted to sift the original from the false reports, it was only the Muslims who were doing so in search of religious truth. Or at least only the Muslims outside Leiden. Those few elite Indonesians who were working at the university under Snouck's direct guidance were given the same sort of training as their Dutch peers. Perhaps the most famous of them was Hoesein Djajadiningrat (1886–1960), a nephew of Aboe Bakar, and the first Indonesian to complete a doctorate at Leiden (in 1913) with his critical study of the *Sajarah Banten*. Already in 1909 Snouck rated him as the very best of all his scholarly charges.[16]

Over the course of the following years, as Snouck took on the role of mentor to the future officials whose examinations he oversaw and to those very few Indies students not drawn to the prestigious fields of law and medicine, he always emphasized the historical aspects of Islam and its role in the Indies. He may not have referred directly in his articles to the writings of ʿAbduh and Rida, or to the activities of the Young Turks, but he had a cautiously optimistic view of the general tenor of their reforms. Beyond this it is clear that he believed that, with the seemingly unstoppable spread of European rule across most Muslim lands, Mecca had become the last redoubt of a "conservative medieval orthodoxy"—or what might even be termed "antique" Islam—and was the source of the "spiritual narrowness and fanaticism brought to the archipelago." It is clear, too, that he still regarded the tariqas as playing a role in this importation of antique values. In his lectures and newspaper columns he still referred to the bastardization of the orders among the common people, reminding his readers that such bodies could still become dangerous instruments in the hands of unscrupulous teachers. That said he felt his ideas had had an impact and that Dutch rule and modern education were increasingly "emancipating" Muslims and seeding a revolution among the elite that the colonial administration had to either lead or allow to develop on its own terms. For even as he applauded the changes in Turkey and Egypt, he wrote to Nöldeke of his "absolute conviction" that "Indonesië" would prove the most likely site of a rapprochement between Islam and humanism, even as the new movements posed a potential threat to the state.[17]

His optimism seems also to have been projected onto the place of women and the declining strength of the Sufis. He even announced to the public that there was less resistance in the Indies to the emancipation of women than in Turkey or Egypt, even though the common people still "clung to the coats of the Sufi divines," or pledged *wayang* performances to the saints. He explicitly voiced the hope that modern times and exposure to Western civilization would put an end to popular affection for the saints. As a historian, however, he declared that one had nonetheless to be grateful to the backward saint-worshippers, for it was in the "heretical mystic writings" that one could see the real *personality* of the "Indies Mohammedans," even as found in the modern schools, where he claimed one could still come across "the most abstruse combinations and comparisons," and "the most ridiculous absurdities."[18]

When it came to comparisons, Snouck could not help but note in passing that certain stories from Indonesia seemed to resonate with those from elsewhere in the Muslim World. In a footnote he suggested that the fate of the heretical Lemah Abang appeared to be an echo of the martyrdom of al-Hallaj. Doubtless he would have communicated this to the French scholar Louis

Massignon (1883–1962), who would stay with him in 1921. His students later wondered how Snouck and Massignon could have cohabited, given that Snouck was famously averse to Catholics and critical of the Frenchman's Arabic, but his letters to Nöldeke demonstrate that there was genuine warmth between them. A warmth that did not, however, prevent Snouck from observing that the sheer weight of Massignon's work rendered it "almost indigestible" to him.[19]

Perhaps this was due to his avowed preference for the lucidity of al-Ghazali over the opacity of Ibn al-ʿArabi. To be sure, al-Hallaj had not been foremost in his mind ten years earlier when he had pronounced upon what it was that "Indies Mohammedans" needed "in order to maintain a place in world affairs." As he had put it, they were "gladly accepting" Dutch leadership in education and development, "given without any precondition that they turn their backs on their old saints in favor of our own." Snouck even concluded the lecture in question by declaring that the great historical task before the Dutch was the eradication of all forms of religious, secular or political narrow-mindedness in the now defined colonial state of Netherlands India. He seems to have had the Indies in mind to the exclusion of the Malay world. While he had outlined the historical impact of Ghazalian reformism on such tariqas as the Sammaniyya, he never attributed the Sanusi family a role in the history he outlined, most probably because its agents were active beyond the zone of Dutch control and at a time later than the periods that most interested him.[20]

This division brings us to the issue of his territorializing language. Immediately after his time in Mecca, where Snouck had watched as the Muslims of the archipelago became ever more aware of a discrete Jawi identity, he began to deploy the terminology has was growing more popular Leiden, referring to those same peoples as "Indonesiërs." Even so, in the 1880s there was still no necessary equation of Netherlands India with Indonesia, with the first being seen as a subfield of the latter, and in writing in *Mekka* of "Muslim Indonesia," Snouck was still acknowledging the existence of non-Muslims both within and beyond the area of Dutch control. This was also the framework used in his report on the Acehnese when he described "Indonesian believers," and "Indonesian Mohammedans," and spoke of things being either "typically Indonesian" (like the "unmistakably Hindu-influenced" practices of the Shattariyya) or else "not specifically Indonesian" (such as the general neglect of daily prayers).[21]

Such terms appeared frequently too in his articles and lectures, though as time went on it appears that "Indies" and "Indonesian" were becoming synonymous.[22] What Snouck never pronounced upon explicitly, though, was the very concept that his work had made possible: "Indonesian Islam" and *its* personality. Rather, that leap would be made by others working in his scholarly shade. Yet for all their liberal sentiment, "Indonesian" was still an abstraction for many Leiden Indologists in the 1910s. The nationalist movement was yet to appropriate the term, for the elite members of the Student Club in Leiden identified, by and large, more with Java than the so-called Outer Islands. This focus is also more than evident in the very title and content of a new journal that many of them would have read. Founded in 1921, *Djåwå* gave space to scholarly articles focusing more often on literature and archaeology than Islam, even if some newly minted officials would see it as an organ for the odd article on that faith.

Tarekat to Sarekat, Sayyid to Shaykh

To be sure, even as he looms large in Indonesian history, Snouck had little to do with developments within reformist circles on Sumatra and Java beyond helping to maintain an atmosphere that was tolerant of their activities. Had he stayed in Batavia beyond 1906, he certainly would have had more to say on the subject of reformist involvement within the burgeoning national movement. Starting in urban contexts like Padang, Batavia, and Surakarta, activists committed to the modernist message, mostly emanating from Cairo and Singapore, set to work establishing networks of schools and societies. In some cases the impetus was competitive, given that missionaries, as well as Arab and Chinese societies, had already taken up the cause of the modern by establishing schools, orphanages, and hospitals.

Some in the colonial government worried about such political developments, but the scholars in charge of the Office for Native Affairs looked upon them as proof positive of a will to modernization among native Muslims. Indeed it is clear that Snouck's minions actively cultivated relationships with the leaders of such organizations, and that they were cultivated in turn. Among the Muslims at the interface between public activism, faith, and power we can count Agoes Salim (1884–1954) and Ahmad Surkati (1872–1943). The first, a gifted Minangkabau trained in Batavia by Snouck and sent to Jeddah under Aboe Bakar Djajadiningrat, would find himself somewhat stranded between the pilgrims he hoped to elevate and the Dutch he tried to emulate. In his white colonial suits, Salim provided a contrast to Aboe Bakar and al-Zawawi, representatives of the traditional order. On his return to Java, changed both religiously and politically after contact with his maternal relative Ahmad Khatib, he would serve as a clerk in the administration.

For his part, the Sudanese Ahmad Surkati had come to Java by a very different path. Recruited from Mecca in 1911, and soon after Salim's departure, he had taught at the al-ʿAttas School (associated with the welfare association Jamʿiyyat al-Khayr) before breaking with his sayyid employers in 1914. In 1915 he was the obvious choice to lead the new reformist movement among the Arabs of less-esteemed birth. Known as al-Irshad, this was patronised by the wealthy entrepreneur and Dutch-appointed head of the Arab community in Batavia since 1902, 'Umar Manqush (d. ca. 1948). Surkati would also serve as an advisor to what was effectively its (older) sister organization, the Muhammadiyah, founded at Yogyakarta in 1912 by Ahmad Dahlan (1868–1923), who had been attracted to the writings of Muhammad 'Abduh and Rashid Rida.

Dahlan was also a local leader of what was becoming, on paper at least, the largest mass movement for Indies natives, Sarekat Islam ("The Islamic Union," SI). This collective had emerged in Surakarta from a small cell of Javanese seeking, with the support of the court, to maintain their economic position in the batik trade against Chinese competition. Quite against the expectations of SI's founders, many of Java's leading towns would soon see sister branches established, whose character often differed widely one from another as in the case of Yogyakarta, which was never allowed to challenge the primacy of Muhammadiyah's interests under Ahmad Dahlan. This is not to say that Sarekat Islam was designed from the first as a welfare movement. Despite plans to establish schools and hospitals akin to the efforts of Muhammadiyah and the students of Ahmad Khatib, little was realized to this end.[23]

Even so, the "Islam" in Sarekat Islam was seen by some members and distant admirers as something that went beyond the mere signification of the indigenous. In some areas initiation rites were not unlike the rituals for pledging loyalty to mystical orders, a development that perturbed the teachers of such orders. But the use of tariqa initiations and pacts by some of the aspirant branches of Sarekat Islam did not deter the Office for Native Affairs from granting it quasi-official backing. Sarekat Islam's leaders made sure that they put their case to the advisors, inviting Hazeu, Rinkes, and Sayyid Uthman to their congresses. The favor was returned in kind. At SI's Solo congress, convened on March 23, 1913, Sayyid 'Uthman introduced himself as "the mufti of Islam to the people" and gave a speech at the invitation of its leader Tjokroaminoto:

Among the benefits of Islam's justice is that it forbids the committing of evil against one's self, against others, and against the state. Secondly, the religion of Islam enjoins that one should respond well to those who do us good or who present us with good works, as well as insisting on our giving thanks to them. Given that Sarekat Islam carries out the good and useful works of the Islamic religion and does not engender anything wicked to the state, we therefore thank His Excellence the Sultan Sunan [Pakubuwana X], by whose blessing and aid the Sarekat Islam has been established with all its good works. May Almighty God grant him good health, long life and honor, Amen! We are furthermore very grateful to the Governing Body of the Sarekat Islam which, by its encouragement, enables all of us Muslims to follow and enact the duties of the Islamic religion and to ward off that which it forbids, thereby enabling honor and security from debasement and evil, as well as advancement and prosperity in this life and the next. We therefore hope that Almighty God shall perfect the good works of Sarekat Islam. It is furthermore incumbent that we all express our thanks to the Dutch Government, which, with its justice and care, enables us to attain happiness in carrying out the duties of religion without interference.[24]

In this year too the Honorary Advisor released his *Sinar istirlam* (Light of the Lantern) in which he attacked objections to Sarekat Islam raised by some Naqshbandi gurus who saw it as a force for Christianization through the alleged dispensation of "Christian water" in its initiations. Pointing to the now yellowing pages of his own tracts, 'Uthman reiterated that Sarekat Islam should be welcomed in keeping with the thanks due to the government for its tradition of non-interference in religious matters.[25] Yet the fact remained that Sarekat Islam was not initially guaranteed this recognition, and some of its members therefore deployed Sayyid 'Uthman's own rhetoric of gratitude in a flyer:

> Here below is a request for just [Government] consideration based on four matters for which the natives are thankful.
>
> Number 1: the natives are extremely grateful for the justice of the Government's "contract" (*kuntrak*) not to interfere in matters of religion.
>
> Number 2: the natives are extremely grateful for the Government's allowing the natives their happiness in carrying out prayers and enlarging mosques and providing wells and the practice of marriage and inheritance and paying the wages of the penghulus of the Raad Agama.
>
> Number 3: the natives are extremely grateful for the justice of the Government's peace and tranquility, preserving natives from difficulties befalling their bodies, their posessions and their religion.
>
> Number 4: the natives are extremely grateful for the policy of the Government to recompense those who teach good to the natives and become useful to the state without any suggestion of their doing evil towards it.
>
> Thus in light of these four matters, the natives earnestly request and place their hopes in the justice of the Government and its blessings that it shall advance the matter of Sarekat Islam....[26]

For his part, Rinkes—now Advisor for Native Affairs following Hazeu's elevation to the post of Director of Education in 1912—certainly played down SI's religious aspect in his report of May 13, 1913, noting the association of *wayang* heroes with key figures like Tjokroaminoto and even listing Islam as one the "unfavorable," but not insurmountable, factors for consideration. As he put it, even if the prominent Ahmad Dahlan was "strongly orthodox, tending to intolerant," he still made a "sympathetic impression." In his view the Pan-Islamism of Sarekat Islam was more social than political, geared to the same sorts of educational demands that one heard among the Arab communities of Batavia and among the Malays of the "Malaccan peninsula."[27]

These arguments apparently convinced the serving Governor General, A.W.F. Idenberg (in office 1909–16), who overruled the objections of regional administrators.

> In my view, the Sarekat Islam is an expression of what one can term the growing self-consciousness of the native. This frame of mind has not come about all of a sudden, but slowly, first in smaller circles, then in wider ones, due to the working of different influences, of which the foremost, according to the advice of Dr. Rinkes, has been the education supplied or enabled by the Government.... It can also be no surprise that in this movement, geared to the cooperation of so many, the religious element, Islam, plays a role.... It must be admitted that one can consider this Islamic element less than desirable, if one sees it as a source of danger. But consider that the Javanese has as good as never demonstrated himself as a fanatical Mahomedan, and that, by and large, Islam on Java does not show an anti-governmental character.[28]

Idenberg went on to point out that regional reports did not indicate present problems but rather worried about future occurrences, and he was satisfied that Rinkes and Hazeu had shown that Sarekat Islam was *not* to be likened to the National Movement in India. Hence he decided to extend recognition to local Sarekat Islam branches that would submit to the oversight of local officials, much as Islamic teaching and the tariqas were to be monitored rather than suppressed by the central administration. Rinkes was therefore appointed to steer the Central Committee in partnership with the amenable Tjokroaminoto, who rapidly rose as the head of the movement, while another ally, Hasan Djajadiningrat (d. 1920), would oversee the Banten Branch from Serang.[29]

The Minister of Colonies, Jan Hendrik de Waal Malefijt (1852–1931), sought reassurance from Snouck, who would back his former assistants in October of 1913. However Snouck also expressed the view that the movement had egalitarian ideals that aimed to undo the traditional oppression of the priyayi class, which did the bidding of the Dutch in an arbitrary way. He recalled, for example, his first years on Java when he had encountered a regent with an unthinking animus against a "harmless" tariqa. In Snouck's eyes, things had finally changed and a major intellectual revolution was being wrought by a Dutch-literate elite building on the foundations of Holle's efforts in the Priangan and inspired by the examples of Japan and Republican China. As far as Islam went, he pointed to his own lectures to the Government Academy in 1911 and affirmed Rinkes's view that the name Sarekat Islam did not signal a religious movement *per se*, but rather was the frame by which natives identified themselves as distinct from the Chinese and Europeans. There was, consequently, no need to equate the birth of Sarekat Islam with the events of Cilegon, and native officials were to be instructed that the formation of organizations for societal ends was by no means dangerous to good government.[30]

Snouck repeated such arguments over the following weeks and months. In the *Indologenblad* and *Locomotief* he outlined a history of oppressive colonial rule and mocked as "pure legend" the notion that Dutch governance had fostered intellectual development. Now in the "Ethical" period, "the desires of the Native population" were to be "harmoniously united" with those of the "so-called motherland." Having seen the rise of Japan and the Chinese Republic, Sarekat Islam was indeed standing up against tyranny, but the Dutch need not fear a religious bloodbath. The literal meaning of the words *Sarekat Islam* (Muslim Partnership) gave no real indication of the nature of the association, which in any case varied widely in its character from place to place.[31]

Snouck and Idenberg alike were probably pleased by the growing relationship between Tjokroaminoto and Rinkes and, later, by the part Agoes Salim would play in the collaborative endeavor "to realize a place for Natives in the world."[32] However, as time would tell, Salim would choose Sarekat Islam as his primary focus of loyalty—a position he expressed in his paper *Neratja*—for his years in Mecca had shown him that Islam had power and that Dutch interests did not necessarily align with his own. Certainly support for Sarekat Islam came from Mecca as well. In 1913 Consul Wolff would report that Muhammad Hasan b. Qasim of Tangerang had issued a treatise there backing Sayyid 'Uthman and calling on all "relatives" to join the movement.[33] Similarly Raden Mukhtar, the Bogor-born son of the former commandant of Manggabesar, in Batavia, would offer his support in the form of a Sundanese poem. This was soon translated into Malay by Kyai Hasan Lengkong, while an Arab called "Gadrawi" would compile his own text on the subject of the movement.[34]

But matters were by no means so clear in the Holy City. Aboe Bakar and 'Abd al-Hamid Kudus would report persistent rumors that the Dutch were laying plans for the Christianization of the Javanese; stemming in part from claims broadcast in Singapore in 1911. Hence Wolff completed his letter of October 1913 with the following observation:

> The Government, already known as no friend to Islam, is now held as a clear enemy.... Following the hadj thousands of pilgrims return to their abodes, and each one tells his circle of what he has seen and heard in the holy land, informing them of the imprinted warnings about Christendom. Contradicting prattle and rumor is a hopeless task. The government can better demonstrate that the principle of religious freedom has by no means been infringed.[35]

The government may have decided that the religious aspect of Sarekat Islam was merely denominational, but ever more Muslims were taking its nomenclature at face value. They saw any policy directed towards it in religious terms. The following year Ahmad Khatib would himself release an Arabic tract in support of the body, and in response to the same sorts of Sufi criticism about which Sayyid 'Uthman had complained. He identified Sarekat Islam as a body established to uphold Islamic principles, to generate trade and agricultural prosperity for its members, and to develop learning that fostered "advancement in faith and the world and the progress of the sons of the homeland."[36] Ahmad Khatib was by no means interested in ecumenical collaboration within a Dutch-run homeland. He was convinced that Sarekat Islam would serve as a redoubt against the creeping miscegenation wrought by contact with the Christians.[37] In fact he had just published another treatise in which he refuted scientific attacks on divine authority, lumping them with Christianity and Judaism as faulty belief systems, in much the same way Snouck—an avowed devotee of evolutionary theory—had been attacked through his controversial protégé Hasan Mustafa in 1903.[38] Ahmad Khatib would probably have been in close agreement with Sayyid 'Uthman once again, but the Batavian most likely never saw these books, for he died in January of 1914, some fourteen months before Ahmad Khatib himself passed away in the Holy City in March of 1916.

CHRISTIAN CONCERNS, BENEVOLENT ADVISORS, ENGLISH ANGST

Dutch officials and Naqshbandi shaykhs were not the only ones alarmed by the formation of Sarekat Islam. Concerns were also raised by the missionaries who had so worried Sayyid 'Uthman and Ahmad Khatib, including those involved with the publication of Kartawidjaja's autobiography. The proceedings of the Dutch Missionary Society for 1914 made little mention of their former poster-convert Kartawidjaja or his freshly printed autobiography compared to the time they devoted to the most recent mass phenomenon in the Indies. Delegates declared that Sarekat Islam was the result of Muslim frustration in the face of the modern world and an attempt by the Javanese in particular to find a place in it by founding schools, newspapers, and hospitals, much as the Dutch themselves had done in quest of converting them.[39] Some of the missionaries even alleged that there was now an uneven playing field. The Director of Missions, M. Lindenborn (1876–1923) insinuated that the emergence of Sarekat Islam was linked to an official partisanship on the part of the colonial administration for Islam. Such charges were by no means new. In 1909, another missionary at Manado, in Sulawesi, had complained that if the state were to allow Muslim schools in areas where time and money had been put into Christian institutions, then the Dutch would be weakening their own investment. After all, given the choice between Islam and the more "rigid" Christianity, natives always inclined to the former.[40]

Based on what was happening behind the scenes one might also argue that the Office for Native Affairs was giving offical sanction to a more rigid form of Islamic practice. This is evident in its oversight of the religious courts and their decisions. Indigenous officials had ruled, for example, that Indo-European women should convert to Islam if they wanted to inherit from their Muslim husbands, and that a certain aspirant to the religious courts should have a more technical knowledge of jurisprudence, and one grounded in Arabic rather than Malay. As Hazeu wrote of one hopeful penghulu in 1908 (and not without some curious errors of transliteration):

> Among the Sjâfi'ites, the most used Fiqh books can be brought back to three groups, being works as compendia and commentaries based on: 1st, the Moeharrar of ar-Râfi'î; 2nd, the Moechtaṣar of Aboe Sjoedjâ'; and 3rd, the Qoerrat al-'ain of Malaibârî. On Java, the most used of the three aforesaid groups of qitâb's, are: the Fathoel-Qarîb, the Fathoel-Moe'în, the Minhâdj at-Ṭâlibîn, the Fath al-Wahhâb, the Toehfah of Ibn-Hadjar, the Nihâjah of ar-Ramlî, the Hasjijah of Ibrahîm al-Bâdjoeri, and a few others. In general it is acknowledged that anyone who wants to be a scholar should have studied one of the [Arabic] texts fully and under the guidance of an accomplished teacher and that one cannot be satisfied by merely studying a few elementary booklets such as the Safînatan-Nadjât and the Qitâb Sittîn, and a few Malay translations of the commentaries, even if, from a juridical standpoint, there is nothing wrong with them. If his own statements are to be trusted, Mas Hadji Moehamad Idris has studied a few simple Arabic fiqh books and, as far as I can determine from the title list, some Malay works, of which a few are by the well known Batavian legist Sajjid Oethman. The latter texts are admirable for what they are, and a few of them were compiled with the aim of providing ig-norant Panghoeloes and members of the Priesterraad with guidance. But none of this changes the fact that one should give preference to the study of one of the aforementioned standard works.[41]

Hazeu, who was legally authoritative if uncomfortable as an Arabist, had also responded to the Manado complaint that year, arguing that the state had to appear the impartial guarantor of religious freedom or face the conse-quences. Six years later, Snouck, who would praise the missionaries for their engagement with Muslims in his American lectures of 1914, responded publi-cally to Lindenborn by stating that he had never sought to curtail mission work among the millions of "Indonesians made Netherlands Indians by his-tory" and that, far from being the manifestation of a mere handful of "devel-oped Muslims," Sarekat Islam was a positive sign that hundreds of thousands sought change, education, and advancement. In the following year he would push the point further, arguing that Sarekat Islam was nothing less than in-debted to the colonial government and to Idenberg himself.[42]

Of course the ever-swelling rallies, even when they were festooned with the Dutch flag and commenced with prayers for the Queen, were not watched with great pleasure by those in the sugar industry, who had long opposed Snouck's policies. The more hawkish colonisers and Christianizers knew full well that they were in danger of losing control of the roman-script media they had once monopolized. Hence missionaries like Hoekendijk devoted even more time to publishing their pamphlets, especially given that the Indies public was now devoted to detective novellas and newspapers. Literacy, the missionaries feared, was posing a threat to the very souls that they themselves had taught to read. It was nonetheless a tool for the further dissemination of their tracts and one that would be exploited by the newly formed Bureau for Public Literature (Volkslectuur) as well. At any rate, the banners of jihad and magical amulets were apparently being given up, and that was all to the good. Missionaries, reformers, and the men of the Office for Native Affairs could all agree about that.[43]

Elsewhere in the archipelago there is evidence that the Office for Native Affairs was casting a sympathetic eye on the activities of Muslim reformers. Writing from West Sumatra in 1914, Van Ronkel reported a general rumor that "the time of the tarikats was past" and that in its place only the new religion of "the orthodoxy" was ascendant, apparently bringing with it kafir-hatred, resistance to authority, and perhaps even the seeds of a new Padri war.[44] In a way, however, Van Ronkel made use of this view, proposed by the local Resident who had called for his investigation, as a straw man.[45] He built a narrative around a conflict between "general" and "universal" Islam, painting the latter as the product of a swift-growing movement in the name of "advancement" *against* what he saw as a specifically *Indonesische Islam*.[46] The latter he saw as a fusion of local lore and tariqa practice, but he stopped just short of lauding the rival position of Ahmad Khatib, much as Veth and Keijzer had pulled short with their regard for the Padris and Wahhabis.

Van Ronkel's approach was informed by his readings of Sufi manuscripts linked to the saintly Burhan al-Din of Ulakan and by oral reports he had received of positions taken by Ahmad Khatib's followers. Foremost among them were the "politicus" Abdallah Ahmad, the "fanaticus" Hajji Rasul, the "practicus" Hajji Muhammad Jamil, and the "rusticus" Hajji Muhammad Tayyib, who had made the previous inter-tariqa rivalries meaningless. It is also clear that Van Ronkel did not see them as Padris reborn, describing the latter as having been merely inspired by the Wahhabiyya, and noting in passing that "the Advisor of 1893" had condemned them less for their theology than their methodology. Since that time, Van Ronkel argued, the vast majority of tariqa books, if they had survived the alleged pyres of Imam Bonjol, had been (re)written by tariqa teachers. While Van Ronkel claimed that many Minangkabau people came back from the Holy Land as ignorant as they had been when they left, a goodly number left the localized tariqa practices of their homeland only to take up new practices in the Holy City, or else returned to campaign against both adat and tariqa. The odd "heretical" teacher might still to be found in the lowlands, but the teachers of older methods were under threat from the new modern schools, whether established by the reformists or the Dutch.[47]

By and large, Van Ronkel seems to have done his best to fall in line with the overall thinking outlined by Snouck, though this is not to say that his assessments were met without criticism. Rinkes pointed out that Van Ronkel's presentation was rather one-sided, particularly in respect to his designation of the reformist Kaum Muda as the bearers of the newest orthodoxy, arguing that the divide could more accurately be characterized as separating a broadly "nationalistic" adat faction and a "social-panislamic" shariʿa faction that was not always modernist.[48] Rinkes, it seems, still had his own independent ideas about how Islam was to be interpreted. Indeed some of his files betray an interest in the occult and superstition.[49] What the querulous official lacked, however, was tact and allies in high places. Certainly there were some in authority who worried he had become too close to his Muslim subjects. Rumors circulated that he had even converted. Beyond this, Rinkes also worried the English in Singapore, and in 1916 there were sighs of relief when he was dispatched to Jeddah for a year. He returned in 1917 to oversee the Bureau for Public Literature, an offshoot of the Office for Native Affairs formed in that year upon the return of Hazeu.[50]

On his unexpected return to the Office for Native Affairs as its High Commissioner, Hazeu found himself overseeing the final changing of the guard, at least in terms of indigenous allies. Sayyid ʿUthman and Aboe Bakar Djajadiningrat were dead, and Hasan Mustafa had decided that enough was enough:

> Certainly their Excellencies Dr. C. Snouck Hurgronje and Dr. G.A.J. Hazeu are aware of what I have done in support of the State, being [concerned with] matters of politics and fanaticism as a part of major happenings such as the Atjeh War, and the Uprising in Banten . . . and, moreover, the propagation of religion by Tarekat gurus. Equally, I have given recommendations and writings of use to the State, such that, at this time, I feel I have spent myself in its defense.[51]

It thus fell to Hazeu to make a recommendation that Hasan Mustafa receive a pension and the title of Honorary Advisor. The time seemed right. Hasan Mustafa's specialties, uprisings and tariqas, were seemingly old news; Muhammadiyah and Sarekat Islam were forging ahead in exciting directions; and there were new scholars to lend their imprimata to the state. Hazeu had already remarked in 1909, for example, that in "these modern times," it was not difficult to find fatwas offering a "broader perspective" on things. He offered as an example one approving the alienation of some endowed lands in West Java for the laying of a railway.[52]

More evidence of amenable muftis may be found in the archives of the 1918

Jawi Hiswara (see below), though that evidence also points to rising tensions within Sarekat Islam, which, it must be said, had been losing steam as its Central Committee (CSI) had few ways of building the cash reserves it would need to support its more grandious schemes. There was also increasing criticism of the advisors, as when the Governor General rejected a request from the CSI for access to funds collected in Java's mosques; funds that had been gathered and dispersed by the State ever since Snouck had carried out his surveys of 1889–91.

> The C.S.I. only asks for information from the High Government regarding the "status and intentions regarding mosque finances," because these days it could be said that almost none of the Muslims in Hindia understand the matter, or yet have a clear idea regarding the beliefs of their religion. This proves that the recommendations of Dr. Snouck-Hurgronje are yet to penetrate their skulls. Bearing in mind the provision of the Indies Constitution ... that states that "all people are completely free to practice their belief," we are mindful of the state of management of mosque finances and what pertains to it these days, for most Muslims feel that they are not free, or are restricted in the practice of their religion. There are even those who feel that Islam in Hindia is led by a non-Muslim government. Is such rule sound? Given this situation we Muslim Natives, who are now consciously striding towards the field of progress, require as clear an acknowledgement as possible from the government as to whether we are not ready to receive progress, because we cannot manage our own house (that is religion). Nay! There should be no such acknowledgement. We are no longer happy to have other people interfering in our house. We are no snobs though. Send Dr. Snouck Hurgronje to study Islam for another two hundred years! He will never know, understand or yet feel our true Islam. And we need not ask a Regent either, for his answer will surely be in accordance with the advice of Dr. Snouck Hurgronje.[53]

While this was not the first time that one of the Advisors had been criticized openly by Sarekat Islam members, the criticism here was far more explicit than before in its Islamic framing.[54] Certainly the colonial administration was increasingly aware that politics were changing and that they could no longer rest on their training and the advice of Snouck. To that end Hazeu, not having trained as an Islamologist, urged the Governor General to expand his office by employing one of Snouck's recent graduates, B.J.O. Schrieke (1890–1945). The son of a Protestant minister, Schrieke had adapted to Snouck's demanding methods in Leiden and defended a thesis on the *Serat Bonang* in 1916. It was in truth something more than a diplomatic study of one of the first texts brought back to the Netherlands. The entire introduction, drawing on published hagiographies and texts in Snouck's library, told the story of the conversion to Islam of the Indies. But despite the author's critical distance, the notion that the founder saints had been conscious advocates of orthodox tariqa knowledge was not rigorously questioned. Schrieke may have doubted Javanese legends claiming that Sunan Bonang had been inducted by Sunan Gunung Jati (and *vice versa*), but it is clear that, much like his own master, he felt that the tariqas must have been an established presence on Java during the lives of both.[55] He similarly followed in his master's footsteps towards the Indies by writing a report on the need for the Office for Native Affairs to keep abreast of Islamic developments globally. He urged that to this end it would be necessary to appoint experts (such as himself) and made specific reference to British manipulations of the caliphate question. Hazeu proffered the report to the Governor General, who obligingly secured Schrieke an appointment in Batavia.[56]

Islam was indeed rising to the fore in many discussions, and it would not be long before one of the more obscure statements, the contribution of an avowed Javanist, tipped the balance. In an article published in the *Jawi Hiswara* in January of 1918, the Prophet was described by Djojodikoro as having been a consumer of alcohol and opium. Java's putihan were outraged and Tjokroaminoto led a huge rally in Surabaya together with Hasan b. Sumayt of al-Irshad. This was followed in early February by their creation, together with Shaykh Rubaya of al-Irshad, of the "Army of the Lord Prophet Muhammad" (Tentara Kanjeng Nabi Muhammad, TKNM).[57]

The Dutch advisors were understandably troubled by this overtly (and so unexpectedly) Islamic turmoil, which spilled over into internecine fights between factions within the Arab community, for the ʿAlawi-sponsored Jamʿiyyat al-Khayr soon organized rallies and speeches of their own. Even so, the advisors felt that they could quell matters and appear neutral. As an advisor on the *Jawi Hiswara* affair, Schrieke defended Djojodikoro's language as the sort of "real-Javanese" wordplay that could found in "mystico-magical" manuals. Later he noted that very similar comments had appeared in the Javanese press (and under the same editor) in 1914, without provoking any reaction.[58] At the time Schrieke probably felt that he could keep both sides in check. He told Idenberg that he had received an offer from a local scholar to produce a fatwa "arguing that one may not involve the (infidel) Government in the matter," but that he had not taken it up "out of deference to his opponent," a sayyid he characterized as "the most influential teacher here who, in all sincerity," had built his hopes on the Government. For his part, Snouck penciled in the margin of his copy of Schrieke's report exactly who was meant by the amenable scholar and his sincere opponent: namely, Ahmad Surkati and ʿAli b. ʿAbd al-Rahman al-Habshi.[59]

Surkati was later said to have had a low opinion of the Dutch (apart from Snouck), and he had campaigned to keep the state out of Muslim affairs. He certainly had respect for some of Snouck's successors, though, whom he now actively sought out in the hopes that they might permit him to take the lead on questions of religion under Dutch rule. A day after Schrieke wrote his report, the Sudanese would renew his offer to Rinkes, writing of having lived under Dutch rule for seven years and of his admiration for the work of "great men" such as the advisors who worked for the moral uplift of the people. Surkati hoped to contribute to this endeavor through sermons that would offer "a clear program treating all the respectable classes, should it please the government." He predicted that this would lead to overall security, greater understanding between ruler and ruled, and improved religious practice, which latter he deemed particularly necessary in the post-war climate.[60]

Al-Habshi, Sayyid 'Uthman's successor, was equally eager to keep the Dutch with the 'Alawis. Though a cordial bond existed between Surkati and the advisors in Java, in Sumatra Schrieke went on to provide further support to the followers of Ahmad Khatib, and 'Abdallah Ahmad in particular, once he was tasked with monitoring the increasingly tense atmosphere on Sumatra's West Coast in 1919. Some of his books, such as the Padang imprint of Ahmad Khatib's attacks, were sourced directly from 'Abdallah Ahmad, who had instigated them in the first place and participated in the al-Imam debates. Schrieke even intervened to grant them recognition as Muslim authorities in contentious public debates on doctrine and seats on the Raad Agama.[61]

Much of what Schrieke thought of the reformist movement as a rational modernizing force can be gleaned from his correspondence with 'Abdallah Ahmad and the conclusions drawn there are given further support by the article he presented to the TBG in February 1920. After commencing with a discussion of the Padri war and dismantling Veth's earlier conflations of the highland Islamists with the Wahhabiyya, Schrieke detailed the issues currently under debate in West Sumatra; from the rise of the Naqshbandiyya and the new Meccan "orthodoxy" under Shaykh Isma'il, to the countermoves of the Adat elite and the 'Alawis in Singapore and Batavia. In so doing he too deliberately emulated his master, pointing out that the correct understanding of "present orthodox Islam" had to be based on "the current interpretation of authoritative texts," by which he had Snouck's writings in mind as much as those of Ahmad Khatib.[62]

Conclusion

Snouck may have been physically absent from Indonesia in the second decade of the twentieth century, but the advisors he had trained were very much on hand. And their mission (or so they thought) was to further Snouck's work by overseeing the transition of Indonesia into the modern world. They thought that they would guide a movement of Indonesians into the orthodox public sphere and away from the otherworldly personal control of mystical teachers. They still cultivated links with elite scholars, but they would have been pleased by the independent yet collaborative voices of Sarekat Islam and the egalitarian tone of the Irshadi movement that was allied with it. For now the state applauded from on high while some of its officers of a less liberal pursuasion watched anxiously. They would have their moment soon enough, however, for matters modern were, it turns out, not so firmly in hand as the advisors supposed.

CHAPTER TWELVE

Hardenings and Partings, 1919–1942

Not all elements of the national movement were as "modern" (or as patient) as the Kaum Muda of Sumatra. In 1916, this newly established Padang branch of Sarekat Islam would swiftly divide between the heirs to Ahmad Khatib and those affiliated with the traditional elite and their (new) Sufi allies led by the Naqshbandi Khatib 'Ali.[1] Two key incidents would mortally wound Snouck's Ethicists in 1919. The first, the May visit to Sulawesi of the Sarekat Islam representative for the "Outer Islands," Abdoel Moeis (1883–1959), led to strikes against corvée labor and the murder of the Controleur at Toli-Toli, J. P. De Kat Angelino. Then, in early June, a minor teacher from Garut and some of his family were shot in their home after refusing the Assistant Resident's demands for the delivery of rice.[2]

The details of the latter incident, sometimes known as the Garut Affair, were soon disputed, especially the alleged number of the followers of this teacher, Hajji Hasan of Cimareme, and whether they were planning an attack on the government soldiers outside the house. Whereas the Dutch commandant was confidant that the occupants were girding themselves to attack, witnesses claimed that they were declaiming the dhikr of the order to which they belonged.[3] But while he was a practitioner of dhikr, Hajji Hasan had a tangential connection at best to what officials later called the "B Section" (Afdeeling B) of the branch of Sarekat Islam at Ciamis, formed after the movement spread into the Priangan highlands and, as at Padang, took in members of the older tariqa networks who now realized that it was more practical to infiltrate SI than to combat it. One Sufi, Hajji Samsari of Tasikmalaya, claimed to have joined Sarekat Islam in 1917 because its program for advancement seemed to enjoy the Government's blessing, but, he complained, the branch had become radicalized following the 1919 visit to Ciamis of Sukino from Batavia and two shaykhs; the amulet seller Hajji Sulayman of Cawi, and Hajji Adra'i, the heir to Muhammad Garut met by Snouck in 1889.

The Afdeeling B had then been established under one Sosrokardono, who declared that members were now Sarekat Islam soldiers committed to regaining independence. Samsari had further been given to understand by Hajji Sulayman that the Afdeeling B was geared to seize control for the people of Java, "so that our independence is in our own hands once more. . . . And if we hold it again, then we can determine the law of the land once more."[4] In contrast to Samsari, Hajji Hasan had merely bought amulets from Sulayman; amulets that failed to protect him as some in the Malay press would sadly note. In his report to Governor General Van Limburg Stirum (in office 1916–21), which was also submitted to the Volksraad (a token parliament established in 1918), Hazeu found that Hajji Hasan had merely been trying to defend his land from being expropriated by the Wedono, who was supported by the high-handed Regent. Hazeu therefore recommended that the native officials involved in the attack be discharged and that their European supervisors, particularly J. L. Kal, the Assistant Resident who had ordered the salvos that killed the villagers, be censured for lack of proper oversight.[5]

Agoes Salim joined in, following the events closely in his paper *Neratja*, which was printed on a press initially subsidised by the Bureau for Popular Literature. At first he cast both the slain official of Toli-Toli and Hajji Hasan alike as fellow victims of an inflexible colonial system. He welcomed the appointment of Hazeu as investigator, and inveighed against the treachery of purveyors of amulets. After all, argued Salim, a true martyr wants to die for his religion and his people and therefore should logically have no use for a protective amulet. He also likened the principled Dutch who fought the Spanish in the sixteenth century to the peoples of Java, Lombok, and Aceh who fought the Dutch in the nineteenth.[6]

Tjokroaminoto too attempted to calm the waters while introducing an indigenous perspective to a Dutch audience. He told one liberal paper:

> We gladly desire the cooperation of those European elements who mean us well, though as to whether this can have an effect on our press I dare not say. For my part I shall gladly work to this end, though there are factors at play which are beyond my control. In recent years there has been a campaign in the European press against the SI and its leaders, which cannot but engender some bitterness that only finds its echo in our press.[7]

Certainly a campaign was being run at the behest of the sugar industry and elements within the Civil Service. Broadsheets like the *Soerabaijasch Handelsblad* would allege that the headstrong Hazeu had snubbed the aristocratic Resident of the Priangan Regencies, L. De Stuers, while the Aceh veteran H. C. Zentgraaff (1874–1940)—who would become a byword for conservative invective—would claim that Hazeu was trying to grandfather his own appointees in the native bureaucracy.[8]

The liberal *Socialistische Gids*, meanwhile, expressed the hope that the Garut affair could allow Sarekat Islam to purge itself of various unwanted elements, and of a no longer nominal one in particular:

> As will be apparent to the reader of the various papers, the S.I. Afdeeling B was primarily established by the more-religious ones, that is, those who see, or wish to see, the S.I. more as an association of true Mohammedans which forms, or which should form, a bulwark against people with other ideas in this land; e.g., against the Christians and adherents of Hinduism

in the wider sense of the word. When one realizes that the most prominent members of the S.I. treat the "sarekat" more as a national association,
such that both groups have, until this point in time, continually opposed
each other in their heart of hearts; and [when one realizes] that the influence of the Arabs is fairly large upon the first group while the foremost
leaders, such as Messrs. Tjokroaminoto, Abdoelmoeis, Hasan Djajadiningrat and Co., have only respected this first group out of fear for their influence on the great mass and ... for the money, then one understands
how great the meaning of the Garoet matter is for the whole S.I. movement. From now on, though, the group of the pure ones shall sing a quieter tune, and the movement shall proceed in a more purely national
direction.[9]

But time would tell, and as it happened it told quite the opposite story. As in
the aftermath of the Gedangan uprising fourteen years beforehand, Hazeu
would be ignored. By November Van Limburg Stirum had watered down his
recommendations at the suggestion of the recently elevated Civil Service Director, F. L. Broekveldt, who declared himself "even less inclined than the Resident De Stuers to look for scapegoats," asserting that Hazeu had merely sum-
marized the opinions of "a few journalists." Broekveldt even rejected the
suggestion that the Wedono and Regent should face sanctions, and it was ultimately decided to save face by reserving punishment for the surviving followers of Hajji Hasan.[10]

Some observers had anticipated such a judgment. With the increasing pressure brought to bear on Sarekat Islam by Dutch officials in September of 1919,
Salim had noted that natives were the only ones being made to feel like crimi-
nals. Still, he could celebrate the capture of Sosrokardono that month, while
the liberal weekly *De Taak* would offer its own analysis of the Hazeu report in
November. Compiled by "a true humanist" and "a model of learning and objec-
tivity," it declaimed that the people sought a hero when oppressed by a government that cared little for their opinions. As such, Hazeu's offering was an unintended monument erected on the grave of the hero of Cimareme.[11]

In reality, though, the events at Cimareme marked the death of Hazeu's of-
ficial career. Broekveldt had proposed the veteran Assistant Resident of Brebes,
R. A. Kern (1875–1958), as a potential replacement for Kal, the failed official
at Garut, though Kern soon found an even more august place in the Office for
Native Affairs once the despondent Hazeu returned to Leiden as Professor of
Javanese.[12] Salim, for his part, rallied his readers and attempted to save Sarekat
Islam from incremental dissolution, first through Tjokroaminoto, and later as
the organization's president when he and Abdoel Moeis called in 1921 for a
more "disciplined" religious course and forced the expulsion of communists
from the body's executive, the CSI. While it appears that Rinkes had failed to
strangle *Neratja* with its "radical" pro-Sarekat Islam platform, he had been able

Figure 11. Agoes Salim, ca. 1927, as reproduced in J. Th. Petrus Blumberger, *De nationalistische beweging in Nederlandsch-Indië*, 2nd ed. Permission for reproduction granted by KITLV is gratefully acknowledged.

to draw both Salim and Abdoel Moeis closer to him by offering them roles within the Bureau for Popular Literature.[13]

Certain Arabs meanwhile continued to squabble over the prestige they were to be accorded, or over whether they could be considered equal participants in the national struggle. As we have seen, some felt that the man who had shed the sobriquet "Arabisch" from his official title favored the Irshadis at the expense of the ʿAlawi sayyids who had served the Dutch and British in shaping knowledge of, and therefore policy on, Islam in the region. Many of these men had been connected to the early genealogies of reformism in the archipelago, and they would continue their dialogue across the years. One was ʿAbdallah al-ʿAttas, whom Snouck had met in Jeddah in 1884, and who remained on the Jawi side of the barricades despite his ʿAlawi heritage. Another was Muhammad Salim al-Kalali of *al-Imam*, who later aided the young H.J.K. Cowan (b. 1907) in deciphering the ancient inscriptions of Pasai.[14]

The same cannot be said of al-Kalali's former colleague, Muhammad b. ʿAqil, who, together with ʿAli b. Ahmad b. Shahab, had become a leading advisor to the British in Batavia and Singapore (as the Dutch well knew). Both were responsible for the drafting of a list of suspect Arabs that was used by the

British to inhibit the free movement of any Irshadis to the Hadramawt, a list in which the British described Bin Shahab as their "first and most reliable and faithful Arab in Java."[15] In the wake of the Great War, W. H. Lee Warner at Singapore still recited a litany that harmonized with sayyid perceptions of their proper role in directing Islam in the archipelago. The TKNM, "clever though it had undoubtedly been," had failed, while other violence could be shown to be a consequence of the famine (actually induced by the wartime British blockade of the neutral Indies) upon "the native in time of national and desperate stress."

> Were such material worked upon either by the pure leaven of fanatic Islam—the 'jehad' type—or by the leaven, less religiously pure, but equally rabid, in that it might work at white heat, of superior educated Arabs backed by European agents provocateurs, that is to say ... by the Said with his religious fire or by the unscrupulous Sjech, backed by German gold, an orgy of murder might well result in the blotting out of whole sections of the Dutch population, especially when the local Dutch naval and military forces were honeycombed—as they are—with Bolshevik tendencies. The Dutch therefore seem to be determined to diminish, to the best of their ability, the power of the Arab elements (to influence the native in a Moslem's most assailable point, his religion), by fanning the Arab interclass disputes, especially those which figure in Al Irshad's programme. The Dutch themselves in common with Arab supporters of the movement, refer to the 'abolition of the old class feuds,' rather than by its proper appellation, namely the fanning of those feuds to flaming point by the mere attempts to abolish them. The Dutch Government knows very well that no Said will give up his privileges without a bitter struggle.

Lee Warner, oblivious to the possibility that the British were themselves fanning the disputes, further accused the "rabidly pro-German" Hazeu of having "prostituted his undoubted knowledge of things Islamic" to aid Manqush in his "anti-British schemes," and in order "to humble Britain's warmest Islamic champions," when his proper duty as a Dutch official should be "to calm, and not to foster, volcanic potentialities."[16]

It can be argued that, by 1919, the Dutch and British had embarked on two different courses for the governance of their Muslim subjects. Broadly speaking, the English favored the trusted elite hands of the past, while the Office for Native Affairs and the Dutch state (which chose to heed the Office) looked to the leadership of new organizations like Muhammadiyah, al-Irshad, and the myriad bodies like Jong Java and the Jong Sumatranen Bond to act as a release valve for nationalist steam. It was only later that the British would become fully aware of the extent to which their policies had been decided by the intrigues of the sayyids Bin Shahab and Bin ʿAqil. Still, ʿAlawi predictions would seemingly come to fruition once Hazeu was forced out in 1920, and W. N. Dunn at Batavia was full of hope for the future in the colonies, if not the academy, where he claimed that the former advisor would doubtless find "ample opportunity to instil into the minds of future generations of Dutch colonial officials his pernicious theories."[17] He also appended the transcript of an August 29, 1919 discussion between Bin ʿAqil and Adjunct Advisor Schrieke which he prefaced with a remark on the advisors, who were "originally intended to serve the Authorities whenever difficult questions of religion or custom arose":

> The Advisor was to be a student not a politician. Hazeu went further and took an active part in native and Arab affairs. He succeeded in gaining the confidence of the Governor General, whose inexperience in matters Oriental was great, and who fell easy victim to the accomplishments of the expert. The direct contact which should exist between the Government and the executive was broken. Hazeu's advice was taken in preference to that of the Residents or of the Director of the Civil Service and, encouraged by his success, he went so far as to meddle with local affairs in various districts, disregarding entirely the officials in charge, whose authority is undermined . . . . In the eyes of the "ethically" inclined Hazeu, everything a native did was either good in itself, or at least excusable. The Koedoes affair [sic], however, shook the Governor's faith in his Advisor, and from that day Hazeu's influence began to wane. It was seen that the "Advisor's" theoretical knowledge could not outweigh the experience of the man on the spot, stronger measures were taken both against European and native political "reformers," and the Advisor's position gradually became untenable.[18]

Dunn must have been chuckling as he read the Schrieke-Bin ʿAqil exchange, in which the former was supposedly left silent in response to the latter's responses regarding the apparent lack of elite Arab support for the Dutch. It was all a matter of "sympathy," said Bin ʿAqil, inquiring (among other things) as to whether the Arabs had ever "attempted to take arms against the Dutch people"; or "ventured to create revolution or even participated with the natives in their revolutionary activities"; or yet "formed any secret societies for the purpose of destroying the peace of the country and of the Dutch people themselves." The interview supposedly warmed up when Schrieke suggested that the Arabs did not support the Dutch.

B.A. This accusation is likewise untrue, because I know there has never been a part of the Netherlands India [sic] taken possession of by the Dutch authorities without the SAIDS helping the Government. Is this a fact or not?

D.S. [*After a momentary pause*] Yes, in many cases.

B.A. In return, what have the Dutch done for the Arabs generally and the SAIDS specially?

[*Here Dr. Schrieke seemed puzzled and ceased to argue the point without giving an answer to the last question, but after a moment remarked:*]

D.S. The Arabs extend their sympathies to other Governments.

B.A. I do not admit they do, but it is natural that a man should like anyone who does him good and should hate anyone who does evil. Towards the man who does good to the Arabs, undoubtebly, they will incline and him they will love and this is not a peculiarity of the Arabs.

D.S. Is there a branch of the Al-Irsjad Society in Singapore?

B.A. No.

D.S. Why?

B.A. Because the British Government is ever watchful and will never allow anything which may produce evil effects to find its way into or prevail in its country.

D.S. Isn't it unfair to prohibit the establishment of an Al-Irsjad branch there?

B.A. Would a civilized Government allow an infectious disease such as cholera to enter it [*sic* M. L.] country?

. . .

D.S. The Al-Irsjad is not really what you believe it to be.

B.A. It is as I have described and can be compared with an infectious disease and if you look at the history of the Netherlands East Indies you will find that the trouble at Padang was the cause of the loss of hundreds of lives which arose from a movement similar in character to the Al-Irsjad, and the same is the case with the trouble now existing between Nejd (the Wahabis) and the Hedjaz whose guns are now busily working in order to suppress the activities of the Wahabis. The British Government does not allow such persons to be admitted simply in order to prevent bad ideas and the activities of the Wahabis from prevailing.

D.S. Do you fear there will be fighting among the Arabs on account of the Al-Irsjad?

B.A. No, because the leaders of the Al-Irsjad are persons who belong to the tribes of highwaymen, thieves, farmers, coolies, and bedouins, who, in their native lands cannot put on the the costumes which you see now being worn by them. They are very low and they realize the difficulties they will have to face, and are absolutely incapable of creating any trouble of fighting, because they have come here for quite a different purpose, although, indisputably, there will occur a rising among the natives owing to the education now being spread by the Al-Irsjad which will create dissension among themselves and finally result in bloodshed. The Dutch Government will find it a most difficult task to extinguish the fire, and then will only realize the fact that they created this trouble by keeping quiet and at the time offering encouragement to the movement of Al-Irsjad. This must be considered as a great mistake. In connection with affairs of this nature, I would refer you to what has befallen Turkey on account of her having allowed mischievous persons to mingle with the natives of the country.

D.S. [*excitedly*] You should not say that the Government offers encouragement to the Al-Irsjad.

B.A. What I have related is a fact well known to the public. How could it be otherwise? The leader of the movement is a Government official (Manggoesj)—a man highly respected by the Government. He does it under the eye of the Government. How could it possibly be that the Government is ignorant of what is known by the public? Not being satisfied he has dragged the Consul General of a foreign Government (Turkish) to support his cause by taking him from one place to another. Their action surely supports the truth of my assertion that the Government is concerned in the movement of the Al-Irsjad.

D.S. [*imperatively*] You should not say so.

B.A. What is the good of your insisting on my not telling a fact which is known by hundreds of thousands of people?

In June of 1920, Dunn advised Lord Curzon that while no replacement had been appointed for Hazeu, three Adjunct Advisors had been nominated; Kern, Hoesein Djajadiningrat, and Schrieke. Of these, Dunn declared Djajadiningrat "the most interesting," observing that he had been educated at Leiden, was a doctor of Oriental languages, and was reputedly very able. Dunn was woefully misinformed about his loyalties, however, believing that, although a "brother to the Regent of Bantam who is a direct descendent of the Emperors of West Java," he was "not over fond of the Dutch."[19]

Perhaps it would have been fairer to say that he would not have been keen on the changing tone of the regime that was to hold sway for two decades more, while the resurgence of the Wahhabiyya would give further ammunition to the sayyid opponents of al-Irshad and to the many reformists with whom they were allied. The dispute eventually became so heated that Schrieke was tasked with monitoring the conflict in the press as well as compiling a report on the struggling Hashimite state that the sayyids by and large supported.[20]

Islam under an Illiberal State

The post of Advisor for Native Affairs entailed that one gave the Government—in the Netherlands Indies, this meant the Governor General—advice on all matters, if he wished to take it. In those days that related to the nationalist movement in all its manifestations and purely Muslim affairs. One can imagine that a G.G. with understanding of and sympathy for nationalism would deem it worthy of taking such advice, whereas, on the other hand, another, who felt the correct way to proceed was by running the country as a police state would feel no inclination to consult the advisor. In his time as advisor Gobée found the truth of this. Personally, he always had the trust of the native population. Rich and poor alike knew the way to his office. He was always ready to hear their complaints and stories in order to help them in times of difficulty or show them the way.[21] (R. A. Kern, obituary for E. Gobée, 1954)

Thus far we have considered the measures that were taken at Leiden, under Snouck, towards the institutionalization of Islamic studies. Snouck's goal was to equip officials with a solid grounding in language, law, and mysticism so that they might serve as benevolent advocates for native rights within a Netherlandic state. He was only ever able to produce a few pallid copies of himself, however, as he was working against the official tide. Ranged against him and his adepts now were staunch critics who believed that the Ethicists had given birth to an incubus that threatened their tropical empire. In a rambling, accusatory essay that drew its title from *De stille kracht*—(The Hidden Force), Louis Couperus's novel on fear of Islam and the native—the embittered former Jeddah Consul, Henny, would publish his once-ignored speculations on the Shattariyya as proof of the dangers of Islamic nationalism as fostered by Snouck. He even accused Snouck of having been asleep to the dangers aroused by figures like Kyai Krapyak, or at least of having encouraged others to follow him blindly as if he were a Sufi shaykh. Among his numerous charges, based at times on selective readings of *Mekka* and *De Atjèhers*, Henny further alleged that the advisor had often put more trust in dubious natives and Arabs than in the members of the Civil Service who had long been concerned by the dangers that they faced, first from the brotherhoods, and now from Sarekat Islam's Afdeeling B.[22]

By the mid-20s the self-declared Ethicists would be on the receiving end of even more such criticism. In the Netherlands itself the reactionary turn would see the establishment of a rival training school at Utrecht in 1925 as a counter to the Leiden establishment seemingly in thrall to an Arabist who had almost become an Arab.[23] In the Indies, meanwhile, some saw the once unassailable ʿAbd al-Ghaffar's decision to marry Ida Maria van Oort (1873–1958) as proof of his lack of sincerity, or at least as reversion to his European religion. Still, one correspondent to *Djawa Tengah* simply averred that Snouck had only ever claimed to be a Muslim in order to write books on Islam, and so now that he was back in the Netherlands, he had married according to the Christian rite. "And rightly so," he said, "for every one should elevate their own religion." In response, the *Darmo Kondo* remarked: "Now we ask ourselves, which religion is actually the real one for the Javanese? According to the S.I. and people in general, it is Islam!"[24]

There would be others, too, whose labors would seemingly confirm that Snouck had had Christian predelictions all along. Having completed a doctorate under Snouck in 1921 (revisiting the sixteenth-century Sufi text first edited by Gunning), Hendrick Kraemer (1888–1965) was entrusted by the Netherlands Bible Society with preparing a new Javanese translation of the Bible and studying recent developments in Islam. His first effort was a report dispatched from Cairo that spoke of recent developments there, including the manifestation of a more stridently anti-colonial tone among the students.[25] Such reports were of course intended to aid the missionaries, and upon his assumption of an advisory post to Jong Java he presented lectures on Christianity. Some of the students then expressed desire to have more lectures on Islam, leading to a split and to the foundation of the Jong Islamieten Bond (JIB), whose journal, *Het Licht*, declared the Sumatran Agoes Salim a principal advisor. The journal was also heavily influenced by the writings of the Ahmadiyah movement in India, and it drew on works of Western scholarship as well. While much has been made of the fact that the work of Snouck Hurgronje was invoked in articles submitted to *Het Licht*, there was no passive acceptance of what he and his epigones had to offer.[26]

The division of interests between the Dutch and their Muslim charges would become set in stone. While Kraemer would increasingly delve into the textual traditions of Sufism, painting Islam as a Middle Eastern entity from which the Indonesians were effectively estranged, he saw the living Muslims of Indonesia as a mission problem. Their elite leaders—even the Dutch-educated ones—were, he believed, exploring the origins of their faith in order both to strengthen it on a stage they saw as global in scope, and to redress their apparent failures to live up to its proper standards. Doubtless the young members of the Jong Islamieten Bond would have been unenthusiastic about the conclusions reached in the first volume of Kraemer's lectures for Christian teachers, in which he proclaimed that while rule-bound Islam was designed to dominate the world, Christianity was destined to renew it.[27]

While the members of the Jong Islamieten Bond would eagerly report the foundation of fraternal papers, such as *Seruan Azhar* in Cairo, they were still interested in what men like Kraemer had to say concerning their evolution from Sarekat Islam and Muhammadiyah.[28] One editorial by Kasman pointed out that the Islamic associations had long been working for an education founded both in Islam and national history that also took account of "science and the demands of modern times."

> If we but take an objective look at our history then we shall see that nowhere, and above all not in our land, has Islam been forced upon the people by a conqueror. Similarly Islam was not brought to us by an immigrant people. No more than nine people brought Islam here. By virtue of the singular example of their lives, they brought the people to their faith which frees one from fear and the worship of numerous spirits and gods, and which makes people free from the caste system in which the entire genuinely indigenous people saw themselves consigned to the lowest caste, while the two highest castes were reserved for those who had come from across the seas and obtained overlordship.[29]

For Kasman, it was Javanese armies that had brought down the Hindu kingdoms before the flood of Western hegemony, and not the Arabs, whom he felt were not inherently deserving of special veneration. It would be far better, he thought, for Indonesians to study the causes that had transformed a half-wild desert people into a world-ruling one, and to answer the charges that Islam disempowered women. Far more space was devoted in *Het Licht* to defending what the editors felt to be a much-slandered faith, especially in regard to its alleged fatalism. As one Tidar would write in June of 1926:

> The Islamite has been called a fatalist. Oh what a word! What an error! They forget that fatalism *does not rest in Islam* but in the person. Islam is pure and free from fatalism. They still confuse Islam with a left-over of Hinduism. Yes, these people don't want to look at Islam up close. They know a little of Islam, and then from a non-Islamite known purely as an Islamologist such as Snouck Hurgronje and Company. These learned men don't know the truth of Islam, even with Arabic under their belts.[30]

After all, as Tidar also noted, the Prophet's own enemies had been perfect Arabic speakers, but they, too, were ignorant of the true character of Islam. Islam's adherents would be nobody's slaves, as the examples of the Turks and Moroccans had so recently demonstrated. This did not mean, however, that these elite Islamites sundered all communication with the Dutch, or even with the Islamologists. An enthusiastic report on the first anniversary of the Jong Islamieten Bond noted the invited presence of the Advisor for Native Affairs after listing an array of associations—including Jong-Java, the Jong-Sumatranen Bond, Jong-Ambon, the Studie-Club "Indonesia," Muhammadi-yah, Partij Sarekat Islam, Jam'iyyat al-Khayr, and the Studie-fonds Kota Ge-dang—who had gathered to celebrate their efforts for the benefit of "our beloved Indonesia."[31]

Of course now in 1926 there were significant parties in the picture, not just the clubs. Communists and secular nationalists were gradually awakening the hopes of the people and winning a lion's share of their attention—and, consequently, of official attention as well. Trials were held, and those convicted of sedition or violation of draconian censorship laws either incarcerated or exiled to such camps as that at Boven Digul, in Dutch New Guinea. Yet for Islam and the Indies government, perhaps the greatest shock would come in the wake of attempted Communist rebellions in West Sumatra and Banten in 1926–27, after which hundreds would make the Hajj to the relative security of Mecca. In the case of the West Sumatran rebellion, Schrieke would be called in yet again and would, in 1928, submit a report assessing the events. Yet the Mecca that the escaping rebels now found had changed. With the death of al-Zawawi, the flight of the Sharifs, and the Wahhabi return under Ibn Sa'ud, there were clear threats to both sayyid prestige and tariqa practices on all sides. What is more, many of the hallowed tombs of the past were slated for demoli-tion. Back in the Indies this news was greeted with disbelief. The abolition of the caliphate by the Turkish National Assembly had generated far more dis-cussion and campaigning, leading to the formation of rival delegations bound for Mecca and Cairo to represent the Muslims of the Indies who were, as it happens, more united than ever, if only in the sense that they wanted to chart their own futures without Arab leadership.[32]

As a part of this shift, and in reaction to the claims of reformists that they represented the sum of Indonesian interests in Mecca, and the parallel claims of the sayyids Bin ʿAqil and Hasan al-ʿAttas to represent all Southeast Asians in Cairo, an alliance of Javanese kyais set about forming a committee of their own to send to Mecca.[33] Thus a new body, "The Awakening of the ʿUlamaʾ" (NU), was born under the auspices of Hasyim Asyʿari of Tebuireng. But what had Asyʿari made of the new movement(s)? In an eschatological treatise, released years after his death, he wrote of the appearance around 1912 of the "wicked faction" of ʿAbduh and Rashid Rida, who attacked the Sunna agreed by the past greats, and the practices of tomb visitation and dhikr in particular. Al-Asyʿari would not describe their errors in depth, however, but would rather turn his full attention to a traditional exposition of the heresy of the pseudo-Sufis and the Wujudiyya, still the greatest threats to the Muslim community in his eyes, followed by, and conflated with, the Materialists, and the Christians (or even the "Magians" for that matter).[34]

Leiden, Cairo, and Mecca

In 1927, Snouck formally stepped down from his professorial post at Leiden University. Over the years he had come to embrace a a line of thinking extremely critical toward a system he felt was incapable of answering the demands of modern Indonesians. His objections are perhaps best summed up in a 1923 article in which he recalled the case of Arshad b. ʿAlwan of Serang, who had been left to languish in exile after the Cilegon Revolt.[35] On the occasion of his retirement, his major works, collected by his student A. J. Wensinck (1882–1939), had been bound together for Orientalist libraries around the world, and many of his pupils and colleagues were on hand, or at least invited, to raise their glasses to the doyen of Islamic studies. His protégés also set about establishing an institute for the study of Islam. Its subscribers included the same mix of invitees as his retirement party: royalty, past governors general and active Orientalists in Europe. The latter included Hazeu and Kern (who had also returned to Holland in frustration in 1926), Louis Massignon in Paris, and R. A. Nicholson in Cambridge. From further afield there were contributions from Muhammad Kurd ʿAli (1876–1953) in Damascus, Ahmad Zaki (1867–1934) in Cairo, ʿUmar Nasif in Jeddah, ʿAbd al-Rahman b. ʿAbdallah al-Zawawi in Mecca, the members of the Office for Native Affairs, as well as ʿUmar Manqush, ʿAli al-Habshi, Abu Bakr and Ismaʿil al-ʿAttas and, of course, the Djajadiningrats. Indeed in his introduction to the special commemorative volume of *Panji Poestaka*, Hoesein Djajadiningrat declared that he and his contemporaries honored Snouck as "the Guru, in an Oriental, mystical sense," adding that all other teachers were obscured by him and even deemed it an honor to be outshone by him.[36]

Absent from the initial celebrations, however, were the names of many of the Honorary Advisors and crucial friends enumerated in *Panji Poestaka*. Although some would not have been able to attend due to age, distance, or reduced finances, it would also seem that there had been a shift from the company of men like Sayyid 'Uthman and Hasan Mustafa to the likes of Ahmad Surkati and Agoes Salim, a shift that had global parallels.[37] Cairo remained an important node in Snouck's networks, and he was well apprised of the debates taking place in that city. Its new state university had been founded in 1908 under the directorship of Ahmad Zaki, and Zaki had even tried to recruit Snouck to his faculty.[38] Snouck also maintained connections with several Cairene intellectuals when they studied in Europe, including Mansur Fahmi and the brothers 'Ali and Mustafa 'Abd al-Raziq, who had all gone to France imbued with the ideas of Muhammad 'Abduh. But though Mansur Fahmi could write enthusiastically in 1925 of his hopes for a modern future under his leadership, he also indicated that the 'Abd al-Raziq brothers would find their path somewhat difficult.[39]

The older of the two, Mustafa 'Abd al-Raziq (1885–1947), graduated from al-Azhar in 1908 and went to the Sorbonne in 1909, where he studied under Émile Durkheim. From 1911 he had studied Islamic Law and Philosophy in Lyon, defending a thesis on al-Shafi'i. After his return to Egypt in 1914 he worked as a journalist and administrator, and was linked to the Umma Party. Following his removal from al-Azhar by King Fu'ad, he served as the inaugural professor of Islamic philosophy at Cairo Unversity from 1927 to 1938, where he edited 'Abduh's papers and wrote on the subject of Sufism. Indeed it appears that Mustafa had bought into the modern, Salafi consensus that Sufism was an antiquarian concern. A hint of his views on the subject may be found in a publication that began as a lecture he presented at Leiden in 1932 and which he published together with Massignon.[40]

Far more controversial was Mustafa's brother 'Ali (1888–1966), who had suggested that the institution of the caliphate was an innovation, perhaps echoing Snouck's lectures on the subject.[41] As Mansur Fahmi had informed Snouck in 1925, this led to him being stripped of his degree, for not all in Cairo were sympathetic to the program of either 'Abd al-Raziq, nor were all of the followers of 'Abduh on good terms with Snouck Hurgronje. Rashid Rida was a vocal critic of any talk of the demise of the caliphate, while Shakib Arslan (1869–1946) took Snouck to task for trying to strip the Muslims of the Far East of their proper loyalty to the wider community of believers and instill in them instead some false sense of national belonging. His dislike for what he took to be Snouck's plan for the creation of "Indonesian" Muslims did not prevent him, however, from relying on Snouck's writings when it came to documenting the history of those same people and the Arabs among them, nor yet did it stop Rashid Rida from sending Snouck a copy of his *Wahy al-muhammadi* (The Muhammadan Inspiration) in 1933, perhaps as an attempt to bring him around to his position.[42] It is also clear that Rida, who had frequented Naqshbandi circles in his youth, had a similar view of the ecstatic brotherhoods. Although he refrained from publishing his long-promised manuscript on the tariqas, his views were clear for he began slowly marching in lock step with the Saudis in the 1920s.

CLOUDS GATHER OVER THE OFFICE FOR NATIVE AFFAIRS

Despite acting as the Chancellor of Leiden University from 1922, Snouck Hurgronje had continued to train (or at least to examine) scholar-officials in his famously uncompromising fashion before they were allowed into the field or, for a small few and after additional studies in Arabic and Acehnese, into the Office for Native Affairs. Two graduates of this grueling program were G. F. Pijper and G.W.J. Drewes. The former completed a dissertation on the *Alf masa'il* under Van Ronkel in 1924 and then was sent to Batavia, where he served as Assistant Advisor, first under Kern and then under Émile Gobée (1881–1954).[43] There he began to develop connections with figures on all sides of Indies society, though he is today best known for his ties to reformists such as Ahmad Surkati, his deputy ʿAbdallah b. ʿAbd al-Qadir Harhara (marked in the British files as "a very dangerous enemy"), and Hamka (ʿAbd al-Malik Karim Amrullah), the prolix son of Hajji Rasul.[44] For his part, Drewes, the son of a Protestant school headmaster, defended his study of three nineteenth-century Akmalis in 1925, then moved to Java to take up a position at the Office for Native Affairs before being transferred to the Bureau for Popular Literature in the following year.[45]

Both Drewes and Pijper were highly admiring of their master, followed his advice, and perpetuated his memory at Leiden and Amsterdam respectively. Yet they were not treated equally. Far from it. Snouck commenced a long and fatherly correspondence with Pijper soon after his seventieth birthday, but it would seem that he never offered the young Drewes his field notes or in fact shared much of anything with him. Drewes thesis certainly lacked any reference to Snouck's manuscripts, which might well well have shed light on his subjects. At one point he resorted to quoting the English (rather than the original Dutch) edition of Snouck's *De Atjèhers* at length.

Despite the lack of his master's blessing—and in addition to other slightings, Snouck later passed him over in 1929 for a post that went to C. C. Berg (1900–90)—Drewes always held himself to his master's standards, emulating his harsh methods, and maintained an interest in the field of Islam past and present. Having attended a lecture in Yogyakarta by the Ahmadi Mirza Wali Ahmad Beg, he would write to his good friend Petrus Voorhoeve (1899–1996) in 1926 commending *Djåwå* as a journal that paid its contributers "pretty well." In that year he published a short article in the journal on Shaykh Yusuf.[46] What he did not mention, however, was that he was on its editorial board, together with Hoesein Djajadinigrat. It thus became the venue for some of his first reviews, which were famously tough, as when he pulled apart a thesis on Hamza Fansuri by J. Doorenbos.[47]

Soon after his arrival in Java, Drewes was appointed as a language official, a post that Pijper first thought quite a sinecure by contrast with his own initially hectic role. Yet, as we shall see below, things would change for Pijper, and indeed the Office in general, after the revolts of the mid-twenties, and he was most certainly not always the first scholar consulted. Rather it was Schrieke, then serving as professor of Ethnology and Sociology in Batavia, who was dispatched to write on the communist revolt in West Sumatra, rising to the post of Director of Education (and thus Pijper's ultimate boss) in 1929. This by no means pleased Pijper, who believed that Schrieke saw him as a rival authority on Islam in Batavia. True or not, Pijper's letters to Snouck, whom he once addressed as his "unattainable ideal," tell the unintended story of a divided Office under pressure to perform its task in the face of a Civil Service with little regard for the Advisors, and certainly little sympathy for Indonesians.

Things had not begun so gloomily for the Adjunct Advisor for Native Affairs. Soon after his arrival, Pijper had accompanied Kern on a tour of Banten in late January of 1926, meeting the then Chief Penghulu, Raden Muhammad 'Isa (b. 1874), another relative of the Djajadiningrats who had claimed to have seen Snouck in Jeddah as a youth. Still, it was a tense time, for the Resident was eager to know what Pijper could learn about the influence of communism on the locals. There was certainly anxiety in the family of the leading Kyai of Banten, Asnawi of Caringin. His son-in-law, (another) Ahmad Khatib, who had succeeded Hasan Djajadiningrat as Sarekat Islam head in Serang in 1920, was said to be the foremost communist in the district, and rumor had it that Asnawi had demanded that Ahmad Khatib divorce his daughter. Ahmad Khatib was by no means eager to do so, given he drew great prestige from the connection to a kyai who, much like Muhammad 'Isa, was related to the Djajadiningrat clan. Its members included the previous Regent of Serang, R. A. Djajadiningrat (d. 1933) and his eldest son, R.A.A. Djajadiningrat, Snouck's former student and then Regent of Batavia.[48]

Much of this information had come from Kyai Ru'yani, who claimed to have seen 'Abd al-Ghaffar himself when he had been in Mecca as a young man. Asnawi also claimed a connection of sorts with 'Abd al-Ghaffar, for his brother-in-law had been Snouck's manservant in Mecca. At least this is what Pijper learned on a return visit in September, when Kyai Ru'yani's tale was confirmed by the infirm Asnawi, after being greeted with utmost deference by the incumbent regent, another member of the extended Djajadiningrat clan. Needless to say, the position of both men and of the Djajadiningrats in general was imperilled when an uprising did break out in November. Although one member of the Raad van Indië predicted that the young Achmad Djajadiningrat was bound for the infamous concentration camp at Boven Digul, history repeated itself and the high-born priyayi escaped censure while the aged kyai was sent into exile.[49]

Such fates seemed not to interest Pijper too greatly at the time, for in his letters to Snouck he more often comments on how the very mention of the latter's alter ego 'Abd al-Ghaffar had opened many doors to him as he interviewed native officials and scholars in Arabic; which he initially practiced with a Palestinian, Tayseer Nabilcy (Taysir Nabulsi), and later with 'Abdallah b. Salim al-'Attas. He also paid regular tribute to the help he was getting from Hoesein Djajadiningrat, who explained all manner of legal rulings to him and backed up his explanations with both the writings of Sayyid 'Uthman and the "inestimable" Ahmad Surkati, who also taught him Arabic for three years.[50]

Another lifetime contact was "the developed" and "very pious" Bantenese, Sjoe'aib Sastradiwirja, who had instructed him in "the secrets" of the study of Islam and prayer since 1926.[51] Yet even after such daily interactions with this protégé of Agoes Salim (not to mention teacher, editor, and Jong Islamieten Bond member), Pijper could still confess to his surprise regarding their piety, as in this report on Hoesein Djajadiningrat, who was "by no means free from things Mohammedan":

> This has become apparent to me on numerous occasions, the last being when I asked him how I should speak of Islam in my lectures to the students of the Government Academy. When I turned to a critical historical introduction concerning the origin and earliest history of Islam, he pointed out its <u>hypothetical</u> character to me. He also asserted that Western scholarship had barely changed in its traditional treatment of Mohammad and his teaching; [but] I should have no particular problem with this teaching. For the moment I doubt this last point. How should I answer when an "enlightened" pupil asks me what to make of the compilation and the origins of the ideas of the Koran? Indeed the impact of European criticism is beginning to make inroads, and in papers and periodicals one finds reaction. In Bantam last year I met a young Assistant Wedana, who was interested in your *Verspreide Geschriften*! I should dearly like some direction from you as to how I should take up the <u>historical</u> aspect of my task.[52]

Snouck responded that he fully understood Pijper's recourse to the Djajadiningrats and Hoesein's increasingly "conservative" course:

> The traditions of his family and fatherland, and perhaps even personal inclination, provide ready inducements. The historical aspect of Islam is

indeed the trickiest to deal with for students from a Moslim milieu. It behooves one to act with extreme tact to transmit what is necessary without causing insult or offence. Sometimes the communication of results intended by the scholars can be objectively separated without implying that the speaker who expressed them is in agreement. Anything that seems like a rebuke can be left out. In later years my audience also consisted of a section of the youth of Mohammedan houses; but I never noted if one thing or another gave offence, for I was always very careful lest I adopt an ironic or disparaging tone.[53]

Snouck's reply seems to have merely triggered Pijper to relate yet another incredulous anecdote, recalling how, despite his Western education, Hoesein agreed with some of Agoes Salim's statements concerning the inherent perfection of Islamic law as it related to women.[54]

But if Pijper worried what Muslims would make of his lectures, and of Dutch scholarship in general, he would in time become more concerned about what his superiors thought of his office. In the field he soon learned that the Office for Native Affairs was held in low regard by members of the Civil Service. Pijper was also unimpressed by the government's reluctance to become involved in clerical matters, which meant that the state had little, if any, need of the solutions proposed by his colleagues.[55] Within a matter of months Pijper's enthusiasm was replaced by a growing sense of confinement in a bureau that he felt allowed him far too little scope for engagement with the peoples of the Indies. He even proposed taking a year's leave in Banten to study local conditions so that he would be better able to draft rulings on so many matters that seemed all too impenetrable too him.[56]

Snouck's response was first concerned with official business, for the legists with whom he had often discussed matters of Islamic law were all of the opinion that the principle of non-interference on the part of the state was only a slogan, and that in practice the state was obliged to take the lead, given that it was the only institution able to back up religious edicts. In this regard Snouck felt that the calls made in native circles for the government and administration to stay out of religious affairs were a mistake.[57] As for Pijper's secret hopes for a study leave, after bemoaning the fact that the only free time *he* had ever enjoyed was on the voyages between Europe and the Indies, a bemused Snouck urged his junior colleague to take stock of his position, for his numerous trips had given him access to many personal experiences and more would doubtless follow.[58]

Things seemed to return to an even keel for a time, but by 1930 there were further indications of pressure being placed on the organization from above, which produced increasing friction among the staff; especially between Gobée and his European underlings who resented the official demands he placed upon them to the cost of the scholarly endeavors they would have preferred to pursue. When Pijper's request to extend a study tour at Ambon was not even answered by the Resident, Pijper too lashed out at Gobée for having sent him on a fool's errand in Ramadan, declaiming that the "curse" of the Office for Native Affairs was the superficial quality of their research.[59] Then there were the Civil Service editors to worry about, as when his official entry on Islam for the *Indisch Verslag* (Indies Report) of 1931 was released, to his mind, "much mutilated and ineptly edited."[60] And in the same year he noted "dark clouds" gathering over the Office for Native Affairs, when the sudden news came in November that the conservative new Governor General, B. C. De Jonge (in office 1931–36), even planned to put the Office under the direct purview of the Civil Service.[61]

Such fears were somewhat alleviated in 1932, when it was felt that Governor General De Jonge had been released from the grip of the opponents of the *Stuw*, the metropolitan movement advocating greater emancipation for Indonesians than the token parliament (Volksraad) allowed. Still, speeches praising the Office for Native Affairs, delivered in the Volksraad by Wiranatakoesoema (1888–1965)—with the support of Mohammed Husni Thamrin (1894–1941) and Wiwoho Probohadidjojo of the JIB—increased Civil Service suspicions. Be that as it may, with the departure of C. O. van der Plas (1891–1977), whose conflicts with Gobée had been particularly fierce, Pijper found himself in an office that was far quieter than when he had first found it. He thus spent more time writing to Snouck about his love of Arabic literature and his admiration for modern Egyptian literati such as Taha Husayn, Mansur Fahmi, and Zaki Mubarak, while evincing a degree of disdain for many of the local Hadramis whom he believed were ever more conscious of being left behind in the race to progress.

Pijper remained, however, concerned with Islamic movements and figures of all types, deeming the framed portrait of ʿAli al-Habshi as useful as that of ʿAbd al-Ghaffar for striking up conversations in his office.[62] He was regularly dispatched to the congresses of Muhammadiyah, the Jong Islamieten Bond, and the hardline Persis of Bandung, and took an interest in the final years at Manado of the tariqa master Arshad Banten, (1854–1934). Also known as Arshad al-Tawil, "the tall one," in contradistinction to the shorter Arshad b. ʿAlwan al-Qasir, he had been exiled to Sulawesi after the Cilegon uprising and had stayed there, despite being allowed to return to Banten in 1918. Indeed he was the leading tariqa shaykh to the Muslim minority, even serving on the Raad Agama. Pijper apparently found the report in which his name appeared interesting for various reasons, including its mention of a tariqa, "apparently still in existence here."[63]

When he died in 1934, Arshad al-Tawil's funeral was attended by Christians and Muslims alike, and the local paper ran an obituary that must have pleased

Snouck, who remembered both Arshads, short and tall, as victims of the colonial system:

> At the age of more than 100 years, bapa Hadji Banten has died in his home in Kampoeng Koemaraka as the oldest internee in Minahasa. He was famous in every corner of Minahasa, throughout Indonesia and the Netherlands, and even in the Hedjaz! Known as Hadji Arsjad Tawil, he was famous in the letters of learned men in Leiden, and bapa Hadji was a close friend of the savant of Islam, Prof. Snouck Hurgronje, the professor in Leiden who teaches at the school for senior judges. The late bapa Hadji came as a young man to Airmadidi via the Glodok prison in Djakarta, for he was accused of being an instigator of the Banten uprising (not the communist one in 1926). In Minahasa bapa Hadji worked as the penghoeloe of the Landraad and as a famous goeroe of Islam and as a leader of santeri Islam. At 5 in the morning, on the 20th of March 1934, the body of bapa Hadji was accompanied by thousands of Muslims and non-Muslims to the Islamic graveyard on Kokaweg. The Muslim community of all Minahasa say that the grave of Bapa Hadji Banten will become a *kramat*.[64]

The account probably pleased Pijper too, who most certainly had his own particularly Christian take on Islam. The agnostic Snouck must have managed to suppress an ironic tone very effectively in his Leiden lectures, given Pijper's free theorizing of the necessary prerequesites for mixing with Muslims. Consider his remarks on the "calm, healthy perspective" of a nominee for the post of Jeddah Consul, C. Adriaanse (1896–1964):

> He comes from a Reformed circle, which will certainly help him come to understand the Moslim thoughtworld, for which one must always, in my opinion, have one of three things: a Reformed background, or a religious background—above all with a Biblical orientation, or yet Semitic blood. By this I mean to say that unless at least one of these three conditions is satisfied, then one's scholarship on Islam will never be worth anything.[65]

It was equally clear that his attendance at a debate between Persis and Ahmadiyah, followed by a congress of the NU, was very much a wasted Easter. At the former meeting, there was lively debate on both sides, though Pijper felt that the Ahmadis, with their techniques honed against the Christians in India, had rhetorical skills that were far superior to the "defenders of orthodoxy, no matter how learned and acute." This was followed, at Batavia, by the congress of "the most right-wing group," the association of the "old fashioned theologians."

This congress lasted for six days, with meetings every morning and afternoon. The physical strain was greater for me than the mental, for it is extremely exhausting to sit on the ground in the *sila*-position for so long. One was surrounded by the finest flower of Java's kjahis, come from Bantam to Banjoewangi. These were men estranged from modern life, with no interest in politics so long as it leaves their own thoughtworld untrammeled. Still, there was engagement with actual topics, such as postmortem examinations and the Sajjid question, though from a very conservative perspective.[66]

Pijper also remarked that all sort of questions were dealt with through reference to the traditional books, such as, for example, whether it could be considered an "emergency" (and thus permissible) for women to go to the market unveiled and unaccompanied, as was standard practice in the Indies. When the question was asked whether women, on attaining Paradise, would get forty male servants, the gathering of beturbanned 'ulama' apparently laughed out loud, a fact that Pijper felt illustrated the spirit of the congress.

> I, the only Saul among the prophets, was treated with great courtesy (at the congresses of modern-oriented Moslims one feels a less friendly mood toward the stranger in their midst), and I felt as though I was (apart from the pain in my joints) sitting in the lap of Abraham. But: it was a loss of six workdays, and nights.[67]

Even if he was more comfortable with "orthodox" traditionalists, Pijper felt he could offer much on modern movements as well, such as al-Irshad and Muhammadiyah, whose leaders he knew well. They included Raden Muhtadi Natadiningrat, the son of Muhammad 'Isa. But Muhtadi, a graduate of the training school for native medics and the head of Muhammadiyah's "seminary" in Yogyakarta, was a friendly discussant. By contrast Pijper had a harder time with an Egyptian-trained tutor who was "fiercely anti-Western."[68]

Of course not all Azharites were so hostile. The son of Kyai Ru'yani, who rose to be deputy head of the Indonesian lodge at al-Azhar in the early 1930s, would be mourned by Indonesians and Dutchmen alike upon his untimely death in 1945.[69] In any case Pijper could live with both sorts of activists. As he wrote, "Moehammadijah maintains itself as a formidable organisation. The members are not, to my mind, always sympathetic, but I have respect for their work."[70] He could also be somewhat patronising to Snouck on the question of what Islam was and the importance of his potential contributions on the modern trends in Indonesia. A softer Snouck, counselling patience at all times, had often urged him to publish, in the words of Friedrich Max Müller (1823–1900), the "chips" from his workshop rather than waiting to build up all the potential pieces of information into one masterwork. In one instance he regretted that while he had come back to Holland burdened with all manner of files that he had planned to exploit for his writings, these were successively pushed back as some new, and more urgent, project was begun, so that they lost their "actuality."[71]

Impelled by such advice, Pijper would gather his chips as his *Fragmenta Islamica*, derived from primary source investigations on the place of women in education and the mosque, divorce and apostasy, and the recent arrival of the Tijaniyya brotherhood.[72] By the time his book appeared, Pijper was at last confident that the Office for Native Affairs was no longer in danger of being placed under the Civil Service, even though those in authority let it be known that Governor General De Jonge still regarded the Office as without obvious utility.[73] He even tempered his rhetoric regarding Schrieke, admitting that he had saved his job when it appeared under threat. Pijper, however, never really came to trust the man who would finally depart for Holland (and Amsterdam's Tropical Institute) in 1935.[74]

Pijper ultimately rose to be the Advisor for Native Affairs in 1936, whereupon he may have gained a better understanding of the pressures that had been placed on his mentors. The increasing mistrust on both sides of Indies society had certainly caused Schrieke great discomfort, and he had been opposed to the internment of many of the nationalists in Boven Digul.[75] He also joined the *Stuw*, as did Drewes, who would moved through the ranks to become director of the Bureau for Popular Literature in 1930, and then succeeded Hoesein Djajadiningrat as director of the Batavian Law School in 1935.

But fewer and fewer Indonesians themselves had the patience for being patronized, either at home or abroad. There was also more questioning of Snouck's legacy among Indonesians and those with an interest in Indonesia. While Shakib Arslan's revised translation of Lothrop Stoddard's *New World of Islam* (published in 1923) now featured a lecture on the Netherlands Indies given in Cairo in 1929 by Snouck's ally Isma'il al-'Attas, it also reported Arslan's exchanges with the doyen of oriental studies. Here he claimed to have challenged the Dutchman's published views, upon which Snouck supposedly acknowledged that the "heretics" among the Jawi Muslims were always more fanatically opposed to the Dutch than the properly religious.[76]

These exchanges began at the Leiden Congress of Orientalists in 1932 at which the celebrated writer Taha Husayn was also present and, apparently, in full voice. For his part a world-weary Snouck—who certainly admired Taha Husayn's powers of recall but grumbled that he lacked the requisite "tact" to mix with normal people—would see his own voice projected further with the English translation of volume two of *Mekka* fresh off the presses.[77] The translator (the former British Consul J. H. Monahan) declared that Snouck's description of the city was "not entirely out of date," but he and the author knew full well of the enormous changes in process there. The subsequent Dutch consuls Gobée, Van der Plas, and D. van der Meulen had kept their master fully informed of events in Arabia, and Prince Faysal b. Sa'ud had even begun sending him photos of a changing city after meeting in Leiden in 1926.[78]

Snouck felt that the relationship between the Netherlands and the current Kingdom of Saudi Arabia were extremely good in comparison with previous regimes, and he probably went to his grave in 1936 with one less worry on that score. There were those in Arabia, however, who wanted to show that relations were equally healthy with the Indies. This was clearly the message in 1937 when a new periodical was launched at Mecca, and by Sumatrans of the sort that Episcopalian Reverend Raymond LeRoy Archer (1887–1970) would have pronounced "orthodox" given the tenor of a report he wrote on the West Coast in that year.[79] Entitled *al-Nida' al-islami / Perseruan Islam*, the Meccan journal was an attempt to bring Jawi students back to the Hijaz. The tone of the articles was decidedly reformist, but Sufism was not so much condemned as its lazy modern shaykhs. The editors concentrated on the achievements of Southeast Asians—named explicitly now as "Malays" and "Indonesians"—and recounted the Islamization of their homelands by Arab traders. This narrative must have seemed only natural to them, but there was a strong reaction when one of the Arab writers, Husayn Ahmad Hasanayn, cited the work of C. C. Berg on the question of the Malay language being riddled with "eccentricities" when used to translate works of Arabic.[80]

A similar annoyance greeted concerns voiced in Medan's *Pedoman Masyarakat* in 1938. Under the rubric "dangerous books," he complained that there were now thousands of Western tracts attacking Islam using the poisonous books in circulation among Muslims themselves. He took special aim at what he described as tales of nonsense and superstition supposedly imported from Persia and India.

> If other people do not study the real truth of Islam, and if the young Western-educated intellectuals see the contents of such books that are in the hands of the Muslims of today, then they will bring down a verdict that Islam is a religion fit for savage peoples at the far ends of islands devoid of culture. When we studied in the *soeraus* of fifteen years ago, the book *Bada-i'oez Zoehoer* was still in favor among students. There it was stated that the world was located on the tip of the horn of a giant cow which, when frightened, would shake its head and cause extreme earthquakes!

Perhaps worse in the author's view was a work known as the *Daqa'iq al-akhbar* (The Details of the Reports), which asserted that the Light of Muhammad had preceded creation, flying through the seven levels of heaven in the form of a parrot. Then there were such "Shi'a" stories, such as that of Muhammad Hanafiyya, and the litanies and magic spells of the tariqas that were so enthralling to villagers and which were all for sale in the bookshops. Some even claimed that God and man were one and that prayers were no longer necessary for the elite!

For such reasons, beyond protesting Western books, Muslim authors and writers must also attend to the illness that plagues their own community in order to prevent us from become a defenseless laughing stock. Remember: Sjech Moehammad Abdoeh gained a great victory when he argued with the philosopher Arnest Renan [*sic*]. Yet he failed when, at the end of the polemic, the philosopher said "I acknowledge that I have been defeated when faced by your arguments, yet the state of the Muslims which I see today makes it impossible for me to capitulate in the face of your information . . ." Take heed![81]

Despite their rhetoric on the physical conditions endured by so many Indonesian Muslims, many reformists believed that the war on medieval deviation among the common people was slowly being won, just as that on colonial rule was set to accelerate. With the gathering storm in Europe and Asia, some would even sniff victory for an identifiable Muslim homeland. On the very eve of Japanese occupation, newspapers with a decidedly Islamic inflection pushed hard for concessions from a shadow state now cut off from the metropole, which had fallen to Germany in May of 1940. Featuring articles by future president Soekarno, Solo's *Islam Raya* even unveiled a new cover showing a pseudo-Moorish minaret set against a rough map of the archipelago. The editors proudly proclaimed of their cover:

> Brothers, you shall certainly recognize it. It's not exactly beautiful, but it is sweet enough! Try, brothers, to pay immediate attention, think on it for a moment. What lesson can we take from it? As with other such images, this one too illustrates, very simply, the Foundation, Aim, and Aspiration and Memories of "Islam Raya." **People of Indonesia!** Imagine. Reflect. Contemplate! How glittering and dazzling can be the land for which we would spill our blood! Secure, peaceful and content. We want to witness its original golden age and . . . even more . . . one to come! Still . . . this is all dreams and aspirations. It needs to be realized. And the conditions? Faith, hope, and action. But the most important thing is that we become AWARE. Take heed, and God shall be with us.[82]

Others too felt that the Indonesia of the future needed appropriately golden Muslim memories. Agoes Salim had marked the Prophet's birthday in 1941 with an extended address entitled *Riwajat Kedatangan Islam di Indonesia* (The Story of the Coming of Islam to Indonesia). Now the ertswhile servant of colonial authority (and believing nemesis of a cynical Pijper) argued that Western literature needed to be reread against non-Western sources, holding that it was an "unsatisfactory" account at best that claimed Islam had only come to his homeland in the thirteenth century. He pointed to Chinese sources that he believed were suggestive of an earlier Muslim presence and invoked Shakib Arslan to wonder whether Islam had in fact come through North African hands in the first place.[83]

Dutch scholars were about to be evicted from their priveleged places, but they were not aware of their fate at the time. It was scholarly business as usual. Pijper gave well-received lectures in Batavia on the loyal Arabs of the Indies, extolling al-Habshi as the inspirational heir to Sayyid 'Uthman, and he continued his discussions with members of al-Irshad and Persatuan Islam on the path to a projected volume on reformism.[84] Drewes, just prior to taking what was intended to be a temporary post in Leiden, published a book with Raden Poerbatjaraka (1884–1964) on the dogged persistence of stories of 'Abd al-Qadir in Indonesian literature. At Utrecht Jan Edel, making use of manuscripts collected by Djajadiningrat and Pijper, defended a thesis under Juynboll on the *Hikayat Hasan al-Din*, in which he was at greater pains to establish the identies of various Bantenese persona than to question the exact nature of references to Khidr or the rites of various Sufi tariqas.[85] In the same vein, Voorhoeve visited Barus in hopes of finding the tomb of Hamza Fansuri, but the locals could only show him what they believed to be that of an Arab called Shaykh Mahmud.[86] In a letter written seven months later, he expressed the hope that Drewes might soon come to Sumatra.[87] However events soon overtook all and sundry. In March of 1942, the Dutch forces and administration were swept away and Japanese converts were sent to select mosques and to the offices once run by Snouck's successors. Despite an abortive Dutch return in 1945–49, the formative era of collaboration and contestation was at an end. And with it Indonesia's colonial past.

Conclusion

The disastrous events of the Afdeeling B and its aftermath did not immediately destroy the relationship between the colonial advisors and the state, but they showed only too clearly that matters modern were not resolved. They also empowered forces whose ascent would result in the practical excommunication of the Office for Native Affairs from key decisions impacting the lives of Indonesians disabused of the promises of colonial tutelege. The campaigners of Sarekat Islam and related bodies would be forced to withdraw as well from a political field increasingly dominated by nationalist and communist agitators, who directed their rhetorical attacks at those they believed had engendered the pervasive backwardness of Indonesians. Their viewpoint could be challenged, but their attacks harmonized with the global scholarly consensus on what real Islam was, both in its vital and its historical states. Times had changed, and Indonesians would have to change as well.

Conclusion

It is my hope that this book will make a meaningful contribution to the study of Islam in Southeast Asia and to broader scholarship on the Muslim World. I have questioned the current consensus on the essence of Indonesia's religious formation by highlighting assumptions formed during the colonial era. This has not been a straightforward path, hence it is worth recounting at this point the overall arc to show how colonial scholarship interpreted the precolonial, and then inflected particular strands of reformist Sufi self-critique into modernist discourse.

A certain amount of preliminary work was necessary to set the stage. The first chapters teased out certain elements of what is known of the region's Islamization and suggested that genealogical claims about Sufi learning have at times overwritten older memories of conversion. Once we rethink such claims, we must also rethink the notion that Sufism inevitably provided the accommodatory mechanism for Southeast Asian conversion or that it explains Indonesia's oft-trumpeted tradition of ecumenical tolerance. I have argued to the contrary that the (generally subsequent) introduction of formalized techniques of Sufi learning was often tied to scholarly intolerance of popular variance that perhaps began as emulation of regal prerogatives. In this sense an observation made by Christopher Bayly seems apposite: what was required in most contexts was acknowledgement of the superiority of the emperor's cult rather than uniformity of belief.[1] Suffice it to say that, by the eighteenth century, increasingly intense connections between Asian courts and Middle Eastern centers of learning engendered appeals to the principle that normative legal practices should define the standard of Islam for most believers. Such appeals were accompanied by the embrace or (less commonly) rejection of foreigners and attempts to restrict Sufi knowledge to a learned elite who could sit in judgement over them. In this regard I have also suggested that the propagation of Egyptian scholarship was crucial in an endeavor arguably global in its scope. From one perspective, however, this project, aimed at the maintenance of regal authority in various Jawi centers, was paradoxically both stalled and enhanced by European interference. The proscriptions of the courts of Java in particular seem not to have mattered as an ever-more consciously Muslim population took advantage of modern transportation networks in order to pursue opportunities for mass education in the name of the sultans of old. But while their retainers and descendents may have nodded appreciatively at the increasing numbers of pesantrens, many were perturbed by the popularity of the newer tariqa learning that was offered by teachers who claimed a firm connection to Mecca and the mantle of the Prophet.

Perhaps the most significant changes to relations between Muslims on the global stage came in the wake of the cataclysmic wars that befell Arabia, Sumatra, and Java when a new classical corpus came into print, overseen by well-known scholars in such centers and Cairo and Singapore. In what may at first seem to be paradox, this corpus was claimed by the popular Sufi masters who represented the broadest spectrum of Shari'a-oriented piety and direct experience of the Holy Places. To be sure, the increasingly antagonistic bodies of official jurists and popular Sufis, each armed with and debating printed texts, was hardly of one, anti-colonial, accord. Rather we can observe the emergence of a Muslim public sphere that was highly contested under Dutch rule, and whose partisans would even seek to engage with that structure of authority in order to pursue their own agendas.

Before exploring such histories, however, I turned in the second part to introduce the Europeans in order that we might rethink the relationship between the trading companies and older metropolitan clerical endeavors, taking aim at the oft-spouted contention that the Dutch were solely concerned with profit in Asia. We should now recognize that there were Netherlandic scholars who attempted to work out how they should treat the members of a faith that they believed they understood perfectly and which the most optimistic among them believed they could even eliminate. Of course knowledge was not enough. Familiarity with Islam and the contempt that it too often bred ensured that little was done systematically to address Islam as a challenge. That moment came only with the incursion of rival Britain at the end of the eighteenth century. From that time onward the increasingly independent pesantrens bared their teeth in Java, and the radical reformists of Sumatra turned their fires of jihad against Western interlopers.

Islam at last loomed as something far greater than a troublesome creed foisted on a mild and passive population by an undifferentiated mix of Arabs and hajjis. The Dutch would therefore attempt to take on Islam in a way that would be of service to their colonial state. Still, the vicissitudes of funding and academic rivalries weakened this effort and resulted in the production of juridical manuals drawn from archives rather than from the field. It was the missionaries once more who made the key breakthroughs in alerting the metropole as to who was, and who was not, a "Muslim," preferring to heed the words of local aristocrats and Arabs over those of the many itinerant hajjis and "priests" who were depriving the former of their authority.

Such histories of misrecognition and misinformation, palpably exposed by the Cilegon massacre of 1888, made the career of the brash young Orientalist Snouck Hurgronje. As we followed his travels and work, we saw how Protestant scholarly concerns became enmeshed with both colonial imperatives and reformist visions of Islam, in an itinerary that whisked us from Mecca to Java and from Cairo to Leiden. Snouck arguably favored the elitist interpretations of his key Muslim allies over their too-populist opponents. Both agreed that the tariqas were the leftovers of a bygone age of Indic-inspired ignorance. In time Snouck, exploiting the textual remnants of learning that had lost its lustre on Java, would train his own coterie of scholar-officials who never questioned the conclusions of their master on the subject of Indonesians past, present, or future. Ironically definitive proof of an engagement between Sufism and Indic syncretism was never to be found in the texts Snouck brought back to Leiden, but this mattered little, for great changes were afoot in the colonies. The Dutch certainly looked with favor on the emergent trends in Islamic discourse spreading from Cairo and Singapore that urged Muslims to react to colonial rule by finding their own modern paths. These would be modern paths that of course would allow them to regain their places at the table of modern nations only at some ill-defined future date.

Snouck and his followers, Dutch and Indonesian alike, enjoyed access to the highest echelons of colonial power and influence only so as long as the modern Muslims they smiled upon set aside their hopes for independence. But as time passed these hopes seemed ever more attainable. Colonial subjects who had for so long collaborated with the colonial state began to condemn it, and their condemnation became all the more voluble once nationalists and the state alike started to abandon their Orientalist middlemen. Indeed, the credibility (and therefore the mutual utility) of the Advisors was irreparably damaged by the end of the 1920s. Still few critics in either camp questioned their historical conclusions. Those are with us still today. There were Islamic tinges to such incidents as that at Garut in 1919 to be sure, but few colonial officials were on the lookout now for Meccan-inspired Sufis. There were more obvious global dangers to hand: socialists and communists, who had done their mingling in Canton or Paris. The modern genie was out of the bottle, and he was no Sufi, for Sufis belonged to far distant pasts. And one can make anything one likes of the past.

Glossary

abangan—Jav. "red ones," those said to be less committed to the formalities of Islamic practice.

adat—Mal. (Ar. ʿada) indigenous traditions often respected or tolerated in Islamic societies.

afdeeling—Du. administrative subdivision.

agama—Mal. religion.

akhlaq—Ar. morals, ethics.

ʿ*Alawi*, pl. ʿ*Alawiyyun*—Ar. patronymic indicating descent from the Prophet by way of a ninth century emigrant to Hadramawt, Ahmad b. ʿIsa (820–924).

ʿ*alim*, pl. ʿ*ulama*'—Ar. learned person, a Muslim scholar.

ʿ*Arafa*—Plain outside Mecca where the ritual of "standing" is observed as part of the Hajj.

*a*ʿ*yan kharija*—Ar. the demonstrable external essences of divinity.

*a*ʿ*yan thabita*—Ar. the "fixed" or "eternal" internal essences of divinity.

baraka—Ar., Mal. divine blessings imparted at holy sites or in the presence of esteemed teachers.

batik—Mal., Jav. traditional Southeast Asian dyed fabric.

batin—Ar. inner nature of things.

*bay*ʿ*a*—Ar. declaration of allegiance.

*bid*ʿ*a*—Ar. innovation.

bilad al-jawa—Ar. Southeast Asia.

bupati—Jav. regent, the highest ranking native in the Dutch bureaucratic hierarchy.

contrôleur—Du. Inspector.

dajjal—Ar. deceiver, Antichrist.

dalang—Mal. (Jav. *dhalang*) puppeteer, most usually of traditional shadow-puppets.

debus—Jav. (Ar. *dabus*) awl used in ritual piercing, associated with the Rifaʿi order.

dhikr—Ar. "recollection" of God through mental or physical régimes often prescribed by a Sufi master.

Ethici—Du. Dutch political reformers who were avowedly concerned for the welfare of Holland's Indies subjects.

fatwa, pl. *fatawa*—Ar. juridical opinion voiced by a Muslim scholar, known specifically as a *mufti*.

fiqh—Ar. Islamic jurisprudence.

habib—Ar. "beloved [of God]," honorific title adopted by some ʿAlawi sayyids.

hadith, pl. *ahadith*—Ar. tradition related or exemplified by the Prophet.

Hajj—Ar. visitation of Mecca and associated ceremonies performed at the beginning of the month of Dhu l-hijja.

hajji, fem. *hajja*—Ar. one who has completed the Hajj.

Hanafi—Ar. of the juridical school attributed to Nu'man b. Thabit Abu Hanifa (699–767).

Hanbali—Ar. of the juridical school attributed to Ahmad b. Hanbal (780–855).

haqq—Ar. ultimate reality; God.

Haramayn—Ar. the two holy sites, Mecca and Medina.

hashiya—Ar. marginal gloss.

Hijra—Ar. emigration of Prophet Muhammad to Medina in 620, taken as the starting date of the Muslim Calendar.

hikayat—Mal. (Ar. *hikaya*) romance, tale, or account.

hilal—Ar. crescent moon.

hulubalang—Mal. Commander.

ihram—Ar. state of ritual purity necessary to undertake the Hajj.

ijaza—Ar. certificate given by an 'alim granting authority to teach a particular text or give instruction in a particular ritual.

ijma'—Ar. consensus, often meant as the scholarly consensus reached by the 'ulama.'

ijtihad—Ar. individual interpretation of Islamic sources.

'ilm—Ar. knowledge.

imam—Ar. leader, most often of communal prayers.

Indologie—Du. study of the Indies and its civilizations.

inlander—Du. native.

insan al-kamil, al-—Ar. "the perfect man," the ideal of Sufi cosmography.

Irshadi, pl. Irshadiyyun—Ar. follower of al-Irshad, the Arab reformist movement on Java.

jaksa—Mal. judge.

Jawa—Ar. Java, Southeast Asia.

Jawi (1)—Ar. anything of or pertaining to Southeast Asia.

Jawi (2)—Mal. modified Arabic script employed to write Malay.

Jawi, pl. Jawa (3)—Ar. inhabitant of Southeast Asia.

jimat—Mal., Jav. talisman (derived from Ar. *'azima*).

jubba—Ar. cloak often worn by the 'ulama' or by holders of authority.

Ka'ba—Ar. central shrine of Mecca and focal point for Muslim prayers.

kafir, pl. *kuffar*—Ar. unbeliever.

kampung—Mal. village, ward.

kaum—Mal. (Ar. *qawm*) a grouping of people, generally understood in Indonesia to be pious Muslims.

Kaum Muda—Mal. young faction, reformists.

Kaum Tua—Mal. old faction, traditionalists.

kayfiyya—Ar. means, a manual for sufi practice.

khalifa—Ar. representative, often of a Sufi shaykh.

khalwa—Ar. isolation, withdrawal.

khatib—Ar. giver of the Friday address, see *khutba*.

khutba—Ar. address given at Friday's congregational prayer.

kitab—Ar. book; Mal. religious book.

kramat—Jav. holy site.

kraton—Mal., Jav. royal enclosure.

kris, keris—Mal., Jav. dagger, often believed to be a receptacle of mystical power.

kufr—Ar. unbelief, rejection of Islam.

kyai—Jav. respected Islamic scholar.

lahir—Mal., Jav. exoteric aspects of Islamic practice.

langgar—Mal. Jav. village school, generally smaller than a pesantren or pondok.

latifa—Ar. subtlety or pressure point.

madhhab, pl. *madhahib*—Ar. juridical school of Islam.

magang—Jav. clerk, the lowest *priyayi* echelon in the Dutch administrative system.

Maliki—Ar. member of the juridical school attributed to Malik b. Anas (711–795).

mansak, pl. *manasik*—Ar. guidebook for the conduct of the Hajj.

ma'rifa—Ar. gnosis, knowledge of the divine.

martabat tujuh—Mal. the seven grades of being.

Masjid al-haram, al-—Ar. the mosque enclosing the Ka'ba in Mecca.

mawlid—Ar. commemoration of the birth of the Prophet.

mufti—Ar. jurisconsult.

muhaddith—Ar. scholar of tradition; cf. hadith.

muhaqqiq, pl. *muhaqqiqun*—Ar. *lit.* those of verification; seekers of the ultimate reality, cf. *haqq, tahqiq.*

murid—Ar. Sufi disciple.

nagari—Minang. village.

nahda—Ar. arising, renaissance.

negara Islam—Mal. Islamic state.

negeri—Mal. polity, town.

ngelmu—Jav. knowledge, see *'ilm.*

orang putih—Mal. "white ones," the religiously pure; analagous Jav. *putihan.*

pangeran—Jav., Mal. prince.

penghulu—Mal. leader or authority, most often a religious official supported by a stipend.

peranakan—Mal. locally born person of foreign extraction.

perdikan, pradikan—Jav. village or school exempt from taxation.

pesantren—Jav. boarding school for religious instruction.

pondok—Mal. hut or residence, also a religious school.

prang sabil—Mal. holy war.

predikant, pl. *predikanten*—Du. clergyman.

priester—Du. priest.

priesterraad, pl. *priesterraden*—Du. court or council with authority over matters of Islamic law.

primbon—Jav. instructional manual.

priyayi—Jav. Javanese aristocratic elite.

putihan—Jav. "white ones," the religiously pure; see also *orang putih.*

qadi—Ar. judge.

qibla—Ar. direction of the Ka'ba in Mecca to which all mosques are oriented.

Raad van Indië—Du. Council of the Indies, the preeminent advisory council in the Netherlands Indies.

rabita—Ar. connection; in Sufism more specifically that made between shaykh and disciple.

Ramadan—Ar. fasting month.

ratib—Ar. litany; Sufi devotional exercise.

rechtzinnig—Du. orthodox.

riwaq, pl. *arwiqa*—Ar. hall of residence at al-Azhar and other major teaching mosques.

Rum—Ar. (Mal. Rum) Ottoman Empire.

rust en orde—Du. peace and tranquility.

salat—Ar. five daily prayers enjoined upon Muslims.

salik—Ar. strider (on the mystical path), see *suluk*.

santri—Jav. student of religion.

sayyid, pl. *sada*—Ar. descendent of the Prophet; cf. *habib*.

sembahyang—Mal. prayer.

Shafi'i—Ar. member of the juridical school attributed to Muhammad b. Idris al-Shafi'i (767–820).

shahada—Ar. declaration of belief in one God and Muhammad as his Prophet.

shari'a—Ar. Holy Law as revealed to Muhammad and interpreted by the 'ulama.'

shaykh, pl. *shuyukh*—Ar. elder or leader, most often a senior 'alim or Sufi master.

sifa—Ar. quality, characteristic.

Sufi—Ar. Muslim mystic.

suluk—Ar. striding on the mystic path; Jav. mystical poetry.

Sunna—Ar. orthodox tradition built on the emulation of the life of the Prophet.

Sunni—Ar. member of the orthodox community.

sura—Ar. chapter of the Qur'an.

surau—Mal. prayer hall.

syair—Mal. poem.

tabligh—Ar. preaching.

tafsir—Ar. exegesis.

tahlil—Ar. the declaration *la ilaha illa llah*, "there is no god other than God."

tahqiq—Ar. verification.

tariqa, pl. *turuq*—Ar. mystical fraternity.

tasawwuf—Ar. mysticism.

tawajjuh—Ar. face-to-face encounter between shaykh and disciple.

tawassul—Ar. intercession granted by a saint.

Tuanku—Mal. religious leader.

umma, pl. *umam*—Ar. community, nation.

Volkslectuur—Du. [Office for] Popular Literature, a.k.a. Balai Poestaka.

vreemde oosterlingen—Du. foreign orientals.

wahdat al-wujud—Ar. unity of being between God and creation.

Wahhabi—Ar. follower of the teachings of the Wahhabiya.

Wahhabiyya—Ar. pietist movement founded in Arabia by Muhammad b. 'Abd al-Wahhab (1703–87).

wakil—Ar. deputy.

wali, pl. *awliya'*—Ar. saint, someone "close to God."

waqf, pl. *awqaf*—Ar. endowment pledged in perpetuity for personal or public use.

wasiyya—Ar. last testament, admonition.

wayang—Mal. and Jav. shadow play.

wedono—Jav. low-ranking official charged with the supervision of a small township.

wujudi—Ar. an adherent of the philosophy of the "unity of being"; cf. *wahdat al-wujud*.

Zabaj—Ar. archaic name for Southeast Asia.

zahir—Ar. the external, see *lahir*.

zakat—Ar. alms.

zawiya—Ar. lodge for Sufis.

ziyara—Ar. visitation, usually of a holy tomb in search of *tawassul*.

Notes

PREFACE

1. Munawar Khalil, "Snouck Hurgronje: Orientalis atau mata-mata ulung?" *Forum Keadilan*, edisi khusus, 8–40 (9 January 2000): 78–79. This account is a summary of P. S. van Koningsveld's *Snouck Hurgronje en de Islam: Acht artikelen over leven en werk van een oriëntalist uit het koloniale tijdperk* (Leiden: Faculteit der Godgeleerdheid, Rijksuniversiteit Leiden, 1988; Indonesian translation, publ. Bandung: Girimukti Pusaka, 1989).
2. Clifford Geertz, *Islam Observed: Religious Developments in Morocco and Indonesia* (Chicago and London: The University of Chicago Press, 1968), 12.
3. Frederick Cooper, *Colonialism in Question: Theory, Knowledge, History* (Berkeley, CA: University of California Press, 2005).

PART ONE: INSPIRATION, REMEMORATION, REFORM

Chapter One: Remembering Islamization, 1300–1750

1. Robert M. Hartwell, *Tribute Missions to China, 960–1126* (Philadelphia: n.p., 1983); M. Flecker, "A Ninth-century AD Arab or Indian Shipwreck in Indonesia: First Evidence for Direct Trade with China," *World Archaeology* 32–33 (2001): 335–54.
2. Oliver Wolters, *The Fall of Śrivijaya in Malay History* (Kuala Lumpur: Oxford University Press, 1970); G. R. Tibbetts, *A Study of the Arabic Texts Containing Material on South-East Asia* (Leiden: Brill, 1979); Michael Laffan, "Finding Java: Muslim Nomenclature of Insular Southeast Asia from Śrivijaya to Snouck Hurgronje," in Eric Tagliacozzo, ed., *Southeast Asia and the Middle East* (Singapore: Stanford and NUS Press, 2009), 17–64; Waruno Mahdi, "Yavadvipa and the Merapi Volcano in West Sumatra," *Archipel* 75 (2008), 111–43; R. E. Jordaan and B. E. Colless, The Mahārājas of the Isles: The Śailendras and the Problem of Śrivijaya (Leiden: Department of Languages and Cultures of Southeast Asia and Oceania, Leiden University, 2009).
3. Elizabeth Lambourn, "Tombstones, Texts, and Typologies: Seeing Sources for the Early History of Islam in Southeast Asia," *JESHO* 51–52 (2008): 252–86.
4. Tibbetts, *Arabic Texts*, 114.
5. Elizabeth Lambourn, "India from Aden: Khutba and Muslim Urban Networks in Late Thirteenth-century India," in: K. Hall, ed., *Secondary Cities and Urban Networking in the Indian Ocean Realm, c. 1000–1800* (Lexington, MA: Lexington Books, 2008), 55–97, esp. 75.
6. R. Michael Feener and Michael F. Laffan, "Sufi Scents Across the Indian Ocean: Yemeni Hagiography and the Earliest History of Southeast Asian Islam," *Archipel* 70 (2005): 185–208.
7. A. H. Johns, "Sufism as a Category in Indonesian Literature and History," *Journal of Southeast Asian History* 2-2 (1961): 10–23; *Hikayat Raja Pasai*, Russell Jones, ed., (Shah Alam [Selangor]: Fajar Bakti, 1987), 12–13; A. H. Hill, ed., "Hikayat Raja-Raja

Pasai: A Revised Romanised Version of Raffles MS 67," *Journal of the Malayan Branch of the Royal Asiatic Society* 33–32 (1961): 56–57; G.W.J. Drewes and R. Poerbatjaraka, *De Mirakelen van Abdoelkadir Djaelani* (Bandung: Nix and Co., 1938), 24.

8. Russell Jones, "Ten Conversion Myths from Indonesia," in Nehemia Levtzion, ed., *Conversion to Islam* (New York: Holmes and Meier, 1979), 129–58, at 134; C. C. Brown, trans., "Sějarah Mělayu or 'Malay Annals': A Translation of Raffles MS 18," *JMBRAS* 25–2/3 (October 1952): 1–275, esp. 12–17, 40–59. Similarly the Bugis dynasty of Luwu', in Sulawesi, claimed a link to the Queen of Sheba. Raja Ali Haji ibn Ahmad, *The Precious Gift (Tuhfat al-Nafis)*, V. Matheson and B.W. Andaya, trans. and ed. (Kuala Lumpur: Oxford, 1982), 2

9. H.A.R. Gibb and C. F. Beckingham, trans. and annot., *The Travels of Ibn Baṭṭūṭa AD 1325–1354*, 4 vols. (London: Hakluyt Society, 1994), IV, 874–87; Tibbetts, *Arabic Texts*, 206; Liaw Yock Fang, *Undang-undang Melaka: The Laws of Melaka* (The Hague: Nijhoff, 1976).

10. Brown, "Sějarah Mělayu," 100–101; Elizabeth Sirriyeh, *Sufi Visionary of Ottoman Damascus: 'Abd al-Ghanī al-Nābulusī, 1641–1731* (London and New York: Routledge-Curzon, 2005), 33; and, more generally, William C. Chittick, *Ibn 'Arabi: Heir to the Prophets* (Oxford: Oneworld, 2005); G.W.J. Drewes, *Directions for Travellers on the Mystic Path: Zakariyyā' al-Anṣārī's Kitāb Fatḥ al-Rahmān and Its Indonesian Adaptations, with an Appendix on Palembang Manuscripts and Authors* (The Hague: Nijhoff, 1977), 218.

11. Cf. W. G. Shellabear, ed., *Sejarah Melayu* (Kuala Lumpur: Dewan Bahasa dan Pustaka, 1967), 148–9; Vladimir Braginsky, *The Heritage of Traditional Malay Literature: A Historical Survey of Genres, Writings and Literary Views* (Leiden: KITLV, 2004), 118; Henri Chambert-Loir, "The *Sulalat al-Salatin* as a Political Myth," *Indonesia* 79 (April 2005): 131–60, at 146.

12. Tibbetts, *Arabic Texts*, 211–29; Ridjali, *Historie van Hitu: Een Ambonse geschiedenis uit de zeventiende eeuw*, Hans Straver, Chris van Fraasen, and Jan van der Putten, intro. and eds., (Utrecht: Landelijk Steunpunt Educatie Molukkers, 2004), 35. For earlier Portuguese mention of such connections, see Brett Baker, "South Sulawesi in 1544: A Portuguese Letter," *RIMA* 39–1 (2005): 61–86, at 73; and on Patani's Chinese links, see Francis R. Bradley, "Piracy, Smuggling, and Trade in the Rise of Patani, 1490–1600," *Journal of the Siam Society* 96 (2008): 27–50.

13. Geertz, *Islam Observed*, 1–11 (see Preface, n.2).

14. G.W.J. Drewes, "Wat valt er te verstaan onder het Javaanse woord suluk?" *BKI* 148–1 (1992): 22–30, 25.

15. Azyumardi Azra, *The Origins of Islamic Reformism in Southeast Asia: Networks of Malay-Indonesian and Middle Eastern 'Ulama' in the Seventeenth and Eighteenth Centuries* (Leiden: KITLV Press, 2004), 124; H. J. de Graaf and T.G.T. Pigeaud, *Chinese Muslims in Java in the 15th and 16th Centuries: The Malay Annals of Semarang and Cerbon*, M. C. Ricklefs, ed. (Clayton, Victoria: Monash University, 1984). On the issue in general, see Denys Lombard and Claudine Salmon, "Islam and Chineseness," *Indonesia* 57 (April 1994): 115–32.

16. On al-Mashhur and his charts, see Ulrike Freitag, *Indian Ocean Migrants and State Formation in Hadhramaut: Reforming the Homeland* (Leiden and Boston: Brill, 2003), 284. See also Kazuhiro Arai, "Arabs Who Traversed the Indian Ocean: The History of the al-ʿAttas Family in Hadramawt and Southeast Asia, c. 1600–c. 1960," PhD

Dissertation, University of Michigan, 2004, 163; ʿAli b. Husayn b. Muhammad b. Husayn b. Jaʿfar al-ʿAttas, *Taj al-aʿras ʿala manaqib al-habib Salih b. ʿAbdallah al-ʿAttas*, 2 vols (Kudus: Minarat Quds, ca. 1979), II, 381.

17. As pamphlets handed out at the tomb of Gunung Jati attest, such a history is not universally acknowledged. See Anon., *Sejarah Sunan Gunungjati* (Cirebon: n.p, n.d.) and Hasan Basyari, *Sekitar komplek makam Sunan Gunung Jati dan sekilas riwayatnya* (Cirebon: Zul Fana, n.d.).

18. Hoesein Djajadiningrat, *Critische beschouwing van de Sadjarah Bantĕn* (Haarlem: Joh. Enschede en Zonen, 1913), 111; Georgius Everhardus Rumphius, *The Ambonese Curiosity Cabinet*, E.M. Beekman, trans., ed., and annot. (New Haven and London: Yale University Press, 1999), 261.

19. Henri Chambert-Loir, "Saints and Ancestors: The Cult of Muslim Saints in Java," in Henri Chambert-Loir and Anthony Reid, eds., *The Potent Dead: Ancestors, Saints and Heroes in Contemporary Indonesia* (Crows Nest, New South Wales: Allen and Unwin, 2002), 132–40.

20. T. Pires and F. Rodrigues, *The Suma Oriental of Tomé Pires, An Account of the East, from the Red Sea to Japan, Written in Malacca and India in 1512–1515, and The book of Francisco Rodrigues, Rutter of a Voyage in the Red Sea, Nautical Rules, Almanack and Maps, Written and Drawn in the East before 1515* (London: The Hakluyt Society, 1944).

21. G.W.J. Drewes, *The Admonitions of Seh Bari: A 16ᵗʰ Century Javanese Muslim Text Attributed to the Saint of Bonaň* (The Hague: Nijhoff, 1969); cf. Chittick, *Ibn ʿArabi*, 71.

22. G.W.J. Drewes, *An Early Javanese Code of Muslim Ethics* (The Hague: Nijhoff, 1978), 14–15, 42–43; M. C. Ricklefs, *Mystic Synthesis in Java: A History of Islamization From the Fourteenth to the Early Nineteenth Centuries* (Norwalk, CT: EastBridge, 2006). See also A. J. Wensinck, "al-Khaḍir (Khiḍr)," in *EI²*, IV, 902–905; and Sanjay Subrahmanyam, "Notes towards a Reconfiguration of Early Modern Eurasia," *Modern Asian Studies* 31–3 (1997): 735–62, esp. 757.

23. Soebardi, "Santri-religious Elements as Reflected in the Book of Tjĕntini," *BKI* 127–3 (1971): 331–49, 346–47; Louis Massignon, *The Passion of al-Hallâj*, Herbert Mason, trans., 4 vols. (Princeton: Princeton University Press, 1982), II, 287. Syam Rahimsyah, *Syekh Siti Jenar (Syekh Lemah Abang)* (Surabaya: Amalia, c. 2002); R. Michael Feener, "A Re-examination of the Place of al-Hallaj in the Development of Southeast Asian Islam," *BKI* 154–4 (1998): 571–92.

24. Anthony Reid, "Aceh," *EI²*, accessed August 23, 2007.

25. Ricklefs, *Mystic Synthesis*, passim.

26. GG en Raden van Indie to Bewindhebbers, Batavia, 27 January 1625, and Corn. Acoley to GG Specx, Banda, 1 September 1631, in *Archief*, V, 223–24 and VI, 159; J. Noorduyn, "Makasar and the Islamization of Bima," *BKI* 143–2/3 (1987): 312–42. From 1631 the Dutch complained about the annual appearance of Makassarese junks and "popes" at Banda following their successes in South Sulawesi; Thomas Gibson, *And the Sun Pursued the Moon: Symbolic Knowledge and Traditional Authority Among the Makassar* (Honolulu: University of Hawaiʻi Press, 2005). Cf. A. C. Milner, "Islam and Malay Kingship," *JRAS* (1981): 46–70.

27. Claude Guillot and Ludvik Kalus, "La stèle funéraire de Hamzah Fansuri," *Archipel* 60 (2000): 3–24.

28. G.W.J. Drewes and L. F. Brakel, *The Poems of Hamzah Fansuri* (Dordrecht: Foris, 1986), 126–37.

29. Claude Guillot and Ludvik Kalus, "En réponse à Vladimir I. Braginsky," *Archipel* 61 (2001): 34–38; "La stèle funéraire," 4–5, 24.

30. Drewes and Brakel, *Poems of Hamzah Fansuri*, 5–6, 44–45.

31. See MCP, based on A. Samad Ahmad, ed., *Hikayat Amir Hamzah* (Kuala Lumpur: Dewan Bahasa dan Pustaka, 1987); S.W.R. Mulyadi, *Hikayat Indraputra: A Malay Romance* (Dordrecht: Foris, 1983); Drewes and Brakel, *Poems of Hamzah Fansuri*; and J. Doorenbos, *De Geschriften van Hamzah Pansoeri* (Leiden: Brill, 1933). Accessed March 16, 2007.

32. Giancarlo Casale, *The Ottoman Age of Exploration* (Oxford: Oxford University Press, 2010); Elizabeth Lambourn, "Khutba and Muslim Networks in the Indian Ocean (Part II): Timurid and Ottoman Engagements," in Kenneth Hall, ed., *The Growth of Non-Western Cities: Primary and Secondary Urban Networking, c. 900–1900* (Lanham, MD: Rowan and Littlefield, forthcoming); Anthony Reid, *Southeast Asia in the Age of Commerce 1450–1680*, 2 vols (Bangkok: Yale University Press and Silkworm Books, 1988–93), II, passim; cf. Muzaffar Alam and Sanjay Subrahmanyam, "Southeast Asia as Seen from Mughal India: Tahir Muhammad's 'Immaculate Garden' (ca. 1600)," *Archipel* 70 (2005): 209–39, at 214; Claude Guillot and Ludvik Kalus, "Inscriptions islamiques sur des canons d'Insuline du XVIe siècle," *Archipel* 72 (2006): 69–94.

33. Siti Hawa bin Haji Salleh, ed., *Bustan al-Salatin*, 2nd edition (Kuala Lumpur: Dewan Bahasa dan Pustaka, 1992), 56.

34. Denys Lombard, "Une autre 'Méditerranée' dans le Sud-Est asiatique," *Hérodote* 88 (1988): 184–92; Anthony Reid, *Southeast Asia in the Age of Commerce*. Cf. Sanjay Subrahmanyam, "Writing History 'Backwards': Southeast Asian History (and the *Annales*) at the Crossroads," *Studies in History* 10–1 (1994): 131–45; and "Notes on Circulation and Asymmetry in Two Mediterraneans, c. 1400–1800," in Claude Guillot, Denys Lombard, and Roderich Ptak, eds., *From the Mediterranean to the China Sea: Miscellaneous Notes* (Wiesbaden: Harrassowitz, 1998), 21–43.

35. Lambourn, "Tombstones, Texts and Typologies," 273, 279; Siti Hawa, *Bustan al-Salatin*, 33–38.

36. John Davis, *The Voyages and Works of John Davis the Navigator*, Albert Hastings Markham, ed. (London: Hakluyt, 1880), 151; J. Lancaster, *The Voyages of Sir James Lancaster to Brazil and the East Indies*, Sir William Foster, ed. (London: Hakluyt, 1940), 96; Azra, *Origins*, 53; Braginsky, *Heritage*, 617; and "Towards the Biography of Hamzah Fansuri: When did Hamzah Live? Data from his Poems and Early European Accounts," *Archipel* 57 (1999): 135–75; A. H. Johns, *The Gift Addressed to the Spirit of the Prophet* (Canberra: Australian National University, 1965).

37. Johns, *Gift*, 9; cf. C.A.O. van Nieuwenhuijze, *Šamsu 'l-Dīn van Pasai: Bijdrage tot de kennis der Sumatraansche mystiek* (Leiden: Brill, 1945), 245–66.

38. Paul Wormser, p.c. April 2009; cf. A. H. Johns, "Shams al-Dīn al- Samaṭrānī," in *EI²* IX, 296–97.

39. Braginsky, *Heritage*, 449; P. Voorhoeve, "Van en over Nūruddīn ar-Rānīrī," *BKI* 107–104 (1951): 353–68, at 357; Azra, *Origins*, 58–59.

40. PUL MS Garrett 476L, f.1b; cf. transcription from al-Raniri's *Fath al-mubin* in Voorhoeve to Drewes, Barchem, 1 February 1979, in KITLV, H 1304. Van Nieuwenhuijze assumed that al-Raniri was merely misrepresenting the teachings of Shams al-Din in regard to the Wujudiyya, while Wormser sees the argument as being deliberately invested in questions of ethnicity. Van Nieuwenhuijze, *Šamsu 'l-Dīn*, 229–30; Paul

Wormser, "La recontre de l'Inde et de l'Égypte dans la vie et l'oeuvre du savant religieux d'expression malaise Nūruddīn ar-Rānīrī (m. 1658)," in Rachida Chih, Denis Gril, and Catherine Mayeur-Jaouen, *Le soufisme en Égypte et dans le monde musulman à l'époque ottomane (16e–18e siècles): Etat des lieux et perspectives* (Cairo: IFAO, 2010), 209–34.

41. Siti Hawa, *Bustan al-salatin*, 44; Voorhoeve, "Van en over Nūruddīn," 362; Braginsky, *Heritage*, 647; Takeshi Ito, "Why did Nuruddin ar-Raniri Leave Aceh in 1054 AH?" *BKI* 134-4 (1978), 489–91. See also PUL, MS Garrett 476L, f.1b. For details surrounding the latter, see Michael Laffan, "When is a Jawi Jawi? A Short Note on Pieter Sourij's 'Maldin' and his Minang Student 'Sayf al-Rijal,'" in *Lost Times and Untold Tales from the Malay World*, Jan van der Putten and Mary Kilcline Cody, eds. (Singapore: NUS Press, 2009), 139–47.

42. Siti Hawa, *Bustan al-salatin*, 4–5, 8.

43. See Azra, *Origins*, 60–61; Voorhoeve to Drewes, Barchem, 1 February 1979, in KITLV, H 1304.

44. PUL, MS Garrett 476L, 15a.

45. PUL, MS Garrett 476L, 15a.

46. Khaled El-Rouayheb, "Opening the Gate of Verification: The Forgotten Arab-Islamic Florescence of the 17th Century," *IJMES* 38-2 (2006): 263–81. Cf. Mufti Ali, "A Statistical Portrait of the Resistance to Logic by Sunni Muslim Scholars Based on the Works of Jalāl al-Dīn al-Suyūtī (849–909/1448–1505)," *ILS* 15-2 (2008): 250–67.

47. PUL, MS Garrett 476L, f.15b.

48. Braginsky, *Heritage*, 450; Voorhoeve, "Van en over Nūruddīn," 359.

49. For al-Misri's account, see the photocopy of an as yet unidentified manuscript held within the papers of R. B. Serjeant at Edinburgh University Libray, hereafter MS *Sirat al-mutawakkil*, see esp. f. 124.

50. Djajadiningrat, *Critische beschouwing*, 49–51, 175.

51. Voorhoeve, "Van en over Nūruddīn," 358; Wormser, "La recontre de l'Inde et de l'Égypte"; Djajadiningrat, *Critische beschouwing*, 51, 63, 176–77; Martin van Bruinessen, "*Shari'a* Court, *Tarekat* and *Pesantren*: Religious Institutions in the Banten Sultanate," *Archipel* 50 (1995): 165–200, esp. 167–68, 193.

52. Ahmad Dahlan, *Khulasat al-kalam fi bayan umara' al-balad al-haram* (Cairo: al-Khayriyya, 1304), 104; C. Snouck Hurgronje, "Een Mekkaansch gezantschap naar Atjeh in 1683," (1887), in *VG* III, 137–47, at 144. See also his work on the fiqh of al-Bajuri and mention of that scholar's resignation to the possibility of female rule in "De beteekenis van den Islâm voor zijne belijders in Oost-Indië" (1883), in *VG* IV-i, 1–26, 22.

53. Engseng Ho, *The Graves of Tarim: Genealogy and Mobility across the Indian Ocean* (Berkeley: University of California Press, 2006), 168; cf. Azra, *Origins*, 78, citing Dahlan, *Khulasat al-kalam*, 104–105.

54. J. Spencer Trimingham, *The Sufi Orders in Islam* (Oxford: Clarendon Press, 1971), 73, 216; Esther Peskes, *Al-'Aidarūs und seine Erben: Eine Untersuching zu Geschichte und Sufismus einer Hadramitischen Sāda-gruppe vom fünfzehnten bis zum achtzehnten Jahrhundert* (Stuttgart: Franz Steiner, 2005), esp. 173–87.

55. On the itinerary and life of 'Abd al-Ra'uf, see P. G. Riddell, *Transferring a Tradition: 'Abd al-Ra'ūf al-Singkilī's Rendering into Malay of the Jalālayn Commentary* (Berkeley: University of California Press, 1990). For references to him as a Jawi, see LOr. 7274; I, ff. 1b–15a; cf. IOL MS Jav. 50, f. 203a, and MS Jav. 77, ff. 30–31.

56. Azra, *Origins*, 16–17, 41–42.

57. I refer here to a copy of the *Shath al-wali* made by ʿAbd al-Ghani al-Nabulsi (1641–1731) in 1727. See IOL Or. 9768/6, ff. 30a–36b. Cf. Voorhoeve, "Van en over Nūruddīn," 365–67; and "Lijst der geschriften van Rānīrī en apparatus criticus bij de tekst van twee verhandelingen," *BKI* 111–1 (1955): 152–61, at 155–56.

58. Voorhoeve, "Van en over Nūruddīn," 367; IOL Or. 9768/6, f. 34a-34b.

59. LOr. 1633, 4b; Braginsky, *Heritage*, 672–75; A. H. Johns, "Daḳaʾiḳ al-Ḥurūf," *JRAS* (1955): 55–73, 139–58.

60. Johns, *Gift*, 10–11; cf M. C. Ricklefs, "A note on Professor Johns's 'Gift Addressed to the Spirit of the Prophet'," *BKI* 129–2/3 (1973): 347–349; and Peter Carey, "A Further Note on Professor John's 'Gift Addressed to the Spirit of the Prophet," *BKI* 131–2/3 (1975): 341–44; P. S. van Ronkel, *Rapport betreffende de godsdienstige verschijnselen ter Sumatra's Westkust* (Batavia: Landsdrukkerij, 1916), 5; and Azra, *Origins*, 85; Riddell, *Transferring a Tradition*, passim.

61. Van Bruinessen notes that Yusuf's pedigree was linked to Nur al-Din's Qadiri uncle, while pointing out that Nur al-Din was better known as a Rifaʿi. Voorhoeve had argued, based on a Bugis manuscript (IOL Add. 12367), that the chain went to al-Raniri himself. See Voorhoeve, "Van en over Nūruddīn," 356; Martin van Bruinessen, "Shaykh ʿAbd al-Qadir al-Jilani and the Qadiriyya in Indonesia," *Journal of the History of Sufism* 1–2 (2000): 361–95, 365; and Azra, *Origins*, 87–108.

62. See colophon of *al-Durra al-fakhira*, PUL, Garrett Collection, MS Yahuda 3872; Azra, *Origins*, 92.

63. See J. Edel, ed., *Hikajat Hasanoeddin* (Meppel: Brink, 1938), 36, 126–44.

64. A. Ligtvoet, "Transcriptie van het dagboek der Vorsten van Gowa en Tello, met vertaling en aanteekeningen," *BKI* 28 (1880), 1–259, at 144 and 154; see also Martin van Bruinessen, "The Tariqa Khalwatiyya in South Celebes," in H. A. Poeze and P. Schoorl, eds., *Excursies in Celebes* (Leiden: KITLV, 1991), 251–69, at 258.

65. On Gervaise and his account, see Christian Pelras, "La première description de Célèbes-sud en français et la destinée remarquable de deux jeunes princes makassar dans la France de Louis XIV," *Archipel* 54 (1997), 63-80.

66. Nicolas Gervaise, *An Historical Description of the Kingdom of Macasar in the East-Indies* (London: Leigh and Midwinter, 1701), 154–55.

67. Gervaise, *Historical Description*, 139–51.

68. Gervaise, *Historical Description*, 133.

69. Gervaise, *Historical Description*, 155–56.

70. Ligtvoet, "Transcriptie," 172, 176; Valentyn, *ONOI* III, ii, 208. Monies had already been gathered in 1689 in an attempt to ransom their then living hero. See Leonard Andaya, *The Heritage of Arung Palakka: A History of South Sulawesi (Celebes) in the Seventeenth Century* (The Hague: Nijhoff, 1981), 276–77.

71. Thomas Gibson, *Islamic Narrative and Authority in Southeast Asia: From the 16th to the 21st Century* (New York: Palgrave, 2007), 67–84; Ligtvoet, "Transcriptie," 154, 165.

72. Ligtvoet, "Transcriptie," 219.

73. M. C. Ricklefs, *The Seen and Unseen Worlds in Java 1726–1749: History, Literature and Islam in the Court of Pakubuwana II* (St. Leonards: Allen and Unwin, 1998), 127–55.

74. Ricklefs, *Seen and Unseen Worlds*, 190, 198.

75. Ricklefs, *Seen and Unseen Worlds*, 22–105. The *Serat Iskandar* had been brought to Mataram after the fall of Surabaya. As an earlier example of Islamic texts being marked by a perhaps Sufi court, we have the mention of the Sultan of Banten, Mawlana Yusuf (r. 1570–80), designating several texts as pious endowments. Djajadiningrat, *Critische beschouwing*, 37.

76. This manuscript also contains Javanese translations of the *Sharab al-ʿashiqin* of al-Fansuri, though the associated pedigree neither includes his name nor reaches to the apparent owner. Ricklefs, *Seen and Unseen Worlds*, 204–205.

77. This is IOL Jav 83. See Ricklefs, *Seen and Unseen Worlds*, 254–59; Drewes, *Directions*, 28.

Chapter Two: Embracing a New Curriculum, 1750–1800

1. Gervaise, *Historical Description*, 125–26 (see ch.1, n.66); Christian Pelras, "Religion, Tradition, and the Dynamics of Islamization in South Sulawesi," *Indonesia* 57 (April 1993): 133–54. On the transmission of religious knowledge of a more technical nature, see Ian Proudfoot, *Old Muslim Calendars of Southeast Asia* (Leiden and Boston: Brill, 2006).

2. MS *Sirat al-mutawakkil*, f. 124; Ricklefs, *Mystic Synthesis*, 212 (see ch.1, n.22).

3. Image of "Haji Baok," enclosed in LOr. 18097, s1 (see frontispiece).

4. Johns, "Sufism as a Category" (see ch.1, n.7); H.A.R. Gibb and Harold Bowen, *Islamic Society and the West*, 2 vols. (London: Oxford University Press, 1950–57), I, 76; Johns, *Gift*, 8 (see ch.1, n.36); Christine Dobbin, *Islamic Revivalism in a Changing Peasant Economy: Central Sumatra, 1784–1847* (London and Malmö: Curzon, 1983), 121–25, and Braginsky, *Heritage*, 399. Cf. A. H. Johns, "Sufism in Southeast Asia: Reflections and Reconsiderations," *JSEAS* 26–1 (1995): 169–83.

5. Jacob Cornelisz. van Neck, *Het tvveede boeck, Iournael oft dagh-register, inhoudende een warachtich verhael ... vande reyse, gedaen ... onder't beleydt vanden admirael Iacob Cornelisz. Neck* (Middelburg: Barent Langhenes, 1601), 41; Davis, *Voyages and Works*, 151 (see ch.1, n.36).

6. Gervaise, *Historical Description*, 64; Drewes, *Admonitions*, 11 (see ch.1, n.21); Martin van Bruinessen, "*Pesantren* and Kitab Kuning: Continuity and Change in a Tradition of Religious Learning," in Wolfgang Marschall, ed., *Texts from the Islands: Oral and Written Traditions of Indonesia and the Malay World* (Bern: Institute of Ethnology, University of Bern, 1994), 121–45; and "*Shariʿa* Court," esp. 172–75 (see ch.1, n.51); Ricklefs, *Mystic Synthesis*, 89. On the alleged foundation of Tegalsari, see Ricklefs, *Seen and Unseen Worlds*, 285–87 (see ch.1, n.73).

7. Ann Kumar, *The Diary of a Javanese Muslim: Religion, Politics and the Pesantren, 1883–1886* (Canberra: Faculty of Asian Studies, ANU, 1985), 32; J.L.V. "Bijdrage tot de kennis der residentie Madioen," *TNI* 17–2 (1855): 1–17, esp. 10 ff.

8. F. Fokkens, "Vrije Desa's op Java en Madoera," *TBG* 31 (1886): 477–517, at 491; Ricklefs, *Mystic Synthesis*, 175–78.

9. LOr. 7931, p. 425b; 655–56, and 1236; Olivia Remie Constable, "Funduq, Fondaco, and Khān in the Wake of Christian Commerce and Crusade," in Angeliki E. Laiou and Roy Parviz Mottahedeh, eds., *The Crusades from the Perspective of Byzantium and the Muslim World* (Washington: Dumbarton Oaks Research Library and Collection, 2001), 145–56; P. J. Zoetmulder, *Old Javanese-English Dictionary*, 2 vols. (The Hague: Nijhoff,

1982) II, 1375; C. A. Mees, ed., *De Kroniek van Kutai*, Proefschrift Universiteit te Leiden (Santpoort, 1935), 150; and J. J. Ras, ed., *Hikajat Bandjar: A Study in Malay Historiography* (The Hague: Nijhoff, 1968), 304–305.

10. Martin van Bruinessen, "*Kitab kuning*: Books in Arabic Script Used in the Pesantren Milieu," *BKI* 146–2/3 (1990): 226–69, esp. 239, n.27. See also Soebardi, "Santri-Religious Elements" (see ch.1, n.23).

11. Holger Warnk, "Some Notes on the Malay-Speaking Community in Cairo at the Turn of the Nineteenth Century," in Fritz Schulze and Holger Warnk, eds., *Insular Southeast Asia: Linguistic and Cultural Studies in Honour of Professor Bernd Nothofer* (Wiesbaden: Harrassowitz, 2006), 141–52; Azra, *Origins*, 120–26 (see ch.1, n.15).

12. For an in-depth study of the Patani tradition, see Francis R. Bradley, "The Social Dynamics of Islamic Revivalism in Southeast Asia: The Rise of the Patani School, 1785–1909," PhD Dissertation, University of Wisconsin, 2010.

13. On the ascent of Palembang, see Barbara Watson Andaya, *To Live as Brothers: Southeast Sumatra in the Seventeenth and Eighteenth Centuries* (Honolulu: University of Hawaii Press, 1993), esp. 115, 190–202, 227–29; see also Ota Atsushi, *Changes of Regime and Social Dynamics in West Java: Society, State and the Outer World of Banten, 1750–1830* (Leiden: Brill, 2005).

14. On the *Fath al-rahman*, see Drewes, *Directions*, 28 (see ch.1, n.10).

15. On the Arab community, see Andaya, *To Live as Brothers*, 219–20. On al-Falimbani, see Mohammed Hussain Ahmad, "Shaykh ʿAbd as-Samad al-Falimbani in the Nexus of 12th/18th Century Muslim Scholars in the Arab and Malay Worlds," PhD Thesis, Sydney, 2009. Cf. Azra, *Origins*, 118, 124; Drewes, *Directions*, 100–05, 106–75.

16. Ahmad, "Shaykh ʿAbd as-Samad al-Falimbani." Cf. Azra, *Origins*, 118; Braginsky, *Heritage*, 566.

17. SOAS MS 11660, esp. ff. 16b–18a, 41a; see also SOAS MS 12225, f. 117b.

18. P. Voerhoeve, "A Malay Scriptorium," in John Bastin and R. Roolvink, eds., *Malayan and Indonesian Studies: Essays Presented to Sir Richard Winstedt on his Eighty-fifth Birthday* (Oxford: Clarendon, 1964), 256–66, at 259; Drewes, *Directions*, 199–207; Teuku Iskandar, "Palembang Kraton Manuscripts," in C.M.S. Hellwig and S. O. Robson, eds., *A Man of Indonesian Letters: Essays in Honour of Professor A. Teeuw* (Leiden: Foris, 1986), 67ff.

19. M. C. Ricklefs, *Jogjakarta under Sultan Mangkubumi 1749–1792* (Oxford: Oxford University Press, 1974), 150–54; G.W.J. Drewes, "Further Data Concerning ʿAbd al-Ṣamad al-Palimbānī," *BKI* 132–2/3 (1976): 267–92; Drewes, *Directions*, 222; Azra, *Origins*, 112–17.

20. [Muhammad Arshad al-Banjari], *Tuhfat al-raghibin fi bayan haqiqat iman al-muʾminin* (Singapore and Jeddah: Muhammad al-Nahdi wa-Awladuh, n.d.), 2; Noorhaidi Hasan, "The *Tuḥfat al-Rāghibīn*: The work of Abdul Samad al-Palimbani or of Muhammad Arsyad al-Banjari?," *BKI* 163–1 (2007): 67–85. On Arshad al-Banjari in general, see Azra, *Origins*, 117–22.

21. Hasan, "Tuḥfat al-Rāghibīn," 81. For Nafis al-Banjari, see Martin van Bruinessen, "Nafis al-Banjari (Muhammad Nafis b. Idrīs al-Banjarī)." *Dictionnaire biographique des savants et grandes figures du monde musulman périphérique, du XIXe siècle à nos jours*, Fasc. no 2 (Paris: CNRS-EHESS, 1998), 24–25.

22. Banjari, *Tuhfa*, 3. Cf. Drewes, "Further Data," 276; Azra, Origins, 131–33, 138; Gril and Mayeur-Jaouen, *Le soufisme à l'époque ottomane*, passim (see ch.1, n.40).

23. Banjari, *Tuhfa*, 18–21; Ian Proudfoot, "An Expedition into the Politics of Malay Philology," *Journal of the Malaysian Branch of the Royal Asiatic Society* 76 (2003): 1–53, at 22.

24. G. Tradescant Lay, "Notes Made During the Voyage of the Himmaleh in the Malayan Archipelago," in *The Claims of Japan and Malaysia upon Christendom, Exhibited in Notes of Voyages Made in 1837, from Canton, in the Ship Morrison and Brig Himmaleh, under Direction of the Owners*, 2 vols. (New York: E. French, 1839), II: 1–295, at 192 and 202. Prof Kawashima Midori has shown me copies of Shattari texts brought back to Magindanao by the putative Islamizer of the Maranao people after the death of his shaykh at Palembang in 1808.

25. Hasan, "*Tuhfat al-Rāghibīn*," 81; cf. C. Snouck Hurgronje, *Mekka in the Latter Part of the 19th century: Daily Life, Customs and Learning of the Moslems of the East-Indian-Archipelago*, trans. J. H. Monahan (Leiden: Brill, 1931), 287.

26. Ann Kumar, "Javanese Court Society and Politics in the Late Eighteenth Century: The Record of a Lady Soldier, Part 1," *Indonesia* 29 (April) 1980: 1–46, 13.

27. "Lijst der, ingevolge Resolutie 9 October 1833 No.13 … Manuscripten, gevonden in den boedel van den naar Soerabaija gerelegeerden titulaieren Sultan van Bantam," Arsip Nasional Indonesia, KBG Dir 0094–95. On al-Mahalli and al-Suyuti, see GAL II, 114, 145. For a Malay translation of the *Yawaqit*, completed in Mecca in 1828 by Muhammad ʿAli b. ʿAbd al-Rashid b. ʿAbdallah al-Jawi al-Qadi al-Sumbawi, see ʿAbd al-Wahhab al-Shaʿrani, *al-Yawaqit wa-l-jawahir fi ʿuqubat ahl al-kabaʾir*, 2nd ed. (Cairo: Mustafa al-Babi al-Halabi wa-awladahu, 1354). On the *Mizan*, see Drewes, *Directions*, 32–33.

28. Rouayheb, "Gate of Verification," 268, 271 (see ch.1, n.46).

29. See Jan Just Witkam, *Vroomheid en activisme in een Islamitisch gebedenboek: De geschiedenis van de* Dalāʾil al-Khayrāt *van al-Ġazūlī* (Universiteitsbibliotheek Leiden: Legatum Warnerianum, 2002); see also Witkam, "The Battle of the Images: Mekka vs. Medina in the Iconography of the Manuscripts of al-Jazūlī's *Dalāʾil al-Khayrāt*," in Judith Pfeiffer and Manfred Kropp, eds., *Theoretical Approaches for the Transmission and Edition of Oriental Manuscripts: Proceedings of a Symposium Held in Istanbul, March 28–30, 2001* (Beirut: Ergon Verlag Würzburg, 2007), 67–82, with images at 295–99.

30. L.W.C. van den Berg, "Het Mohammedaansche godsdienstonderwijs op Java en Madoera en de daarbij gebruikte Arabische boeken," *TBG* 31 (1887): 518–55, at 519; C. Snouck Hurgonje, "Brieven van een Wedono-Pensioen," (1891–92), in *VG* IV-i, 111–248, at 160–61; M. Lindenborn, "Langgars en Pesantrèns," *MNZG* 61 (1917), 119–27, 120.

31. Muhammad Zayn al-Din al-Sumbawi, *Siraj al-huda pada menyatakan ʿaqidat ahl al-taqwa* (Mecca: al-Mirriyya, 1303), 20.

32. On the *Alf Masaʾil*, a series of questions supposedly put to the Prophet by a Jewish leader, see G. F. Pijper, *Het boek der duizend vragen* (Leiden: Brill, 1924); G.W.J. Drewes, "Javanese Versions of the 'Questions of ʿAbdallah b. Salam'," *BKI* 142–2/3 (1986): 325–27; and Ronit Ricci, "Translating Conversion in South and Southeast Asia: The Islamic *Book of One Thousand Questions* in Javanese, Tamil and Malay," Doctoral Dissertation, University of Michigan, 2006. According to a report written in the 1830s, the *Sittin* was still in standard use in Java as a follow-up to the "semoro-kandi" (i.e., the catechism of Samarqandi). J. A. van der Chijs, "Bijdragen tot de geschiedenis van het inlandsch onderwijs in Nederlandsch-Indië," *TBG* 14 (1864): 212–323, at 232.

33. A.W.T. Juynboll, "Een Moslimsche catechismus in het Arabisch met eene Javaansche interlineare vertaling in pegonschrift: Uitgegeven en in het Nederlandsch vertaald," *BKI* 29 (1881): 215–31, at 217–21. For an incomplete nineteenth-century example from Java, bound together with the *Umm al-barahin* and what pupports to be a synopsis of the *Maʿrifat al-islam*, see PUL, Islamic Manuscripts, Third Series, 645.

34. Sumbawi, *Siraj al-huda*, 2, 36ff.

35. Sumbawi, *Siraj al-huda*, 36–37.

36. LOr. 7084, *[Bab] maʿrifat al-islam wa-l-iman*, 7a; C. Snouck Hurgronje, "Nieuwe bijdragen tot de kennis van den Islâm," (1882) in *VG* II, 1–58, at 49.

37. IOL, Add. 2645, at folios 5r and 116 r. Cf. M. C. Ricklefs and P. Voorhoeve, *Indonesian Manuscripts in Great Britain: A Catalogue of Manuscripts in Indonesian Languages in British Public Collections* (Oxford: Oxford University Press, 1977), 45.

38. Johns, *Gift*, 11–12; LOr. 7274; I ff. 1b–15a; IOL MSS Jav. 50, 203a–202b and IOL MSS Jav. 77, 30–31. See also LOr. 7369 (where the pedigree ends with Babah Ibrahim of Kampung Tinggi) and LOr. 7424 (no. IV) and LOr. 7397.

39. *Kayfiyyat khatm qurʾan* (Bombay: Fath al-Karim, 1298), 120–22.

40. *Kayfiyyat khatm qurʾan*, 127–30. Pages 131–34 are then given over to the rites of the Sammaniyya order passed down by three other Patani scholars.

41. IOL MS Jav. 77, after p. 36 (MS not paginated hereafter).

42. IOL MSS Jav. 50, f. 203a.

43. Dale F. Eickelman and Armando Salvatore, "Muslim Publics," in Dale F. Eickelman, ed., *Public Islam and the Common Good* (Leiden: Brill, 2004), 3–27.

44. A. H. Johns, "Quranic Exegesis in the Malay World: In Search of a Profile," in Andrew Rippin, ed., *Approaches to the History of the Interpretation of the Qurʾān* (Oxford: Clarendon, 1988), 257–87; Braginsky, *Heritage*, passim (see ch.1, n.11).

45. Nico Kaptein, "The *Berdiri Mawlid* Issue Among Indonesian Muslims in the Period from Circa 1875 to 1930," *BKI* 149–1 (1993): 124–53, esp. 127, 130–31.

46. Michael Sells, "Ascension," in Jane Dammen McAuliffe, ed., *Encyclopaedia of the Qurʾān* (Georgetown University, Washington DC: Brill, 2007); Johns, *Gift*, 78–79; Shaʿrani, *Yawaqit*, 8; Ricklefs, *Seen and Unseen Worlds*, 66; Kartawidjaja in Lindenborn, "Langgars en Pesantrèns," 126.

Chapter Three: Reform and the Widening Muslim Sphere, 1800–1890

1. Ahmad b. Zayni Dahlan, *al-Futuhat al-islamiyya baʿda mudiyy al-futuhat al-nabawiyya*, 2 vols (Mecca: al-Mirriyya, 1302), II, 202–06.

2. Dahlan, *Futuhat*, II, 206, 209.

3. Dahlan, *Futuhat*, II, 207 ff.; IOL, Add. 12389, f 58b. The visit to Bone probably occurred after 1806 and before the death of Ahmad al-Salih (r. 1775–1812). The tomb of Ahmad al-Badawi is actually in Tanta, Egypt.

4. Dobbin, *Islamic Revivalism* (see ch.2, n.4); cf. Jeffrey Hadler, *Muslims and Matriarchs: Cultural Resilience in Indonesia Through Jihad and Colonialism* (Ithaca and London: Cornell University Press, 2008). For Sumbawa, see H. Zollinger, "Verslag van eene reis naar Bima en Soembawa, en naar eenige plaatsen op Celebes, Saleijer en Floris, gedurende de maanden Mei tot December 1847," *VBG* 23 (1850): 1–224, esp. 169–70.

5. Dobbin, *Islamic Revivalism*, 123. Cf. E. P. Wieringa, "A Tale of Two Cities and Two Modes of Reading: A Transformation of the Intended Function of the *Syair Makah dan Madinah*," *Die Welt des Islams* 42–2 (2002): 174–206, at 191. On the notion

of the "remaking" of tariqa practices, see Mark Sedgwick, *Saints and Sons: The Making and Remaking of the Rashidi Ahmadi Sufi Order, 1799–2000* (Leiden: Brill, 2005).

6. See the depiction of Imam Bonjol in fig. 4 as taken from H.J.J.L. de Stuers, *De vestiging en uitbreiding der Nederlanders ter westkust van Sumatra*, 2 vols. (Amsterdam: van Kampen, 1849–50), II, facing 163; though compare that of a follower in *TNI* 1–2 (1839), between 140 and 141. Other scholars remarked on Padri consumption of coffee, which they believed the Wahhabis eschewed. See H. A. Steijn Parvé, "De secte der Padaries (Padries) in de Bovenlanden van Sumatra," *TBG* 3 (1855): 249–78, at 269, n.1.

7. Steijn Parvé, "De secte der Padaries," 261, 264 n.2. Cf. Dobbin, *Islamic Revivalism*, 134.

8. See JALAL AL-DIN. Cf. E. Ulrich Kratz and Adriyetti Amir, *Surat keterangan Syeikh Jalaluddin karangan Fakih Saghir* (Kuala Lumpur: Dewan Bahasa dan Pustaka, 2002).

9. JALAL AL-DIN, 37ff. By contrast Steijn Parvé presented the movement as having essentially been the fruit of Hajji Miskin. See Steijn Parvé, "De secte der Padaries," 254–61.

10. JALAL AL-DIN, 16, 31, 47; cf. Dobbin, *Islamic Revivalism*, 135.

11. JALAL AL-DIN, 38ff.; Hadler, *Muslims and Matriarchs*, 24.

12. Wieringa, "Tale of Two Cities," 182, 195–96.

13. Cf. Wieringa, "Tale of Two Cities," 190–91; Suryadi, "Shaikh Daud of Sunur: Conflict Between Reformists and the Shaṭṭāriyyah Sūfī Order in Rantau Pariaman in the First Half of the Nineteenth Century," *Studia Islamika* 8–3 (2001): 57–124.

14. On ʿAbdallah b. ʿAbd al-Qahhar, see Van Bruinessen, "*Shariʿa* Court," 182 (see ch.1, n.51). For references to the Naqshbandiyya (among other orders) in Bantenese texts, see Djajadiningrat, *Critische beschouwing*, passim (see ch.1, n.18); and Edel, *Hikajat Hasanoeddin*, esp. 36 and 138–39 (see ch.1, n.63). For an analysis of such retrospective castings in the seventeenth century, see Martin van Bruinessen, "Najmuddin al-Kubra, Jumadil Kubra and Jamaluddin al-Akbar: Traces of Kubrawiyya Influence in Early Indonesian Islam," *BKI* 150 (1994): 305–329.

15. This was Ismaʿil b. ʿAbdallah al-Jawi al-Mankasari. The Bone MS is now held by the Aga Khan Museum in Toronto. With thanks to Annabel Gallop.

16. Arnold Snackey, ed., *Sair Soenoer Ditoeroenkan dari ABC Melajoe-Arab dan Diterangkan oleh Arnold Snackey* (Batavia: Albrecht en Co., 1888), 10–14. Cf. A.W.P. Verkerk Pistorius, *Studiën over de inlandsche huishouding in de Padangsche Bovenlanden* (Zalt-Bommel: Noman en Zoon, 1871), 199, 201, 211–12. For Daʾud's self-identification, see LOr. 12.161 f.17.

17. Hamka (Haji Abdul Malik Karim Amrullah) *Ajahku: Riwayat hidup Dr. H. Abd. Karim Amrullah dan perdjuangan kaum agama di Sumatera* (Jakarta: Widjaja, 1967), 34–35; cf. Snackey, *Sair Soenoer*, 12.

18. B. Schrieke, "Bijdrage tot de bibliographie van de huidige godsdienstige beweging ter Sumatra's Westkust," *TBG* 59 (1919–21): 249–325, at 263, 266.

19. E. B. Kielstra, "Onze aanrakingen met Troemon," *IG* 10–2 (1888): 1191–1207, at 1192–93; Sjafnir Aboe Nain, *Naskah Tuanku Imam Bonjol* (Padang: Pusat Pengkajian Islam dan Minangkabau, 2004) ms pp. 39–54, esp. 50; Cf. Hadler, *Muslims and Matriarchs*, 27–28; LOr. 1751.

20. P.B.R. Carey, *Babad Dipanagara: An Account of the Outbreak of the Java War (1825–1830)* (Kuala Lumpur: M.B.R.A.S., 1981), xxxviii–ix; this has since been super-

seded by his magisterial *The Power of Prophecy: Prince Dipanagara and the End of an Old Order in Java, 1785–1855* (Leiden: KITLV, 2008).

21. Unless otherwise noted, reference to Dipanagara's personal history is from Cary's *Power of Prophecy* and M. C. Ricklefs', "Dipanagara's Early Inspirational Experiences," *BKI* 130-2/3 (1974): 227–58.

22. Carey, *Babad*, 258, n. 99, records that the main 'ulama' centers at the time were at Dongkelan, Kasongan, Papringan, Plasa Kuning, and Purwarĕja. On Kyai Maja and his link to Dipanagara, see *Babad*, 262, n.110; where Carey notes that Maja's own son, Kyai Imampura, had studied at Tegalsari.

23. One of the Javanese copies of the *Tuhfa al-mursala* was owned by the Yogyakartan aristocrat and friend to Dipanagara, Raden Ayu Danureja (b. ca. 1771), whose family had supported Taftayani on their lands at Melangi before May of 1805. A later successor at Melangi, meanwhile, seems to have been a student of Kyai Maja. Carey, "Further Note"; and *Power of Prophecy*, 90–91

24. On the 2nd Makassar notebook, see Carey, *Babad*, xxxi; *Power of Prophecy*, 113–14, 744–45.

25. "Diponegoro," Manado, 15 December 1919, in LOr. 8652 K (3).

26. J. P. Schoemaker, "De gevangenneming van Kiai Modjo: Schets uit den Java-oorlog," *TNI* 5–3 (1899): 277–307, at 281.

27. Ricklefs, "Dipanagara's Early Inspirational Experiences," 253–54.

28. Carey, *Babad*, xliv; Ricklefs, "Dipanagara's Early Inspirational Experiences," 241–45.

29. Carey, *Babad*, xvlvii.

30. Cornelis Fasseur, *The Politics of Colonial Exploitation: Java, the Dutch, and the Cultivation System*, R. E. Elson and Ary Kraal, trans. (Ithaca: Southeast Asia Program, Cornell University, 1992).

31. J.L.V. "Bijdrage," 11 (see ch.2, n.7); S. E. Harthoorn, "De zending op Java en meer bepaald die van Malang," *MNZG* 4 (1860): 103–36, 212–52, at 237.

32. Fokkens, "Vrije Desa's," 499–500; Snouck Hurgronje, "Brieven," 178 (see ch.2, n.30).

33. Both al-Saqqaf and Salim b. Sumayr are reported as having been active in Singapore after the arrival of Raffles. Al-Saqqaf died in Gresik around 1875, and Bin Sumayr died at Batavia in 1853. C. B. Buckley, *An Anecdotal History of Old Times in Singapore* 2 vols. (Singapore: Fraser and Neave, 1902), II, 564–65; Van den Berg, "Mohammedaansche godsdienstonderwijs," 519, 526–27 (see ch.2, n.30); Snouck Hurgronje, "Brieven," 182.

34. On 'Abd al-Ghani and his relationship with Junayd Batavia, see Snouck Hurgronje, *Mekka*, 262–63 (see ch.2, n.25); and LOr. 7931, 425.

35. Heer's bibliography lists some three dozen titles ranging from elementary jurisprudence to works of saintly biography and Sufism in general. Nicholas Heer, *A Concise Handlist of Jawi Authors and their Works* (Seattle: n.p., 2007).

36. LOr. 7931, 140ff.

37. LOr. 7931, 229, 799.

38. LOr. 7572; Sugahara Yumi, "Kitab Jawa: Islamic Textbooks Written in Javanese (Pegon)," in Kawashima Midori, Arai Kazuhiro, Yamamoto Hiroyuki, eds., *Proceedings of the Symposium on Bangsa and Umma* (Tokyo: Sophia University, 2007), 113–31, 40–48.

39. Martin van Bruinessen, "Saleh Darat," in *Dictionnaire biographique des savants et grandes figures du monde musulman périphérique, du XIXe siècle à nos jours,* (Paris: CNRS-EHESS, 1998) Fasc. no 2., 25–26.

40. Lindenborn, "Langgars en Pesantrèns," 121, 123. Alongside the *Safina* and *Sittin,* Kartawidjaja mentioned the *Sullam al-tawfiq* of ʿAbdallah b. al-Husayn b. Tahir (d. 1855). Cf. Van den Berg, "Mohammedaansche godsdienstonderwijs," 519, 527.

41. Lindenborn, "Langgars en Pesantrèns," 124–26 (see ch.2, n.30).

42. M. C. Ricklefs, *Polarising Javanese Society: Islamic and other visions, c. 1830–1930* (Singapore: NUS Press, 2007), 72.

43. J.L.V. "Bijdrage," 14–15. For comparison, in nearby Bagelan in 1843, hajjis had accounted for only 17 individuals, and santris 206, out of a total population of "geesteli-jken" numbered at 8,000: P. Bleeker, "Opgave der Mohammedaansche geestelijkheid in de res. Bagelan," *TNI* 2 (1850), 19.

44. Harthoorn, "De zending op Java," 240–1; Ricklefs, *Mystic Synthesis,* 203–204 (see ch.1, n.22); Carel Poensen, "Een en ander over den godsdienstigen toestand van den Javaan," *MNZG* 8 (1864): 214–63.

45. Butrus Abu-Manneh, "The Naqshbandiyya-Mujaddidiyya in the Ottoman Lands in the Early 19th Century," *Die Welt des Islams* 22 (1982): 1–36.

46. Abu-Manneh, "Naqshbandiyya-Mujaddidiyya," 13, 15–16.

47. Butrus Abu-Manneh, "Khalwa and rabita in the Khalidi order," in M. Gaborieau, A. Popovic, and T. Zarcone, eds., *Naqshbandis: cheminements et situation actuelle d'un ordre mystique musulman* (Istanbul: Isis, 1990), 283–302.

48. Itzchak Weismann, *Taste of Modernity: Sufism, Salafiyya, and Arabism in Late Ottoman Damascus* (Leiden: Brill, 2001), 102.

49. Michael Laffan, "'A Watchful Eye': The Meccan Plot of 1881 and Changing Dutch Perceptions of Islam in Indonesia," *Archipel* 63–1 (2002): 79–108.

50. G.W.J. Drewes, *Drie Javaansche goeroe's: Hun leven, onderricht en messiasprediking,* Doctoral Dissertation (Leiden: Vros, 1925).

51. I. J. [*sic*] van Sevenhoven, "Java: ten dienste van hen die over dit eiland wenschen te reizen," *TNI* 2–1 (1839): 321–55, at 350–51.

52. LOr. 7931, 73, 77; Drewes, *Drie Javaansche goeroe's,* 10–18.

53. See letters of Ahmad Rifaʿi, in KITLV, D Or.22, esp 22–26; and Resident of Yogyakarta, Van Baak, to GG, 31 October 1881, secret, in MR 1881, no. 1041.

54. Kumar, *Diary* (see ch.2, n.7).

55. For Mas Rahmat's claims, see Kumar, *Diary,* 65, 81–94. On the anonymous *Bayan al-sirr,* see Drewes, *Directions,* 35 (see ch.1, n.10). The *Tuhfa* here is more likely that of al-Haytami rather than that of al-Burhanpuri. It is also clear from Dutch reports that some Akmali teachers were in possession of the *Fath al-rahman* and the *Hikam.* See J. J. Verwijk in MR 1889, no. 41.

56. This was the *Fath al-mubin.* S. Keijzer, *Onze tijd in Indie* (Den Haag: Susan, 1860), 54. It is claimed that ʿAbd al-Mannan Dipomenggolo (d. 1862), the founder of the Pesantren Tremas in 1830, and grandfather of Mahfuz Tremas (1868–1920), had studied in Egypt under al-Bajuri, much as his grandson favored contact with Egyptian scholars in Mecca like Abu Bakr Shattaʾ. Martin van Bruinessen, "Mahfuz b. ʿAbd Allah al-Tarmasi (K. H. Mahfudz Tremas, d. 1338/1920)," *Dictionnaire biographique,* Fasc. no 1., 30–31.

57. Alfred von Kremer, *Aegypten: Forschungen über Land und Volk während eines zehn*

jährigen Aufenthalts, 2 vols. (Leipzig: Brockhaus, 1863), II, 279; Ignaz Goldziher, "Universitäts-Moschee El-Azhar," in Georg Ebers, ed., *Aegypten in Bild und Wort*, 2 vols. (Stuttgart and Leipzig: Hallberger, 1879), II, 71–90, at 88. According to an Azharite visitor to Leiden in 1883, some Jawis, dissatisfied with education at home, had since moved to al-Azhar. C. Snouck Hurgronje, "Een en ander over het inlandsch onderwijs in de Padangsche bovenlanden" (1883), in *VG* IV–1, 27–52, 37, n.2.

58. ʿUmar ʿAbd al-Jabbar, *Siyar wa-tarajim: Baʿd ʿulamaʾina fi l-qarn al-rabiʿ ʿashr lil-hijra*, 3ʳᵈ ed. (Jeddah: al-Kitab al-ʿArabi al-Saʿudi, 1982), 288; Chaidar, *Sejarah Pujangga Islam: Syech Nawawi al-Banteni Indonesia* (Jakarta, 1978); and Hj. Wan Mohd. Shaghir Abdullah, "Bahasa Melayu bahasa ilmu: Mininjau pemikiran Syeikh Ahmad b. Muhammad Zain al-Fattani," *Jurnal Dewan Bahasa*, 34 (March 1990): 201–206.

59. Van den Berg, "Mohammedaansche godsdienstonderwijs," 523.

60. MR 1889, no. 41; Drewes, *Drie Javaansche goeroe's*, 49.

61. LOr. 5567, *Wulang Haji*, copied September 1873.

62. Zamakhsyari Dhofier, "Kinship and Marriage among the Javanese Kyai," *Indonesia* 29 (April 1980): 47–58.

63. Ricklefs, *Polarising Javanese Society*, 70.

64. K. F. Holle, "Mededeelingen over de devotie der Naqsjibendijah in den Ned. Indischen Archipel," *TBG* 31 (1886): 67–81, esp. 67, 69–76; Martin van Bruinessen, "Controversies and Polemics Involving the Sufi Orders in Twentieth-Century Indonesia," in F. de Jong & B. Radtke, eds., *Islamic Mysticism Contested: Thirteen Centuries of Controversies and Polemics* (Leiden and Boston: Brill, 1999) 705–28, at 710–12; ʿUthman b. ʿAbdallah b. ʿAqil, *al-Nasiha al-aniqa lil-mutalabbisin bi-l-tariqa* ([Batavia]: n.p., n.d.), 2.

65. ʿAbd al-Jabbar, *Siyar wa-tarajim*, 71; H. W. Muhd. Shaghir Abdullah, *Syeikh Ismail Al Minangkabawi: Penyiar Thariqat Naqsyabandiyah Khalidiyah* (Solo: Ramadhani, 1985); William G. Shellabear, "A Malay Treatise on Popular Sufi Practices," in *The Macdonald Presentation Volume* (Princeton and London: Princeton University and Oxford University Presses, 1933), 349–70, at 351–53.

66. On Ahmad Lampung, see Snouck Hurgronje, *Mekka*, 259–61; and *AA* III, 1874. Muhammad Maʿruf b. ʿAbdallah served as the Friday preacher at Palembang in the 1870s; Drewes, "Further Data," 227. For brief notice on Muhammad Ismaʿil b. ʿAbd al-Rahim al-Bali, see his Meccan edition of the *Fath al-ʿarifin* of AH 1323.

67. LOr. 7931, 19–21.

68. *Kayfiyyat khatm qurʾan*, 150.

69. Van den Berg, "Mohammedaansche godsdienstonderwijs," at 521 and 526; Snouck Hurgronje, "Een en ander," 41; LOr. 7931, passim.; *Mekka*, 192

70. Bernard Lewis, *What Went Wrong: Western Impact and Middle Eastern Response* (Oxford: Oxford University Press, 2002). Cf. Orlin Sabev, "The First Ottoman Turkish Printing Enterprise: Success or Failure?" in Dana Sajdi, ed., *Ottoman Tulips, Ottoman Coffee: Leisure and Lifestyle in the Eighteenth Century* (London: Taurus, 2008), 63–89.

71. The pass is reproduced in Alastair Hamilton, *Arab Culture and Ottoman Magnificence in Antwerp's Golden Age* (N.p.: The Arcadian Library and Oxford University Press, 2001), 86.

72. Ian Proudfoot, "Mass Producing Houri's Moles, or Aesthetics and Choice of Technology in Early Muslim Book Printing," in P. G. Riddell and A. D. Street, eds.,

Islam: Essays on Scripture, Thought and Society: A Festschrift in Honour of Anthony Johns (Leiden: Brill, 1997), 161–84.

73. Cf. Nile Green, "Journeymen, Middlemen: Travel, Trans-Culture and Technology in the Origins of Muslim Printing," *IJMES* 41–42 (2009): 203–24.

74. Ian Proudfoot, *Early Malay Printed Books: A Provisional Account of Materials Published in the Singapore-Malaysia Area up to 1920, Noting Holdings in Major Public Collections* (Kuala Lumpur: Academy of Malay Studies and The Library, University of Malaya, 1993), 14 and 464; and Proudfoot, "Malays Toying with Americans: The Rare Voices of Malay Scribes in Two Houghton Library manuscripts," Harvard Library Bulletin 11–1 (Spring 2000): 54–69.

75. Jan van der Putten and Al Azhar, intro. and eds., *Di dalam berkekalan persahabatan: "In everlasting friendship," Letters from Raja Ali Haji* (Leiden: Department of Languages and Cultures of Southeast Asia and Oceania, 1995), 11, n.2.

76. H. von Dewall, "Eene inlandsche drukker te Palembang," *TBG* 6 (1857): 193–98. Von Dewall offered them in turn to the Dutch Government for ƒ30. See Von Dewall to Resident of Palembang, Riau, 8 September 1857; and Von Dewall at Riau, 19 February 1858, in Perpustakaan Nasional H25.

77. N.J.G. Kaptein, "An Arab Printer in Surabaya in 1853," *BKI* 149–2 (1993): 356–62. Copies of the *Sharaf al-anam* as produced by al-Habshi are yet to surface. For a later example produced in Bombay ca. 1906 as part of a prayerbook destined for the Southeast Asian market, see n.n., *Majmūʿat mawlud* (Bombay: Muhammadiyya, 1324). See fig. 10.

78. J. van der Putten, "Printing in Riau: Two Steps Toward Modernity," *BKI* 153–4 (1997): 717–36, at 721.

79. Proudfoot, *Early Malay Printed* Books, 181–82. An eighteenth-century copy of the *Bidayat al-mubtadi bi-fadl allah al-mahdi* as held by the PNRI is W17.

80. Yusuf al-Ghani b. Sawwal al-Sumbawi, *Bidayat al-mubtadi waʿumdat al-awladi* (Istanbul: n.p., 1305), 118–20.

81. See *Katalog Manuskrip Melayu Koleksi Perpustakaan Negara Malaysia* (Kuala Lumpur: Perpustakaan Negara Malaysia, 2000), 66. Based on a copy made in 1862, the Malaysian catalogue suggests that the author was Arshad al-Banjari, but this is perhaps a reference to the transcription of Arshad al-Jawi's sponsorship of the print edition of 1861.

82. Sumbawi, *Bidayat al-mubtadi*, 118–20.

83. In later life Ahmad served as the *shaykh al-sadat* in Mecca, where he is buried. Whereas ʿAbd al-Jabbar refers to ʿAbd al-Rahman as a former mufti of the Shafiʿi school, he seems to mean Ahmad, the father of ʿAlawi al-Saqqaf (1839–1916). Another son of ʿAbd al-Rahman, Muhammad (d. 1906), would serve as Ottoman Consul at Singapore. See Buckley, *Anecdotal History*, II, 564–65; ʿAbd al-Jabbar, *Siyar wa-tarajim*, 137, 147.

84. Sumbawi, *Bidayat al-mubtadi*, 17, 23, 113–15.

85. Sumbawi, *Bidayat al-mubtadi*, 20, 37. Elsewhere (p. 88), al-Sumbawi is explicit about the beneficial use of "Barus camphor" for cleansing the corpse.

86. The *Kayfiyyat khatm [al-]Qurʾan* had been in existence for some decades. A partial MS from the mid-nineteenth century is held by Malaysia's national library. See MSS 2269(c), described in *Katalog Manuskrip Melayu*, 21–22. A Cairene edition of

1923 lacks many of the sections discussed here; cf. *Kayfiyyat khatm qur'an* (Cairo: al-Halabi), 1342.

87. *Kayfiyyat khatm qur'an*, 117, 152.

88. *Kayfiyyat khatm qur'an*, 172–78; cf. ʿAbd al-Jabbar, *Siyar*, 71; Van Bruinessen, "Kitab kuning," 252 (see ch.2, n.10).

89. Muhammad Zayn al-Din al-Sumbawi, *Manasik al-hajj* ([Bombay:] Fath al-Karim, 1305); *Minhaj al-salam* (Istanbul: al-Khayriyya, 1305); *Siraj al-huda* (see ch.2, n.31).

90. LOr. 7931, 78–80, 90, 169.

91. Proudfoot, *Early Malay Printed Books*, 29.

92. Snouck Hurgronje, "Brieven," 183.

93. Azyumardi Azra, "A Hadrami Religious Scholar in Indonesia: Sayyid ʿUthmân," in Ulrike Freitag and William G. Clarence-Smith, eds., *Hadhrami Traders, Scholars and Statesmen in the Indian Ocean, 1750s–1960s* (Leiden, New York and Cologne: Brill, 1997), 249–63; Nico Kaptein, "Sayyid ʿUthmān on the Legal Validity of Documentary Evidence," *BKI* 153–1 (1987): 85–102; and "The Sayyid and the Queen: Sayyid ʿUthmān on Queen Wilhelmina's Inauguration on the Throne of the Netherlands in 1898," *Journal of Islamic Studies* 9–2 (1998): 158–77.

94. *Qamar al-zaman*, verses 77–79. With thanks to Nico Kaptein (p.c. November 27, 2006).

95. Cf. [al-Banjari], *Tuhfat al-raghibin* 18 (see ch.2, n.20).

96. ʿUthman b. ʿAbdallah b. ʿAqil b. Yahya, *Manhaj al-istiqama fi l-din bi-l-salama* (Jakarta: Maktabat al-Madaniyya, n.d. [reprint of edition of 1890]), 15–16, 41–43, 45–46, and 59.

97. ʿUthman b. ʿAbdallah b. ʿAqil, *al-Wathiqa al-wafiyya fi ʿuluww sha'n tariqat al-sufiyya* ([Batavia]: n.p., 1303), esp. 14 and 19.

98. Ahmad b. Zayni Dahlan, *Risala raddiyya ʿala risalat al-shaykh Sulayman Afandi* (Mecca: al-Miriyya, 1301), 1.

99. ʿUthman b. ʿAbdallah b. ʿAqil b. Yahya, *Arti tarekat dengan pendek bicaranya* (Batavia: n.p., 1301), 11; cf. C. Snouck Hurgonje, "Een rector der Mekkaansche universiteit (met aanhangsel)," (1887) in VG III, 65–122, 72. On ʿAbd al-Wahhab Langkat, see Abdullah, *Syeikh Ismail*, 62–75; and Van der Putten, "Printing in Riau," 726.

100. Annabel Gallop, pc, November 2008; Gallop, "From Caucasia to Southeast Asia: Daghistani Qur'ans and the Islamic Manuscript Tradition in Brunei and the Southern Philippines, I," *Manuscripta Orientalia* 14–1 (2008): 32–56.

101. Dahlan, *Risala raddiyya*, 5.

102. The letters from Deli and Lankat bore the signatures of Muhammad Saʿid Qasati Banjar, ʿAbd al-Rahman Banjar, Zayn al-Din Rawa, and Muhammad Yunus b. ʿAbd al-Rahman. See Dahlan, *Risala raddiyya*, 12.

103. Snouck Hurgonje, "Een rector," 71.

104. Snouck Hurgonje, "Een rector," 91.

105. Snouck Hurgronje, *Mekka*, 286–87. The colophon of al-Sumbawi's *Siraj al-huda*, published in April 1886, indicates that al-Fatani was not the overall director of the press, with that role being taken by ʿAbd al-Ghani Afandi Shuwayki Zadeh.

106. Abdullah, "Bahasa Melayu bahasa ilmu," 201–206. Elsewhere Wan Shaghir has suggested that al-Fatani tried to convince al-Halabi to print Malay books in 1876, which they only seem to have done in the 1890s. Mohammad Shaghir Abdullah, *Wa-*

wasan pemikiran Islam: Ulama Asia Tenggara, 7 vols (Kuala Lumpur: Khazanah Fathani-yah, 2000), II, 95–96.

107. On Ahmad al-Fatani, see V. Matheson and M.B. Hooker, "Jawi Literature in Patani: The Maintenance of an Islamic Tradition," *JMBRAS* 61–1 (1988): 1–86, esp. 28–30. For Mecca, Snouck Hurgronje, basing himself on the "Hijaz Almanac" for AH 1303, states that it was in 1883 and that it listed twelve Malay books; Snouck Hurgonje, "Een rector," 70.

108. N.J.G. Kaptein, *The Muhimmât al-nafâ'is: A Bilingual Meccan Fatwa Collection for Indonesian Muslims from the End of the Nineteenth Century* (Jakarta: INIS, 1997).

109. Muhammad b. ʿAbdallah al-Khani al-Khalidi, *al-Bahja al-saniyya fi adab al-tariqa al-ʿaliyya al-khalidiyya al-naqshbandiyya* (Cairo: al-Maymuniyya, 1319), 3.

110. Muhsin Mahdi, "From the Manuscript Age to the Age of Printed Books," in George N. Atiyeh, ed., *The Book in the Islamic World: The Written Word and Communication in the Middle East* (Albany, NY: State University of New York Press/Library of Congress, 1995): 6–7; see also Dale F. Eickelman and Armando Salvatore, "Muslim Publics," in Armando Salvatore and Dale F. Eickelman, eds., *Public Islam and the Common Good* (Leiden: Brill, 2004), 3–27, at 12–13; and Martin van Bruinessen, "After the Days of Abû Qubays: Indonesian Transformations of the Naqshbandiyya Khâlidiyya," *Journal of the History of Sufism* 5 (2008): 225–51.

111. On the al-Khanis and al-Shaʿrani, see Leila Hudson, "Reading al-Shaʿrānī: The Sufi Genealogy of Islamic Modernism in Late Ottoman Damascus," *Journal of Islamic Studies* 15–1 (2004): 39–68. According to Van den Berg's informants in Semarang, Levantine copies of the *Jamiʿ al-usul* printed in AH 1287 (1870–71) were well known in Java. L.W.C. van den Berg, "Over de devotie der Naqsjibendîjah in den Indischen Archipel," *TBG* 28–2 (1883): 158–75, at 171. Four years later Van den Berg associated this text, and two others (*al-Ghunya li-talab al-tariqa* by Salih ʿAbd al-Qadir b. Musa [d. 1165–66] and *al-Fath al-rabbani wa-l-fayd al-rahmani* by ʿAfif al-Din b. al-Mubarak) with students of Sulayman Afandi teaching in Cirebon, Semarang, Surabaya, Bangil, and Madura. Van den Berg, "Mohammedaansche godsdienstonderwijs," 553. This was confirmed by Snouck Hurgronje in 1889 when he found Khalidi teachers in possession of even earlier Istanbul editions of the *Jamiʿ al-usul* from AH 1276 (1859–60); LOr. 7931, 165.

112. Ahmad Khatib b. ʿAbd al-Ghaffar Sambas, *Futuh al-ʿarifin yaitu bicara tariqat al-qadiriyya al-naqshbandiyya li-mawlana al-shaykh ʿAbd al-Qadir al-Jilani* (Singapore: ʿAbdallah al-Khatib al-Falimbani, Inciʾ Muhammad Sidin and al-Hajj Muhammad Yahya, 1287).

113. For a later edition of 1323 AH, see Shellabear, "Malay Treatise."

114. The *Mawahib* was a Malay translation of a work by Muhammad b. ʿAbd al-Daʾim b. bt. Maylaq, and 1883 would see the first publication at Singapore of a manual for the Naqshbandiyya. Proudfoot, *Early Malay Printed Books*, 212, 342.

115. Cf. Wieringa, "Tale of Two Cities," 183, 187.

116. See Snouck's handwritten note in the Leiden University copy of the Meccan edition of 1305 (1886–87), shelf-number 8187 A 28; and *AA* II, 1218. A Jakartan MS copy of a printed work is PNRI ML 149.

117. See LOr. 7310. On the library of Hajji Harun, see *AA* III, 1856–75.

118. *Kayfiyyat khatm qurʾan*, 23, 51, 120–52.

119. For example, a copy of the *Bidayat al-hidaya* or the *Fath al-muʿin* purchased in

Mecca in the mid-1880s would cost fifteen piastres, while the smaller Javanese *Fayd al-rahman* would cost about eight. See the list of prices for twenty-eight books sent by Aboe Bakar Djajadiningrat to Snouck, and received 5 April [1886?], in LOr. 7111.

120. Proudfoot, *Early Malay Printed Books*, 28.

121. A later version appeared from the press of Muhammad Arshad of Semarang. *Sha'ir shari'a dan tariqa* (Singapore: ca. 1880s).

122. Proudfoot, *Old Muslim Calendars*, 87 (see ch.2, n.1). Cf. J. Skovgaard-Petersen, *Defining Islam for the Egyptian State: Muftis and Fatwas of the Dār al-Iftā* (Leiden and New York: Brill, 1997); and Sayyid 'Uthman, *al-Qawanin al-shar'iyya li-ahl al-majalis al-hukmiyya bi tahqiq al-masa'il li-tamyiz lahum al-haqq min al-batil* = *Segala aturan hukum syara' bagi ahli-ahli majlis hukum syara'* (Batavia: n.p., 1324), ch.14.

123. Sartono Kartodirdjo, *The Peasants' Revolt of Banten in 1888: Its Conditions, Course, and Sequel* (The Hague: Nijhoff, 1966).

124. 'Uthman, *Arti tarekat*, 3–7 (see n.99 above).

125. C. Snouck Hurgronje, "Eenige Arabische strijdschriften besproken" (1897), in *VG* III, 149–88. Cf. Thomas Eich, "Publish or Perish in 19th Century Sufism: New Materials on Abu'l-Huda al-Sayyadi," forthcoming. Among the participants in such debates was Amin b. Hasan al-Madani (d. 1898).

126. Dahlan was known as the teacher of Haddadi prayers to such elite students as the son of the Penghulu of Bagelan and 'Abd al-Kafi in Samolangu, Kebumen. See LOr. 7931, pp. 231 and 256. On the Cirebon-born 'Abdallah b. 'Alawi b. Hasan al-'Attas (1860–1916), who is said to have founded the 'Attasiyya sub-branch of the Haddadiyya in India in 1886, see Arai, "Arabs Who Traversed," 173; and 'Attas, *Taj al-a'ras*, II, 702 (see ch.1, n.16).

127. I owe this observation to Nico Kaptein.

128. Snouck Hurgronje, "Eenige Arabische strijdschriften," 168–69.

129. *Kayfiyyat khatm qur'an*, 142; 'Abdallah b. 'Alawi al-Haddad, *al-Nafa'is al-'uluwiyya fi l-masa'il al-sufiyya* (n.p.: Dar al-Hawi, 1993), ix, 16–21.

130. Snouck Hurgronje, *Mekka*, 268–72, 284.

131. Pak Sonhaji, p.c., Pesantren Wahid Hasyim, Gaten, Yogyakarta, 2002.

132. Heer, *Handlist*, 6–7.

133. Sumbawi, *Siraj al-huda*, 8–9.

PART TWO: POWER IN QUEST OF KNOWLEDGE

Chapter Four: Foundational Visions of Indies Islam, 1600–1800

1. Frederik de Houtman, "Cort Verhael van Frederik de Houtman," in W. S. Unger, ed., *De Oudste reizen van de Zeeuwen naar Oost-Indië* (Gouda, 1880), 64–111, at 110.

2. Jan Huygen van Linschoten, *Reys-geschrift vande navigatien der Portugaloyers in Oriente* and *Itinerario, voyage ofte schipvaert van Jan Huygen van Linschoten naer Oost ofte Portugaels Indien inhoudende en corte beschryvinghe der selver landen ende zee-custen* (Amsterdam: Cornelis Claesz., 1595–96). For a useful overview of the Dutch literature from Van Linschoten to 1942, see B. J. Boland and I. Farjon, *Islam in Indonesia: A Bibliographical Survey 1600–1942* (Dordrecht and Cinnaminson: Foris, 1983).

3. Willem Lodewijcksz., *Prima Pars: Descriptionis itineris navalis in Indiam Orientalem* (Amsterdam: Nicolai, 1598), 26a.

4. Davis, *Voyages and Works*, 140–53 (see ch.1, n.36).

5. Frederick de Houtman, *Spraeck ende woord-boeck, inde Maleysche ende Madagaskarsche talen, met vele Arabisch ende Turcsche woorden* (Amsterdam: Jan Gerritsz. Cloppenburgh, 1603).

6. Van Neck, *Tvveede boeck*, 26a (see ch.2, n.5).

7. Van Neck, *Tvveede boeck*, 26b.

8. Van Neck, *Tvveede boeck*, appendix, not paginated.

9. De Houtman's dialogue commences with the arrival of a ship in port, and a later passage has his Dutchman announcing: "We are good people, come from a far-away country" (*Kyta oran baick, datan dérri negry iáou*). While God (*Alla*) is mentioned in the attached vocabulary, religion is not. *Spraeck ende woord-boeck*, 11, 27–28, 112.

10. Houtman, "Cort Verhael," 97–98.

11. Houtman, "Cort Verhael," 99, 102–103, 111.

12. Karel Steenbrink, *Dutch Colonialism and Indonesian Islam: Contacts and Conflicts, 1596–1950* (Amsterdam and Atlanta, GA: Rodopi, 1993), 16, 33–35; cf. Van Neck, *Tvveede boeck*, 41b–43a; *ONOI*, III, i, 27.

13. Van Linschoten, *Itinerario*, plates 66 and 67.

14. "Resolutie der vergadering van de zeventien," 27 February 1603, in *Archief*, V, 1 (see list of abbreviations).

15. "Contract met Henricus Slatius," 2 May 1606, in *Archief*, V, 4–6. See also G. J. Schutte, ed., *Het Indisch Sion: De gereformeerde kerk onder de Verenigde Oost-Indische Compagnie* (Hilversum: Verloren, 2002).

16. Joh. Wogma to Bewindhebbers OIC, Amboina, 14 August 1608 and Jan Maertsoon van Campen to Kerkeraad te Amsterdam, [Ambon], [1611], in *Archief*, V, 7, 19.

17. *Plakaatboek*, I, 7–9.

18. "Consideratien en advis vant Classis van Delff en Delflant," 7 April 1614, in *Archief*, V, 31–37, esp. 35.

19. *Plakaatboek*, I, 108 (see list of abbreviations). Cf. [J.A. Grothe], "Het Seminarie van Walaeus," *Berigten der Utrechtsche Zendings-Vereeniging* 23 (1882): 17–27, 33–44, and 49–57, at 19–20.

20. "Resolutie der vergadering van de zeventien," 24 February 1621, in *Archief*, V, 126–27.

21. Hugo de Groot, *Bewijs van den waren godsdienst* (n.p., 1622), 102–11, esp. 103; Martine Julia van Ittersum, *Profit and Principle: Hugo Grotius, Natural Rights Theories and the Rise of Dutch Power in the East Indies, 1595–1615* (Leiden: Brill, 2006).

22. Jaap R. Bruijn and Femme Gaastra, "The Dutch East India Company's Shipping, 1602–1795, in a Comparative Perspective," in Jaap R. Bruijn and Femme Gaastra, eds., *Ships, Sailors, and Spices: East India Companies and Their Shipping in the Sixteenth, Seventeenth, and Eighteenth Centuries* (Amsterdam: NEHA, 1993), 177–208.

23. Peter G. Riddell, "Rotterdam MS 96 D 16: The Oldest Surviving Qur'an from the Malay World," *Indonesia and the Malay World* 30/86 (March 2002), 9–20; G.W.J. Drewes, *Een 16de Eeuwse Maleise Vertaling van de Burda van al-Bûṣîrî (Arabisch Lofdicht op Mohammad)* (The Hague: Nijhoff, 1955); Muhammad Naguib al-Attas, *The Oldest Known Malay Manuscript: A 16th Century Translation of the Aqai'd of al-Nasafi* (Kuala Lumpur: University of Malaya Press, 1988).

24. This text is LOr. 1928. See B.J.O. Schrieke, *Het Boek van Bonang* (Leiden, 1916); and Drewes, *Admonitions* (see ch.1, n.21).

25. This was LOr. 266, studied successively by J.G.H. Gunning, *Een Javaansch ge-schrift uit de 16de eeuw, handelende over den Mohammedaanschen godsdienst* (Leiden: Brill, 1881); H. Kraemer, *Een Javaansche Primbon uit de zestiende eeuw* (Leiden: Trap, 1921); and G.W.J. Drewes, *Een Javaansche Primbon uit de zestiende eeuw, Newly Edited and Translated* (Leiden: Brill, 1954).

26. Aḥmad ibn Qāsim al-Ḥajarī, *Kitāb Nāṣir al-dīn ʿalā 'l-qawm al-kāfirīn (The sup-porter of religion against the infidels)*, P. S. van Koningsveld, Q. al-Samarrai, and G. A. Wiegers, trans. and eds. (Madrid: Consejo Superior de Investigaciones Científicas, Agencia Española de Cooperación Internacional, 1997), 198–99.

27. Harold J. Cook, *Matters of Exchange: Commerce, Medicine, and Science in the Dutch Golden Age* (New Haven and London: Yale, 2007).

28. Ibn al-Ḥajarī, *Kitāb Nāṣir al-dīn*, 181–82. Ibn al-Hajari further confessed his amazement that the lands whence cloves were brought could be subject to a Muslim sultan, let alone two sharing the same island.

29. Antonio Pigafetta, *Magellan's Voyage: A Narrative Account of the First Circum-navigation*, R. A. Skelton, trans. and ed. (New York: Dover Publications, 1994), 128–30 and 172–77.

30. See note 16 above, and Caspar Wiltens to Classis/Kerkeraad van Amsterdam, Ambon, 31 May 1615, in *Archief*, V, 42–67, at 56.

31. Kees Groeneboer, *Gateway to the West: The Dutch Language in Colonial Indonesia 1600–1950*, Maya Scholz trans. (Amsterdam: Amsterdam University Press, 1998), 30–31; Jacobus Richardus Callenbach, *Justus Heurnius: Eene bijdrage tot de geschiedenis des Christendoms in Nederlandsch Oost-Indie* (Nijkerk: C. C. Callenbach, 1897), 36–37.

32. Jasper Janssen to Bewindhebbers, Amboina, 12 Juli 1612, in *Archief*, V, 21.

33. Casper Wiltens to Classis/Kerkeraad van Amsterdam, Ambon, 31 May 1615, in *Archief*, V, 49–50.

34. Callenbach, *Justus Heurnius*, 37.

35. J. P. Coen to Bewindhebbers, Jacatra, 5 August 1619, in *Archief*, V, 117.

36. "Extract uit het resolutieboek van Amboina," 28 September 1617, in *Archief*, V, 79–80.

37. Steven van der Haghen to Bewindhebbers, Amboina, 14 August 1617, and Adr. Blocq to Steven van der Haghen, Bantam, 6 November 1617, in *Archief*, V, 84, 87–89.

38. Aert Gijsels to Bewindhebbers, Amboina, 5 August 1619, in *Archief*, V, 110–16.

39. Herman van Speult to Bewindhebbers, Amboina, 10 August 1619, in *Archief*, V, 118–19.

40. "Corte beschrijvinghe hoe ende op wat maniere de Rosengeynders (volgens haer versoeck) om Christen te worden gehandelt is," in *Archief*, V, 152–67.

41. Ibid. 162.

42. Ibid. 163.

43. Grothe, "Het Seminarie," 37, 42 (see n.19 of this chapter).

44. Justus Heurnius, *De legatione evangelica ad Indos capassenda, admonito* (Leiden: Elsevier, 1618), as quoted in Grothe, "Het Seminarie," 22.

45. Caspar Wiltens, et.al., *Vocabularium, ofte, Woorden-Boeck, nae ordre van den alpha-beth, in't Duytsch en Maleys* (Amsterdam, 1650); George Henrik Werndly, *Maleische Spraakkunst, Uit de eige schriften der Maleiers opgemaakt* (Amsterdam: Wetstein, 1736), 231–35, 288, 293.

46. Kerkeraad te Batavia to Bewindhebbers, Batavia, 20 December 1638, in *Archief,* VI, 395. See also L. J. Joose and A. Th. Boone, "Kerk en zendingsbevel," in Schutte, *Indisch Sion,* 25–42 (see n.15 of this chapter).

47. *Tafsir,* for example, is consistently misspelled as *tacxir,* and the "angel of death" (*malikul ma'oeth*) is simply glossed as "death." *Dictionarium Malaicobelgicum,* Bodleian Library, MS Marsh 712, 78b.

48. Based on the watermark, the dictionary was written on paper produced between 1633, a year after the closure of the college, and 1652, that of Heurnius's death.

49. *Dictionarium Malaicobelgicum,* 3b.

50. *Dictionarium Malaicobelgicum,* esp. 54b. It is worth noting that the verb *mengaji* remains in use in Indonesian today for the study of religious texts.

51. C. Snouck Hurgronje, "De Islâm," (1886), in *VG* I, 183–294, at 190.

52. Cook, *Matters of Exchange,* 204–206.

53. On Voetius, see J. van Amersfoort en W. J. van Asselt, *Liever Turks dan Paaps? De visies van Johannes Coccejus, Gisbertus Voetius en Adrianus Relandus op de islam* (Zoetermeer: Boekencentrum, 1997), 19–23. Cf. Steenbrink, *Dutch Colonialism,* 49–52.

54. *ONOI* IV, i, 123; R.R.F. Habiboe, *Tot verheffing van mijne natie: Het leven en werk van François Valentijn (1666–1727)* (Franeker: Van Wijnen, 2004), 28, 30.

55. F. de Haan, "Uit oude notarispapieren I," *TBG* 42 (1900): 297–308. St. Martin also had numerous manuscripts on Persian topics by Herbert De Jager.

56. De Haan, "Oude notarispapieren," 306–307.

57. De Haan, "Oude notarispapieren," 307.

58. Rumphius, *Curiosity Cabinet,* ciii, 392 (see ch.1, n.18).

59. Rumphius, *Curiosity Cabinet,* ciii, 235, 280, 290, 392. Cf. Cook, *Matters of Exchange,* 329–32. While there is no longer a village of Ely on Ambon, it is preserved in the name of the leading family in Assilulu. Wim Manuhutu, p. c., October 19, 2008.

60. Rumphius, *Curiosity Cabinet,* 238.

61. Rumphius, *Curiosity Cabinet,* 239.

62. Rumphius, *Curiosity Cabinet,* 267.

63. See Rumphius, *Curiosity Cabinet,* 264. Both the Golian and Leijdecker dictionaries defined an *'azima* (*Adjimath / azmet*) as just such an object. See *Dictionarium Malaicobelgicum,* 3a; *Maleisch en Nederduitsch Woordenboek met Arabisch Karakter vermoedelijk het Manuscript van Dos. Leidekker,* KITLV, Or. 165, 34b.

64. Snouck Hurgronje, "De Islâm," 186–87; Van Amersfoort and Van Asselt, *Liever Turks,* 23–28.

65. Van Amersfoort and Van Asselt, *Liever Turks,* 108.

66. Van Amersfoort and Van Asselt, *Liever Turks,* 119.

67. Snouck Hurgonje, "Een rector," 77 (see ch.3, n.99). For manuscripts passed from Valentijn to Relandus, see LOr. 1692 and LOr. 1945 described in Jan Just Witkam, *Inventory of the Oriental Manuscripts of the Library of the University of Leiden* (Leiden: Ter Lugt, 2007), II, 219, 291.

68. Valentyn, *ONOI,* IV, i, 223.

69. H. E. Niemeijer, "Orang Nasrani: Protestants Ambon in de zeventiende eeuw," in Schutte, *Indisch Sion,* 127–45, esp. 142–44; Habiboe, *Tot verheffing,* 52–57. See also François Valentyn, *Deure der waarhijd voor 't ooge der Christenwereld geopend* (Dordrecht, 1698).

70. Ridjali, *Historie van Hitu*, 25 (see ch.1, n.12).

71. "Kerknieuws," *Boekzaal der Geleerde Werelt* (November 1727): 610–32, at 619; Habiboe, *Tot verheffing*, 118.

72. *Catalogus Exquisitissimorum & Excellentissimorum Librorum . . . Viri Reverendi Fr. Valentyn . . .* (The Hague: Alberts & Van der Kloof, 1728), 5–6; cf. Habiboe, *Tot verheffing*, 121–22. One of Valentijn's copies of the *Ma'rifat al-islam* is now held in Kuala Lumpur while another variant of the text is held in Jakarta. Cf. Werndly, *Spraakkunst*, 355.

73. "Verklaaringe vande Muhhamedaansche Godts-geleertheijt," LUB, BPL 310; LOr. 1700 and LOr. 14.383; Werndly, *Spraakkunst*, 354–55.

74. *ONOI*, III, i, 19–27.

75. *ONOI*, III, ii, 148–235, esp. 233.

76. *ONOI*, III, ii, 233.

77. *ONOI*, IV, ii, 1–2. Ibn al-Hajari's information had been less enlightening. Likely basing himself on Pedro Texeira's *Relaciones del origen, descendia y succession de los Reyes de Persia, y de Harmuz, y un viaje hecho por el mismo autor dende la India Oriental hasta Italia por tierra* (Antwerp, 1610), he merely mentioned the conversion of Java from cannibalism 130 years beforehand. See Ibn al-Ḥajarī, *Kitāb Nāṣir al-dīn*, 182.

78. *ONOI*, IV, ii, 4.

79. Werndly, *Spraakkunst*, 241.

80. Werndly, *Spraakkunst*, 354–55.

81. The *Kanz al-khafi* was also noted by Valentijn. See *ONOI*, III, i, 27; see also Voorhoeve, "Lijst der geschriften," 156-57 (see ch.1, n.57).

82. Werndly, *Spraakkunst*, 354–57; Proudfoot, "Expedition," 20 (see ch.2, n.23).

83. For the "Leijdekker" dictionary, see KITLV, Or. 165, [Part I] 26b, 90a, 92a; [Part II] 12a, 31a–b. For mention of Shaykh Yusuf's retinue, see F. De Haan, *Priangan: De Preanger-regentschappen onder het Nederlandsch bestuur tot 1811*, 4 vols. (Batavia: Bataviaasch Genootschap van Kunsten en Wetenschappen, 1910–12), III, 283.

84. *Plakaatboek*, VII, 392–407. Cf. P. A. van der Lith, "De koloniale wetgeving tegenover de Europeesche en de Inlandsche Rechtsbegippen," *De Gids* 3 (1882): 193–231, at 221.

85. See instructions of 1757 and 1759 reported in BL MSS Eur/Mack Private 32, "Realia Livre A, Volume III," 308–309.

86. "Korte verhaal van de Javasche oorlogen sedert den jare 1741 tot 1757," *VKI* 12 (1830): 77–254, at 185–89; cf. G. W. van der Meiden, "A Turkish Mediator between Mangkubumi and the Dutch East India Company (1753–1754)," *RIMA* 14–1 (1980): 92–107.

87. Sri Margana, *Java's Last Frontier: The Struggle for Hegemony of Blambangan, c. 1763–1813* (Leiden, CNWS/TANAP, Faculty of Arts, Leiden University, 2007).

88. J. M. Mohr to Jan Jacob Schultens, Batavia, 28 April and 1 November 1759, LUB, BPL 245 xii.

89. Werndly, *Spraakkunst*, 350, 354. For the *Kanz al-khafi*, cf. *ONOI* III, i, 27.

90. Habiboe, *Tot verheffing*, 63.

91. An edict of 1651 had banned all Muslim meetings and assemblies, yet in 1654 there were complaints about "Moorish, Chinese and Javanese" schools in operation in Batavia, and a survey of 1674 found six places of worship. Steenbrink, *Dutch Colonialism*, 70.

92. Max de Bruijn and Remco Raben, eds., *The World of Jan Brandes, 1743–1808:*

Drawings of a Dutch Traveller in Batavia, Ceylon and Southern Africa (Amsterdam: Rijksmuseum, 2004); G. L. Balk et.al., eds., *The Archives of the Dutch East India Company (VOC) and the Local Institutions in Batavia (Jakarta)* (Leiden and Boston: Brill, 2007); Oiyan Liu and Eric Tagliocozzo, "The National Archives (Jakarta) and the Writing of Transnational Histories of Indonesia," *Itinerario* 32–1 (2008): 81–94.

93. Huib J. Zuidervaart and Rob H. van Gent, "'A Bare Outpost of Learned European Culture on the Edge of the Jungles of Java': Johan Maurits Mohr (1716–1775) and the Emergence of Instrumental and Institutional Science in Dutch Colonial Indonesia," *Isis* 95 (2004): 1–33.

94. "Voorbericht," *VBG* 1 (1779): 29–30. (Note that pagination of the various imprints of the first volume varies.)

95. De Bruijn and Raben, *The World of Jan Brandes*, 215–18.

96. A rare exception was the Sundanese lexicon of Jonathan Rigg. See his *Dictionary of the Sunda Language of Java* (Batavia: Lange, 1862).

97. Ricklefs, *Mystic Synthesis*, 175 (see ch.1, n.22).

98. Ricklefs, *Mystic Synthesis*, 176–79.

Chapter Five: New Regimes of Knowledge, 1800–1865

1. Cees Fasseur, *De Indologen: Ambtenaren voor de Oost, 1825–1950*, 3rd edition (Amsterdam: Aula, 2003).

2. Peter Boomgaard, "For the Common Good: Dutch Institutions and Western Scholarship on Indonesia around 1800," in Peter Boomgaard, ed., *Empire and Science in the Making—Dutch "Colonial" Scholarship around 1800 in Comparative Perspective*. Forthcoming.

3. J. A. van der Chijs, "Bijdragen," 212 (see ch.2, n.32).

4. In so doing though they were no worse than the Dutch. The Deventer collection of Malay manuscripts was booty from a 1784 expedition against Selangor, and many other texts were gathered for the English through the cooperation of local regents. See D. E. Weatherbee, "Raffles' Sources for Traditional Javanese Historiography and the Mackenzie Collections," *Indonesia* 26 (October 1978): 63–95, esp. 67–68.

5. Even with the destruction of the *Fame*, it is clear that most of Raffles's earlier collection was spared, to be bequeathed to the Royal Asiatic Society in 1830. See Ricklefs and Voorhoeve, *Indonesian Manuscripts*, xxvii.

6. William Marsden, *The History of Sumatra: Containing an Account of the Government, Laws, Customs, and Manners of the Native Inhabitants, with a Description of the Natural Productions, and a Relation of the Ancient Political State of that Island* (London: Thomas Payne and Son, 1783), iv.

7. Marsden, *History of Sumatra*, 3rd edition (London: M'Creery, 1811), iv.

8. Marsden, *History of Sumatra* (1783), 35–36.

9. Marsden, *History of Sumatra* (1783), 163–65.

10. IOL Add. 26568, 117b–18a; Werndly, *Spraakkunst*, 343–47 (see ch.4, n.45).

11. John Bastin, "John Leyden and the Publication of the Malay Annals, 1821," *JMBRAS* 75–2 (2002): 99–115.

12. Van der Chijs, "Bijdragen," 214.

13. Van der Chijs, "Bijdragen," 215–19.

14. Mentioned were the "alip-alipan (abc boek), toeroetan, pateka, njasin, koran, aliphlam, kitab asmoro kandi, kitab zitim, kitab doerat, kitab nahoe, kitab sarap, kitab

amil, kitab joeroemia." Of these, the elementary catechisms of al-Samarqandi and al-Sanusi, and the grammar of Ajurrumi, stand out. At Kedu, by contrast, the listing referred solely to the disciplinary designations of "nahwoe, tasrip, hoesoeb, pekik en tapsir." Van der Chijs, "Bijdragen," 217–18.

15. For example, Cirebon counted some 190 pesantrens with some 2,763 students, Semarang was said to encompass 95 schools with 1,140 pupils, while Surabaya and Jipan had 410 langgars with 4,397 santris. Van der Chijs, "Bijdragen," 228–30.

16. Report of the Patti, Chief Jaksa and Chief Panghulu of Japara, as cited in Van der Chijs, "Bijdragen," 321.

17. Van der Chijs, "Bijdragen," 234.

18. Van der Chijs, "Bijdragen," 231.

19. *VBG* 9 (1825): xix.

20. J. I. van Sevenhoven, "Beschrijving van de hoofdplaats van Palembang," *VBG* 9 (1825): 39–126, esp. 68–69, 76, 80–81.

21. [H.G. Nahuijs], H. Eric Miller, trans., "Extracts from the Letters of Col. Nahuijs," *JMBRAS* 19-2 (1941): 169–209, at 187.

22. Nahuijs, "Extracts," 191.

23. R. N. Cust as cited in *Actes du Sixième Congrès International des Orientalists, tenu en 1883 à Leide*, 4 volumes. (Leiden: Brill, 1884–1885), I, 56.

24. Annabel Teh Gallop, "Early Malay Printing 1603–1900: An Exhibition at the British Library 20 January to 4 June 1989," British Library Exhibition Notes, 1989; see also Proudfoot, *Early Malay Printed Books*, 9 (see ch.3, n.74).

25. Kees Groeneboer, *Van Radja Toek tot Goesti Dertik: Herman Neubronner van der Tuuk als veldlinguïst in negentiende-eeuws Indonesië* (Amsterdam: Koninklijke Nederlandse Akademie van Wetenschappen, 2000), 9.

26. W. H. Medhurst, "Mission of the London Missionary Society in Java," *Missionary Herald* 25 (June 1829), 192–93.

27. See ʿAbdallah Munshi, *Hikayat Abdullah*, A. H. Hill, ed. and trans. (Kuala Lumpur: Oxford University Press, 1970), 195–96; and C. B. Buckley, *Anecdotal History*, I, 11–12 (see ch.3, n.33).

28. PUL, Garrett Collection, 480L, 37b. While Jesus is referred to as the "spirit of God" in the Qur'an (4: 169), this phrase also played into an apocalyptic tract from the 1860s, where a very militant Jesus does battle with the hosts of Hell. W. Hoezoo, "Het Javaansche geschrift 'Achir-ing-djaman'," *MNZG* 27 (1883): 1–42, at 35.

29. De Houtman, "Cort verhaal," 97ff. (see ch.4, n.1); De Haan, "Oude notarispapieren." (see ch.4, n.55)

30. *Tahlil pada menyatakan peri Kitab Allah*, PUL, Garrett Collection, 481L; Proudfoot, *Early Malay Printed Books*, 422–24.

31. These are the alleged words of Joseph le Bron de Vexela (1793–1853) addressing a group of Kyai Maja's followers in November 1828 as quoted in Schoemaker, "Gevangenneming van Kiai Modjo," 291 (see ch.3, n.26).

32. G.W.J. Drewes, "De etymologie van *padri*," *BKI* 138, 2–3 (1982): 346–50; J. Kathirithamby-Wells, "The Origin of the Term *Padri*: Some Historical Evidence," *Indonesia Circle* 41 (November 1986): 3–9; Marcia Hermansen, "Wahhabis, Fakirs and Others: Reciprocal Classifications and the Transformation of Intellectual Categories," in Jamal Malik, eds., *Perspectives of Mutual Encounters in South Asian History, 1760–1860* (Leiden: Brill, 2000), 23–48; Veth in De Stuers, *Vestiging*, I, 33–34, n.2 (see ch.3,

n.6); R.P.A. Dozy, *Het Islamisme* (Haarlem: Kruseman, 1863), 290 n; KITLV, Or. 22, 23–26; Henry Yule and Arthur Coke Burnell, eds., *Hobson-Jobson: Being a Glossary of Anglo-Indian Colloquial Words and Phrases* (London: Murray, 1886), 496–97.

33. Nahuijs, "Extracts," 187–88.

34. Sophia Raffles, *Memoir of the Life and Public Services of Sir Thomas Stamford Raffles* (London: Murray, 1830), 429, 562.

35. Nahuijs, "Extracts," 189–90.

36. LOr. 1743, flycover note.

37. JALAL AL-DIN, 52.

38. Ricklefs, *Mystic Synthesis*, 217 (see ch.1, n.22).

39. KITLV, Or. 163; De Stuers, *Vestiging*, II, 8–14.

40. Annabel Teh Gallop, "The Library of an 18th-century Selangor Bibliophile," unpublished paper presented to the 20th ASEASUK Conference, the Horniman Museum, London, October 12, 2002. See also Voerhoeve, "Malay Scriptorium," 259 (see ch.2, n.18).

41. Van Sevenhoven, "Beschrijving." For a reconstruction of the Palembang library, see Drewes, *Directions*, 199–200 (see ch.1, n.10).

42. John Crawfurd, *History of the Indian Archipelago: Containing an Account of the Manners, Arts, Languages, Religions, Insitutions, and Commerce of its Inhabitants*, 3 vols. (London: Cass, 1967 [1820]), II, 259–71, esp. 260–61, 269.

43. On the school, see Fasseur, *Indologen*, 147; Kenji Tsuchiya, "Javanology and the Age of Ranggawarsita: An Introduction to Nineteenth-century Javanese Culture," in George McTurnan Kahin and Takashi Shiraishi, eds., *Reading Southeast Asia: Translation of Contemporary Japanese Scholarship on Southeast Asia* (Ithaca: Cornell University Southeast Asia Program, 1990), 75–108, esp. 79–81.

44. P. P. Roorda van Eysinga, *Handboek der land- en volkenkunde, geschied-, taal-, aardrijks- en staatkunde van Nederlandsch Indië*, 4 vols (Amsterdam: Van Bakkenes, 1841–50); Boland and Farjon, *Islam in Indonesia*, 7. (see ch.4, n.2)

45. Fasseur, *Indologen*, 50.

46. P. J. Veth, *Specimen e litteris orientalibus exhibens majorem partem libri As-Sojutii de nominibus relativis inscripti* Lubb al-Lubab (Leiden: Luchtmans, 1840), esp. xix.

47. Paul van der Velde, *Een Indische liefde: P. J. Veth (1814–1895) en de inburgering van Nederlands-Indië* (Nijmegen: Balans, 2000), 96, 261.

48. Albertus Meursinge, *Specimen e litteris orientalibus, exhibens Sojutii librum de interpretibus Korani, ex Ms. codice Bibliothecae Leidensis editum et annotatione illustratum* (Lugduni Batavorum: Luchtmans, 1839); and *Handboek van het Mohammedaansche regt, in de Maleische taal; naar oorspronkelijke Maleische en Arabische werken* (Amsterdam: Jan Müller, 1844) (cf. LOr. 1633); J. J. de Hollander, *Handleiding tot de kennis der Maleische taal* (Breda: Broese, 1845); *Handleiding bij de beoefening der Maleische taal en letterkunde* (Breda: Nys, 1856).

49. Compare JALAL AL-DIN, 52, with LOr. 1743, 28.

50. Fasseur, *Indologen*, 149.

51. S. Keyzer, *Kitab Toehpah, Javaansch-Mohammedaansch Wetboek* (The Hague: n.n., 1853). For an earlier approach to Islamic legal texts, see J.F.W. van Nes, "Boedelscheidingen op Java volgens de kitab saphihi," *TNI* 12–2 (1850): 257–61. On the efforts of Meursinge and Keijzer in general, see Léon Buskens, "Twee negentiende eeuwse ontdekkers van het Islamitisch recht te Delft: Een begin van het debat over theorie en

praktijk," in Paulien van der Grinten and Ton Heukels, eds., *Crossing Borders: Essays in European and Private International Law, Nationality Law and Islamic Law in Honour of Frans van der Velden* (Deventer: Kluwer, 2006), 153–72.

52. Taco Roorda, *Kitab Toehpah: Een Javaansch handboek voor het Mohammedaansch regt* (Leiden: Brill, 1874), v–vi; *AA* III, 1844; on Engelhard's importance, see Weatherbee, "Raffles' sources," 69ff.

53. Roorda, *Kitab Toehpah*, x.

54. S. Keijzer, *Handboek voor het Mohammedaansch regt* (The Hague: Belinfante, 1853), i–iii. His later work on criminal law, based on Arabic and Indonesian sources, and a study of Abu Shujaʿ (d. after 1196), displayed the same attitude. S. Keijzer, *Mohammedaansch Strafrecht naar Arabische, Javaansche en Maleische Bronnen* (The Hague: Susan, 1857); and *Précis de Jurisprudence musulmane selon le Rite châféite par Abou Chodjâ* (Leiden: Brill, 1859).

55. W. L. Ochsenwald, "The Jidda Massacre of 1858," *Middle Eastern Studies* 13–3 (1977): 314–26.

56. Keijzer, *Onze tijd*, 52. (see ch.3, n.56)

57. Keijzer, *Onze tijd*, esp.120–26.

58. Marc Gaborieau, "Muslim Saints, Faquirs and Pilgrims in 1831: According to Garcin de Tassy," in Malik, *Perspectives*, 128–56 (see n.32 above).

59. G. K. Niemann, *Inleiding tot de kennis van den Islam, ook met betrekking tot den Indischen Archipel* (Rotterdam: M. Wijt and Zonen, 1861), 325–27, 356–57.

60. S. Keijzer, ed., *François Valentijn's Oud en Nieuw Oost-Indiën* (Amsterdam: Van Kesteren, 1862).

61. Veth, in De Stuers, *Vestiging*, I, xcix, 33–34, 36.

62. R.P.A. Dozy, *Het Islamisme* (Haarlem: Kruseman, 1863). On the series and its genesis, see A. L. Molendijk, *The Emergence of the Science of Religion in the Netherlands* (Leiden: Brill, 2005), 55–63.

63. Dozy, *Het Islamisme*, 275, 290–92.

Chapter Six: Seeking the Counterweight Church, 1837–1889

1. Tradescant Lay, "Notes," II, 192 (see Chapter 2, n.24).

2. See [J. T. Dickinson], "Notices of the City of Borneo and its Inhabitants, Made During the Voyage of the American Brig Himmaleh in the Indian Archipelago, in 1837," *The Chinese Repository* 7 (1838): 121–36 and 177–93; and Lay, "Notes."

3. Lay, "Notes," 186.

4. Dickinson, "Notices," 185.

5. Lay, "Notes," 209–10.

6. Dickinson, "Notices," 134.

7. Gallop, "From Caucasia to Southeast Asia," 32–56 (see ch.3, n.100); Gallop, "Seals, Sufis and Saints: The Unveiling of Maʿruf al-Karkhi," paper presented to the Simposium Internasional Pernaskhahan Nusantara II, Fakultas Sastra Universitas Indonesia, Depok, November 26, 1998.

8. Spencer St. John, *Life in the Forests of the Far East*, 2 vols (Kuala Lumpur: Oxford in Asia Historical Reprints, Oxford University Press, 1974), II, 258–59.

9. See also [Van Hoëvell], "Verdraagzaamheid der Mohammedanen op Java," *TNI* 12–2 (1850): 74-75.

10. "Mohammed en de Koran," *De Gids* 9-2 (1845) 294-309, 346-57, 393-421, 461-

78, 525–46; W. R. van Hoëvell, *Nederland en Bali: Eene stem uit Indië tot het Nederlandsche volk* (Groningen: Oomkens, 1846); cf. Van der Velde, *Indische liefde*, 124 (see ch.5, n.47).

11. W.R. Van Hoëvell, *Reis over Java, Madura en Bali in het midden van 1847, uitg. onder toezigt van P.J. Veth*, 3 vols (Amsterdam: Van Kampen, 1849–54), I, 2.

12. Van Bruinessen, "Shaykh ʿAbd al-Qadir," 368, 374–75 (see ch.1, n.61).

13. Van Hoëvell, *Reis over Java*, I, 25–27.

14. P. J. Veth, in Van Hoëvell, *Reis over Java*, I, 25–26, n.

15. Van Hoëvell, *Reis over Java*, I, 156–57.

16. Van Hoëvell, *Reis over Java*, I, 162. For similar sentiments expressed by Van Hoëvell in relation to Islam in Banten, see his "Verdraagzaamheid."

17. Of the guessed texts, one was perhaps the elementary *Umm al-barahin*, while Veth declared the crowning text to have been the *Tariqat al-fuqaha'*. Van Hoëvell, *Reis over Java*, II, 53–54.

18. cf. Weatherbee, "Raffles' Sources" (see ch.5, n.4).

19. Van Hoëvell, *Reis over Java*, II, 55–57.

20. Van Hoëvell, *Reis over Java*, II, 91.

21. Van Hoëvell, *Reis over Java*, I, 143.

22. Van Hoëvell, *Reis over Java*, I, 183.

23. Groeneboer, *Van Radja Toek*, 11. As but one example, we may point to the *Mir'at al-mu'min* of Shams al-Din with the translation of Van der Vorm. See LOr. 1700.

24. V.d.H. "Oorsprong der Padaries, eene secte op de Westkust van Sumatra, en hare uitbreiding," *TNI* 1–1 (1838) 113–31; Anon. "Het heilige graf van Girie," *TNI* 2–1 (1839): 60–66; W. R. van Hoëvell, "MOHAMED," *TNI* 2–1 (1839): 365–92, esp. 391–92; "Tafeleeren uit der aanvang der Padriesche onlusten in het landschap Agam," in De Stuers, *Vestiging*, II, 243–51 (see ch.3, n.6).

25. W. R. van Hoëvell, "Heilige graven," *TNI* 3–1 (1840): 172–76.

26. Van Sevenhoven, "Java 349–53 (see ch.3, n.51).

27. Van Sevenhoven, "Java," 351–52.

28. "Over de edelen, geestelijken en beambten," note appended to Moenier's "Het boek der Nawolo-Pradhoto," *TNI* 6–1 (1844): 261–434, at 335–39.

29. "Algemeen overzigt van den toestand van Nederlansch Indie, gedurende hat jaar 1846," *TNI* 10–1 (1848): 78–120, at 96–97.

30. P. Bleeker, "Fragmenten eener reis over Java," *TNI* 9–2 (1849), 17–55, 117–145, 170–90, 241–70 and 10–1 (1850): 1–50, 89–113, 165–91, 245–73, 309–14, 397–415.

31. Van Hoëvell, "Verdraagzaamheid."

32. A. D. Cornets de Groot, "Bijdrage tot de kennis der zeden en gewonten der Javanen," *TNI* 15–1 (1853): 81–103, esp. 93–97.

33. Van Nes, "Boedelscheidingen op Java." (see ch.5, n.51)

34. Harthoorn, "De zending op Java," 240–1 (see ch.3, n.31); Poensen, "Godsdienstigen toestand van den Javaan," esp. 227–28 (see ch.3, n.44); Ricklefs, *Polarising Javanese Society*, 36–38, 84–104 (see ch.3, n.42).

35. J.L.V. "Bijdrage," 16 (see ch.2, n.7).

36. J.L.V., "Bijdrage," 10, n.

37. Jan Frederik Gerrit Brumund, *Het volksonderwijs onder de Javanen* (Batavia: Van Haren, Noman and Kolff, 1857), esp. 4–29.

38. Brumund, *Volksonderwijs*, 20–21.

39. Brumund, *Volksonderwijs*, 21–22.

40. On Niemann's use of Brumund, see his *Inleiding*, 361–62 (see ch.5, n.59).

41. Fasseur, *Indologen*, 151 (see ch.5, n.1).

42. *TNI* 24–1 (1862): 195.

43. P. J. Veth, "Het onderwijs der Javanen," *De Gids* 22–3 (1858): 747–49, 757–58; cf. Van der Velde, *Indische liefde*, 150.

44. Fasseur, *Indologen*, 197.

45. Van der Putten and Al Azhar, *Berkekalan persahabatan*, 5–8 (see ch.3, n.75).

46. See, for example, Von de Wall to Resident of Banten, 17 January 1857, in Perpustakaan Nasional H29, 281.

47. A. B. Cohen Stuart to Resident of Surakarta, Surakarta, 29 January 1857, in Perpustakaan Nasional H29, 583–84.

48. See the list of seven titles in Arabic, Malay, and Sundanese supplied by Muhammad Musa of Garut on 3 January 1857 in Perpustakaan Nasional H29, 351.

49. See "[Handschriften] In het bezit van Sj. Ali te Soerabaja," Sourabaja, 17 Maart 1857, in Perpustakaan Nasional H29, 702.

50. Harthoorn, "De zending op Java," 229–37 (see ch.3, n.31); "Een en ander over den godsdienstigen toestand van den Javaan," *MNZG* 9 (1865): 161–202, esp. 162–64; [G.J. Grashuis], "Eene Soendanesche Pasantren," *Bataviaasch Zendingsblad* 2–3 (1864): 33–38; and "De eerste leerboeken van den santri," *Bataviaasch Zendingsblad* 2–4 (1864): 49–54.

51. M. Lindenborn, *West-Java als zendingsterrein der Nederlandsche Zendingsvereeniging* (Utrecht: Algemeene Boekhandel door Inwendige- en Uitwendige Zending, [1922]), 101, 128; cf. 447, n. 23.

52. Lindenborn, *West-Java*, 102–103; Fasseur, *Indologen*, 227; Kees Groeneboer, *Een vorst onder de taalgeleerden: Herman Neubronner van der Tuuk, Afgevaardigde voor Indië van het Nederlandsch Bijbelgenootschap, 1847–1873* (Leiden: KITLV, 2002).

53. He seems to have ended his career by auctioning off his library in 1899. *Catalogus van boeken, plaatwerken, enz., gedeeltelijk nagelaten door de heeren Mr. C. P. Henny . . . en anderen, waarbij gevoegd is de bibliotheek over oostersche taal-, land- en volkenkunde van Mr. G. J. Grashuis* (Arnhem: Gouda Quint, 1899). His manuscripts, on the other hand, only came into the collection of Leiden University in 1935. P.S. van Ronkel, "Eene nieuwe uitgave van de Kroniek van Koetai," *BKI* 100 (1941): 405–14, at 408.

54. G. J. Grashuis, *Zedeleer naar Ghazzāli* (Leiden: Sijthoff, 1874); *Soendaneesch Leesboek* (Leiden: Sijthoff, 1874); *Soendanesche bloemlezing: Fabelen, brieven en verhalen* (Leiden: Sijthoff, 1881); *Soendanesche bloemlezing: Legenden en Moslimsche leerboekjes* (Leiden: Sijthoff, 1891).

55. *Bataviaasch Zendingsblad*, 2–3 (1864): 31.

56. Grashuis, "Eerste leerboeken," 49.

57. Grashuis, *Bloemlezing*, 1881, xi.

58. Grashuis, "Eerste leerboeken," 50.

59. Grashuis, "Eerste leerboeken," 51.

60. Grashuis, *Bloemlezing*, 1881, xxiii–xxiv.

61. Grashuis, "Eerste leerboeken," 52–53.

62. Van der Chijs, "Bijdragen."

63. On Verkerk Pistorius, see P. A. van der Lith, "Levensbericht van A.W.P. Verkerk Pistorius," *Jaarboek van de Maatschappij der Nederlandse Letterkunde* (1895): 168–86.

64. A.W.P. Verkerk Pistorius, *Studiën over de Inlandsche huishouding in de Padangsche Bovenlanden* (Zalt-Bommel: Noman, 1871), esp. 188–240.

65. Verkerk Pistorius, *Studiën*, 210. The cited titles were "Sarof," "Nahoe," "Pakihi," "Tafsir," "Hadis," "Salajoe" and "Piei." The last two would appear to be references to texts compiled by 'ulama' of Piei in the district of Salayu (XIII Kota), already famous for its large school. Cf. Verkerk Pistorius, *Studiën*, 222.

66. Verkerk Pistorius, *Studiën*, 199, 201, 211–12.

67. Verkerk Pistorius, *Studiën*, 211.

68. Verkerk Pistorius, *Studiën*, 232.

69. Snackey, *Sair Soenoer*, 14 (see ch.3, n.16).

70. Verkerk Pistorius, *Studiën*, 233–34.

71. Verkerk Pistorius, *Studiën*, 235–36.

72. C. Poensen, *Brieven over den Islām uit de binnenlanden van Java* (Leiden: Brill, 1886), 67. Poensen also dismissed Freiderich's choice of an image of a kindly hajji.

73. Poensen, *Brieven*, 69–70.

74. Poensen, *Brieven*, 70.

75. See especially P. J. Veth, *Java: Geographisch, ethnologisch, historisch*, 3 vols. (Haarlem: De Erven F. Bohn, 1875–82).

76. See also his *Catalogus der afdeeling Nederlandsche Koloniën van de Internationale Koloniale en Uitvoerhandel Tentoonstelling (van 1 Mei tot ult. October 1883) te Amsterdam* (Leiden: Brill, 1883).

77. Juynboll, "Moslimsche catechismus," 215–31 (see ch.2, n.33) and "Samarkandi's Catechismus opnieuw besproken," *BKI* 29 (1881): 267–84.

78. Van den Berg, "Mohammedaansche godsdienstonderwijs," 518–55 (see ch.2, n.30).

79. C. Poensen, "Een mohammedaansche tractaatje," *MNZG* 32 (1888): 1–23, 11.

80. Poensen, "Mohammedaansche tractaatje," 4.

81. R. A. van Sandick, *In het rijk van de vulkaan* (Zutphen: Thieme, 1890); and *Leed en lief uit Bantam* (Zutphen: Thieme, 1892); Sartono, *Peasants' Revolt of Banten* (see ch.3, n.123); Laffan, "A Watchful Eye'" (see ch.3, n.49).

82. L.W.C. van den Berg and R.H.T. Friederich, *Codicum Arabicorum in bibliotheca societatis artium et scientiarum quae Bataviae floret asservatorum catalogum* (Batavia and the Hague: Bruining, Wijt and Nijhoff, 1873); L.W.C. van den Berg, *De beginselen van het mohammedaansche recht, volgens de imâm's Aboe Hanîfat en asj-Sjâfe'i* (Batavia and the Hague: Bruining, Wijt and Nijhoff, 1874); *Verslag van eene verzameling Maleische, Arabische, Javaansche en andere handschriften, door de regeering van Nederlandsch Indië aan het Bataviaasch Genootschap van Kunsten en Wetenschappen ter bewaring afgestaan* (Batavia: Bruining, 1877). See also S. J. van den Berg, "Levensbericht van Mr. L.W.C. van den Berg," *Jaarboek van de Maatschappij der Nederlandsche Letterkunde*, 1928: 16–30.

83. *Minhâdj at-Tâlibîn, Le guide des zélés croyants: Manuel de jurisprudence musulmane selon le rite de Châfi'i*, 2 vols. (Batavia: Imprimerie du Gouvernement, 1882–84).

84. Van den Berg, "Devotie der Naqsjibendîjah" (see ch.3, n.111).

85. Van den Berg, "Devotie der Naqsjibendîjah," 175.

86. Holle, "Mededeelingen over de devotie der Naqsjibendijah" (see ch.3, n.64).

87. L.W.C. van den Berg, *Le Hadhramout et les colonies Arabes dans l'archipel Indien* (Batavia: Imprimerie du Gouvernement, 1886).

88. Van den Berg, "Mohammedaansche godsdienstonderwijs," 521.

89. Van den Berg, "Mohammedaansche godsdienstonderwijs," 547, 554.
90. Van den Berg, "Mohammedaansche godsdienstonderwijs," 521.
91. Resident of Soerakarta, Spaan, to GG, Soerakarta 15 October 1888, geheim; in MR 1888, no.728.
92. V.S., "Mohamedaansche-godsdienstige broederschappen," *TNI* 20–2 (1891): 187–205. Cf. Louis Rinn, *Marabouts et khouan: Étude sur l'Islam en Algérie* (Algiers: Jourdan, 1884). Rinn served as chief of the Central Service of Indigenous Affairs to the Governer General of Algeria.
93. MR 1889, no. 41.

PART THREE: ORIENTALISM ENGAGED

1. C. Snouck Hurgronje, "Mohammedaansch recht en rechtswetenschap: Opmerkingen naar aanleiding van twee onlangs verschenen brochures," (1885) in *VG* II, 231–47, at 233–34. Emphasis original.

Chapter Seven: Distant Musings on a Crucial Colony, 1882–1888

1. LOr. 7935–i, 2.
2. LOr. 7935–e.
3. See Fahmi's appended note on the book on a business card found within LOr. 7935–e.
4. C. Snouck Hurgronje, "De laatste vermaning van Mohammed aan zijne gemeente, uitgevaardigd in het jaar 1880 N.C. vertaald en toegelicht," (1884) in *VG* I, 125–44, at 144.
5. C. Snouck Hurgronje, "Nieuwe bijdragen," 1 (see ch.2, n.36).
6. C. Snouck Hurgronje, Review of L.W.C. van den Berg, *Minhâdj at-Tâlibîn, Le guide des zélés croyants: Manuel de jurisprudence musulmane selon le rite de Châfi'i*, (1883) in *VG* VI, 3–18.
7. Al-Madani's pamphlets would be used by Snouck in the 1890s, while his sale offerings would enrich the holdings of Leiden University via Messrs Brill. Snouck Hurgronje, "Eenige Arabische strijdschriften," 149–88 (see ch.3. n.125); J. J. Witkam, "Inleiding," in C. Snouck Hurgronje, *Mekka in de tweede helft van de negentiende eeuw: Schetsen uit het dagelijks leven*, J. J. Witkam, ed. and trans. (Amsterdam/Antwerp: Atlas, 2007), 21; Carlo Landberg, *Catalogue de manuscrits arabes provenant d'une bibliothèque privée à al-Medina et appartenant à la maison E. J. Brill* (Leiden: Brill, 1883). Al-Madani was not the only Arab met by Snouck in Leiden in 1883, and he later referred to discussions with the Azharite Khalid b. 'Abdallah b. Abi Bakr. Snouck Hurgronje, "Een en ander," 37, n.2 (see ch.3, n.57).
8. Van der Velde, *Indische Liefde*, 283 (see ch.5, n.47); Marieke Bloembergen, *Colonial Spectacles: The Netherlands and the Dutch East Indies at the World Exhibitions, 1880–1931*, Beverley Jackson (trans.) (Singapore: NUS Press, 2006).
9. Cust, *Actes du Sixième Congrès*, I, 56 (see ch.5, n.23). On Cust, see Katherine Prior, "Cust, Robert Needham (1821–1909)," in *Oxford Dictionary of National Biography*, H.C.G. Matthew and Brian Harrison, eds. (Oxford: Oxford University Press, 2004), http://www.oxforddnb.com/view/article/32685 (accessed October 31, 2008).
10. C. Snouck Hurgronje, "Het Leidsche orientalisten-congres: Indrukken van een Arabisch congreslid vertaald en ingeleid," (1883) *VG* VI, 240–272, 269.

11. Snouck Hurgronje, "De beteekenis van den Islâm," 8–9 (see ch.1, n.52).

12. Veth, *Catalogus*, 319–25 (see ch.6, n.76).

13. At least this was the impression of Poensen. See his *Brieven*, 63 (see ch.6, n.72). On Kuenen, Tiele, and the study of "world" or "principal" religions, see Molendijk, *The Emergence of the Science of Religion* (see ch.5, n.62); and Tomoko Masuzawa, *The Invention of World Religions: Or, How European Universalism Was Preserved in the Language of Pluralism and Diversity* (Chicago: University of Chicago Press, 2005).

14. For Snouck, Kuenen, and the Hibbert Lectures, see Snouck to Bavinck, Leiden, 12 December 1881, in SB, 40–42; Snouck Hurgronje, "Beteekenis van den Islâm," 13–15; cf. Carel Poensen, "Gato-Lotjo (Een javaasch geschrift," *MNZG* 17 (1873): 227–65.

15. Snouck Hurgronje, "Beteekenis van den Islâm," 15, 22. Cf. Poensen, "Godsdienstigen toestand van den Javaan," 232 (see ch.3, n.44).

16. L.W.C. van den Berg to Directeur van Onderwijs, Eeredienst en Nijverheid, Batavia, 15 September 1881, secret, in MR 1881, no. 978.

17. Van der Tuuk to *NBG*, 31 July 1870, as cited in Groeneboer, *Van Radja Toek*, 31 (see ch.5, n.25).

18. J. C. Neurdenburg, "De beteekenis van den Islâm voor zijne belijders in Oostindië," *MNZG* 28 (1884), 96–106.

19. K.F.H. van Langen, *Wordenboek der Atjehsche taal* (The Hague: Nijhoff, 1889).

20. Snouck Hurgronje, "Een en ander," 27–52.

21. Snouck Hurgronje, "Een en ander," 42. Snouck to Bavinck, Leiden, 18 April 1882, in SB, 43; Snouck also praised Grashuis in a piece written for the *Indisch Gids* in May. See C. Snouck Hurgronje, "Prof. de Louter over Godsdienstige wetten, volksinstellingen en gebruiken," *IG* 5–2 (1883): 98–103, at 104. For Snouck's copies of Grashuis's manuscripts, see LOr. 7084.

22. Snouck Hurgronje, "Een en ander," 41.

23. Poensen, *Brieven*, 65; Snouck Hurgronje, "Een en ander," 44–46; cf. Harthoorn, "De zending op Java," 229 (see ch.3, n.31).

24. Snouck Hurgronje, "Een en ander," 47, cf. Gunning, *Een Javaansch Geschrift*, xii–xvi (see ch.4, n.25); Van den Berg, "Devotie der Naqsjibendîjah," 165, n.1 (see ch.3, n.111).

25. Snouck Hurgronje, "Een en ander," 49.

26. Snouck Hurgronje to Van der Chijs, 22 December 1885, in Witkam, "Inleiding," 135.

27. Snouck Hurgronje, "Laatste vermaning"; and *AA* III, 1896–1912.

28. M. J. De Goeje, "Nieuweste reizen in Arabië," *De Gids* 9 (1882): 1–22.

29. Snouck Hurgronje to Keuchenius, 1 October 1888, in Witkam, "Inleiding," 172.

30. Jeddah Diary, as quoted in Witkam, "Inleiding," 41.

31. Snouck Hurgronje, *Mekka*, 184 (see ch.2, n.25); "Some of My Experiences with the Muftis of Mecca," *Jaarverslagen van het Oostersch Instituut te Leiden 1934–40*, 4 (1941): 2–16, 14.

32. Muhammad Salih al-Zawawi, *Kayfiyyat al-dhikr 'ala l-tariqa al-Naqshbandiyya al-Mujaddadiyya al-Ahmadiyya* (Riau: al-Ahmadiyya, 1313). This was not the last Sufi text produced in Riau, and at least two other Naqshbandi manuals (neither by a Zawawi) came off the Ahmadiyya Press in 1904 and 1905 respectively. See Van der Putten, "Printing in Riau," 728, n. 20 (see ch.3, n.78).

33. Jeddah Diary, as cited in Witkam, "Inleiding," 42.

34. Jeddah Diary, as cited in Witkam, "Inleiding," 58.

35. Snouck Hurgronje to Van der Chijs, Mecca, 5 March 1885, in Witkam, "Inleiding," 94–96.

36. Cf. Jan Kommers, "Snouck Hurgronje als koloniaal etnograaf: De Atjehers (1893–1894)," *Sharqiyyât* 8–2 (1996): 87–115; and "Snouck Hurgronje als etnograaf van Mekka," *Sharqiyyât* 10–2 (1998): 151–77.

37. Jeddah diary, 10 December 1884, as quoted in Witkam, "Inleiding," 65.

38. Snouck Hurgonje, "Een rector," 91 (see ch.3, n.99); Witkam, "Inleiding," 123, 155, 175.

39. In fact Snouck had even been continuing the battle from Jeddah: "Zelfverdediging of zelfverlaging?" (1884), in *VG* II, 223–30.

40. In response to Van den Berg's attempts to defend himself, Snouck unleashed a further book-length assault in the *Indische Gids* in the third edition of his *Beginselen van het Mohammedaansche recht*. C. Snouck Hurgronje, "Mr. L.W.C. van den Berg's beoefening van het Mohammedaansche recht," (1884) in *VG* II, 59–221.

41. "Van den Berg's beoefening," 61; and "Brief," (1886) in *VG* II, 264–271, at 267–68.

42. Snouck Hurgronje, "Mohammedaansch recht," 235.

43. C. Snouck Hurgronje, "De Islâm," 194 (see ch.4, n.51). Blunt's *Future of Islam* had been one of the many tomes Snouck had been forced to abandon in Mecca.

44. Snouck Hurgronje, "De Islâm," 268–69.

45. Snouck Hurgronje, "De Islâm," 272–73; cf. Dozy, *Het Islamisme*, 209, 224–25 (see ch.5, n.32).

46. Snouck Hurgronje, "De Islâm," 278–79.

47. Snouck Hurgronje, "De Islâm," 287.

48. C. Snouck Hurgronje, "C. Poensen, brieven over den Islâm uit de binnenlanden van Java" (1886), in *VG* IV–1, 55–67.

49. 'Uthman b. 'Abdallah b. 'Aqil al-'Alawi, Atlas 'arabi (Leiden: [Brill], 1886); Snouck Hurgronje, *Mekka*, 272.

50. Snouck Hurgronje, "Een Arabisch bondgenoot der Nederlandsch-Indische Regeering," (1886), in *VG* IV–1: 69–85, 73.

51. Ibid. 75.

52. Ibid. 76; On Rinn, see ch.6, n.92.

53. Snouck Hurgronje, "Arabisch bondgenoot," 81.

54. Ibid. 85.

55. Sayyid 'Uthman to Snouck Hurgronje, Batavia, 30 August 1886, LOr. 8952.

56. Sayyid 'Uthman to Snouck Hurgronje, Batavia, 4 January 1887, LOr. 18.097, s 32. As Kaptein notes, Van den Berg was already favorably disposed to him. Nico Kaptein, "Arabophobia and *tarekat*: How Sayyid 'Uthmān Became Advisor to the Netherlands Colonial Administration," in Ahmad Ibrahim Abushouk and Hassan Ahmed Ibrahim, eds., *The Hadhrami Diaspora in Southeast Asia* (Leiden and Boston: Brill, 2009), 33–44.

57. "Lijst v. boeken ontvangen van Aboe Bakar December 1885," in LOr. 7111.

58. "Nota dari peladjaran mangadji akan Igama Islam," and "Nota Darie adanja boekoe (of kitab) jang die pake boewat adjar die Pesantren Tegalsari," in LOr. 7572.

59. Jeddah Diary, 10 December 1884, in Witkam, "Inleiding," 65; C. Snouck Hurgronje, "Vergeten jubilé's," (1923) in *VG* IV–2, 415–36.

60. ? to Bergsma, Brangsong, 4 March 1886, in LOr. 7572.

61. [Notes on pesantrens], 5–6, in LOr. 7572.

62. Reference to the "Djawahir" could be to Kyai Salih Jawahir of Pekalongan, cf. LOr. 7931, 23.

63. C. Snouck Hurgronje, "De Sjattarijjah-secte," (1888), in *VG* VI: 281–83. Cf. "Godsdienstige verschijnselen en toestanden in Oost-Indië (Uit de Koloniale Verslagen van 1886 en 1887)," *MNZG* 32 (1888): 172–86.

64. Resident of Surakarta, Spaan, to GG, Surakarta, 15 October 1888, secret, in MR 1888, no.728.

65. "De resident van Bantam vraagt inlichtingen over het te Mekka verblijvende hoofd van een islam-sekte," and Resident of Bantam to GG, Serang, 20 September 1888, both in MR 1888, no. 662.

66. Snouck, as quoted in K. F. Holle to GG, Waspada, 14 October 1888, secret, in MR 1888, no.727.

67. Snouck Hurgronje, *Mekka*, 291

68. Witkam, "Inleiding," 168.

69. Ibid. 153–54, 159.

70. Snouck to L.W.C. Keuchenius, Leiden, 1 October 1888, in Witkam, "Inleiding," 168–172.

Chapter Eight: Collaborative Encounters, 1889–1892

1. Masuzawa, *Invention*, 126–27 (see ch.7, n.13).

2. Snouck to Van der Chijs, Leiden, 8 December 1888, in Witkam, "Inleiding," 32.

3. "Soerakarta: Dari Correspondent BB," *Bintang Barat* 123 (31 May 1889), 4.

4. Snouck to Bavinck, Weltevreden, 16 July 1890, in SB, 50–53.

5. Snouck to Nöldeke, Garut, 12 November 1889, in VK, 13–15.

6. Grashuis, *Soendanesche bloemlezing*, xxiv (see ch.6, n.54).

7. *AA* III, 1980–86.

8. LOr. 7931, 1.

9. LOr. 7931, 2.

10. See, for examples, Hasan Mustafa to Snouck, 13 September 1912 and 14 October 1913, in LOr. 8952. With thanks to Nico Kaptein.

11. "Hadji Hasan's voor 't bestuur gemaakt lijst der in de Preanger gebruikelijk kitabs 1889," in LOr. 18097, s12.

12. LOr. 7931, 89.

13. LOr. 7931, 22, 77, 89b, 90b. For a 1903 report on Adi Kusuma, see *AA* II, 1189–93. For notes on other Shattari teachers, including the Penghulu of Cirebon, see: LOr. 7931, 21b, 23b–24, 74, 77, 169. For copies of Malay guides used by gurus in Caringin, see LOr. 7356.

14. C. Snouck Hurgronje, *The Achehnese*, A.W.S. O'Sullivan, trans., 2 vols. (Leiden: Brill, 1906), II, 11, n.1; LOr. 7397.

15. See notes from Purbalingga, LOr. 7931, 181; notes from Perapen, 728; and "Undang pondok di Kyai Saleh Darat," 735. Cf. Snouck Hurgronje, "Brieven," 172 (see ch.2, n.30). For 'Ubayda, see LOr. 7931, 6, 8 and 9; cf. Van den Berg, "Mohammedaansche godsdienstonderwijs," 522 (see ch.2, n.30).

16. LOr. 7931, 73b, 90, 392–93; and LOr. 7572, 3.

17. See LOr. 7931, 12–13.

18. These men included (1) Muhamad Razi of Sukamana, who had studied the Alfiyya in Madura; (2) Raden Hajji Yahya, who was then the chief penghulu of Garut; (3)

the faqih Muhammad ʿArif of Sumedang (d. 1888/9); (4) Muhammad Sahidi in Bumi-
kasih, who had gone on to study with ʿUbayda; (5) the grammarian Kyai Bunter of
Tanjung Sari, Sumedang, who had died in Mecca; (6) the Qurʾan reciter Hasan Basri of
Kiara Kareng, Suci (d. 1865); and (7) Kyai Ci Pare of Wanaraja. See Snouck's notes on
pesantrens in LOr. 7572, 6; cf. LOr. 7931, 5–7, 1147 b.

19. On Imampura, see LOr. 7931, 227. For the "Risalat tariqa al-khalwatiyya wa-
naqshbandiyya," see LOr. 7337.

20. Ie., LOr. 7931, 16.

21. LOr. 7111; LOr. 7931, 8, 15, 26.

22. LOr. 7931, 73–74, 77, 269; Drewes, *Drie Javaansche goeroe's*, 10–18 (see ch.3,
n.50).

23. LOr. 7931, 22b, 77, 78b–79b. Khalwatis were not welcomed by some officials
either. See MR 1889, no. 41.

24. LOr. 7931, 123–24; 164b–165. Also, see Ilyas described as the Naqshbandi
"Mohamad Iljas of Soekaredja Lor," whose pesantren was supported by the breeding of
goats, in MR 1889, no. 41.

25. LOr. 7931, 74, 80.

26. Snouck Hurgronje, "Brieven," 188–89

27. Ibid., 185–87, 192.

28. Ibid., 194–95.

29. *AA* II, 1187–88.

30. Van Sandick, *Leed en lief*, esp 22–26, 141–142, 172–176 (see ch.6, n.81). Cf.
Anon., "De woerding en het verloop van de Tjilegonsche troebelen in Juli 1888," *IG*
13-2 (1891): 1137–1206; C. Snouck Hurgronje, "Nieuws over Bantam?" (1893) in *VG*
IV-1, 249–56; "Een onbezonnen vraag," (1899) in *VG* IV, i, 369–86. Van Sandick appears to have deliberately ignored Snouck's work, including his chapter on the Jawa as
serialised in *De Locomotief: De Djawa te Mekka* (Semarang: Van Alphen, 1890).

31. V. S., "Mohamedaansche-godsdienstige broederschappen," 201 (see ch.6, n.92).

32. *The Achehnese*, I, 154–5, 165–66; II, 18–20, 222–23.

33. C. C. Berg, "The Islamisation of Java," *Studia Islamica* 4 (1955): 111–42, at 121.

34. Until that time Hasan Mustafa had continued to draw an allowance of ƒ50 per
month for his efforts. C. Snouck Hurgronje, Leiden, 22 December 1913, in HAZEU (5),
7.

35. Hasan Mustafa to Snouck, Kota Raja, 1 June 1893, in LOr. 18097, s12a.

36. See summaries of Hasan Mustafa's interviews conducted in late December of
1893 in Hasan Mustafa to Snouck, Kota Raja, 2 January 1894, in LOr. 18097 s12a.

37. Mufti Ali, "A Study of Hasan Mustafa's Fatwa: 'It is Incumbent Upon the Indonesian Muslims to be Loyal to the Dutch East Indies Government,'" *Hamdard Islam-
icus* 27-2 (April-June 2004): 67–84; and LOr. 18097, s9.

38. Hasan Mustafa to Snouck, Kota Raja, n.d., received 17 December 1894, in LOr.
18097, s12a. On Teungku Kota Karang, cf. Snouck, *Achehnese*, I, 18, 183–88.

39. On ʿAbdallah's visit, see Van Langen to Snouck, Kota Radja, 25 April 1893 and
the various pictures by Sayyid Qasim, all in LOr. 18097, s12a.

40. Samman Tiro b. ʿAbdallah b. Muhammad b. ʿAbd al-Salam ila l-sada al-
ʿarabiyyun [*sic*] al-ladhina yakhdimun qabr al-Sayyid Abu Bakr, Kampung Jawa, 18
Shawwal 1304, in LOr. 18097, s8. On T. Anjong, see Snouck Hurgronje, *The Achehnese*,
I, 156.

41. Teukoe Waki Kama, Idi Cut, 1 Safar 1309, in LOr. 18097, s10.

42. Alfons von der Kraan, *Lombok: Conquest, Colonization and Underdevelopment, 1870–1940* (Kuala Lumpur and Hong Kong: Heinemann, 1980), 17, 231.

43. See sketches in LOr. 18097, s1.

Chapter Nine: Shadow Muftis, Christian Modern, 1892–1906

1. Sayyid ʿUthman to Snouck, Batavia, 28 Shawwal 1305, in LOr. 8952; *AA* III, 1844–45; Sayyid ʿUthman, *al-Qawanin* (see ch.3, n.122); C. Snouck Hurgronje, "Sajjid Oethman's gids voor de priesterraden," (1894), in *VG* IV–1: 283–303; Nico Kaptein, "Sayyid ʿUthmân: De adviseur," in Rosemarijn Hoefte et. al., eds., *Tropenlevens: De [post]koloniale biografie* (Amsterdam: Boom, 2008), 208–209; "Arabophobia and *tarekat,*" 43 (see ch.7, n.56).

2. Hajji Muhammad Tayyib b. ʿAbdallah al-Khalidi to ʿAbd al-Ghafir [*sic*], Tanjung Beringin, 14 Rabiʿ II 1311; Pangeran ʿAbd al-Majid to Snouck, Bandung, 4 March 1898; and [unclear], Cirebon, 19 March 1898, all in LOr. 18097, s1.

3. Hajji ʿAbd al-Rahman b. Ahmad b. Jamal al-Layl to Hajji ʿAbd al-Ghaffar, Palembang, 15 Muharram 1311, in LOr. 18097, s1.

4. Ibid.

5. Al-Hajj ʿAbd al-Rahman and Kiagus Hajji Mun, Palembang, 28 Safar 1311, in LOr. 18097, s1; Snouck Hurgronje to Assistant Resident of Surabaya, Batavia, 19 August 1895, in *AA* III, 1928–30; for more details, see M. F. Laffan, "What Can Collaborators Tell Us about the Idea of an Islamic Indies?" in Kawashima Midori et al., eds., *Proceedings*, at 123, n.11 (see ch.3, n.38).

6. Hajj ʿAbd al-Rahman to GG, Palembang, 11 December 1904 and ʿAbd al-Rahman to Snouck, Palembang, 11 Shawal 1322, both in LOr. 18097, s1; Dja Endar Moeda to Snouck Hurgonje, Padang, 13 May 1905, in: Shakyh Padang Kandis, *'Aqa'id al-iman* (Padang: Snelpersdrukkerij Insulinde, 1901), LUB, shelfmark 8197 D 49. A pedigree of Muhammad Salih Padang Kandi [*sic*], who also taught the Shadhiliyya dhikr, is copied in Hazeu's papers. See Hazeu (92).

7. On Palembang, see Hazeu (8), 34–41. For the attack on Islam, see "Karangan dan pekabaran dari pada Pembantoe Pembantoe: Hikayat amal beramal," in *Selompret Melajoe*, 36–10 (23 January 1896), 1–2, in LOr. 18097, s12.

8. Snouck to Bavinck, Weltevreden, 16 July 1890, in SB, 50; Aboe Bakar to Snouck, Jeddah, 19 March 1897, in LOr. 8952; "De week," *Soerabaiasch Handelsblad* 45 (20 February 1897), 1, in LOr. 18097, s12.

9. Aboe Bakar to Snouck, Jeddah, 19 March 1897, in LOr. 8952.

10. C. Guillot, *L'Affaire Sadrach: Un esai de Christianisation à Java au XIXe siècle* (Paris: Association Archipel, 1981).

11. Kartawidjaja, *Van Koran tot Bijbel* (Rotterdam: Nederlansche Zendingsvereeniging, n.d.). See also Lindenborn, "Langgars en Pesantrèns," 119–27 (see ch.2, n.30).

12. Kartawidjaja, *Van Koran tot Bijbel*, 3.

13. Of the two sayyids, we might tentatively identify one as Tahir b. Yahya.

14. Kartawidjaja, *Van Koran tot Bijbel*, 27.

15. Ibid., 52–54.

16. *ONZ* 40–3 (March 1900): 43–44; 40–4 (April 1900): 53. For the original dispatches of Hoekendijk, see: Archief Raad voor de Zending der Ned. Herv. Kerk, Het Utrechts Archief, Toegang 1102, nummer 104.

17. *ONZ* 40–5 (May 1900): 74.

18. *ONZ* 40–6 (June 1900): 93; and 40–8 (August 1900): 127.

19. *Misbah al-sharq*, 28 Sha'ban 1320. The article is copied in LOr. 7205.

20. LOr. 7205, 14.

21. *Injaz al-wa'd*, LOr. 7205, 15a–25b, esp. 16, 24–25.

22. Sayyid 'Uthman to Hasan Mustafa, 14 Dhu l-qa'da 1320, in LOr. 7205, 35.

23. *Injaz al-wa'd*, 38–39.

24. Anon., "Ta'assub al-urubiyyun didd al-muslimin," *al-Liwa'* 1425 (16 August 1904), 1.

25. *Traoesa Pertoeloongan Goeroe lagi boeat Bladjar Bahasa Inggris-Blanda-Melajoe [Engelsch-Maleisch-Hollandsch en Maleisch-Engelsch-Hollandsch Samenspraken en Woordenlijst]*, 3e druk, (Surabaya: Van Ingen, n.d.), 98.

26. Vb 16 July 1904, no. 6 and 13 August 1904, no. 30. Cf. Sartono Kartodirdjo, *Protest Movements in Rural Java: A Study of Agrarian Unrest in the Nineteenth and Early Twentieth Centuries* (Singapore: ISEAS and Oxford University Press, 1973), 80–86.

27. Snouck Hurgronje to GG, 6 June 1904, in Vb 16 July 1904. For Snouck's characterization of Van Heutsz, see Snouck to Bavinck, Weltevreden, 1 June 1904, in SB, 60.

28. "Barid al-Islam: Jawi," *al-Liwa'* 1506 (4 September 1904), 1; Jan Schmidt, *Through the Legation Window, 1876–1926: Four Essays on Dutch, Dutch-Indian and Ottoman History* (Istanbul: Nederlands Historisch-Archaeologisch Instituut, 1992), esp. 108–42; Snouck Hurgronje to GG, Batavia, 6 July 1905, in *AA* III, 1969–73; G.A.J. Hazeu, "De Gedangan zaak," Hazeu (6), 4; Sartono, *Protest Movements*, 81.

29. Hazeu, "Gedangan zaak," 151–52.

30. Hajji 'Abd al-Jabbar b. Muhammad Jalal al-Din Sambas to "Tuan Mufti Duqtur Snukum Khrunye," Singapore, 17 Rabi' II 1322, in L.Or. 18097, s1.

31. Henny, Jeddah, 31 May 1905, excerpt from: "Zeer vertrouwelijke nota betreffende de broederschap, de tarega der SJATHARIA," in MinBuZa, 451, 201.

32. Ibid.

Part Four: Sufi Pasts, Modern Futures

1. Snouck to Nöldeke, Leiden, 13 June 1909, em. original, in VK, 147.

Chapter Ten: From Sufism to Salafism, 1902–1911

1. G.F. Pijper, "De Ahmadîyah in Indonesia," in *Bingkisan Budi: Een bundel opstellen aan Dr. Philippus Samuel van Ronkel door vrienden en leerlingen aangeboden op zijn tachtigste verjaardag 1 augustus 1950* (Leiden: Sijthoff, 1950), 247–54, at 247.

2. Ahmad b. Muhammad Zayn b. Mustafa al-Fatani, *al-Fatawa al-fataniyya* ("Siam": al-Fataniyya, 1957), 179–80. Whereas the letter is dated here as 13 Ramadan 1322, a copy reproduced by Wan Shaghir gives 14 Ramadan 1323: Abdullah, *Syeikh Ismail*, 87–89 (see ch.3, n.65). Cf. Kraus, "Sufis und ihre Widersacher in Kelantan/ Malaysia: Die Polemik gegen de Ahmadiyya zu beginn des 20. Jahrhunderts," in De Jong and Radtke (eds) *Islamic Mysticism Contested*, 729–56, at 744 (see ch.3, n.64).

3. Kraus, "Sufis und ihre Widersacher in Kelantan, 741–2; Sedgwick, *Saints and Sons*, passim (see ch.3, n.5). On the Idrisiyya and its offshoots, see also Trimingham, *Sufi Orders*, 114–21 (see ch.1, n.54).

4. Abdullah, *Syeikh Ismail*, 87–89. Cf. al-Fatani, *al-Fatawa*, 179–210, esp. 180–81; and Kraus, "Sufis und ihre Widersacher," 745; R. Gramlich, "Madjdhûb," *EI²*, V, 1029.

5. Fatani, *al-Fatawa*, 181–83, 188–89.

6. Ibid., 191–92, 195, 204–205, 209.

7. ʿAbd al-Jabbar, *Siyar wa-tarajim*, 38–43 (see ch.3, n.58). It should be noted that ʿAbd al-Jabbar's use of the term Salafi is connected to more recent Saudi usage.

8. Wan Shaghir claimed that the answer of al-Fatani was published in a work entitled *Mir'at al-a'ajib*, though I have been unable to locate it. Abdallah, *Syeikh Ismail Al Minangkabawi*, 89.

9. Ahmad Khatib b. ʿAbd al-Latif, *Izhar zaghl al-kadhibin fi tashabbuhihim bi-l-sadiqin* (Padang Pondok: Baümer, 1324), 1; cf. Van Bruinessen, "Controversies and Polemics, 705–28 (see ch.3, n.64).

10. Ahmad Khatib, *Izhar zaghl al-kadhibin* (1324), 25.

11. Ibid., 33–34, 36–37, 103–106, 144.

12. Ibid., 57, 146.

13. Hala Fattah, "'Wahhabi' Influences, Salafi Responses: Shaikh Mahmud Shukri and the Iraqi Salafi Movement, 1745–1930," *Journal of Islamic Studies* 14–2 (2003): 127–48; Itschak Weismann, "Between Ṣūfi Reformism and Modernist Rationalism: A Reappraisal of the Origins of the Salafiyya from the Damascene Angle," *Die Welt des Islams* 41–42 (2001): 206–37.

14. Sumbawi, *Siraj al-huda*, 31, 39–40 (see ch.2, n.31).

15. Zawawi, *Kayfiyyat al-dhikr* (see ch.7, n.32).

16. Shaykh Saʿd, the most important Khalidi in Sumatra after Shaykh Ismaʿil, had studied in Mecca in 1894. Abdullah, *Syeikh Ismail*, 59–60.

17. Ahmad Khatib b. ʿAbd al-Latif, *Izhar zaghl al-kadhibin fi tashabbuhihim bi-l-sadiqin*; *al-Ayyat al-bayyinat li-l-munsifin fi izalat khurafat ba'd al-muta'assabin*; *al-Sayf al-battar fi mahq kalimat ba'd ahl al-ightirar* (Cairo: al-Taqaddum al-ʿIlmiyya, 1326).

18. Ahmad Khatib, *al-Sayf al-battar*, esp. 6–7 and 20–21.

19. Ibid., 25.

20. Ibid., 27–28.

21. "Ahli Naqshbandiyya" to Habib ʿUthman, Bukit Tinggi, 30 Muharram 1325, in Hazeu (91).

22. ʿUthman b. ʿAbdallah b. ʿAqil b. Yahya to "Ahli Naqshbandiyya," Batavia, 24 Safar 1325, in Hazeu (91).

23. See Ass. Res. of Batavia, 20 April 1907, in Hazeu (92).

24. Noer repeated claims that copies of *al-ʿUrwa al-wuthqa* were smuggled into the Javanese port of Tuban, although it seems from contemporary observations that copies were in free circulation among Indies Arabs. Deliar Noer, *The Modernist Muslim Movement in Indonesia 1900–1942* (Kuala Lumpur: Oxford University Press, 1973), 32; Van den Berg, *Hadhramout*, 174 (see ch.6, n.87).

25. William R. Roff, *The Origins of Malay Nationalism* (New Haven and London: Yale University Press 1967); Barbara Watson Andaya, "From Rūm to Tōkyō: The Search for Anticolonial Allies by the Rulers of Riau, 1899–1914," *Indonesia* 24 (1977): 123–56; Abu Bakar Hamzah, *Al-Imam: Its role in Malay Society 1906–1908* (Kuala Lumpur: Media Cendekiawan, 1991); Abdul Aziz Mat Ton, *Politik al-Imam* (Kuala Lumpur: Dewan Bahasa dan Pustaka, 2000); and Michael F. Laffan, *Islamic Nationhood and Colonial Indonesia: The Umma Below the Winds* (London and New York: RoutledgeCurzon, 2003).

26. *al-Imam*, 2–9 (5 March 1908): 277.

27. *al-Imam*, 2–11 (1 May 1908): 349–51.

28. "Surat kiriman," *Utusan Melayu*, 85 (23 May 1908): [3].

29. *al-Imam*, 2–12 (1 June 1908): 381–83.

30. Hazeu to Resident of Batavia, Weltevreden, 29 December 1908, in HAZEU (10), 39–40.

31. *al-Imam*, 2–7 (3 January 1908): 219–22.

32. "Surat kiriman," *Utusan Melayu*, 94 (13 June 1908) [3].

33. *al-Imam*, 3–1 (30 July 1908): 41–45.

34. *al-Imam*, 3–2 (29 August 1908): 77–83. See *al-Bahja al-saniyya fi adab al-tariqa al-ʿaliyya al-khalidiyya al-naqshbandiyya* (Cairo: Maymuniyya, 1319).

35. "al-Rabita ʿind al-naqshbandiyya wa-taʿat al-murid li-shaykhih," *al-Manar* 11–7 (30 Rajab 1326): 504–14, esp. 506–507.

36. According to Freitag, his co-editor was Hasan b. Shihab. Freitag, *Indian Ocean Migrants*, 287 (see ch.1, n.16).

37. "Ruʾasaʾ al-ʿarab bi-jawa," *al-Watan* 1–1 (17 Safar 1328): 3; ʿUthman b. ʿAbdallah b. ʿAqil, *Tariq al-salama min al-khasran wa-l-nadama* (Batawi, 1329), 5–6; W. R. Roff, "Murder as an Aid to Social History: the Arabs of Singapore in the Early Twentieth Century," in Huub de Jonge and Nico Kaptein, eds., *Transcending Borders: Arabs, Politics, Trade and Islam in Southeast Asia* (Leiden: KITLV Press, 2002), 91–108, at 103.

38. "Kaum Melayu," *Neracha* 2–42 (2 Shaʿban 1330): 1.

39. Hamka (Haji Abdul Malik Karim Amrullah) *Ajahku: Riwayat hidup Dr. H. Abd. Karim Amrullah dan perdjuangan kaum agama di Sumatera*, 3rd ed. (Djakarta: Widjaja, 1958), 50–52; ʿAbd al-Jabbar, *Siyar wa-tarajim*, 38.

Chapter Eleven: Advisors to Indonesië, 1906–1919

1. Snouck Hurgronje, "Brieven," 192 (see ch.2, n.30); Snouck Hurgronje to Nöldeke, Weltevreden, 26 January 1890, in VK, 15–17; *AA* II, 1202–03.

2. Hogenraad to Snouck, Semarang, 31 January and 8 February 1896; and Snouck to Hogenraad, Batavia, 12 February 1896, in LOr. 18097, s12.

3. See the documents gathered in HAZEU (16).

4. C. Snouck Hurgronje, "De opleiding van ambtenaren voor den administratieven dienst in Nederlandsch-Indie," (1906) *VG* IV–2: 51–76 and 91–95.

5. G.A.J. Hazeu, *Bijdrage tot de kennis van het Javaansche tooneel* (Leiden: Brill, 1897).

6. P. S. van Ronkel, *De Roman van Amir Hamza* (Leiden: Brill, 1895), 3; G. F. Pijper, "Levensbericht Ph.S. van Ronkel," *Jaarboek van het Koninklijk-Nederlandsche Instituut van Wetenschappen, Letterkunde en Schoone Kunsten* (Amsterdam: Noord-Hollandsche, 1955–56), 285–97.

7. Notes of C. D. van Vliet, "Kennis van de godsdienstige wetten, instellingen en gebruiken der Mohamedanen in Nederlandsch Indië in verband met het Moslimsch Recht," KITLV, H 1037, 178–79; cf. G.W.J. Drewes, "D. A. Rinkes: A Note on His Life and Work," *BKI* 117–4 (1961): 417–35, esp. 419.

8. Snouck to Nöldeke, Weltevreden, 13 April 1900, in VK, 79. For Adriani's perspective on Islam and the Christian missions, see his 1907 lecture "Het mohammedaansche gedeelte van Nederlandsch Indië als zendings-gebied," in M. Adriani-Gunning, ed., *Verzamelde Geschriften van N. Adriani*, 3 vols. (Haarlem, Bohn, 1932), I, 160–70.

9. Snouck to Nöldeke, Weltevreden, 18 June 1904, in VK, 101.

10. C. Snouck Hurgronje, *Het Gajōland en zijne bewoners* (Batavia: Landsdrukkerij, 1903); Snouck to Nöldeke, Batavia, 8 September 1904, in VK, 104.

11. Snouck to Pijper, Leiden, 9 September 1930, in PS; Witkam, "Inleiding," 178 (see ch.7, n.7).

12. See correspondence in HAZEU (8) 75–92, esp. 78–82.

13. Ibid., 78–79.

14. Hazeu to GG, Weltevreden, 30 August 1906, in HAZEU (90).

15. D. A. Rinkes, *Abdoerraoef van Singkel: bijdrage tot de kennis van de mystiek op Sumatra en Java* (Heerenveen: Hepkema, 1909); D. A. Rinkes, *De heiligen van Java* (Batavia: Lange, 1910–13).

16. Snouck to Nöldeke, Leiden, 13 June 1909, in VK, 147.

17. C. Snouck Hurgronje, "De Hadjii-politiek der Indische regeering," (1909) in *VG* IV–2, 173–98; esp. 193ff.; "Het Mohammedanisme," (1911) in *VG* IV–2, 199–220, at 215; "De Islam in Nederlandsch-Indië," (1911) in *VG* IV–2, 359–91, 372 and 388; Snouck to Nöldeke, Leiden, 13 June 1909, in VK, 147–48.

18. Snouck Hurgronje, "De Islam in Nederlandsch-Indië," 373, 383–84, 386–87.

19. Snouck Hurgronje, ibid., 385; Voerhoeve to Drewes, [Barchum], 26 August 1966 copy in possession of Dr. Nico Kaptein, Leiden; Van Donzel (p.c. Leiden 2007); Snouck to Nöldeke, Leiden, 4 January 1919 and 24 November 1922, in VK, 267, 300.

20. Snouck Hurgronje, "De Islam in Nederlandsch-Indië," 389, 391.

21. Compare "Aus allen muslimschen Ländern Indonesiens," in *Mekka* (The Hague: Nijhoff, 1889), II, 347 and the Dutch translation of 1890, "Uit alle Moslimsche landen van Indonesië," *De Djawa te Mekka*, 73 (see ch.8, n.30); *De Atjèhers* (Batavia: Landsdrukkerij, 1894), II, 12, 18, 295, 335–36.

22. Snouck Hurgronje, "Het Mohammedanisme," 207; and "Politique musulmane de la Hollande," (1911) *VG* IV–2: 221–306, at 225.

23. Takashi Shiraishi, *An Age in Motion: Popular Radicalism in Java, 1912–1926* (Ithaca: Cornell University Press, 1990), 44.

24. Sayyid 'Uthman, [23 March 1913], in HAZEU (34), 84–85

25. 'Uthman b. 'Abdallah b. 'Aqil, *Sinar istirlam pada menyatakan kebenaran Syarikat Islam* (Batavia, 1331), 2, 7, 10–15. Cf. Nico Kaptein, "Grateful to the Dutch Government: Sayyid 'Uthmân and Sarekat Islam in 1913," in Anthony Reid and Michael Gilsenan, eds., *Islamic Legitimacy in a Plural Asia* (London and New York: Routledge, 2007), 98–116.

26. See HAZEU (34), 82; and (99).

27. *Bescheiden betreffende de vereeniging "Sarekat Islam"* (Batavia: Landsdrukkerij, 1913), esp. 26–27 and 33–36.

28. Extract uit het Register der Besluiten van den Gouverneur-Generaal van Nederlandsch-Indië, Buitenzorg, 2 July 1913, in HAZEU (20), 19–33, esp. 22–28.

29. Shiraishi, *Age in Motion*, 69–79.

30. Snouck to Minister of Colonies, Leiden, 4 October 1913, in HAZEU (13) 11–28; cf. C. Snouck Hurgronje, *Nederland en de Islâm: vier voordrachten, gehouden in de Nederlandsch-Indische Bestuursacademie* (Leiden: Brill, 1911).

31. "De bestuurswerkkring in Nederlandsch Indië voorheen en thans," *Indologenblad* 5 (1913–1914) in HAZEU (13) 1–10.

32. HAZEU (13), 10.

33. Kaptein, "Grateful to the Dutch Government," 111.

34. Wolff to GG, Jeddah, 22 October 1913, in Hazeu (34), 79–81; Schrieke, "Bijdrage tot de bibliographie," 267 (see ch.3, n.18).

35. Wolff to GG, Jeddah, 22 October 1913, in Hazeu (34), 81.

36. Ahmad al-Khatib b. ʿAbd al-Latif, *Tanbih al-anam fi radd ʿala risalat Kaff al-ʿawamm ʿan al-khawd fi Sharikat al-Islam* (Cairo: Dar al-Kutub, 1332), 4.

37. Ibid., 6.

38. Ahmad al-Khatib b. ʿAbd al-Latif, *Irshad al-hayara fi izalat baʿd al-shubah al-nasara* (Cairo: Dar al-Kutub, 1332).

39. Archief Raad voor de Zending der Ned. Herv. Kerk, Het Utrechts Archief, 1102, 8 (Notulen) and 108 (Vermeer 1914–23).

40. See M. Lindenborn, "De heilige oorlog en de zending," in *Nieuwe Rotterdamsche Courant, Avondblad* (18 May 1915): 6; and Ass. Res. of Sangi and Talud Islands, Post, to Resident of Manado, Taroena, 24 December 1909, in Hazeu (8), 14–15.

41. Hazeu to Resident of Batavia, Weltevreden, 22 October 1908, in Hazeu (39b), 41–42. For the 1908 advice concerning the "wilde echt" of Eliza Netti Clark and the Hoofd Penghulu's use of al-Bajuri, see Hazeu (39a), 93–96.

42. Hazeu to GG, Weltevreden, 19 February 1909, in Hazeu (8), 20–24; C. Snouck Hurgronje, *Mohammedanism: Lectures on Its Origin, Its Religious and Political Growth, and Its Present State* (New York and London: Putnam, 1916) 173–74; "De Islam en de Zending," (1915) in *VG* IV–2, 403–06, 405; "De Sarikat Islam in het credit van koloniaal bestuur," (1916) in *VG* IV–2, 407–10.

43. On Hoekendijk's concerns, see the review "Van een nuttig werk," *Nieuwe Zondagsbode* 26–30 (28 July 1917): 1; and J. G. Hoekendijk, *De papieren zendeling* (n.p.:1924), 5–6.

44. Van Ronkel, *Rapport* (see ch.1, n.60).

45. J. Ballot to GG, Padang, 28 February 1913, in Hazeu (98).

46. Such usage may also have informed Schrieke's use of the term *Indonesisch* in relation to political matters three years later. Cf. R. E. Elson, *The Idea of Indonesia: A History* (Cambridge: Cambridge University Press, 2008), 28.

47. Van Ronkel, *Rapport*, 9.

48. See Rinkes to Dir. Onderwijs, 11 December 1914, in Van Ronkel, *Rapport*, 91–94.

49. See LOr. 8652 K.

50. Doris Jedamski, "Balai Pustaka: A Colonial Wolf in Sheep's Clothing," *Archipel* 44 (1992): 23–46.

51. Hasan Mustafa to Resident of the Preanger, Bandung, 4 October 1917, in Hazeu (5), 8–9.

52. Hazeu to Directeur van Binnenlansch Bestuur, Weltevreden, 10 September 1909, in Hazeu (8), 71–73.

53. "Hal kas masdjid," *Oetoesan-Hindia*, 196 (14 October 1916), as transcribed in Hazeu (39b), 177–79.

54. Cf. Shiraishi, *Age in Motion*, 82–84.

55. B.J.O. Schrieke, *Het boek van Bonang* (Utrecht: Den Boer, 1916); 48–49. The *Serat Bonang* was subsequently attributed to Seh Bari by Drewes, *The Admonitions of Seh Bari* (see ch.1 n.21).

56. Hazeu to GG, Weltevreden, 2 May 1917, and [B.J.O. Schrieke] "NOTA," in Kern (225), 1–44.

57. Shiraishi, *Age in Motion*, 106–107.

58. Schrieke to GG, secret, Weltevreden, 21 Feb 1918, in HAZEU (76): 18–19; Schrieke, "Bijdrage tot de bibliographie," 288, n.4 (see ch.3, n.18).

59. Schrieke to GG, secret, Weltevreden, 21 Feb 1918, in LOr. 18097, s3.

60. G.F. Pijper, *Nederland en de Islam*, (Leiden: Brill, 1955), 17; *Studiën over de geschiedenis van de Islam in Indonesia 1900–1950* (Leiden: Brill, 1977), 118; Surkati to Rinkes, Weltevreden, 22 February 1918, in HAZEU (117).

61. See HAZEU 111, 106, 125 and 148; a note on the collophon of the Padang edition of the *Izhar* collected by Schrieke in 1919 (LUB shelf mark 800 E 75); and Kaptein, "The *Berdiri Mawlid* Issue," 145 (see ch.2, n.45).

62. Schrieke, "Bijdrage tot de bibliographie," 253.

Chapter Twelve: Hardenings and Partings (1919–1942)

1. Schrieke, "Bijdrage tot de bibliographie," 307–308 (see ch.3, n.18).

2. Shiraishi, *Age in Motion*, 113 (see ch.11, n.23).

3. Raes, Patrouillie-rapport v/m 5 t/m 11 Juli 1919, in HAZEU (36a), 550–55.

4. HAZEU (36a), 616–19.

5. See draft of Hazeu to GG, 29 August 1919, in HAZEU (36a), 262–346.

6. See transcriptions of *Neratja* for 9 July, 14 July and 11 August 1919 in HAZEU (36a), 386, 545–46, 583–86.

7. Interview with Tjokroaminoto, *De Socialistische Gids*, 25 September 1919, transcribed in HAZEU (36a), 207.

8. *Soerabajasch-Handelsblad*, 23 July 1919, and [H.C.] Zentgraaff, "Niewe zwenking," *Soerabajasch-Handelsblad*, 24 September 1919, transcribed in HAZEU (36a), 211–16, 458.

9. "De Garoet-affaire als zuiveringsproces?" *De Socialistische Gids*, 1 Oct. 1919, transcribed in HAZEU (36a), 168.

10. Broekveldt to GG, Weltevreden, 10 November 1919, and 1st Gov. Sec., Welter, to Dir. BB, Broekveldt, Buitenzorg, 18 November 1919 in HAZEU (36a), 118–19.

11. "SI Garoet," *Neratja*, 8 September 1919, in HAZEU (36a), 255–57; "Ditangkap," *Neratja*, 20 September 1919, in HAZEU (36a), 222–26; "Het rapport-Hazeu," *De Taak*, 29 November 1919, transcribed in HAZEU (36a), 103–109.

12. Kern, the son of the leading Dutch Indologist, had commenced his career in the Priangan in 1896. He returned to the metropolitan government academy before being sent to Brebes and Mojokerto from 1914. His writings on Islam came much later and included "De Javaan als Moslim," in J. Poortenaar en W. C. Coolhaas, eds., *Onder palmen en waringins: Geest en godsdienst van Insulinde* (Naarden: Uitgeverij in den toren, 1945), 156–73; the translation and introduction to Hadji Hasan Moestapa, *Over de gewoonten en gebruiken der Soendaneezen* (The Hague: Nijhoff, 1946); and the compact *De Islam in Indonesië* (The Hague: Van Hoeve, 1947). On Kern, see G. W. Drewes, "In Memoriam R. A. Kern, 26 september 1875–23 maart 1958," *BKI* 114–4 (1958): 345–58.

13. Shiraishi, *Age in Motion*, 225–31; cf. William A. Oates, "The Afdeeling B: An Indonesian Case Study," *Journal of Southeast Asian History* (March 1968): 107–17; Jedamski, "Colonial Wolf," 34–36.

14. Pijper to Snouck, Benkoelen, 4 September 1933, in PS; H.K.J. Cowan, "Bijdrage tot de kennis der geschiedenis van het rijk Samoedra-Pasè," *TBG* 78–2 (1938): 204–14, at 209, n.4.

15. "Index of Arabs in the Netherlands East Indies. Anti-Britain and Friendly," in IOR R/20/A/1409; see also Hazeu to GG, 10 November 1919, in HAZEU (10), 68–69.

16. Lee Warner to the Under Secretary of State, 14 July 1919, in IOR R/20/A/1409.

17. W. N. Dunn to Curzon, Batavia, 10 April 1920, enclosure in Batavia dispatch Secret No. 50 of 10 April, Semarang 28 March 1920, in IOL L/PS/10/630.

18. Ibid.

19. W. N. Dunn to Earl Curzon, Batavia, 7 June 1920, in IOL, L/PS/10/630.

20. [B.J.O.] Schrieke, "De strijd onder de Arabieren in pers en literatuur," *Notulen van de Algemeene en Directie-vergaderingen van het Bataaviaasch Genootschap van Kunsten en Wetenschappen* 58 (1920): 189–240.

21. R. A. Kern, Obituary for E. Gobée, in *Jaarboek van de Maatschappij der Nederlandse Letterkunde te Leiden* (1953–1955): 59–64.

22. C. Henny, "Stille kracht: (opgedragen aan het Binnenlandsch Bestuur)," *IG* 43 (1921): 808–30; 895–919.

23. Utrecht also managed to secure Snouck's student Juynboll for its staff, which Snouck deemed the ultimate betrayal. Snouck to Pijper, Leiden, 9 September 1930, in PS.

24. IPO No.20/1919.

25. Kraemer, *Een Javaansche Primbon* (see ch.4, n.25); Rapport van H. Kraemer aan het hoofdbestuur van het Nederlandsch Bijbelgenootschap over zijn verblijf in Cairo van 15 November 1921 tot 13 maart 1922; in KERN, 375.

26. Cf. Steenbrink, *Dutch Colonialism*, 137 (see ch.4, n.12).

27. H. Kraemer, *Agama Islam: Djilid jang pertama* (Bandung: Nix, 1928), 95.

28. "Onze broeders in Egypte," and "Wat de Heer Dr. H. Kraemer van ons zegt," *Het Licht* 2–1 (March 1926): 9–10.

29. Kasman, "De Jong Islamieten Bond," *Het Licht* 1–7 (September 1925): 146–53, at 150.

30. Tidar, "De Iman," *Het Licht* 2–4 (June 1926): 84–86.

31. "De viering van het eenjarig bestaan van den Jong Islamieten Bond afd. Batavia," *Het Licht* 2–4 (June 1926): 88–91.

32. B. Schrieke, "The Causes and Effects of Communism on the West Coast of Sumatra," in *Indonesian Sociological Studies*, 2 vols. (The Hague, etc.: Van Hoeve, 1955) I, 83–166; Michael Charles Williams, *Communism, Religion, and Revolt in Banten* (Athens, Ohio: Ohio University Press, 1990); Martin van Bruinessen, "Muslims of the Dutch East Indies and the Caliphate Question," *Studia Islamika* 2–3 (1995): 115–40.

33. Mohammad Redzuan Othman, "Conflicting Political Loyalties of the Arabs in Malaya," in De Jonge and Kaptein, *Transcending Borders*, 25–40, at 48 (see ch.10, n.37).

34. Muhammad Hashim al-Ash'ari, *Risalat ahl al-sunna wa-l-jama'a fi hadith al-mawta wa-ashrat al-sa'a wa-bayan mafhum al-sunna wa-l-bid'a* (Tebuireng: Maktabat al-Turath al-Islami, 1418), esp. 12–13.

35. Snouck Hurgronje, "Vergeten jubilé's," (see ch.7, n.59).

36. Hosein Djajadiningrat, "Inleiding," *Panji Poestaka* ("Nomor Snouck Hurgronje," 1927), ii.

37. Ronen Raz, "The Transparent Mirror: Arab Intellectuals and Orientalism, 1798–1950," PhD Dissertation, Princeton University, 1997.

38. Both Van Krieken and Benda refer to Snouck having been offered a post at the University (in 1911), based on the biography of Van der Maaten (see I, 52ff.) This proposal may have first been mooted around 1909, when Snouck reported the visit of the

University's secretary, 'Abd al-Hamid Lutfi. See Harry J. Benda, *The Crescent and the Rising Sun: Indonesian Islam under the Japanese Occupation, 1942–1945* (The Hague: Van Hoeve, 1958) 209, n.57; G. S. van Krieken, *Snouck Hurgronje en het panislamisme* (Leiden: Brill, 1985), 5; Snouck to Nöldeke, Leiden, 12 October 1909, in VK, 152.

39. Mansur Fahmi to Snouck, Cairo, 28 July 1925, in LOr. 7935–e.

40. Luwis Masinyun and Mustafa 'Abd al-Raziq, *al-Islam wa-l-tasawwuf*, Ibrahim Zaki Khurshid, et.al., eds. (Beirut, 1984).

41. Compare C. Snouck Hurgronje, "The Caliphate," (1924) in *VS* VI, 435–52; and 'Ali 'Abd al-Raziq, *al-Islam wa-usul al-hukm: bahth fi l-khilafa wa-l-hukuma fi l-islam* (Cairo: Matba'at Misr, [1925]).

42. Michael F. Laffan, "Another Andalusia: Images of Colonial Southeast Asia in Arabic Newspapers," *Journal of Asian Studies* 66–3 (2007): 689–722; Snouck to Pijper, Leiden, 23 October 1933, in PS.

43. Pijper, *Het boek* (see ch.2, n.32).

44. "Index of Arabs in the Netherlands East Indies," in IOR R/20/A/1409; see also PIJPER.

45. A. Teeuw, "In Memorium G.W.J. Drewes, 28 November 1899–7 June 1992," BKI 150–1(1994): 27–49.

46. Drewes to Voorhoeve, Weltevreden, 23 Feb 1926, in KITLV, H 1304 (1); G.W.J. Drewes, "Sech Joesoep Makasar," *Djåwå* 6–2 (1926): 83–88.

47. G.W.J. Drewes, "Review of J. Doorenbos, *De geschriften van Hamzah Pansoeri uitgegeven en toegelicht*," TBG 73 (1933): 391–98.

48. "Dagboek van eerste reizen naar Bantam," LOr. 26.337 (61). See also Else Ensering, "Banten in Times of Revolution," *Archipel* 50–1 (1995): 131–63, at 137.

49. Pijper to Snouck, Weltevreden, 25 May 1929; and Batavia-Centrum, 31 May 1933, both in PS.

50. Pijper to Snouck, Weltevreden, 10 May 1927, in PS.

51. Pijper to Snouck, Weltevreden, 25 May 1929, in PS.

52. Pijper to Snouck, Weltevreden, 10 May 1927, in PS.

53. Snouck to Pijper, Leiden, 6 July 1927, in PS.

54. Pijper to Snouck, Weltevreden, 2 August 1927, in PS.

55. Pijper to Snouck, Weltevreden, 15 and 31 Januari 1928, in PS.

56. Pijper to Snouck, Weltevreden, 13 February 1928, in PS.

57. Snouck to Pijper, Leiden, 20 March 1928, in PS.

58. Snouck to Pijper, Leiden, 20 March 1928; see also Snouck to Pijper, Leiden, 7 November 1927, in PS.

59. See especially, Pijper to Snouck, Makassar, 13 March 1930, in PS.

60. See typescript in LOr. 26.337 (41).

61. Pijper to Snouck, 9 November 1931, in PS.

62. Pijper to Snouck, Weltevreden, 30 Mei 1930, in PS.

63. Pijper to Snouck, Batavia-Centrum, 3 September 1932, in PS.

64. "Meninggal doenia ditempat pemboeangan," *Pemandangan*, 19 May 1934, transcribed in Pijper to Snouck, Batavia-Centrum, 29 May 1934, in PS.

65. Pijper to Snouck, Weltevreden, 28 Juli 1930, in PS.

66. Pijper to Snouck, Batavia-Centrum, 31 May 1933, in PS.

67. Pijper to Snouck, Batavia-Centrum, 31 May 1933, in PS.

68. Pijper to Snouck, Batavia-Centrum, 26 Juli 1934, in PS.

69. "Uitknipsels over Bantam," in LOr. 26.337 (61).

70. Pijper to Snouck, Batavia-Centrum, 26 Juli 1934, in PS.

71. Snouck to Pijper, Leiden, 1 August 1930, in PS.

72. G. F. Pijper, *Fragmenta Islamica: studiën over het islamisme in Nederlandsch-Indië* (Leiden: Brill, 1934); Pijper to Snouck, Batavia-Centrum, 24 October 1933 in PS.

73. Pijper to Snouck, Batavia-Centrum, 26 Juli 1934, in PS.

74. Pijper to Snouck, Batavia-Centrum, 24 October 1933, in PS.

75. On Schrieke, see J. Vogel, *De opkomst van het Indocentrische geschiedbeeld: leven en werken van B J.O. Schrieke en J. C. van Leur* (Hilversum: Verloren, 1992), especially 33–107.

76. Lothrop Stoddard, *Hadir al-ʿalam al-islami*, ʿAjjaj Nuwayhid, trans., Shakib Arslan, ed., 4 vols. (Cairo: al-Halabi, 1352), I, 364–75; III, 372–74.

77. Snouck to Pijper, Leiden, 4 September 1932, in PS.

78. J. H. Monahan, ["Introduction"], in *Mekka* (1931), vi; "Prins Faisal Bin Abdal-Aziez Al-Saʿoed," (1926) in *VS* VI: 465–70; Snouck to Pijper, Leiden, 26 June 1932, in PS.

79. Cf. Raymond LeRoy Archer, "Muhammedan Mysticism in Sumatra," *JMBRAS* 15–2 (1937): 1–126.

80. Laffan, "Another Andalusia," 717.

81. "Kitab-kitab jang berbahaja," *Pedoman Masjarakat* 4–6 (1938); 101ff., as transcribed in LOr. 26.337 (41).

82. *Islam Raya* 4–2 (20 January 1942): 20.

83. A. Salim, *Riwajat Kedatangan Islam di Indonesia* (Batavia-Centrum: Soemberilmoe, 1941). Ismaʿil al-ʿAttas—whose Cairene lecture was reproduced by Arslan—had also pointed to Arab agents and used the Cantonese colony for proof. Cf. Stoddard, *Hadir al-ʿalam*, III, 366.

84. Pijper, lecture given at the Volksuniversiteit, 12 March 1937, in LOr. 26.337 (35); the resulting volume was his *Studiën over de geschiedenis van de Islam i* (see ch.11, n.60).

85. Drewes and Poerbatjaraka, *Mirakelen van Abdoelkadir* (see ch.1, n.7); Edel, *Hikajat Hasanoeddin* (see ch.1. n.63).

86. Voorhoeve to Drewes, Pematangsiantar, 24 June 1939, in KITLV, H 1034 (1).

87. Voorhoeve to Drewes, Pematangsiantar, 29 January 1940, in KITLV, H 1034 (1).

CONCLUSION

1. Christopher Bayly, *The Birth of the Modern World 1780–1914: Global Connections and Comparisons* (Oxford: Blackwells, 2004), 3.

Index

Princeton Studies in Muslim Politics